Approaches to Preschool Curriculum

Approaches to Preschool Curriculum

Michael C. Anziano
Associate Professor of Psychology
Fort Lewis College, Colorado

Jane Billman
Teaching Associate
Department of Human Development and Family Studies
University of Illinois at Urbana-Champaign

Marjorie J. Kostelnik
Professor and Acting Chairperson
Department of Family and Child Ecology
Michigan State University

Cathleen S. Soundy
Associate Professor
Early Childhood and Elementary Education
Temple University, Pennsylvania

GLENCOE
McGraw-Hill

New York, New York
Columbus, Ohio
Mission Hills, California
Peoria, Illinois

Send all inquiries to:
Glencoe/McGraw-Hill
936 Eastwind Drive
Westerville, OH 43081

ISBN 0-02-802096-0 (Student Edition)
ISBN 0-02-802097-9 (Instructor's Guide)
ISBN 0-02-802098-7 (Study Guide)
ISBN 0-02-802099-5 (Test Bank)

Printed in the United States of America

1 2 3 4 5 6 7 8 9 10   POH   00 99 98 97 96 95 94

Library of Congress Cataloging-in-Publication Data

Approaches to preschool curriculum / Michael C. Anziano . . . [et al.].
        p.   cm.
    Includes bibliographical references and index.
    ISBN 0-02-802096-0 (Student ed.) — ISBN 0-02-802097-9
(Instructor's guide) — ISBN 0-02-802098-7 (Study guide)
    1. Education, Preschool — United States — Curricula.   2. Curriculum planning — United
States.   I. Anziano, Michael Curran.
    LB1140.4.A67   1995
    372.19 — dc20   94-6686
                                                       CIP

Co-developed by
Glencoe/McGraw-Hill
and Visual Education Corporation
Princeton, NJ

Reviewers

Polly Ashelman
Assistant Professor and Graduate Coordinator
Department of Early Childhood and Family Studies
Kean College of New Jersey

Barbara L. McCornack
Assistant Professor and Director
Early Childhood Laboratories
Department of Human Development and Family Studies
Colorado State University

Joseph O'Brien
Assistant Professor
Department of Curriculum and Instruction, School of Education
University of Kansas

Credits and Acknowledgments

Special thanks to:

Carnegie Family Center, Princeton, NJ

The Harmony Schools, Princeton, NJ

Janssen Child Development Center, A Quality Program of Resources for Child Care Management, Titusville, NJ

Princeton University League Nursery School, Princeton, NJ

Mercer Children's Center, Mercer Medical Center, Trenton, NJ

Photo Credits:

Dwight Cendrowski: 247, 350–351

David Crow: 325, 388, 392

H. Armstrong Roberts: Title page, 133, 205, 224, 245, 287, 297, 384

  C. Barr: 195

  J. Nettis: 303

  L. O'Shaughnessy: 241

  B. Taylor: 269

  Zefa: 202

Ken Lax: 352, 374

Library of Congress: 7

Cliff Moore: 2–3, 13, 15, 17, 20, 28, 33, 44, 46, 47, 56, 61, 76, 79, 83, 95, 102, 107, 108, 111, 117, 120, 131, 139, 148, 162, 165, 171, 198, 203, 210, 213, 217, 223, 228, 233, 264, 275, 288, 294, 301, 309, 323, 362, 368

Rita Nannini: 231, 238, 276, 305, 306, 362

PhotoEdit:

  Robert Brenner: 180, 340

  Mary Kate Denny: 191

  Myrleen Ferguson: 342

  Tony Freeman: 174

  Stephen McBrady: 182

  James L. Shaeffer: 283

  Ulrike Welsch: 122, 151, 270, 320, 377

  David Young-Wolff: 4, 93, 188

Photolink/Jon Reis Photography: 314

Kathy Sloane: 69, 128, 253, 336

Terry Wild Studio: 10, 227, 394

Shirley Zeiberg: 22, 42, 59, 65, 71, 86, 89, 146, 160–161, 178, 206, 221, 258, 334, 352, 361, 365

Preface

Curriculum planning at the preschool level revolves around two basic themes of education—how children learn and what they should learn. Different views on these key issues have led to a variety of approaches to preschool curriculum. This book describes the leading curriculum approaches and discusses the focus, goals, structure, and implementation techniques of each approach. The book also illustrates how curriculum goals can be developed by teachers and how different kinds of classroom activities can help meet these goals.

Content

Part 1 of the book focuses on the role of curriculum in providing structure in the daily life of the classroom. In addition to defining the leading approaches to curriculum, the book presents views of supporters and critics of each approach. It also provides numerous examples of how these different approaches translate into practice.

The first chapter of the book begins with a survey of different types of care for young children—including family day care, group home care, child care centers, and preschools. In subsequent chapters, the umbrella terms *preschool* and *preschool setting* are used to refer to all types of care for young children unless otherwise specified. Throughout the book, the word *teacher* is used broadly to include teachers and caregivers. Typical situations, stages, and problems encountered in preschool education are illustrated in examples in the text. The children featured in these examples usually are identified as either male or female to avoid awkward he/she and him/her constructions.

Other chapters in Part 1 also cover the role of play in the curriculum, the physical environment, and methods for creating curriculum goals, objectives, and written plans.

Part 2 relates curriculum to the various developmental domains of early childhood: physical, emotional, social, cognitive, and creative. Each of these chapters begins with a short overview of leading theories of child development or main issues related to the particular area of development. The chapters provide practical techniques for developing and using curriculum activities to help children acquire the skills, knowledge, and attitudes relevant to each area.

Part 3 summarizes the key ideas on the social and cognitive goals of curriculum. It provides an overview of the developmental tasks of the primary years and summarizes the types of experiences that preschool teachers can provide to prepare children for kindergarten and elementary school.

Each chapter in the book begins with learning objectives and a list of important terms. Within the chapter, these terms are highlighted in *italics*; they are defined again in the Glossary at the back of the book. Author and publication date for each source are cited in the text—for example (Erikson, 1972); full bibliographic information is provided in the References at the back of the book.

Special Features

The book's practical approach to preschool curriculum is reinforced in a section called *Applications* and in a series of "*Focus on*" features on topics of concern to preschool teachers.

The *Applications* section that concludes each chapter provides hands-on suggestions for teaching strategies and activities that relate to the curriculum elements discussed in the chapter. The *Applications* section addresses the reader directly as "you," to create a more immediate connection between author and reader.

Focus on Cultural Diversity shows how multicultural issues affect the development of preschool curriculum and the implementation of activities. There are two variations on the theme: one is intended to encourage sensitivity and awareness in teachers; the other focuses primarily on teaching children about diversity. Both offer tips and guidelines for making multiculturalism an integral part of the classroom. The theme of multiculturalism runs throughout the text as well.

Focus on Communicating presents discussions of everyday problems as well as extremely sensitive topics. Written in dialogue format, this feature illustrates one way—not necessarily the best—that a teacher might communicate with parents or children. It invites students to consider other ways of handling the communication and of using curriculum activities to address the issue.

Focus on Activities presents typical activities related to the topics covered in the chapter. This feature includes a rationale or objective for the activity, materials, and suggestions for effectively carrying out the activity.

End of Chapter Materials

Each chapter ends with a comprehensive chapter review. These materials include a *Summary* of important points covered; *Acquiring Knowledge,* a section that can be used to review chapter content; and *Thinking Critically,* a section that raises questions early childhood educators need to consider. *Observations and Applications* proposes various situations in which students can practice observational skills and apply their knowledge of curriculum development. *For Further Information* lists books, curriculum guides and resource books, and, in some chapters, videotapes.

Supplementary Materials

The **Instructor's Guide** is a useful teaching support tool. It includes *Teaching Strategies* for each chapter in the text, *Chapter Tests,* and a list of sources for teaching curriculum development.

The **Study Guide** is a workbook that provides students with a means of checking their mastery of the material covered in the text. *Study Questions* review the content, concepts, and vocabulary of each chapter. *Observation Activities* direct students to observe in the field firsthand the kind of activities and behavior they are studying in the text. *Application Activities* require students to apply their knowledge to case studies and current issues in curriculum development and teaching at the preschool level.

Test Bank. The computerized *Test Bank* provides a variety of questions that can be used to build a customized test for students. The software leaves room for instructors to add their own questions. Answers are included.

Contents

Part 1
The Role of Curriculum 2

Chapter 3:
The Building Blocks of Curriculum   56

Chapter 4:
Play and the Curriculum   76

Part 2:
Curriculum and the
Developing Child   160

Chapter 7:
Physical Development   162

Chapter 11:
Cognitive Development: Language   264

Chapter 12:
Cognitive Development: Thinking and Learning   294

Part 3:
Curriculum and the Child's
Expanding World   **350**

Chapter 15
Looking Ahead to the School Years   374

Approaches to Preschool Curriculum

PART 1

The Role of Curriculum

1

Preschool Care, Learning, and Curriculum

OBJECTIVES

Studying this chapter
will enable you to

- Describe how attitudes toward childhood have changed over time
- Describe the history and development of preschools and identify current trends in early childhood education
- Enumerate the kinds of early childhood education programs available for children prior to kindergarten
- Discuss how children grow and learn in their first five years of life
- Explain how preschools and child care centers can enhance the learning and development of children

CHAPTER TERMS

child care center
cooperative preschool
corporate child care center
curriculum
developmentally at risk
family day care
group home care
preschool
Project Head Start

SONYA Miller was excited. It was her first day of student teaching at a local preschool. Sonya was assigned to assist Carla Paone with her class of four- and five-year-olds. The first thing Sonya noticed was that Ms. Paone's classroom was large, brightly decorated, and divided into several distinct areas. As Sonya looked around the room, she could see a thickly carpeted area with big, soft pillows and a brightly painted set of shelves displaying books. Another area was partitioned off by a 4-foot-high pegboard with coat hooks holding dress-up clothes. Next to the pegboard were two boxes filled with hats, scarves, and other accessories. Another area had low shelves filled neatly with toys and musical instruments such as tambourines and little tom-tom drums. One corner of the room contained artists' easels near a sink and more low shelves with paper, scissors, and markers. In the center of the classroom, several children were clustered around two large low tables. One group of children was playing with modeling clay, and another group was drawing together with crayons on one large piece of paper.

"We're going to plant flower seedlings outside this afternoon," Ms. Paone told Sonya. "Maybe you can lead the children in a discussion about gardens. We'll discuss ideas after the children have gone home."

"Oh yes, I'd love to," Sonya said.

"You could talk to them about different kinds of flowers and the differences among flowers that grow on trees and bushes and flowers that grow in the ground and from bulbs," said Ms. Paone. "Tomorrow, we'll talk about the differences between fruits and vegetables."

"That will be fun," said Sonya. "Do you have some pictures to illustrate each kind of plant?"

"Yes, I have some here. We can also have samples of vegetables like carrots, tomatoes, and cucumbers for the children to taste, smell, and feel," said Ms. Paone. "But don't go on for too long, or they'll lose interest. Ask them questions, and give them plenty of opportunities to ask questions and make comments in return," she said.

Sonya and Ms. Paone took the children outside and set them to digging in the garden plot that Ms. Paone had prepared for the tomato plants.

"While we're planting the seedlings, I'll talk about watering and weeding and plant food," Sonya said. After a moment she added, "It's amazing how much you can teach the children just from one little project like this."

"Yes, but we don't want to make this too much like elementary school," laughed Ms. Paone. "In preschool, we want to focus on helping the children to be curious and excited and to have fun and learn just for the sheer pleasure of it. That's what preschool is all about," she said.

Parents and siblings contribute in countless ways to each child's growth and development in the first five years of life. Preschools provide young children with many valuable experiences and opportunities that build a foundation for growth and learning.

This chapter shows how a young child's learning begins in the home and it provides an overview of the key areas in which the preschool setting extends that learning and enriches a child's life in the first five years and beyond. It also presents a history of early childhood education and describes the various kinds of preschools in existence in the United States. The chapter includes a discussion of current trends in the field of early childhood education. Changes that are taking place now in preschool practices and curricula will shape early childhood education in the coming years and affect the lives of today's children long into the future.

The Beginning of Child Development

The attitude of adults toward children has changed substantially over the years. Before the 18th century, little thought was given to how children developed and how they should be educated. For the most part, children were regarded as miniature adults, as sources of labor, and as property. The function of education was generally to teach children the rules of society and to

During the Industrial Revolution, young children were put to work in factories, where they labored 14 to 16 hours a day in unhealthy and dangerous conditions.

train them to fulfill their assigned roles. In agrarian communities, children were put to work at an early age, herding animals or tilling fields. In cities and towns, children had to learn the crafts or trades of their parents.

With the coming of the Industrial Revolution, many people moved to cities. Young children were put to work in factories and mines, where they labored long hours in unhealthy and dangerous conditions. However, in the academic world, philosophers and teachers began to examine the nature of childhood and to formulate theories about child development and education.

The English philosopher John Locke (1632–1704) was one of the first philosophers to recognize and write about the fact that children possessed individual differences in intelligence and personality traits. He was one of the first to assert that children learn through play. The French philosopher Jean-Jacques Rousseau (1712–1778) believed that children are born inherently good and innocent and that they should be allowed to naturally "unfold" as they grow without social restrictions being imposed on them. He advocated that children should be allowed to follow their own natural interests and curiosities and that not until adolescence should they begin to be taught actual lessons. Rousseau set forth his view of education in a work entitled *Émile*, the story of a young boy and his private tutor.

In the 20th century, psychoanalysts such as Sigmund Freud (1856–1939) and Erik Erikson (1902–) and theorists such as Jean Piaget (1896–1980) began to study the psychological, physical, and intellectual development of children from infancy to adolescence. Their theories, many of which are discussed throughout this book, still strongly influence the practices and principles of early childhood educators.

Early Childhood Education Settings

Today, early childhood education takes place in a wide variety of settings—in the home, in religious institutions, in preschools, and in child care centers. Sociological and economic changes, as well as government policies, have contributed to the shaping of education for young children. This section reviews historical influences on early childhood education and describes the types of child care options available today.

The History of Early Childhood Education

American early childhood education evolved from models in Europe, particularly Switzerland, Germany, Italy, and England. Rousseau's ideas about the nature of childhood made a strong impression on Johann Pestalozzi (1746–1827), a Swiss educator. Pestalozzi's school for children of the poor was based on Rousseau's philosophy of education. He emphasized learning through the senses and hands-on activities that reflected the interests of the children. German philosopher Friedrich Froebel (1782–1852) was also influenced by Rousseau's ideas. In the late 1830s, Froebel established the first schools for children between the ages of three and six. He called these schools *kindergartens,* or child's gardens, because of his view that schools should encourage the natural development of children, much like flowers in a garden. His schools were places where young children could play, grow, and learn for their own benefit—rather than to meet the preset ideals of adults. Froebel's concept of schools for young children gradually spread over Europe and to the United States.

During the early 19th century and into the 20th century, many schools for young children were started specifically to help orphans and children from poor and working-class families. Cotton mill owner Robert Owen established the first "infant school" in Scotland in 1816 for the children of his mill workers. In 1907, an Italian physician, Maria Montessori, opened a school in a slum district in Rome. The school emphasized cleanliness and health and individualized, sequential learning using a wide variety of special sensory materials that Montessori developed. Montessori schools spread all over the world and are still very popular in the United States.

In England, between 1908 and 1910, Rachel and Margaret McMillan established the first "nursery school" to provide care for children of working mothers. The school, which operated from early morning until evening, served as an inspiration for many of the early American schools for young children (McMillan, 1921).

FOCUS ON Cultural Diversity

Multiculturalism in the Preschool Classroom

Seihyun, a four-year-old Korean boy, grasped his mother's hand tightly as they walked into the Early Horizons Preschool. His eyes quickly scanned the room for some familiar trace of home. None of the children looked like him. However, he saw a set of blocks just like the set he had at home, and he relaxed a little.

The entire class stopped what they were doing and simply stared. Then Seihyun's mother kissed him good-bye and told him that she would be back later. The teacher introduced Seihyun to the class and made a place for him to sit in the circle.

The children studied Seihyun at close range. They had never seen a Korean boy before.

"Why doesn't he talk?" whispered one little girl to the teacher.

"He's shy right now. He doesn't know us yet," the teacher replied, sitting down next to Seihyun.

Seihyun felt his face grow hot. He stared at the floor and wished that he would disappear.

Enrollment in preschools and child care centers throughout the country is becoming more culturally diverse. Today's preschool population in the United States includes children of many different races and ethnic groups—Asian American, black, Native American, Hispanic, and others.

Today, educators, including early childhood educators, recognize the importance of acknowledging every child's cultural background. A multicultural curriculum includes daily activities and materials that focus on the everyday life of cultures and ethnic groups in the United States, not just on special holidays or outdated representations.

The goals are for children to associate favorable feelings with multicultural experiences and to recognize similarities and to respect differences among cultures. For example, activities may show children that we all eat and sleep, but our foods and beds may look different.

Early childhood educators believe that children can be enriched by diversity, as Seihyun's classmates will be. A preschool curriculum that supports cultural diversity will help children form positive attitudes that will stay with them long past the preschool years. A curriculum that does not may hurt children now and in their future.

Early Childhood Education in the United States

Early childhood education arrived in the United States in the 19th century. Margarethe Schurz (1833–1876), a German immigrant and a student of Froebel's, started a small kindergarten for her own children and the children of relatives in Wisconsin in 1856. She introduced Elizabeth Peabody to Froebel's methods, and Mrs. Peabody started the first kindergarten for English-speaking children in Boston in 1860.

The 1920s through the 1950s. In the 1920s, a number of experimental and laboratory schools opened around the country under the auspices of colleges and universities and with the help of private grants. Two of the most important of these programs were the Merrill-Palmer Institute in Detroit, which was established to teach girls how to be mothers, and the

Laura Spelman Rockefeller Memorial, which established child study centers for research at Yale, Columbia, and several other major universities. Many of these centers also included programs focusing on home economics for a family emphasis.

During the Great Depression in the 1930s, the federal government supported the operation of 3,000 nursery schools around the United States. The schools were intended to provide employment to women as well as to educate young children. An estimated 75,000 children attended these schools during the Depression years. Federal support for nursery schools and other forms of child care continued throughout World War II, allowing the mothers of young children to work in defense plants. Some companies also provided on-site child care to keep mothers working.

After World War II, government support of these schools dried up, and most of the schools closed. Public schools started with the first grade, not kindergarten. During this period, public schools began to adopt the idea of enrolling five-year-old children in half-day kindergartens. By 1960, more than 70 percent of public school districts had established kindergartens.

The 1960s.   The Civil Rights movement of the 1960s brought a resurgence of government support for education, including education for the very young and the socioeconomically disadvantaged. The federal government established *Project Head Start*, a program for children from low-income families and children with physical disabilities. This program is designed to give the children a "head start" so that they will be more likely to succeed in school. It also provides medical, dental, and nutritional services, as well as other special services for children with disabilities. Some home-based Head Start programs were started in the 1970s, and involvement of parents and other family members is still a high priority of the programs today. Head

Project Head Start was designed in the 1960s to give children from low-income families and children with physical disabilities a "head start" in school. These four-year-olds are working on fine motor and social skills as they build with blocks together.

Start is the major government-supported early childhood education program in the United States. Since its inception in the 1960s, Head Start has served more than 11 million children throughout the United States. Although the funding for Head Start has increased significantly in recent years, the program still serves only about 50 percent of eligible children.

The 1970s and the 1980s.   Enrollment in privately owned and operated schools and child care for young children continued to increase steadily during the 1970s and the 1980s as more and more women joined the work force. Parents and educators became concerned about the quality of these settings and the quality of the training of early childhood educators and child care providers. Many community colleges added early childhood education programs to their curricula to meet the demand for more trained teachers and caregivers. In addition, the federal government established the Child Development Associate program (CDA) in the mid-1970s. This program offers training for child care providers who are not seeking a formal bachelor's degree in education or child study. It also sets minimum licensing and certification standards for CDA graduates.

All states set standards for operations providing prekindergarten care and require a license to operate. In the 1970s, standards for licensing were developed by the U.S. Office of Child Development, with input from licensing agencies across the country and national and state early childhood organizations. In the mid-1980s, the National Association for the Education of Young Children (NAEYC), an association of early childhood professionals, established accreditation standards that are higher than the minimal state standards. Accreditation, however, is not mandatory, and only 2,500 of the 80,000 licensed child care centers nationwide are accredited. To be accredited as offering a high-quality program by the NAEYC, a school is reviewed by a team of experts and must conform to a rigid set of standards governing facilities, teacher training, teacher-child ratio, and curriculum.

Types of Child Care Today

In the scenario at the beginning of this chapter, Sonya began her practice teaching at a preschool with four- and five-year-olds. Other student teachers may start out in any of a wide variety of situations, such as caring for infants at a child care center, working with three-year-olds at a Montessori school, or supervising kindergarten and elementary school students in an after-school program. The various early childhood education settings are defined in the following section.

Preschools and Child Care Centers.   *Preschools* (also called prekindergarten schools or nursery schools) are designed primarily to provide early educational experiences for three- to five-year-olds. Preschools typically offer half-day (for example, 9 A.M. to 11:30 A.M.) or part-week programs (for example, Monday, Wednesday, and Friday). *Child care centers*, sometimes called *day-care centers*, also provide early educational experiences for young

FOCUS ON Communicating with Parents

Parents Who Are Anxious about Putting Their Child in Preschool

Karen, the head teacher at the New Beginnings Preschool, glanced at her watch. They had been sitting in Karen's office for almost an hour, discussing Mrs. Marcus's questions. Before that, Karen had given her an extensive tour of the preschool.

It is not unusual, Karen knew, for parents to be particular about checking preschools before enrolling a child. Even so, Mrs. Marcus seemed to have more concerns than most. Perhaps she was feeling guilty about going back to work and leaving three-year-old Katy in someone else's care. Or maybe she was worried that Katy would take it as rejection from her mother.

MRS. M.: Did I ask you about the school's credentials?

KAREN: We're accredited by the National Association for the Education of Young Children. We're also licensed by the state.

MRS. M.: Are teachers trained in first aid?

KAREN: Most of them are. At least one on every shift is trained. It's rare that anything serious

happens, but if it does, we will notify you immediately at work. We keep a file with parent and doctor emergency phone numbers.

MRS. M.: I'm just a little nervous. Is it okay for parents to visit?

KAREN: You can visit as often as you like, and no prior notice is required. You also can call any of the teachers at school or at home. Of course, I imagine you'll be quite busy at work.

MRS. M.: They do learn, right? I mean they don't just play?

KAREN: At this stage in their development, children learn by playing and interacting with other children. You should look carefully at how our curriculum is structured and then see if you think that it will suit Katy. You know her best.

What else might Karen have done to make Mrs. Marcus feel more comfortable about enrolling her daughter in preschool? Should Karen have asked Mrs. Marcus if she had guilty feelings about returning to work?

children, but they are geared to the schedules of working parents. In addition, many child care centers provide infant care and early morning and afternoon care for school-age children. They typically offer full-day programs that operate from early morning to evening five days a week. Many parents who use child care during the day do so because they work. Others, including teen parents, attend school or are pursuing independent activities.

It is important to note that the distinctions between types of care for young children have become blurred in recent years. Many preschools have lengthened their hours of operation to accommodate working parents, and child care centers have added more educational components to their programs. A 1990 survey by the NAEYC found that 80,000 early childhood programs, including preschools and child care centers, were serving four million preschoolers and one million elementary school children.

In addition to caring for her own three-year-old daughter, this family day care provider offers care for two other children in her home.

Family Day Care.   Another type of early child care is *family day care*, where providers take care of small groups of children in their own homes. The providers often combine caring for their own children with caring for the children of relatives, friends, and neighbors. Another type of family day care, called *group home care*, involves two or more providers and an average of 7 to 12 children in a home setting. Most states set limits on the number of children that can be cared for by one provider, and they require licensing for health and safety reasons. In most states, providers are not required to meet any minimum educational standards, unless they are seeking to be accredited by NAEYC. Family day care providers comprise a large segment of early childhood care providers. The 1990 NAEYC survey estimated that there were about 118,000 licensed family day-care operations, approximately 2,800 of which are accredited by the NAEYC, and as many as 1.2 million unlicensed ones. Together, these operations provide care for as many as 3.8 million children.

Sponsors of Child Care

Preschools and child care centers are supported by public funding from the federal, state, or local government; by private funding, usually fees paid by parents or corporations; or by a combination of public and private funding. Since the 1960s, the federal government has played an increasingly important role in establishing child care policies, such as tax credits for adults with child care costs, and appropriating funds to make sure that as many children as need child care receive it. Corporations and businesses, too, are increasing their interest in and support of child care issues and creating new options to meet the growing child care needs of their employees.

Publicly Funded Child Care.   Some preschools, such as Head Start, are public, nonprofit operations. Federal legislation has also provided funding for early childhood education. For example, the Education for the Handicapped Act of 1975, Public Law (PL) 94–142, mandates free public education for children with physical disabilities beginning at age three. Public Law 99–457, passed in 1986, amends the Education for the Handicapped Act to provide funding for educational services to infants and toddlers with disabilities, in addition to children ages three to five. Other legislation includes the Act for Better Child Care Services (ABC), approved by Congress in 1990. This legislation enables states to improve the quality and availability of child care services and to help families with low and moderate incomes to pay for child care. One government agency, the U.S. Department of Defense, directly sponsors preschools and child care programs for its employees. It operates more than 500 preschools on military bases around the world to serve the needs of military personnel, and it enforces very high standards.

States and public school districts also fund and operate preschools throughout the country. Some school districts around the country have established prekindergartens in recent years to accommodate working parents. Other programs provide compensatory education to disadvantaged four-year-olds so that they will be on a par with other youngsters when they enter kindergarten. Other school districts provide full-day kindergartens or offer two years of kindergarten to children who are *developmentally at risk*—that is, children whose language or motor skills are significantly below the norm. In addition, a few school districts with large numbers of teenage mothers offer child care and home economics programs at high schools so that the mothers can complete their educations and learn effective parenting skills. Some publicly funded preschools are fully funded by the government; others are partially subsidized and also are supported by fees paid by parents, sometimes on a sliding scale based on household income.

Privately Funded Child Care.   Most preschools are privately owned and operated centers to which parents pay fees for services. One common type of private preschool is the *cooperative preschool* where parents cooperatively govern all facets of the school. Fees are lower at cooperative schools because parents volunteer to serve as assistant teachers or to perform cleaning and maintenance work around the school. Many religious institutions, YMCAs, and YWCAs sponsor preschools. Usually, the school is housed in a church, temple, or Y building and may be partially funded by the organization.

Some preschools have become chain operations with facilities in many cities and a standardized curriculum. One of the largest of these operations is Kindercare Learning Centers, Inc., which has close to 2,000 centers across the country. Certain privately operated preschools, such as Montessori schools, follow a specialized curriculum (see Chapter 2) and may require

At corporate child care centers, parents can take their children to their place of business and visit them during the day, such as on their lunch hour.

specialized teacher training. Montessori schools remain popular in the United States, and there are 690 schools affiliated with the American Montessori Association. Today, Montessori and many other types of preschools have a waiting list for enrollment.

A few large corporations and hospitals have established subsidized on-site or *corporate child care centers* so that parents can take their children to their places of business and then visit them during the day. Some companies provide employees with vouchers to help pay for child care. Other companies form cooperative services with neighboring companies, contract with nearby child care centers for services, or offer information and referral services to their employees. Although these programs can be expensive to operate, many business managers believe that they actually save the companies money because satisfactory child care arrangements reduce employee turnover and absenteeism. Some companies use their child care services to attract—and keep—well-qualified personnel who have children. Some hospitals operate round-the-clock child care centers to enable employees to work changing shifts.

Universities and community colleges that offer child care or education degrees often run their own laboratory or research schools where students can practice-teach and perform research on child development. These schools often offer child care services for university faculty members, employees, and students, as well as for local residents.

The Path to Learning

During the first five years of life, children grow and develop rapidly, changing miraculously from helpless infants to capable, independent young children. As they grow, children acquire an enormous amount of information about themselves, about other people, and about their world. They learn to use their senses; to walk, run, and climb; to speak their native languages; and to establish relationships with others. They form many basic concepts about objects and people in their environments, and about how things work and relate to each other. They also form ideas about themselves that can affect their thinking and behavior all their lives.

The First Five Years

Almost from the moment they are born, children are hard at work learning about the world. They stare at their own fingers; they see, taste, and feel the objects around them; they begin using their muscles to sit up, crawl, and walk; and they learn to distinguish their mother's voice and touch from those of other people. They listen intently to human speech and practice making sounds themselves. Soon they are beginning to talk and communicate with others.

As they grow, children develop and gain skills in five broad areas—physical, emotional, social, cognitive (intellectual), and creative. As their bodies mature, children develop the large and small muscle control that enables them to walk, run, climb, and manipulate objects. Emotionally and socially, they learn to trust other people, to communicate with others, and to express their feelings to others. Intellectually, they develop the ability to remember things they have learned in the past, to solve problems, to imagine themselves playing various roles, and to sort and classify objects according to common properties. Creatively, young children learn to explore and devise new uses for materials and to discover novel solutions to challenges and problems, sometimes referred to as creative thinking.

By the age of two, children have become avid explorers and scientists constantly testing their environment. They are learning to talk well and to express their needs and desires in words rather than by crying. With the acquisition of language, cognitive development blossoms because language enables children to talk about their experiences, ask questions, form concepts, and understand events more effectively.

Around age three, children begin to become involved in a wider world. Their daily experiences and increased language skills allow them to interact more with people and places in the neighborhood and community—stores, playgrounds, restaurants, and perhaps preschools. Of course, some young children may already have been in child care settings with other children during their infant and toddler years. They begin to play with other children and to develop social skills and moral values. They feel tremendously confident about their abilities.

Three- and four-year-olds spend a lot of time in fantasy play, which helps them develop important problem-solving skills. This type of play also helps children work out their feelings in various situations and provides an opportunity to practice language skills. In everyday activities, children at this age begin to ask endless questions and conduct endless experiments to see how things work and what happens next.

By the time children are four or five, their senses have nearly matured, and their large and fine motor skills are improving. They can climb a set of monkey bars or hold a crayon with equal ease. Their attention span has also increased so that they can work with greater concentration on puzzles, art, and building projects. They can follow directions and enjoy simple board games. Most early childhood education experts agree that young children still learn best through hands-on activities such as Ms. Paone's tomato plant project. Preschoolers at this age are typically very energetic and enthusiastic.

Learning at Home

Children traditionally begin learning at home, and their parents and siblings are their first teachers. When a baby's mother plays peekaboo or patty-cake with her, when her father reads a storybook to her, or when her sister builds a house with plastic bricks while she watches, the baby is soaking up new knowledge and experiences. Children's first environment is their home and yard and the objects in them. They learn about the functions of different rooms, and they are surrounded by toys and household objects that they can manipulate and study.

Children learn many physical skills at home, such as running, climbing, riding a tricycle, buttoning a sweater, and taking lids off jars. In addition, children are stimulated intellectually by all the objects and experiences in their home environments. Most children first encounter toys, pets, counting rhymes, songs, books, colors, and art materials at home.

Socially, children develop their first relationships with family members. Their emotional development is greatly affected by how they are treated within the family. A child who has warm and nurturing primary care-givers—for example, parent, guardian, and/or full-time babysitter—will have a very different self-image than a child who has cold and distant primary caregivers. The social and emotional development of children is also influenced by their birth order within the family. For example, firstborn children tend to be somewhat more aggressive and dominating because their parents are often very demanding with high expectations, whereas younger siblings tend to be more accommodating. In addition, children learn their first social skills at home. They learn to put away their toys, share a treat with their siblings, take turns using the bathroom, and say "please" and "thank you."

Parents usually see their major roles as those of caregivers, nurturers, and disciplinarians, but they are also teaching their children about the world and human relationships as they carry out their parental responsibilities. Children's experiences at home are limited and controlled by the creativity and resources of their families. A child who is exposed to books at home may learn to read more readily than a child who grows up in a home devoid of books. Similarly, children whose parents or caregivers take them to restaurants, museums, concerts, and zoos will know more about the wider world than children whose parents stay close to home.

Home is a child's first learning environment. Children begin to develop many basic skills through reading stories with their parents, playing games, and experimenting with art materials.

Learning in the Preschool Setting

Parents decide to put children into preschool or another form of child care for a variety of reasons. Single parents or two-parent working families need child care for their young children. Other parents may feel that an only child

FOCUS ON / **Activities**

Observing in the Preschool Setting

Observation—closely watching children's behavior—is an important part of teaching. It is a helpful tool in identifying problems and opportunities, making teaching decisions, establishing relationships with the children, and assessing their progress. Good observation takes practice!

Try observing one activity or one child. Before you begin, establish an objective for the observation. Specifically, what will you be looking for? For example, you might try observing how the teacher greets the children at the beginning of the day.

Carry a small notebook to record your observations. Confine yourself to factual statements; don't interpret. For example, note that "Stephen smiled when the teacher said hello and asked about his birthday party over the weekend," rather than "Stephen liked it when the teacher said hello"—unless you hear the child say so. Use action words such as *hug* or

laugh and descriptive words such as *loud* or *carefully*. Stay close enough to the teacher and children to hear what they say (write down everything they say), but do not talk to them.

Record the date and the activity that you are observing. Then, focus on "clues" that relate to your observation objective. Did Stephen engage in conversation with the teacher? What did he do after the teacher had finished greeting him? Did the teacher greet every child in the same way? If not, what did he or she do differently?

Afterward, share your observations with the classroom teacher. He or she might shed some light on the situation. For example, Stephen may be a new child, or English may be his second language, and the teacher may be paying extra attention to conversations with him. Discussions with colleagues are helpful in objectively evaluating classroom observations.

needs to socialize with other youngsters. Many parents also see preschool as a means of giving their children a head start educationally. They may feel that the preschool setting offers a richer environment for learning and socialization than their homes do.

Long-term Benefits.   Several leading studies have concluded that children, especially those from a culturally or socioeconomically deprived background, experience certain long-term benefits from attending preschool. A longitudinal study conducted by the High/Scope Educational Research Foundation has been following approximately 60 children from low-income families who attended the Perry Preschool Program in Ypsilanti, Michigan, in the 1960s. The researchers found that the children who had attended preschool had greater academic achievement and participated more in sports and after-school activities than did children in a control group who did not attend preschool. Longer term, they were also more likely to graduate from high school, to go on to college or vocational school, and to obtain and hold a job than did children in the control group. Further findings of this longitudinal study determined that children who attended preschool were more likely to have lower rates of juvenile delinquency and drug use and were also less likely to become teenage parents or to go on welfare. The researchers attributed many of these benefits to the fact that preschool programs help foster children's positive sense of self-esteem (Celis, 1993; Schweinhart, Weikart, & Larner, 1986; Spodek & Brown, 1993).

Another similar longitudinal study found that children who attend preschool are less likely to repeat a grade or to need special education (Lazar, Darlington, Murray, Royce, & Snipper, 1982). Although not all studies agree on the long-term benefits of preschool, researchers do agree that the preschool programs should be high quality in order for children to reap the greatest benefits. Factors that contribute to a high-quality program—trained teachers, an enriched environment, and a varied social environment—are discussed in the following sections.

Trained Teachers.   Teaching preschool children is different from teaching children in elementary or high school. The preschool teacher is trained to be a facilitator and guide rather than a leader or director of learning. While some preschool teachers may model or demonstrate activities, most do not formally instruct their students or require them to complete academic assignments. The preponderant view of early childhood is that preschoolers are not developmentally ready for formal instruction. When they are pushed or hurried beyond their years and abilities, they develop symptoms of stress (Elkind, 1986).

Instead, preschool teachers are trained to teach in a pleasant, informal manner by responding to and encouraging the interests and enthusiasms of the children. For example, Ms. Paone knows that young children love to plant seeds and to watch them grow. With her class, she will capitalize on this interest in exploring different kinds of plants and learning how to care for them. Preschool teachers are trained to make learning a joyful experience because enjoyment is one of the best possible motivations for learning (Sava, 1987; Weider & Greenspan, 1993). The Association of Teacher Educators and the NAEYC recommend that individuals seeking to work in early childhood professions, including preschool teachers, demonstrate competencies in the following core areas as they relate to young children:

- Growth, development, and learning
- Family and community relations
- Curriculum development, content, and implementation
- Health, safety, and nutrition
- Field experiences and professional internship
- Professionalism

An important element of preschool teacher training is learning how to develop a curriculum. In the preschool setting, *curriculum* is generally defined as the process of identifying goals and formulating plans to provide early educational experiences for young children. A curriculum may focus on various elements, including content and activities (What will the children do?);

The preschool environment is a busy, engaging place that offers young children a rich variety of materials to explore. Many preschools provide equipment, such as water tables, that are not usually available to children at home.

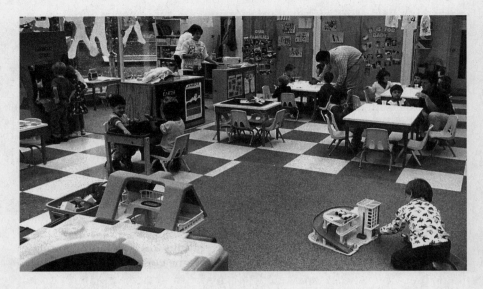

implementation (How will the activities be carried out?); cognitive development (What will the children learn from the activities?); social and emotional development (Are the children enjoying the activity or practicing any social skills?); or a combination of these elements. Different approaches to curriculum are discussed in more detail in Chapter 2 and throughout the book.

Enriched Environment.   Providing children with a wide variety of materials gives them opportunities to explore, manipulate, practice language skills, and learn about the environment. In the preschool setting, these materials can and often do include supplies and equipment not available to children at home. Large crayons and paintbrushes, child-sized scissors, water tables, different kinds of blocks, and puzzles are standard equipment for little hands that are still learning how to manipulate objects. Outside, preschools typically have movable and stationary climbing and play equipment, sandboxes, areas to ride tricycles, and more.

The preschool environment helps children cultivate a sense of order by providing different places and spaces for toys and activities (see Chapter 5 for a more detailed discussion on the physical setting). Ms. Paone's room includes a cozy area for story time, an area for dress-up play, an art corner with easels, and a low table for group art and construction projects to facilitate the children's activities in the preschool environment. Children also become accustomed to conforming to a routine, including periods of indoor and outdoor play, story time, and lunch and snack times.

In Ms. Paone's room, as in most preschool settings, toys, games, and equipment are kept on low shelves so that children can choose their own activities. Having the freedom to choose activities and work on their own gives preschoolers an "I can do it myself" feeling, a sense of independence, and the opportunity to explore new experiences without pressure. Preschools and child care centers also present many opportunities for young children to learn about new environments and people away from home. New experiences for preschoolers that greatly expand their knowledge of their immediate world may include bus rides; field trips to parks, nature centers, and museums; and classroom visitors such as a pilot or a doctor.

Varied Social Environment.   In preschool settings, children learn how to get along with other children, and they learn to master basic social rules. Preschool children have many important opportunities to practice social skills, such as sharing toys and treats, taking turns, communicating with other children, and making friends. Children acquire social skills through practice. Once they have mastered these skills, they are more likely to be liked by other children and to develop high self-esteem. In addition, social interaction in the preschool environment may help a shy child become more outgoing, calm an overactive child, or give a nonverbal child the confidence to talk more.

   Children in family day-care or preschool settings also learn how to relate to adults outside the family. Children often become close to preschool teachers and new caregivers, and they feel loved and cared for by a number of adults. This experience helps children build trust with other adults, which will serve them well during their school years. Child care settings can also provide opportunities for children to get to know children and adults of other races, ethnic groups, or backgrounds. These multicultural experiences foster tolerance, respect, and understanding in children.

Trends in Early Childhood Education in the 1990s

Americans will continue to need and demand high-quality, affordable child care and preschool programs. The number of two-worker (or dual-income) families has increased 13 percent since 1980 (U.S. Bureau of Labor Statistics), while the number of single-parent families has grown enormously in recent years. In fact, one-fourth of American children live in single-parent homes. As of 1991, there were more than eight million single-parent homes (U.S. Bureau of the Census), and in many of those homes, the parent works full-time and needs affordable child care. Also, about 17 percent of women in the work force have children under the age of six (U.S. Bureau of Labor Statistics), and more than 55 percent of mothers of young children under age six are entering or returning to the work force (Zinsmeister, 1988). The increase in working mothers has created a demand not only for more infant day care but also for more child care options throughout the years prior to kindergarten.

   In addition, pending changes in state and federal welfare policies will encourage or mandate that single mothers on welfare join the work force. These changes in turn will greatly increase the need for affordable child care for those families. In fact, a recent study conducted at Harvard Graduate School of Education found that working-class parents face some of the worst shortages of preschool in the country (Chira, 1993).

Preschool teaching is a rewarding career that is gaining status. Professional organizations are working toward increased pay, providing more ongoing professional training, and increasing public awareness of the value of early educational experiences for young children.

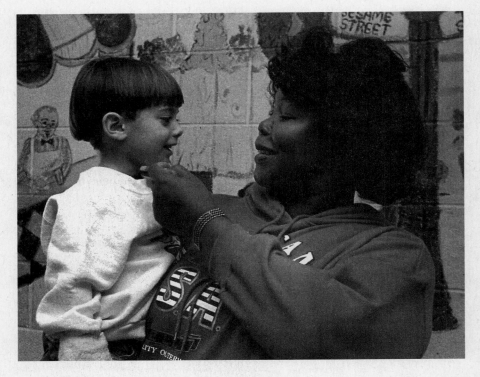

Corporations are expected to continue their involvement in providing and supporting child care options for their employees' children. In 1991, an estimated 5,600 companies offered some form of child care options, such as child care referral networks, job-sharing arrangements, or on-site child care centers (Friedman & Galinsky, 1991). Increasingly, more companies have adopted policies such as parental leave that enable parents to deal with family needs or crises without fear of losing their jobs or incomes. The Family and Medical Leave Act of 1993 protects all eligible employees of companies totaling 50 employees or more from losing their jobs if they take unpaid temporary leave for the birth, adoption, or foster care placement of a child or to care for a child or another family member with a serious health condition.

The federal, state, and local governments and school districts continue to increase funding and enrollment in programs such as Head Start, prekindergartens, and extended kindergartens (two-year kindergartens for children who, through testing, are found to need an extra year of kindergarten before first grade). Under the Act for Better Child Care Services, the federal and state governments are also continuing to strive for higher academic, health, and safety standards for child care centers and preschools. Professional organizations, such as the NAEYC and the National Council for Accreditation of Teacher Education (NCATE) will continue to set teacher standards for accreditation and continuing education options throughout the 1990s. Teachers and child care professionals have been demanding more ongoing professional training, such as workshops, home study, and refresher courses.

The early childhood professional organizations such as NAEYC are working to raise the public's awareness of the need for high-quality child care, such as those schools accredited by NAEYC, and fair compensation for child care professionals. State licensing is becoming more complex as states move to age-based instead of grade-based licenses. Pay and compensation for child care professionals has historically been very low, even when compared with other traditional "women's jobs" such as elementary school teachers and secretaries. In 1991, the weekly median salary for child care providers was $132, while secretaries earned $359 and elementary school teachers earned $537 (U.S. Bureau of Labor Statistics).

Early childhood educators can expect to see further changes in preschool settings as preschools adopt new curriculum elements. Some of these elements will include computer literacy programs, multicultural and anti-bias curriculum, and developmentally appropriate practices, which will be discussed in Chapters 2 and 3. As child study centers in universities and colleges continue to conduct research on the intellectual, emotional, social, and physical growth of children, new findings will continue to affect preschool curriculum practices. In addition, the sociological and economic trends and changes discussed in this chapter will support the need for well-trained and dedicated preschool teachers long into the 21st century.

CHAPTER 1 REVIEW

SUMMARY

- In earlier centuries, children were regarded as miniature adults and cheap laborers. Only in the last few centuries have philosophers and educators begun to study child development, recognizing the differences between children and adults, and striving to identify and to meet the specific needs of children.

- Preschools began in Europe in the 1800s. German educator Friedrich Froebel started the first kindergartens in which fostering the development of the child was emphasized. Many early preschools were established to help orphans and children of the poor.

- The preschool movement began to grow in the United States in the 1920s. The government supported nursery schools during the Depression and World War II. In the 1960s, the government established Head Start preschools to provide early education to children from low-income families and children with disabilities.

- Types of child care today include preschools, which emphasize child growth, development, and early educational experiences; child care centers, with hours designed to meet the needs of working parents; and family day care, which is in-home, small-group child care.

- The federal and state governments and many school districts sponsor child care programs and services throughout the United States.
- Privately owned nonprofit and for-profit child care centers serve hundreds of thousands of children. These include cooperative schools, centers that are sponsored by religious organizations, day-care chain operations, and corporate on-site child care centers.
- Children grow and develop rapidly in the first five years. They learn to use their senses, walk and talk, form their own identities, and develop relationships with others.
- Children first begin to learn about their world at home as they explore their home environments and form their first relationships with family members.
- Preschools can provide a richer learning environment than the home. Research shows that children who attend high-quality preschools may be more successful in school.
- Preschools can provide varied social environments where children learn to get along with other children, befriend and trust adults, experience other cultures, and interact with children from other ethnic groups.
- The increasing number of two-worker families and working single parents will continue to increase the demand for high-quality child care in the United States.
- Government agencies, corporations, and professional organizations will strive to upgrade the quality of child care and to increase compensation for child care professionals.
- As child study centers in universities and colleges continue to research child development and how children learn, the preschool curriculum will change and evolve to better serve the needs of young children. This change will also support the need for well-qualified preschool teachers and child care professionals.

ACQUIRING KNOWLEDGE

1. Describe the attitudes of adults toward children that were most common before the 18th century.
2. How did the Industrial Revolution lead to changes in attitudes toward children?
3. What theories about children did Locke develop?
4. What recommendations did Rousseau make for a child's education?
5. On whose theories was Pestalozzi's school based? What type of education did this school emphasize?
6. Why did Froebel use the word *kindergarten* to describe his school?
7. What did the schools for young children established by Owen, Montessori, and the McMillans have in common?

8. How did the federal government during the Great Depression change the growth of preschools in the United States?

9. What is Project Head Start? What are its primary goals?

10. What are the main differences between a preschool and a child care center? How are these distinctions becoming less rigid?

11. What is family day care?

12. Describe three sources of public funding for preschools.

13. How do cooperative preschools keep fees low?

14. What are some of the options that corporations and companies offer to provide child care benefits to employees?

15. Give three examples of social skills that children learn at home.

16. How can birth order affect a child's development?

17. How does the parent of a young child fulfill a role as teacher?

18. What are some of the long-term benefits of attending a high-quality preschool?

19. Why are preschool teachers trained differently from elementary school teachers?

20. What can happen if preschool children are pushed to learn academic lessons that are too difficult for them?

21. How do preschools provide an enriched environment?

22. Why are low shelves used for storage in most preschools?

23. How does the preschool setting help children develop social skills?

24. What trends in early childhood education will probably continue in the next ten years?

THINKING CRITICALLY

1. Early pioneers in the field of child development, such as Locke and Rousseau, faced both resistance and indifference to their ideas. How do you think that they convinced people to change their attitudes toward children? What arguments might they have used?

2. Many studies have supported the long-term benefits of high-quality preschool education. How could these studies be used to support an increase in public funding for preschool education? Do you think that publicly funded preschools benefit society as a whole? Why or why not?

3. Many businesses offer child care for their employees, but many others do not yet offer this benefit. How might employees at a company that does not provide child care persuade their employer to change this policy? What advantages might the company gain?

4. The National Association for the Education of Young Children established accreditation standards in the 1980s. However, accreditation is not mandatory to operate a preschool. Why do you think the NAEYC decided to begin this program? Why might a preschool seek accreditation from an association such as NAEYC?

OBSERVATIONS AND APPLICATIONS

1. Visit two different preschool settings, such as a private preschool and a family day-care setting, or a Head Start preschool and a corporate day-care center. How many children are there in each setting? How many caregivers are there? Describe in detail the different activities going on in the two settings. What kinds of materials are the children using? What are some of the differences you observe between the two settings, such as group size, noise level, and room size? Try to be as specific as possible. At the preschool, check with the head teacher to determine if the center is nonprofit or for-profit and whether it is accredited.

2. Spend part of a morning or afternoon at a preschool. Make a detailed list of the activities and materials you see that you think might not typically be available at the children's homes. These might include group story reading, playing with musical instruments, or a water table.

3. Gina is a bright four-year-old girl, who happily plays at home during the week while her mother watches her. Gina's mother makes a special effort to "teach" Gina about various concepts that relate to her daily play, such as filling different-sized pails with sand or looking for the color green in the pictures of a storybook. Gina's mother believes that home is the best learning environment for her daughter at this time, but Gina's father disagrees. He wants to send Gina to preschool for a few days each week. What elements of the preschool setting might he discuss with his wife to help her see his point of view?

4. Brett is a four-year-old boy in your preschool class. When his mother came to pick up Brett, she voiced a concern to you. At home, Brett has often been playing by himself lately with imaginary friends, acting out different scenarios such as eating at a restaurant or going to the doctor. Brett's mother is worried because Brett seems to prefer these imaginary friends to real people. What can you tell her to allay her fears?

FOR FURTHER INFORMATION

Adams, G., & Sandfort, J. (1992). State investments in child care and early childhood education. *Young Children, 47*(6), 33–35.

Ayers, W. (1989). *The good preschool teacher: Six teachers reflect on their lives.* New York: Teachers College Press.

Baker, A. C. (1992). A puzzle, a picnic, and a vision: Family day care at its best. *Young Children, 47*(5), 36–38.

Boyer, E. L. (1993). Ready to learn: A mandate for the nation. *Young Children, 48*(3), 54–57.

Bredekamp, S. (Ed.). (1991). *Accreditation criteria and procedures of the National Academy of Early Childhood programs* (rev. ed.). Washington, DC: National Association for the Education of Young Children.

Elkind, D. (1987). The child yesterday, today, and tomorrow. *Young Children, 42*(4), 6–11.

Friedman, D. (1986). *Child care makes it work—A guide to employer support for child care*. Washington, DC: National Association for the Education of Young Children.

Greenberg, P. (1990). Before the beginning: A participant's view. *Young Children, 45*(6), 41–52.

Hendrick, J. (1987). *Why teach: A first look at working with young children*. Washington, DC: National Association for the Education of Young Children.

Hymes, J. (1987). Public school for four-year-olds. *Young Children, 42*(2), 51–52.

Jensen, M., & Goffin, S. (Eds.). (1993). *Visions of entitlement: The care and education of America's children*. Albany, NY: State University of New York Press.

Katz, L., Evangelou, D., & Hartman, J. (1990). *The case for mixed-age grouping in early education*. Washington, DC: National Association for the Education of Young Children.

Klein, A. (1992). *The debate over child care: 1969–1990*. Albany, NY: State University of New York Press.

Maynard, G. (1986). *The child-care crisis: The thinking parent's guide to day-care*. New York: Penguin.

McMahan, I. (1992). Public preschool from the age of two: The ecole maternelle in France. *Young Children, 47*(5), 22–28.

Neugebauer, R. (1989, February). Child care 1989: Status report on for-profit child care. *Child Care Information Exchange*, pp. 19–23.

Osborn, D. K. (1991). *Early childhood education in historical perspective*. Athens, GA: Daye Press.

Phillips, D., Scarr, S., & McCartney, K. (1987). Dimensions and effects of child care quality: The Bermuda study. In D. Phillips (Ed.), *Quality in child care: What does the research tell us?* (pp. 43–56). Washington, DC: National Association for the Education of Young Children.

Shuster, C., Finn-Stevenson, M., & Wart, P. (1992). Family day care support systems: An emerging infrastructure. *Young Children, 47*(5), 29–35.

Stevens, J. (1982). The national day-care home study: Family day-care in the United States. *Young Children, 37*(4), 59–66.

Theilheimer, R. (1993). Something for everyone: Benefits of mixed-age grouping for children, parents and teachers. *Young Children, 48*(5), 82–87.

Willer, B. (1992). An overview of the demand and supply of child care in 1990. *Young Children, 47*(2), 19–22.

Curriculum Approaches and Developmental Tasks

OBJECTIVES

Studying this chapter
will enable you to

- Discuss four leading theories of child development
- Explain how preschool programs are developed from theories of child development
- Compare and contrast the characteristics of child-initiated and teacher-directed programs
- Discuss how curriculum activities relate to the ages and stages of preschool children

CHAPTER TERMS

academic approach
behaviorist theory
child-initiated curriculum
cognitive-developmental theory
curriculum web
developmental-interactionist theory
developmental task
developmental/whole child approach
developmentally appropriate
hierarchical learning
High/Scope
key experience
maturationist theory
Montessori
object permanence
preoperational stage
project approach
psychosocial
scheme
teacher-directed curriculum

JASMINE, age five, saw the large fishbowl filled with bright objects as soon as she arrived in her classroom in the Sunny Days Preschool. At first, she thought that the bowl was filled with jelly beans, just like the "How Many Jelly Beans?" contest at the public library. As she moved closer, though, she saw that the bowl was filled with buttons. Unable to resist the lure of the bright buttons, Jasmine dipped her hand into the bowl, and, as she began stirring the buttons, several other children drifted over to the table, each wanting a turn.

Jasmine's teacher, Barbara Jones, called to the children to come and look. Then she asked, "What's in the fishbowl?"

Avi, age five, answered, "Buttons . . . lots of buttons. They must have come from a whole bunch of stores! Can we play with them?"

The children all spoke at once: "Can we?" "Me, too!" "Me first!"

"Everyone will have a turn," Ms. Jones said. As the children settled at her table, she suggested a task for the four-year-olds. "Juan, Karen, Nathan, and Rickie, here are some buttons for each of you." She gave each child a handful of buttons and asked them to find the blue buttons and put them in one pile.

Next, Ms. Jones turned her attention to the five-year-olds. "Avi, Jasmine, and Alice. Let's see if you can find all of the blue buttons that have only two holes." The children didn't realize it, but Ms. Jones had given a more complex task to the older children.

Jasmine worked in her group for a few minutes, trying to sort the blue buttons with two holes. She threw them down in frustration. "I can't do this," she said to Ms. Jones. "Can I help find the blue buttons instead?"

As Ms. Jones found, all the children were interested in the button sorting, but not all children of the same age were able to perform the same tasks. For example, although Jasmine was five years old, she preferred the simpler task of just finding the blue buttons rather than looking for two characteristics—color and number of holes. This suggests that she might not yet have reached the developmental level typical of five-year-olds.

How Young Children Learn

Researchers and experts in the field of child development have tried to explain exactly how children are able to learn so much during their first five years. Although no one explanation describes how all children learn, a number of ideas have been advanced. This section will consider three main views: that children learn in stages, that children learn from experiences, and that children learn from play. These views are not mutually exclusive—that is, they can be considered separately or together as an explanation of how children learn.

One view of learning, *hierarchical learning*, holds that learning proceeds in stages. For example, young children learn to climb stairs by first crawling up each step. Next, they hold onto the banister while placing both feet on the same step. Finally, they alternate placing one foot on each step. Each stage requires children to use existing skills while developing new and more advanced skills.

Another commonly accepted idea suggests that young children learn best through their own hands-on experiences. In other words, they learn by doing (Elkind, 1986; Kamii, 1985). For example, it is easier for children to learn about sponges by dipping one in water, squeezing it, and wiping up spilled milk with it, than by seeing a picture of a sponge. Very young children have limited language abilities and a limited ability to understand symbols or representations, such as a picture of a sponge. Adults often use only the sense of sight, but children rely on many senses to help them discover and learn.

Another illustration of this view is the way a child learns to ride a bicycle. Although an adult can demonstrate how to ride and can explain to a child how to balance his body on the bicycle, the child cannot learn to ride until he gets on the bicycle and tries it himself.

FOCUS ON Activities

Adapt an Activity to Different Ages

Cooking allows children to explore a variety of concepts related to mathematics (measurement, time, sequence), science (temperature, liquid to solid), and language (recipe instructions), as well as to follow directions. Most cooking projects are easy to adapt to different age levels in the same classroom.

It's best to choose a simple recipe—corn bread is a good choice. Keep the group size to three to five children at a time.

For two-year-olds, use a prepared corn bread mix. Premeasure the corn bread mix in plastic bags and the water (or milk) in plastic containers. If an egg is required, break it open beforehand and place it in a container. Prepare a chart of the recipe in pictures (picture of a measuring cup, carton of milk, and so on) so that children can follow the process.

For five-year-olds, use a simple corn bread recipe, not a mix. Label measuring cups and

spoons in large writing. Use a picture chart similar to the one described above. Set up the ingredients to be easily accessible (for example, flour emptied into a canister is better than flour in a 5-pound bag).

For either group, plan the activity so that everyone has an active role, not just watching the teacher. Try giving every child a job, such as measuring and stirring in the milk. Many recipes can be halved, or quartered, so that a new group of children can make their own batch of corn bread.

Begin with a discussion of cooking. What kinds of foods do the children's families cook? What is a recipe? Have they tasted corn bread? Show the materials and proceed through the recipe, demonstrating each step. Let the children watch as you put the pans in the oven. When the corn bread is done, enjoy!

Yet another idea is that children learn through play. Play helps children develop physical skills, strength, and coordination. In addition, play provides children with the opportunity to practice language skills. When preschoolers play together, they learn and practice social skills such as sharing and cooperating. Play allows children to create and act out different situations or to replay actual experiences but with a different outcome. A child may play with dolls, acting out her mother's tucking her into bed, but unlike her mother, she "allows" the child doll to play with her teddy bears before the mother turns out the light.

These ideas describe some of the ways in which children learn. It is also important to know that children develop as individuals, not as a group. Each child develops under different circumstances and at different times and rates. Early childhood professionals need to know and understand theories of how children learn, grow, and develop. They must also know how this information influences curriculum for preschoolers.

This chapter will show how the most commonly accepted theories of child development have shaped various curricula. The chapter will focus on two leading preschool curriculum approaches. It will include a summary of the advantages and disadvantages often associated with each of the approaches. The chapter also summarizes the design of other well-known preschool curriculum models, including the developmentally appropriate curriculum model.

Theories of Child Development

Educators who work with preschool children create programs and curricula that reflect their beliefs about how children learn, grow, and develop. Although these beliefs vary, early childhood professionals and preschool teachers tend to agree that, on the whole, two-year-old children are very different from three-year-old children, and three-year-olds from four-year-olds, and so on—physically, emotionally, and cognitively.

Theories of how children develop and learn are the foundations on which early childhood educational programs are based. Understanding these theories will help early childhood professionals evaluate existing programs and formulate new programs. Many of these theories, however, focus on different aspects of child development. No one theory addresses all factors of child development—such as the range of abilities of "average" children or the effects of diverse backgrounds on learning—with equal emphasis. This section describes four leading theories of child development: cognitive-developmental, psychosocial, behaviorist, and maturationist.

Cognitive-Developmental Theory

Proponents of the *cognitive-developmental theory* believe that children learn by interacting with their world (DeVries & Kohlberg, 1990; Franklin & Biber, 1977). Children actively question, analyze, experiment, and test what they see and hear against what they already know, as Jasmine did with the bowl of "jelly beans"/buttons. By interacting with their environment, children acquire ever-increasing amounts of information and develop more efficient ways of processing this information. This processing in turn, leads them to further develop cognitive skills.

Much of cognitive-developmental theory was formulated from the work of Swiss psychologist Jean Piaget in the 1920s and later. Through his observations, Piaget reasoned that children strive to understand their world through a combination of assimilation, or incorporating new information into their conceptual framework, and accommodation, or adjusting their conceptual framework to fit the new information. Jasmine's original *scheme*—a general, established mental concept or structure—told her that small, shiny, multicolored objects were jelly beans. Through accommodation, she changed that scheme to the following concept: small, shiny, multicolored objects can be many things, including jelly beans and buttons. Cognitive development occurs as children bring their knowledge and conceptual framework into balance and move to the next level.

Piaget's observations of his own children led him to define four distinct stages of intellectual development. From birth to between 18 and 24 months of age, children are in the sensorimotor stage and learn through the senses

Most preschoolers are in Piaget's second stage of cognitive development, the preoperational stage. These four-year-olds are practicing their ability to match different shapes.

and movement. Much of the infant's and toddler's experiences with objects and people during this time become the basis for future conceptualization. The major intellectual accomplishments of this period include understanding *object permanence* (knowing that objects exist even if they are out of sight), learning about cause and effect, beginning to develop a sense of self-identity, acting on an idea, and developing short-term memory.

Piaget's second stage of intellectual development is called the *preoperational stage.* It represents the preschool years and lasts from about age two to about age six or seven. During this stage, children learn to use language; start to develop the ability to reason, classify, use mental images, and think intuitively; and come to understand the concept of number. Children at this stage of development occasionally exhibit behaviors characteristic of the previous or the next stages. For example, the ability to sort objects based on more than one characteristic indicates a higher cognitive level than being able to sort based on only one characteristic. Although Jasmine was able to sort buttons based on color, she was not yet able to sort for two characteristics (color and number of holes), an ability typically reached by age five or six. The preoperational stage is discussed in greater detail in Chapter 12.

Children from about age 6 or 7 to about 11 or 12 are in the third Piagetian stage of cognitive development—concrete operations. They are developing the ability to think logically and use reasoning to draw conclusions, just as Avi did when he wondered about the source of so many buttons. Children at this stage can classify, explore, experiment, and integrate new information at a higher cognitive level than before.

The last Piagetian stage of formal operations begins about age 12. This stage is the start of mature, logical, abstract thinking, which continues to develop into adolescence and adulthood. Children in this stage are able to

FOCUS ON   Communicating with Parents

Talking about Your Curriculum Approach

Sheri Hamilton, head teacher at the Great Start Preschool, smiled as she noticed Mr. Delgado's puzzled look. His reaction was typical of parents who were unfamiliar with child-initiated curriculum.

Sheri imagined how the school must appear to Mr. Delgado—an uncontrolled environment where children did as they pleased with little guidance from the teachers. Yet, the scene before them was the result of hours of teacher preparation, based on experience with each child's strengths, weaknesses, interests, and skills.

MR. D: This isn't exactly what I expected to see. When I placed my other daughter in preschool, where we used to live, the teachers led arts and crafts and other planned activities. Things haven't changed that much in just a few years, have they?

SHERI: No, but our preschool takes a different approach—it's called child-initiated.

MR. D: Do the children just play? What do the teachers do?

SHERI: Some preschools follow a teacher-directed approach. The teacher decides what the children will do each day and when activities will start and stop. With our approach, the teachers plan a variety of activities and provide appropriate materials, but the children choose to do what they find most interesting. We've found that this keeps them highly motivated. They learn at their own pace, as they develop their independence.

MR. D: It sounds like I could leave my daughter at home and achieve the same result.

SHERI: It may seem that way, but you would need to do a lot of work behind the scenes. For example, the wheels in that corner will introduce the children to how things move along the ground. Later in the week, we'll put out some boxes, pulleys, and other materials. We began this unit because several of the children made their own "delivery truck" with our red wagon.

MR. D: I see. Well, I'd like to think about what I've seen today.

SHERI: Of course. Take as much time as you need. And remember, you can always bring your daughter in for a trial period.

What are some other points Sheri could have made to help Mr. Delgado feel more comfortable? Why might a teacher-directed program have benefits over a child-initiated program?

consider hypothetical possibilities and abstract concepts such as freedom, and they are able to visualize and choose among alternative solutions. However, it is not clear how many people ever reach this stage of cognition. Some early childhood experts believe that formal operational thinking is attained only after a sufficient number of appropriate experiences and may also be tied to cultural influences (Byrnes, 1988; Santrock, 1990).

Another adaptation of developmental theory is called the *developmental-interactionist theory*, which expands upon Piagetian theory. Whereas Piagetian theory focuses primarily on cognition, or intellectual development, the developmental-interactionists take a broader view of the child. They believe that learning takes place not only through the interaction of the child with his environment but also through interaction of the child's various "selves"—cognitive, physical, emotional, social, and creative. For example, developmental-interactionists believe that a child's emotional self affects his cognitive self. That is, if he feels good about himself, he will be more curious and interested in learning. Further, if he feels competent in physical skills and/or makes friends easily, this competency will help him feel masterful and good about himself, which in turn prepares him for new experiences.

Psychosocial Development

Another stage-oriented theory was formulated by Erik Erikson, an American psychoanalyst born in Germany. He theorized that during childhood and adulthood, the individual goes through a series of eight stages that shape basic attitudes, expectations, and emotions. As with Piaget's stages of cognitive development, each stage presents a more complex set of challenges than the one before it. Further, the attitudes shaped by the resolution of the conflicts within each stage stay with people throughout the rest of their lives.

Unlike Piaget, who stressed cognitive development, Erikson focuses on social and emotional development. His theory is sometimes referred to as *psychosocial*, since it addresses the psychological and emotional aspects of people, as well as how people interact with one another. Erikson's first three stages occur during early childhood. Infants experience the first stage—trust versus mistrust—when they learn whether the adults in their lives are trustworthy or not. A baby who is fed regularly learns to trust others to fulfill her food needs.

The second stage—autonomy versus shame and doubt—occurs when children are between 18 and 24 months. During this time, children have a "sudden violent wish to have a choice" (Erikson, 1963, p. 252) and to become more independent of their primary caregiver. They begin to make decisions and to act on them, such as wanting a specific toy and then finding it. They often use the word *No!*, especially when asked to perform a task. Saying "No!" helps them create a barrier or separation to show their independence. When caregivers try to control children at this age too strictly and prevent or restrict them from making their own decisions, children feel shame as well as doubt about their self-worth.

Between the ages of two and five, children feel a struggle between initiative and guilt. They become more involved with their environment, exploring and experimenting, testing the effects of their actions, and enjoying imaginative play. The threat of failure, however, in achieving their own goals of accomplishment, may plague the child with feelings of guilt or anxiety. To be successful in resolving this stage, and the previous stage, initiative must dominate. Although Jasmine was eager to initiate play with the buttons, she might have become doubtful or anxious about her abilities if she had not found a way to be successful with a less-complicated task. (Turn to Chapter 8 for a more detailed discussion of Erikson's stages.)

Behaviorist Theory

The *behaviorist theory* of child development is rooted in behaviorist psychology. B. F. Skinner, one of the leading American psychologists working in this area, formulated a theory of behavior based on his observations of animals and people. Skinner believed that a child develops and learns as a result of forces, sometimes called stimuli, controlled by someone other than the child. Further, a child tends to repeat behaviors or responses that are reinforced or rewarded in some way that is meaningful to the child.

Behaviorists believe that the reverse is also true. Children tend to discontinue behaviors that are not rewarded. Based on his experiments, Skinner concluded that children learn when specific stimuli and meaningful rewards are combined to produce appropriate responses. This is a direct contrast to the cognitive-developmental view that children learn through internal forces generated by their own interaction with the environment.

Maturationist Theory

Arnold Gesell developed the *maturationist theory* by observing children of all ages to determine at what age and in what order they learn to perform tasks and behaviors. Gesell's observations, conducted during the 1940s, were used to chart the normal stages of development that children go through as they mature. As a result of his studies, Gesell concluded that children who are the same age will generally master the same skills and perform the same behaviors. Although Gesell's original work was done 50 years ago, researchers doing similar studies have found that Gesell's average ranges of child development are still accurate (Brenner, 1990).

Unlike the behaviorists, who believe that children's behavior and learning are primarily molded by external influences, advocates of the maturationist theory assert that children are born with the genetic program for all their abilities. These abilities emerge at a specified time. Most children's abilities evolve in generally the same order and at about the same age. The process of maturation is the key mechanism for children to reach each successive stage.

Critics of Gesell's theory assert that, with respect to some aspects of development, it is inappropriate to "wait" until the child matures to a certain stage (Mason & Sinha, 1993). For example, research has shown that poor readers in first grade remain poor readers in later grades (Juel, 1988; Mason, Kerr, Sinha, & McCormick, 1990). For this reason, it is preferable to involve these children in early literacy activities in preschool and not to wait until the ability to read appears in time.

Understanding Developmental Tasks

Approaches to curriculum flow directly from various theories of child growth and development. Activities within a curriculum are determined by many factors. This section focuses on the link between curriculum activities

TABLE 2.1
Overview of Developmental Tasks

Areas of Development	Two- and three-year-olds	Four- and five-year-olds
Physical—Gross Motor	Walk, run, climb, hop	Smoother, more skilled movements: run faster, jump higher, skip, throw ball, jump rope
Physical—Fine Motor	Gradually gain more control over hands and fingers: string large beads, turn pages, solve simple puzzles	Lace, cut, draw simple geometric shapes; cut neatly around objects with pre-drawn lines; color within lines; dress selves
Social	Play near other children but not with them; participate in simple group activities; know gender identity; develop friendships	Interact with other children during play, also play alone; may be obedient and eager to please but may also challenge adults to get peer approval
Emotional	Feel secure in routines; begin to separate selves from primary caregiver; begin to develop self-control; respond to affectionate behavior	Proud of new skills; express feelings; may have frequent but short quarrels; can control behavior even when adults are absent
Cognitive	Experiment with tactile objects, tastes, and smell; begin to label, match, and associate objects; represent actions, events, and objects in symbolic way; understand functions of objects	Begin to reason; match, make associations; ability to discriminate between and among things improves; role-playing becomes more sophisticated
Language	Converse with friends and family; develop concepts and communicate with them verbally; enjoy talking and asking questions	Expand oral vocabulary; speak in full sentences; respond to conversations; verbalize concepts; describe objects; reason with others

and the ages and stages of preschool children. Whether working in teams or individually, it is important for teachers to understand the capabilities and limitations of children between the ages of two and five in order to plan an effective curriculum (Greenberg, 1990).

What are developmental tasks? *Developmental tasks* were defined by Robert Havighurst (1952) as tasks individuals have to master at different ages in order to be happy and to function well in society. More than 40 years later, this definition is still valid. Another way to look at the term is that developmental tasks are the particular abilities or skills that children master over time. Also, these abilities or skills gradually become more complex. These tasks fall into the general areas of physical, emotional, social, and cognitive development. Tasks within these areas are often expressed as being achieved by a certain age—for example, walking by one year or throwing a ball by four years. Table 2.1 provides an overview of developmental tasks, and Appendix A provides more detail.

FOCUS ON   Cultural Diversity

A Glimpse into a Japanese Preschool

Five-year-old Yoshi attends a Japanese preschool in Osaka called a *hoikuen* (day-care center) six days a week including Saturday. His mother takes him to school on her way to work at about 8 A.M. Yoshi always helps the younger children put away their lunch boxes and other belongings as they arrive. He knows that this task is the responsibility of the older children like him.

After everyone arrives, the day begins with a ritual—a 30-minute morning meeting for the whole school. Yoshi and his friends sing songs and perform calisthenics. Today, they are going to hear an inspirational speech.

In the classroom, the children formally bow and greet their teacher each day, another ritual of Japanese schools. There is one teacher for every 40 children. Yoshi is especially excited today because the teacher has chosen him to be the *toban*, or monitor, for the day. He will assist with activities, gather the class together, and distribute tea at lunch.

After the morning ceremony, Yoshi and his friends participate in organized play, such as arts and crafts, nature walks, story time, and games that will help the children prepare for academic study. At lunch the children say a formal thank-you for their meal. Afterward,

Yoshi enjoys a period of free play before the children settle down for a nap. Then there is time for a snack and more free play or an organized activity until Yoshi's mother comes to pick him up.

Nearly all preschools in Japan are privately owned and require tuition. There are two early education options: the *yochien* for three- to five-year-olds and the *hoikuen*, which accept children from infancy to first grade. The two types of preschools used to have different curricula, but today the only real distinction is in their schedules. *Yochiens* are in session four to five hours a day, while *hoikuens* remain open for the full day. Both schools operate six days a week. The traditional curriculum covers health, society, nature, language (communication with others), drawing, and music/rhythm. Most schools do not provide any academic instruction, even at a preliminary level. The Japanese believe that preschool children are too young to benefit from such study.

In many ways, Japanese preschools are similar to their Western counterparts. They are considered successful if the children develop good social relations and hygiene habits and become interested in learning about the world.

Physical Development

During the preschool years, young children gain weight, grow taller, move more smoothly, and control their bodies with more precision and skill. Part of preschoolers' physical development involves the refinement of gross motor and fine motor skills. Running is a gross motor skill; tying shoelaces is a fine motor skill. Sometimes, these skills are called large muscle and fine muscle skills. Some examples of physical developmental tasks for young children are walking backward (12 to 24 months), then walking on a line (three to four years); kicking a ball (two to three years), then throwing it overhand (three to four years).

Emotional and Social Development

Preschoolers are beginning to learn about what feelings are and how to express feelings without hurting others. They are learning to share, to help others, and to feel good about themselves. Emotionally healthy children are self-confident and can focus their energies on learning and growing without worry or insecurity. Children with strong social skills interact well with other children or adults, are more likely to make friends easily, enjoy a sense of well-being, and function well in new settings. Two examples of social developmental tasks are beginning dramatic play—such as pretending to squirt water on a fire (three to four years)—and engaging in dramatic play with more cooperative roles—one child acts as a fire truck driver, another climbs ladders, another turns on the water while another holds the hose (four to five years).

Cognitive Development

During the preschool years, children develop many intellectual skills, including language and memory; use of symbols to represent objects or actions; and the ability to pay attention, reason, and draw conclusions. Two examples of cognitive developmental tasks are understanding past and present in a general sense (three to four years) and understanding "next week" (six years).

Variability in Development

Although all children grow and develop physically, emotionally, socially, and cognitively, they develop at different rates in different areas. For example, five-year-old Jasmine was not at the same cognitive level as the other children her age, yet she was self-confident enough to ask Ms. Jones if she could change her activity. Development in one area affects development in another. Emotionally self-confident children are more likely to participate in new activities, which may in turn enhance their cognitive development.

Some of the variability in development rates can be attributed to heredity, parenting background, health history, and other environmental factors (Greenberg, 1992). Even though teachers should take variability into account, developmental averages provide useful guides or benchmarks.

Curriculum Content

Curriculum development starts from the teacher's knowledge of the theories of child development, understanding of how children learn, and understanding of the developmental tasks of the age group in the class. The content of curriculum, or the focus of activities to address the growth and development of young children, can be approached in different ways. The two leading approaches to curriculum content are developmental/whole child and academic. Whereas some preschools strongly emphasize one approach or the other, many may use a combination of approaches.

In addition to the following discussion, throughout this book you will see many examples of different kinds of curriculum content, and you will learn how curriculum activities foster the growth and development of young children.

The Developmental/Whole Child Approach

In the *developmental/whole child approach*, activities are designed to encourage development of the "whole child"—physically, emotionally, socially, cognitively, perceptually, and creatively. Activities usually address more than one developmental area; for example, outdoor climbing affects physical, social, and perceptual development. This approach reflects the developmental-interactionist theory of child development—focusing on growth through the interaction of the child's physical self, emotional self, social self, and so on. Curriculum activities provided by the teachers are based on their observations of each child's interests and developmental progress.

Activities designed with the developmental/whole child approach typically reflect the maturationist theory of child development. Each activity is neither too difficult nor too easy but geared to the developmental level of the child to provide challenges for further growth. Teachers provide activities that capture the children's interest and are challenging but not so difficult that the children become frustrated or threatened. Ms. Jones tried to structure the button activity to suit the different abilities of the children in her class. Although she initially divided the group by age, she now knows that Jasmine may belong in the group primarily made up of four-year-olds, at least for certain kinds of activities.

The Academic Approach

In the *academic approach* to preschool curriculum content, the majority of activities are specifically designed to help children develop the skills they will need in grade school, such as reading and writing. Different areas of the curriculum may be called "subjects," such as art, blocks, cooking, math, physical education, woodworking and construction, crafts, and dramatic play. Language arts might include such skills as reading, writing, drama, vocabulary, and storytelling. Science might include such areas as health, hygiene, geography, history, current events, and family life. The academic approach, influenced by the behaviorist theory of child development, is often utilized in teacher-directed programs, which are discussed in the next section.

Curriculum Implementation

Once the curriculum content is determined, there are a variety of styles, or approaches, in which it can be implemented. The two leading approaches for implementing the curriculum are child-initiated and teacher-directed. Other important approaches discussed in this chapter and throughout the book include the developmentally appropriate curriculum, Montessori, the

TABLE 2.2
Variations in curriculum based on the structure and content

Curriculum Structure	Focus of Curriculum Content	
	Developmental/Whole Child	*Academic*
Child-Initiated	Child chooses activities, how to use materials, and duration of activity. Child moves around classroom freely. Activities are designed to address all aspects of child's development.	Activities and materials have academic focus, and materials are to be used in certain way. However, child chooses activities and duration of activities. Child moves around classroom freely.
Combination	Mixes aspects of child-initiated and teacher-directed structures. Some parts of day are dedicated to free choice of activities for children; other parts of day are directed by teacher. Activities address many developmental areas.	Mixes aspects of child-initiated and teacher-directed structures. Some activities are directed by teacher, and others are free choice. Activities are focused on academic content.
Teacher-Directed	Curriculum content reflects many aspects of child development, but teacher directs most activities. Curriculum may include developmental activities, but teacher decides what children will do, duration of activities, and how materials will be used.	Curriculum focuses on academic skills only. Teacher directs most activities and decides time and their duration. For example, teacher tells children when and how to participate in science, premathematics, prereading, and reasoning activities.

project approach, and High/Scope. As illustrated in Table 2.2, many preschools and child care centers utilize a combination of approaches to curriculum content and implementation.

The Child-Initiated Curriculum

The *child-initiated curriculum* is based on the cognitive-developmental theory of child development—that children learn by doing, playing, and experimenting with objects rather than by being taught about them. This approach is also driven by the idea that young children learn through play.

Structure. All the activities in a child-initiated program are developed by the staff to interest the children and stimulate their own natural curiosity. Early childhood educators who use the child-initiated approach believe that if activities are designed to attract the children's attention, then the children will enjoy becoming involved in the activities they choose and will stay focused longer.

Although the day appears to be unstructured, teachers in child-initiated programs play an important behind-the-scenes role. They research, devise, and make available to the children a variety of activities. They prepare materials for all areas of the classroom, such as cooking, art, and dramatic-play

In a child-initiated program, teachers provide a choice of activities and materials.

materials. They choose books, find songs, and plan for special trips and visitors.

In a child-initiated program, the children decide what activities to do, when to do them, for how long, and how to use the materials available. For example, a child may choose to paint in the morning. She will also decide what to paint and when to stop. There is little or no direct instruction from the teacher.

A typical day in a child-initiated preschool is relatively unstructured. Children might meet as a group and talk about a particular topic—for example, how birds built a nest outside one of the classroom windows. For much of the day, however, children choose and participate in individual activities. Several activities may be happening simultaneously. At other times, children may all be involved in playground activities outdoors.

Proponents of child-initiated programs believe that children who participate in activities they enjoy will perform them well and acquire a sense of competence and a feeling of achievement or accomplishment. This feeling in turn increases their self-esteem—that is, they feel good about themselves as successful learners. Early childhood educators who use the child-initiated approach generally believe that children themselves are the best source for building self-esteem. Self-esteem and competence are discussed in more detail in Chapter 8.

Child-initiated programs depend on having the children actively involved in their learning (Kamii & DeVries, 1978). Such programs need abundant resources and substantial opportunities for children to experiment. They require teachers who will support the children in their exploration and experimentation.

The teachers act as resources and facilitators to encourage children to develop strategies for learning (Forman & Kuschner, 1983). In child-initiated programs, teachers tend to ask questions that encourage children to discuss, reflect, and examine. In general, the process of "doing" and developing ways of thinking is emphasized more than the specific content of what is learned.

Advantages and Disadvantages.   Every curriculum approach has its supporters and its critics. Supporters of the child-initiated approach believe that children choose the activities they consider most interesting. Not only does free choice keep the children highly motivated and engaged in their activities, it also means that the teacher may have fewer discipline problems.

Other advantages attributed to child-initiated programs are that children learn to set priorities, develop independence, and make decisions. Children are encouraged to pursue their own interests rather than doing what may be meaningful only to the teacher or to another child.

In a child-initiated program, the children learn how to think about and process new information, a skill that supporters say can be used in any situation, not just school. Also, since children in these programs learn at their own pace, they generally are not pressured to learn a prescribed set of skills within a specified time frame.

Critics of the child-initiated curriculum say that teachers have less control over where children play and how they use materials. For example, a child may consistently choose to work in the art area, avoiding the block or science areas entirely. Such a response by the child, critics assert, could lead to a severely limited preschool experience. The question arises, for example, as to whether this child will be prepared for kindergarten.

Child-initiated programs that utilize the developmental/whole child approach require teachers to observe and identify on an ongoing basis each child's strengths, weaknesses, interests, and skills. To address all of these ever-changing developmental and individual needs adequately, critics say, requires substantial resources.

The Teacher-Directed Curriculum

The *teacher-directed curriculum* typically incorporates behaviorist theories about how children learn. In this approach, the teacher decides what activities the children will do, when they will do the activities, for how long, and how the materials will be used. For example, the teacher may provide only red and yellow paint and tell all the children to paint flowers for 15 minutes. No other activities are available until the painting activity is completed. This approach is in direct contrast to the child-initiated approach, where children would be likely to choose their own colors and decide what to paint.

Structure.   A typical day in a teacher-directed program has more obvious structure than a child-initiated program and less time for free play. Teachers are careful to prepare children for later grades. They tend to teach subjects as a series of skills, each more complex than the one before it. Activities are designed to teach these skills by dividing them into small segments. The idea

In a teacher-directed program, the teacher typically leads children in most activities. Here, a caregiver explains the different parts of a tree to a group of three-year-olds.

is that these interim steps help children learn without frustration. As children master sequential steps, teachers gradually progress to activities directed at more challenging skills. Many teachers reinforce or reward children who perform the desired behaviors or tasks with verbal approval, an extra privilege, or a symbolic reward such as a star. Children who do not perform well may have to repeat assignments or may be denied some privilege or activity that is meaningful to them, such as free outdoor play.

One program that provides immediate feedback to children is DISTAR, developed by Carl Bereiter and Siegfried Engelmann in 1966. The DISTAR program was originally designed to guide children from socioeconomically disadvantaged backgrounds through a specific sequence of academic skills. Children must master each skill before they can move forward. Appropriate responses are immediately reinforced. Chapter 11 includes more discussion of the DISTAR curriculum.

Advantages and Disadvantages.   The teacher-directed approach has been both praised and criticized. Supporters suggest that immediately reinforcing desired behaviors reduces errors in learning. Children will not have to unlearn errors. The teacher, however, must be skilled in reinforcing behaviors, directing children to the next level of mastery, and making sure that children learn skills in each content area.

Advocates of teacher-directed programs also consider it an advantage that teachers have more control over the activities in which the children participate. Teachers, they say, have more freedom in determining the content of the curriculum and can set a well-rounded curriculum for all the children. Also, many people are more comfortable with the idea that an adult is in charge.

Critics say that the teacher-directed approach is too heavily controlled by external (teacher) rather than internal (child) forces (Seefeldt, 1990). By directing learning, teachers ignore the child's thoughts and feelings in favor of an imposed curriculum and tend to treat children as passive objects rather than active learners.

Since all activities are teacher-directed, critics assert that children have little sense of autonomy or self-control. They must do as they are told. For example, a child may become frustrated if he is allowed to play at a preferred activity for only 15 minutes a day. Another child may be told to play in a certain area where she does not want to play. Many critics see the reinforcement aspect of the teacher-directed approach as manipulative and consider it an improper teaching method.

The Developmentally Appropriate Curriculum

In the mid-1980s, early childhood programs such as kindergartens became increasingly funded by state and local governments as part of public school systems. During this time, early childhood educators became increasingly concerned that they would no longer have control over the curriculum. In response to their concern, the National Association for the Education of Young Children published a position statement entitled *Developmentally Appropriate Practice in Early Childhood Programs Serving Children from Birth through Age 8* (Bredekamp, 1987). The book sets forth the NAEYC's definition and description of developmentally appropriate and inappropriate practices in early childhood education programs.

In a *developmentally appropriate* curriculum, activities are geared to the developmental level of the child. Both child-initiated and teacher-directed preschool programs can utilize a developmentally appropriate approach through activities designed with the delicate balance of presenting challenges without causing frustration.

A developmentally appropriate curriculum has two dimensions: age appropriateness and individual appropriateness. The concept of age appropriateness is related to the work of Gesell, as discussed earlier in the chapter. Children grow physically, emotionally, socially, and cognitively in a sequence that follows a predictable pattern. By understanding the changes that children experience at each age, teachers are better able to provide activities that are appropriately challenging.

Individual appropriateness addresses the unique differences among children, including "individual pattern and timing of growth, as well as individual personality, learning style, and family background" (Bredekamp, 1987, p. 2). Although children progress through the same ages and stages,

A developmentally appropriate program is geared to the varying abilities and interests of preschoolers. Discovery and learning take place through hands-on activities. These four-year-olds are exploring how different shapes feel.

they do so at different rates and in different patterns. Individually appropriate programs provide activities that respond to the child's needs regardless of what they might be. Curriculum activities need to be modified to support children who, for example, are physically challenged or extremely shy.

Developmentally appropriate programs are flexible and accommodate the needs of the children, rather than forcing the children to mold themselves to a preset program (Bredekamp, 1987). In the scenario at the beginning of the chapter, Ms. Jones modified the button-sorting tasks to fit the differing abilities of the children in her class. By definition, developmentally appropriate experiences are those in which children experience success and accomplishment and are challenged without feeling overwhelmed. Successful experiences foster feelings of self-confidence and strengthen emotional development. Children feel good about themselves and are more willing to take risks and to try new activities.

The term *developmentally appropriate* refers to all aspects of the program: the content, materials, teaching strategies, and activities. Proponents of this approach assert that programs that are not developmentally appropriate may cause the child to become frustrated, confused, or withdrawn. Those that are developmentally appropriate will encourage the child's growth and development (Bredekamp, 1987).

Other Curriculum Approaches

As stated earlier, many early childhood education programs combine aspects of the teacher-directed, academic curriculum with the child-initiated, developmental curriculum. Three examples of these variations are Montessori, the project approach, and High/Scope.

Montessori. Activities in a *Montessori* preschool, a variation of the academic approach, are designed to develop independence, a sense of empowerment, and self-help in children. The Montessori curriculum is influenced by the maturationist view of child development. All activities are structured and directed by the teachers and are academic in focus. The activities focus on mathematics concepts, reading and language, geography, science, physical activities, and practical life skills, such as keeping one's environment clean and neat.

Montessori programs consist of a rich sensory environment with specially designed materials to develop the senses of touch, smell, and hearing, as well as visual development. Materials include, for example, cloth swatches, rods, blocks, sticks, smelling jars, bells, and sound boxes.

Teaching follows a prescribed format. The teacher models, demonstrates, or explains the new skills to the children (in some instances, only to the child or children who are ready). The children observe the teacher and then immediately imitate the skill—for example, sorting rods into groups by size. Once the correct procedures are learned, the child is encouraged to independently engage in the activity to reinforce learning. The activities represent steps that the children must learn in the process of acquiring skills. Only those children who have successfully learned one step will be taught the next. The curriculum also includes some opportunities for children to choose their own activities.

A typical Montessori activity might look like the following. Jamal and Lisa unroll a small rug on the floor. Then they get blocks from the shelves, starting with the shorter blocks first, and place them on the rug. They lay out the blocks in the pattern of an increasingly large spiral. When they have used all the blocks, Jamal watches as Lisa walks inside the spiral, making one step next to each block. When she reaches the center, she turns and walks out in the same way. Next it's Jamal's turn. The children return the blocks to the shelf in the prescribed order and roll and put away the rug. See Appendix C for an example of a daily plan and Appendix D for an example of an activity plan in a Montessori preschool.

In a strict Montessori preschool, there is only one way to perform activities and use materials. Early childhood professionals wishing to teach in Montessori schools must receive special training, in addition to appropriate state certification.

Although the Montessori approach has many followers, it has been criticized for focusing too heavily on intellectual development and too little on emotional and physical development. There is also little creative thinking because children use materials in the Montessori-prescribed way.

Project Approach. The project approach, promoted by Lilian Katz in the United States, is a variation on the child-initiated approach. The *project approach* allows groups of children to explore one topic, from several different aspects, over the course of several days or weeks, depending on the interest and the ages of the children. It is similar to the concept of units, or themes, but uses more input from the children.

The Montessori approach is designed to help children gain a strong sense of independence. It utilizes a variety of specially designed sensory materials to foster growth and development.

The topics for projects tend to be broad based and drawn from the children's experience. For example, children living in a rural or suburban area might learn about the bus that takes them to school. One group of children might study all the different kinds of lights inside and outside the bus. Another group might measure the bus and count the number of seats. Another group might compare the bus door to other kinds of doors or school buses to other kinds of buses. Another group might draw pictures of what it is like to take a ride on a bus. It is important that the project provide a context to sustain the interest of the groups (Katz, 1988). Projects generally require advance planning, cooperative work, research, and the active participation of all children in the group.

Katz and many other early childhood educators in the United States admire the preschool programs in Reggio Emilia, Italy, which have used the project approach for decades. Teachers use projects to allow children to practice their developing skills and to pursue their interests in all areas of the classroom—such as drawing, dramatic play, and language arts. The teachers stay attuned to the children's progress, looking for ways to expand the children's interest in and knowledge of the topic. Teachers observe, ask questions, and may add new props or materials to extend the project in new directions. Because these projects involve a high level of teacher-child interaction and often lead to new ideas for curriculum activities, Reggio Emilia may be considered a combination of the teacher-directed and child-initiated approaches to curriculum (New, 1992).

Katz and her associates refer to project work as a way of teaching and learning. Designing curriculum in a project format also helps determine the content of what is learned and taught. Katz and Chard believe that project work included in an early childhood curriculum promotes intellectual development by engaging the children's minds (Katz & Chard, 1989). Project work might not replace the entire curriculum, but should provide an opportunity for children to contribute to group efforts and to try out newly learned skills. See Appendix C for an example of a daily plan in a preschool that uses the project approach.

One aspect of this approach is called a *curriculum web,* in which children's interests serve as a starting point from which different activities grow. Each activity relates to a central concept—for example, water. A web of activities extends from the central concept into different areas, such as weather, animals that live in the water, and songs about water. Curriculum webs support the developmental-interactionist theory of child development; that is, curricula should reflect the interdependence of all aspects of the child (Workman & Anziano, 1993). See Figure 2.1 for an example of a curriculum web. See Appendix D for an example of an activity plan related to a curriculum web.

High/Scope.   The *High/Scope* curriculum is based on the cognitive-developmental view of child development. It supports the idea that children construct knowledge from interaction with their environment and that they must be actively involved in their learning. Curriculum activities are

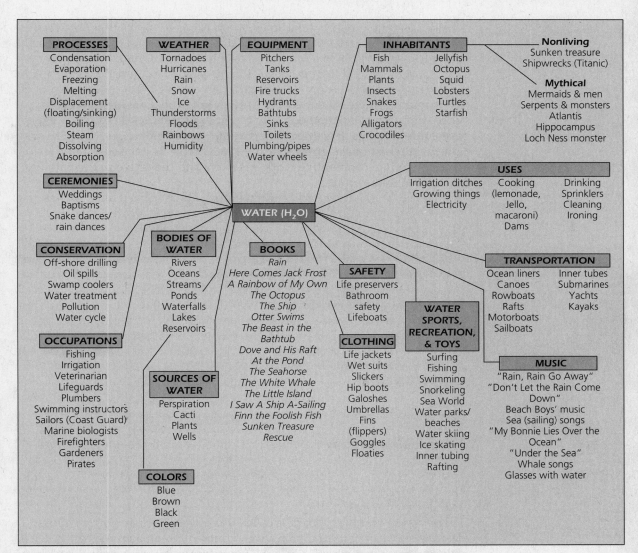

FIGURE 2.1   Example of a Curriculum Web. This curriculum web shows how a central concept—water—can form the basis for a wide variety of activities throughout the curriculum. Reprinted from "Curriculum Webs: Weaving Connections From Children to Teachers" by S. Workman and M. C. Anziano, 1993, *Young Children*, *48*(2), p. 5. Copyright © 1993 by the National Association for the Education of Young Children. Used by permission.

focused on exposing the children to *key experiences*, a preset group of experiences designed to stimulate teacher-child discussion and problem-solving tasks. One key experience, for example, is grouping. After a discussion with the teacher about all the things that go into a house, the children might sort a boxful of household items into cooking items and cleaning items.

In a process called "Plan-Do-Review," the teacher and the children plan activities one-on-one or as a group, carry out the activities, and then review them (Hohmann, Banet, & Weikart, 1979). For example, a child might decide to play in the housekeeping area. She first places her name tag on a hook in the group time area under a picture of the kitchen. Later in the day, the teacher might talk to her about her housekeeping play, ask her to tell a story about it to a small group of children, or have her draw a picture about it.

As in the child-initiated approach, teachers who use the High/Scope curriculum must plan and set up the classroom environment carefully. Extensive written materials and teacher training are provided by the developers of the High/Scope curriculum. See Appendix C for an example of a daily plan and Appendix C for an example of an activity plan that might be used in a High/Scope preschool.

Applications

Teachers need to know the developmental levels of preschool children in order to plan developmentally appropriate activities. It is important to remember that the needs of children change as they develop and that children develop at different rates. The following lists relate some of the different needs of children ages two and three and children ages four and five to curriculum materials and activities. Part II of this book discusses all these areas in greater detail. Age-specific needs aside, all preschool children require adult supervision and safe, adequate outdoor and indoor play areas and play equipment.

Developmental Needs of Two- and Three-Year-Olds

Physical development:
- Because two- and three-year-olds need space to experiment physically, preschools should provide adequate play spaces and equipment.
- Toddlers need adequate rest time and frequent, nutritious snacks, so it is important to make time for naps and to incorporate food into some of the activities, such as simple cooking projects.

Emotional and social development:
- Because many toddlers are just beginning to interact with others, create activities that can be done in pairs.
- Two-year-olds do not know how to share. For example, if there are four children playing with trucks, there should be four trucks.

Cognitive development:
- Two- and three-year-olds primarily use their senses to learn about their environment, so make available a variety of interesting tactile materials. Encourage children to touch and manipulate materials.
- Because toddlers are just beginning to increase their language skills, start to include stories, rhymes, and songs.
- Toddlers have limited cognitive understanding and a limited attention span; keep instructions simple and short.

Developmental Needs of Four- and Five-Year-Olds

Physical development:
- Because they are increasing large muscle coordination, children should have outdoor and indoor equipment for gross motor development that they can move themselves.
- For the development of fine motor skills, four- and five-year-olds need objects to explore and manipulate, such as toy cars and trucks, puzzles, and dolls with clothes that button and zip.

Emotional and social development:
- Four- and five-year-olds want to feel that they are contributing to the group. Try to create opportunities for them to handle daily responsibilities.
- Children this age are learning to work with others. Include some activities that require small group cooperation.

Cognitive development:
- Four- and five-year-olds are becoming increasingly verbal. Leave ample time to discuss, converse, sing, share ideas, express opinions, and talk. Expect the classroom to have a higher noise level. Talking is healthy—a sign of language development.
- Because they are developing prereading skills, read to the children often, and also leave unstructured time in your curriculum plans for children to spend with books.
- To challenge their classifying skills, present materials to practice sorting and matching by different characteristics.

CHAPTER 2 ▪ REVIEW

SUMMARY

- Although no one explanation describes how all children learn, several views have emerged: children learn in stages, through their own hands-on experiences, and through play.
- Cognitive-developmental theorists such as Jean Piaget believe that children learn by interacting with their world.
- Piaget established four distinct stages of intellectual development: sensorimotor, preoperational, concrete operations, and formal operations.
- Erik Erikson developed a stage theory focusing on social and emotional development. The first three stages affect the preschool years: trust versus mistrust, autonomy versus shame and doubt, and initiative versus guilt.
- Behaviorists believe that children learn as a result of external forces (for example, teachers and parents). Children tend to repeat behaviors that are reinforced or rewarded.

- Maturationists believe that children are born with all their abilities. As they grow and mature intellectually, physically, socially, and emotionally, most children's abilities evolve in generally the same order and at about the same age.

- Developmental tasks fall into the areas of physical, emotional, social, and cognitive development. Most children learn to perform the same sequence of tasks, although some develop at variable rates.

- There are many approaches to curriculum content, but the most common are developmental/whole child and academic. The developmental/whole child approach focuses on developing all the "selves" of the child—physical, emotional, social, cognitive, and creative. The academic approach focuses on activities that help children develop the skills they will need in grade school.

- The two primary approaches to curriculum implementation are child-initiated and teacher-directed.

- The child-initiated curriculum is based on the theory that children learn by interacting with their environment. Teachers devise the learning environment and may structure time periods for certain types of activities, but children choose their own activities.

- In a teacher-directed curriculum, the teacher decides what activities the children will do and how the children will use the materials. These programs are often based on behaviorist theories about how children learn.

- Many preschools utilize a combination of approaches to curriculum structure and content.

- The developmentally appropriate curriculum has two dimensions—age appropriateness and individual appropriateness—and is an important influence on early childhood education programs today. Activities are designed with the children's developmental levels in mind to interest and challenge them without causing frustration.

- Montessori preschools are designed to develop independence and a sense of empowerment in children. Most activities are structured, directed or modeled by the teachers, and academically focused.

- In the project approach, small groups of children explore one topic over the course of several days or weeks.

- The High/Scope curriculum is focused on exposing the children to key experiences, a preset group of experiences designed to stimulate teacher-child discussion and problem-solving tasks. In a process called "Plan-Do-Review," the teacher and children plan activities together, carry out the activities, and then review them.

ACQUIRING KNOWLEDGE

1. Describe three ways in which children learn.
2. How does a child develop new skills and abilities according to the theory of hierarchical learning?

3. What is the primary belief of the cognitive-developmental theory?
4. According to Piaget, what is the difference between assimilation and accommodation?
5. What skills are achieved by infants during the sensorimotor stage of intellectual development?
6. What cognitive skills are achieved during Piaget's preoperational stage?
7. How does the theory of developmental interaction differ from Piaget's constructivist theory?
8. How does Erikson's theory of psychosocial development identify stages of emotional-social learning?
9. How is behaviorism a direct contrast to the cognitive-developmental theory?
10. What is the maturationist theory?
11. Why is it important to identify developmental tasks before designing a preschool curriculum?
12. What is the difference between gross motor and fine motor skills?
13. Give one example of each of the following: a social developmental task, an emotional developmental task, a cognitive developmental task.
14. What are the most important differences between the developmental/whole child approach and the academic approach to curriculum content?
15. Describe how activities are selected and explored by preschoolers in a child-initiated curriculum.
16. What is the role of the teacher in a child-initiated curriculum?
17. How does a teacher-directed curriculum support the theory of behaviorism?
18. What have critics identified as disadvantages of the teacher-directed curriculum approach?
19. What is a developmentally appropriate curriculum?
20. What is the Montessori approach?
21. What are some advantages of project work over individual activities?
22. How do curriculum webs support the developmental-interactionist theory of child development?
23. How can an effective curriculum strengthen children's self-confidence?
24. Why is it important to provide tactile materials for two- to three-year-olds?
25. How can teachers compensate for the limited attention span of a three-year-old?
26. Describe some steps teachers should take to encourage cognitive development in four- to five-year-old children.

THINKING CRITICALLY

1. The theory of behaviorism centers on providing children with stimuli and rewards that are meaningful to the child. What types of rewards might be used to reinforce desired behavior in preschool children? Do you think

that it is a good idea to try to shape behavior by providing rewards? Why or why not?

2. Many preschool curricula today follow a child-initiated approach. Discuss the advantages of this approach. What do you think might be some disadvantages in moving away from an academic approach?

3. It is not always easy to tell whether or not an activity is developmentally appropriate. What should a teacher consider when evaluating a new activity?

4. In some small preschool programs, children of ages three to five are grouped together throughout the day. How might the teacher adapt an activity to make it more challenging for the older children?

5. Parents often have high expectations about their children's development of new skills. Some parents put demands on preschools to teach their children skills that the teacher may not feel are developmentally appropriate. How might a teacher respond to such demands from parents or guardians?

OBSERVATIONS AND APPLICATIONS

1. Observe a teacher and a group of children in the block area of a preschool classroom. In what ways did the teacher interact with the children? Did he or she appear to be directing their play by suggesting things for them to build or props for them to use? Did the teacher stay on the sidelines and watch? Did the teacher respond to things the children said, even if they were not directly addressing him or her?

2. Observe four- or five-year-old children during story time. What was the story about? Did the children seem interested, and did the story hold their attention all the way to the end? If not, at what point did they become distracted or bored? What kinds of comments or questions did they make to one another or to the teacher? Did the teacher seem interested in the children's remarks, or did he or she respond to them as an interruption?

3. In a preschool that follows a child-initiated curriculum, the teacher has taped a long sheet of brown paper along one wall and set up a plastic sheet and pots of paint on the floor. Later that morning, the teacher talks with the children about murals and explains that a mural is a kind of painting that a group of people can make together. Nell and Leroy insist that they paint a farm mural, but Matt and Emma want to paint a mural with astronauts and rockets. The children shout at one another, and one begins to cry. How might the teacher try to resolve the situation without directing instruction?

4. In a preschool that utilizes the project approach, the group of three-year-olds has shown a great interest in fish. The class has visited an aquarium, and there are three pet goldfish in the classroom. What kinds of activities could turn the children's interest in fish into a multifaceted project that will address different developmental areas?

FOR FURTHER INFORMATION

Beardsley, L. (1990). *Good day, bad day: The child's experience of child care.* New York: Teachers College Press.

Biber, B. (1977). A developmental intersection approach: Bank Street College of Education. In M. C. Day & R. K. Parker (Eds.), *The preschool in action* (2nd ed.) (pp. 423–460). Boston: Allyn & Bacon.

Christie, J. (1992). How much time is needed for play? *Young Children, 47*(3), 28–32.

DeVries, R., & Kohlberg, L. (1990). *Constructivist early education: Overview and comparison with other programs.* Washington, DC: National Association for the Education of Young Children.

Elkind, D. (1984). Montessori education: Abiding contributions and contemporary challenge. *Young Children, 38*(2), 3–10.

Elkind, D. (1987). *Miseducation: Preschoolers at risk.* New York: Knopf.

Greenberg, P. (1990). Why not academic preschool? Part 1. *Young Children, 45*(2), 70–80.

Greenberg, P. (1992). Why not academic preschool? Part 2. *Young Children, 47*(3), 54–63.

Hohmann, M., Banet, B., & Weikart, D. P. (1979). *Young children in action: A manual for preschool educators.* Ypsilanti, MI: High/Scope Press.

Jones, E., & Reynolds, G. (1992). *The play's the thing: Teachers' roles in children's play.* New York: Teachers College Press.

Katz, L. (1988, Summer). What should young children be doing? *American Educator,* pp. 28–33, 44–45.

Katz, L., & Chard, S. (1989). *Engaging children's minds: The project approach.* Norwood, NJ: Ablex Publishing Corporation.

Kessler, S., & Swadener, B. (Eds.). (1992). *Reconceptualizing the early childhood curriculum.* New York: Teachers College Press.

Levin, D. E. (1986). Weaving curriculum webs: Planning, guiding and recording curriculum activities in the day care classroom. *Day Care and Early Education, 13*(4), 16–19.

Mallory, B., & New, R. (1993). *Diversity and developmentally appropriate practices: Challenges for early childhood education.* New York: Teachers College Press.

Montessori, M. (1967). *The discovery of the child.* Notre Dame, IN: Fides.

New, R. (1990). Excellent early education: A city in Italy has it. *Young Children, 45*(6), 4–10.

Rambusch, N. (1962). *Learning how to learn: An American approach to Montessori.* Baltimore: Helicon.

Scales, B., Almy, M., Nicolopoulou, A., & Ervin-Tripp, S. (Eds.). (1991). *Play and the social context of development in early care and education.* New York: Teachers College Press.

Workman, S., & Anziano, M. (1993). Curriculum webs: Weaving connections from children to teachers. *Young Children, 48*(2), 4–9.

OBJECTIVES

Studying this chapter
will enable you to

- Describe how the preschool
  curriculum can contribute to the
  development of children's positive
  self-concept and attitudes towards
  others
- Name five skill categories that the
  preschool curriculum is designed
  to develop
- Compare and contrast how
  knowledge is acquired by
  preschool children in teacher-
  directed and child-initiated
  curricula
- Explain why it is important to
  adapt the curriculum to meet the
  individual needs of preschoolers
- Discuss how the teacher's attitudes
  can affect the outcome of
  curriculum activities

CHAPTER TERMS

anti-bias curriculum
attitude
autonomy
disposition
multicultural curriculum
perceived competence
receptivity
self-concept
self-esteem

AFTER the first few days,
Ms. Garcia was less apprehensive
about Beth's joining her class.
She found that although Beth wore a leg
brace to compensate for a birth defect, she
was fitting in well with the four-year-old
class at Community Preschool.

Today, as Ms. Garcia's glance swept the
room, she noticed that Beth was in the
dramatic play corner with two other girls.
She could hear them talking as they began
sorting through the prop box filled with
old clothes, hats, and jewelry.

"Let's pretend we're living on that farm,"
said Josey. The children had visited a
nearby farm last week.

"I'll be the farmer, and you are my
helpers," Lucy said. "We'll put on these
pants and straw hats." As Lucy and Josey
started to put on the denim overalls, Beth
hesitated, afraid that the overalls would
not fit over her brace.

Ms. Garcia noticed Beth's hesitation and
acted quickly but unobtrusively. She
walked over to the dress-up bin,
rummaged around, and found a denim
wraparound skirt. She wrapped the skirt

around Beth's waist and tied a neat bow in front. Then, Beth put a straw hat on her head, just like Lucy and Josey.

"It's time to feed the horses," Beth announced with a smile on her face. "Let's get started." The children picked up their imaginary feed bags and placed them on their horses, just as they had seen the farmer do.

Preschool programs set the stage for children's future growth and learning. Preschools provide children with their first early educational experience in a school environment, introducing them to teachers, classroom routines, group play, and organized learning. Alert and sensitive teachers like Ms. Garcia know that children sometimes require a little assistance to participate in preschool activities. For young children to enjoy a positive preschool experience, the curriculum must address a variety of areas and be flexible enough to adapt to the children's needs. A flexible preschool program increases the likelihood that young children will enter elementary school ready to learn (Epstein, 1993).

There is considerable variation in the style and format of preschool curricula. Basically, however, they all share the same goal: to help young children form positive attitudes about themselves and others, master certain skills, and acquire knowledge through hands-on experiences related to a variety of topics.

To design or implement a curriculum with these general objectives (specific curriculum objectives are discussed in Chapter 6), teachers must know and understand what types of attitudes, skills, and knowledge children typically acquire or develop during the preschool years (Spodek & Brown, 1993). These three elements can be thought of as the building blocks of the preschool curriculum. This chapter discusses how interacting with other children and adults in the preschool setting helps children develop positive attitudes about themselves and about others. It also shows how the curriculum helps young children develop and practice many skills and explore various areas of interest to build and broaden their knowledge.

Early childhood curricula reflect the school's philosophy of education and the talents and interests of the staff. They also tend to reflect the needs and goals of the communities they serve (Robison & Schwartz, 1982). For example, some programs might have a stronger international orientation. Others might be more academic or might focus primarily on the development of social skills.

Curriculum Building Block #1: Self-Concept

During the preschool years, young children are developing their self-concept. *Self-concept* refers to the perception people have of themselves. It includes many aspects of the self—physical, psychological, gender, ethnic makeup. Preschoolers, however, most often describe themselves in physical or action-oriented terms—such as "I can ride a bike" (Damon, 1983; Keller, Ford, & Meacham, 1978). As children grow older, their self-concept divides

Curriculum activities to practice physical skills, such as jumping, help foster a positive, "I can do it" attitude. When children feel good about themselves, they are eager to try new experiences.

into different areas. For example, children may perceive themselves as being competent physically but not socially, or as interacting well with peers but not with adults (Marshall, 1989). Preschool teachers need to understand that the developmental level of the different children in the class will affect how the children define themselves. For example, five-year-olds are more likely to differentiate various aspects of themselves than three-year-olds are.

To help build children's self-concept, preschool teachers must identify children's strengths and provide appropriate opportunities within the curriculum in which they can succeed, as Ms. Garcia did for Beth. Such experiences have a cumulative effect. Success leads to other successful experiences, and children who are successful feel good about themselves. They are also more willing to try new experiences. Helping children develop a positive self-concept should be considered the core building block of curriculum. Without a positive self-concept, young children will not feel confident enough to try new skills, participate in activities, or show interest in new topics and ideas that will broaden their knowledge.

One aspect of self-concept is *self-esteem*—that is, how one evaluates or judges one's own worth as a person. Self-esteem is influenced in part by how the child thinks others perceive her. For example, she might wonder, "Do other children want to be friends with me?" or "Do other children think I'm good at catching the ball?" Self-esteem is also influenced by the child's own *perceived competence*—her beliefs about her ability to succeed at particular tasks (Marshall, 1989).

Another important element in developing positive self-concept is *autonomy*, the ability to make choices and to do things on one's own. This ability helps children feel good about themselves. A curriculum that supports children's autonomy helps improve children's own perceptions of their competence, self-worth, and sense of mastery (Ryan, Connell, & Deci, 1985).

FOCUS ON Activities

Creative Movement for the Physically Challenged

Early childhood programs that include one or more children with disabilities may need to make adjustments in some activities. Take creative movement, for example, which helps children become aware of their bodies and use their imaginations. Can children with disabilities enjoy creative movement along with children who are not disabled?

They can—if you use a little creativity and focus on each child's abilities and strengths.

Warm up by asking the children to move one part of their bodies to the beat of the music. Some children may move their trunk and head, others may wiggle their toes. You may also want to pair a child who has disabilities with one who does not.

Change the music to signal the start of the movement session. (A prerecorded tape of slower and faster music works well.) Provide specific descriptive scenarios for the children to act out, focusing on a variety of body parts

so that all children will feel that they can participate. Here are some ideas.

- "What if your arms were the branches of a tree in a rainstorm . . . or a flower blooming?" "What if your foot was a groundhog coming out of its burrow to see if spring is here?"
- "Pick a part of your body to show me the way the music makes you feel."
- "What expression would you make with just your face if you were upset . . . or scared?" "What if you used just one hand to show you were angry . . . or happy?"

Encourage enthusiasm, but draw the line between acceptable movement and "running wild."

Close the session with a cooldown, such as a finger play or other slow, simple movement. Don't be afraid to ask the children for feedback in preparation for the next movement session.

The preschool curriculum can help foster autonomy in many ways. The High/Scope curriculum, described in Chapter 2, helps children develop a sense of autonomy and positive self-esteem by involving them in their own learning through developmentally appropriate activities (Weikart & Shouse, 1993). In a process called Plan-Do-Review, teachers plan activities with individual children or small groups of children. The children then carry out the activities and review what they have done. The teacher asks the children open-ended questions to help them think about the experiences. For example, Ben makes a "plan" to work in the block center for 45 minutes during center time. His plan is verified by his sticking his name on the Velcro pad in the block center. The teacher notices that Ben and several boys are building a rocket ship. She suggests that a wooden block could represent a computer to help chart their course in space. This faciliates communication and adds a new dimension to the boys' play. Later, in "review," or recall time, Ben and the other boys draw pictures of their ship.

A curriculum that offers children choices—a core teaching strategy in a developmentally oriented or child-initiated approach—fosters autonomy. Teachers who utilize this type of curriculum approach let children choose their own activities in the classroom. They may let children choose from a variety of materials, such as different kinds of markers and paper for drawing, and they may let them choose a book for story time or a music game for circle time.

Another way the curriculum contributes to the development of a positive self-concept is through activities that help children understand and feel good about their cultural background and heritage. By learning more about themselves and what they have in common with others, as well as how their cultural backgrounds make them unique, children take pride in who they are. In the process, they learn to respect other points of view and in turn are respected by their classmates (Ramsey, 1982). The role of curriculum in helping young children learn more about their own culture and other cultures is discussed later in this chapter and in Chapter 9.

In addition to specific curriculum elements, teachers can help foster autonomy by giving children small classroom responsibilities, such as watering the plants or feeding the classroom pets. Although these activities may seem routine to adults, they provide children with the opportunity to develop and demonstrate their growing independence.

Curriculum Building Block #2: Skills

The preschool years are an important time for developing skills. Preschoolers acquire and practice skills through their senses, experimentation, and play—especially by manipulating real, concrete objects and materials, and by imitating others. This skill building occurs in five major areas—physical, emotional, social, cognitive, and creative.

The preschool curriculum fosters the development of many types of skills—including emotional skills, such as learning to handle disappointment.

Physical skills are usually separated into two main types—large motor skills and small motor skills. Large motor skills require the use of the large muscle groups in the arms and legs and are developed in running, jumping, and climbing activities. Small motor skills use the small muscle groups—for example, in the hands. Small-muscle skills, such as eye-hand coordination and cutting with scissors, are developed in art activities and block play, even in dramatic play (for example, in buttoning a doll's coat). Other physical skills addressed by the curriculum relate to physical fitness. For example, children learn about the importance of nutrition, safety, hygiene, and exercise.

Emotional skills affect the well-being and development of children. Emotional skills include learning how to handle emotions—such as fear, frustration, or disappointment—and learning how to behave emotionally in acceptable ways in various situations—such as a child learning not to sulk if she does not get her way. Emotional skills also include learning how to express negative emotions such as anger in acceptable ways and learning how to understand the ways in which one's own emotions and actions affect others' feelings.

The curriculum also should address helping young children develop and strengthen positive attitudes about themselves and their own abilities. When the curriculum provides daily opportunities for children to experience success and feel competent, this experience in turn contributes to their emotional health and well-being.

Social skills are skills that help children interact in a positive, constructive way with other children and adults. Two of the most important social skills children master in good early educational programs are how to get along with other people and how to work effectively in a group. Related social skills include helping, sharing, making friends, and seeing another's point of view. Several elements of the preschool curriculum foster the development of emotional and social skills. These elements include cooperative group play, dramatic play, block play, play with puppets, and circle games.

Preschoolers develop intellectual abilities through curriculum activities such as problem solving, grouping similar objects, or discovery activities (for example, testing whether different objects dropped into water will sink or float). These intellectual abilities include the ability to concentrate, reason, and think, and perceptual skills such as visual discrimination. The combination of hands-on experiences, exploration, and learning information forms the basis for developing concepts, symbolic representations, and long-term memory.

In addition, intellectual skills include language skills. Young children acquire more complex language skills by learning and practicing new words and remembering details, and telling longer, more intricate stories. For example, the curriculum may foster the development of language skills through activities such as a word bank. A word bank is a collection of new vocabulary words written on cards and kept in a ring binder. The child uses her word bank to write or dictate stories, and the teacher helps her add new words each week. Language skills also are integral to the development of emotional, social, and creative skills, as language helps children communicate their feelings, needs, thoughts, and ideas.

Creative skills include the ability to experiment with and express oneself through art and manipulative materials, movement, and dramatic play. Creative skills fostered through art activities often involve small-muscle skills, such as learning to paint with a brush or learning to hold a crayon. Creative skills also include thinking of original ideas or solutions to problems, or coming up with novel uses for materials. The creative process contributes to children's feelings of self-worth. By providing curriculum activities that focus on creative exploration, making choices, and experimenting with a variety of materials and media, teachers help children discover the joy of the creative process as well as the finished product. Children who are encouraged to be creative are likely to continue to be throughout school and life.

Curriculum activities and materials to support the development of these five categories of skills should be both concrete and relevant to the children (Kamii, 1985). In her book *Developmentally Appropriate Practice in Early Childhood Programs Serving Children From Birth Through Age 8*, Bredekamp writes: "Children need years of play with real objects and events before they are able to understand the meaning of symbols such as letters and numbers. Learning takes place as young children touch, manipulate, and experiment with things and interact with people" (Bredekamp, 1987, p. 4).

FOCUS ON Communicating with Parents

Holding a Parent Conference

Bob Davis greets Arlene Weiss with a big smile to hide his nervousness. Even after teaching for several years at the Tiny Tots Preschool, Bob still gets a little anxious before parent conferences. However, he is always well prepared and spends hours gathering samples of the children's work and compiling observations. Conferences help him learn more about the children and also about their parents' expectations. These meetings also provide the parents with a better understanding of the preschool's program and their child's growth and development.

BOB: Hello, Ms. Weiss. I'm Bob Davis, Erin's teacher. I'm glad you're so prompt—we'll have the full 20 minutes to talk together. Let's start with my general impression of Erin. She is doing very well in the intellectual area, what we call cognitive development. She is a quick learner, she already has mastered her shapes and colors, and she is one of the first children in the class to learn new songs. Developmentally, she is ahead of the average three-year-old.

MS. W: Thank you—that's a relief.

BOB: Were you worried that Erin would have problems adjusting to preschool?

MS. W: Yes, a little. She's an only child and doesn't have many friends. I thought that might keep her from fitting in.

BOB: Well, that may help explain her behavior. Although Erin is learning very fast, she is not interacting much with the other children. Let's talk about how we can help her become more comfortable. What do you think about pairing Erin with different children in the class who like to do the same things she does? We'll focus on activities that require two or more children. For example, I know Erin likes colors. I might have an art activity where pairs of children create a painting together, using colors they choose together.

MS. W: That sounds like it might work.

BOB: Great. I'll try it over the next few weeks and let you know what happens. Now, would you like to take a look at some of Erin's work?

How do you think Bob handled the conference? Did he do too much of the talking? How do you think Bob handled Erin's reluctance to socialize? Do you think he focused too much on cognitive skills?

As discussed in Chapter 2, activities in all areas of the curriculum should be developmentally appropriate to reflect different age levels within the preschool program. For example, cognitive and creative arts activities should reflect the fact that the attention span of a two-and-a-half-year-old is much shorter than that of a five-year-old.

Activities can often be designed to provide the opportunity to work on more than one skill simultaneously. For example, a small group of children who are building a house with blocks are developing fine-motor skills (physical), communicating with each other (cognitive and social), and carrying out a plan together (cognitive and social). See Chapter 2 and Appendix A for more in-depth information about the skills preschool children learn.

Curriculum Building Block #3: Knowledge

The preschool years are a time of great discovery for young children as they acquire knowledge about many different topics—families, the community, nature and animals, cars and transportation, numbers and letters, and more. Knowledge, in the preschool setting, is the information that teachers believe children should acquire to be successful both in preschool and in the primary grades. That spectrum of knowledge can vary greatly, depending on the curriculum approach. Some programs emphasize knowing the names of shapes, colors, and parts of the body, or pre-academic activities such as counting or learning the alphabet. Others emphasize knowing the properties of basic objects and how they work; knowing how to solve simple problems; knowing about families and the community; or knowing how to relate to others. Although theories of child development help teachers decide how to teach young children, they do not tell them what to teach (Spodek & Brown, 1993). The curriculum content comes from the teacher or school administrators.

Preschool curricula differ in the types of knowledge that are taught and in how that knowledge is taught or experienced by the children. In teacher-directed early education programs, the teacher directs the learning process and decides what will be taught. Activities typically focus on memorizing information, such as the names of parts of a tree, and imitating skills modeled by the teacher, primarily cognitive skills. The development of physical, emotional, social, and creative skills is a secondary goal.

As discussed in Chapter 2, teacher-directed programs usually reflect a behaviorist approach to child growth and development. Teachers reinforce correct responses and appropriate behavior with rewards or verbal praise. The teacher assumes that all children learn in a similar way and in a predictable order. Concepts and ideas are taught in small, sequential steps.

In child-initiated programs, the children's own interests form the framework for activities. For example, children may show an interest in colors or insects or babies. The teacher devises activities that will expand the children's knowledge of these topics. The project approach and curriculum webs described in Chapter 2 help children gain information and knowledge in this way.

Some child-initiated curricula are pre-academic in orientation and, like teacher-directed programs, organize knowledge into "subjects." For example, they use children's interests as the basis for activities that foster pre-mathematics skills, such as classification and one-to-one correspondence.

Preschool programs that follow a child-initiated approach generally reflect cognitive-developmental theories of child growth and development. The teacher's role primarily involves observing the children's interests and expanding their knowledge with developmentally appropriate materials and activities, making suggestions, asking questions, and providing positive feedback. In this sense, the teacher acts as a guide, intervening in the children's activities only in an indirect manner and only when necessary. The teacher also designs activities to encourage hands-on participation by the children.

Children learn to recognize differences in people, including skin color, at a very early age. An anti-bias curriculum helps children develop positive attitudes about themselves and others.

Curriculum Building Block #4: Attitudes

In addition to fostering a positive self-concept, the development of certain skills, and the acquisition of knowledge, the preschool curriculum influences children's *attitudes*—their feelings, beliefs, and opinions about themselves and others. Children's attitudes are formed early and largely reflect those expressed by the adults in their lives, including parents, guardians, preschool teachers, and other caregivers.

Children's attitudes are influenced by other external factors, too. For example, biased attitudes represented on television, or even the pressure of living in overcrowded housing or an unsafe neighborhood, can negatively impact young children's developing attitudes. Preschool teachers must be aware of these forces and how they might affect the attitudes of young children.

A strong early childhood curriculum includes opportunities, materials, and activities to foster unbiased, inclusive attitudes in children and to counteract negative influences. Furthermore, the curriculum should address the individual needs of children who have special needs—for example, those who are differently abled, from a minority culture, or from a disadvantaged background; those who have a single parent; or those who speak English as a second language (Spodek & Brown, 1993).

The preschool curriculum plays a vital role in helping many children develop positive attitudes. With so many parents working longer hours away from the home and with the increase in alternative living arrangements, preschools may be the most stable aspect of a preschooler's life (Townsend-Butterworth, 1992). Consequently, preschools play an important role in shaping children's attitudes about themselves, their classmates, and others.

Developing Positive Dispositions

In addition to developing their self-concept, skills, and knowledge, preschoolers are also developing *dispositions*—personality traits and tendencies to respond to situations or experiences in a certain way. Dispositions develop primarily as children watch and listen to the people around them.

The curriculum can play an important role in fostering positive dispositions in young children. For example, if the curriculum is designed around cooperation rather than competition, then children have a better chance of developing a disposition that could be described as "helpful to others." Child-initiated curriculum approaches can help promote independence, curiosity, and autonomy. Teacher-directed approaches can help foster *receptivity*—that is, having personality and temperamental characteristics that make the child receptive to new experiences, reflective, attentive to others, perceptive, and curious. Teacher-directed approaches also promote traits such as compliance and perseverance.

Preschoolers need opportunities to develop acceptable dispositions. Age-appropriate and individually appropriate activities in the preschool curriculum give children the experiences they need to build positive dispositions. When the teacher praises their actions, children are more likely to repeat the action in the future (Katz, 1988).

Anti-Bias Curriculum and Attitudes

An *anti-bias curriculum* is designed to promote positive attitudes in young children toward themselves and toward other people based on gender, race, differing abilities, and culture. In response to anti-bias issues in early childhood education, Louise Derman-Sparks and her associates developed *The Anti-Bias Curriculum,* published in 1989 by the National Association for the Education of Young Children. This book provides guidelines for early childhood educators who want to reduce bias in their curriculum. It also suggests various activities to help young children form unbiased attitudes.

It is not too early to address children's attitudes about other people in the preschool setting, since children notice differences among themselves at a very early age (Katz, 1982). By age four or five, children begin to behave in a manner defined by their social or cultural group (Derman-Sparks & the A. B. C. Task Force, 1989). They also begin to act in accordance with gender stereotypes promoted by parents, the media, and others. During the preschool years, children's attitudes about the differences they perceive can become either positive or negative. The preschool teacher, by example and through curriculum activities, can help children develop positive attitudes.

Research has shown, however, that creating an anti-bias curriculum is not easy for most teachers and that teachers still tend to display very traditional attitudes. For example, a study that examined classrooms that included children who were differently abled found that none had pictures of people who were differently abled, nor did the teachers make verbal references to people who were differently abled (Froschl & Sprung, 1983). Another study

FOCUS ON   Cultural Diversity

Confronting Your Own Biases

Everyone has biases. Whether hidden or expressed openly, all adults have varying positive and negative attitudes about race, gender, ethnicity, physical disabilities, and different life-styles. For child care professionals, these attitudes influence the way they interact with young children.

Creating an unbiased teaching style requires thoughtful preparation. The first step is to learn more about yourself. There are a number of activities that will help increase your self-awareness.

- **Start a list.** Write down situations involving people with disabilities that make you feel uncomfortable. These situations might include dealing with people in wheelchairs, people with visual impairments, or people with mental disabilities. Create similar lists of life-styles you find unacceptable, such as people living on welfare, homosexual couples, or permissive parenting. With a friend or colleague, review your lists and talk about areas that cause you discomfort.
- **Change your point of view.** It is often hard to see a situation from another's viewpoint. Try experiencing a day with a self-imposed

disability; for example, use a wheelchair or a blindfold. Alternatively, experiment by living on the income received by a family on welfare for a week. In each case, pay special attention to how your routines must change to accommodate the particular disability or life-style.
- **Challenge your perceptions.** Try changing the gender or race of the main character in a fairy tale or popular children's story. How might the story line have to change? Would you feel comfortable reading the new story to your class? Why or why not?
- **Observe the children**. Observation provides clues as to whether your teaching style is unbiased. Do both sexes in your class choose the same types of toys? Are boys or girls excluded from play at any time? Do you allow boys to interrupt more than girls? Do you always call on girls when asking questions?
- **Organize a support group.** Whether two people or ten, a support group is important to provide objective feedback—to evaluate mistakes, plan strategies, and, importantly, to celebrate successes.

revealed gender bias attitudes in preschool teachers who tended to "over-help" girls and children with disabilities. This bias also included a tendency to praise girls for their cooperative spirit and appearance and boys mainly for their achievements (Hoffman, 1983).

Such studies suggest that the effectiveness of an anti-bias curriculum depends largely on the teacher. For example, placing children who are differently abled together in one classroom with children who do not have disabilities does not ensure that the two types of children will play together. The teacher's actions and attitudes, however, can encourage children who are differently abled, children of color, and children from diverse cultural backgrounds to become integrated into the life of the classroom (Hanline, 1985). Teachers must also be honest and straightforward while stressing the similarities among the children and helping them learn to respect and appreciate their differences.

Teachers need to evaluate their own attitudes and their curricula. See the "Focus on Cultural Diversity" feature in this chapter for more information about evaluating your own biases. Through the evaluation process, teachers are able to identify and then to reduce the effects of bias in their classrooms. This evaluation will help the teacher to effectively challenge all stereotypes, confront misconceptions about disabilities, encourage children to stand up for themselves and others, and communicate that girls and boys are able to perform the same activities (Spodek & Brown, 1993). For example, cooking and woodworking activities should be discussed with and made available to boys and girls equally, without the usual stereotypical attitudes. Teachers should use a matter-of-fact approach in presenting these types of activities. Strategies to help teachers implement their curriculum without bias are discussed in the "Applications" section later in this chapter.

Multicultural Curriculum and Attitudes

As stated earlier, children's attitudes about other races and cultures form during the preschool years. The *multicultural curriculum*, a kind of subset of the anti-bias curriculum, seeks to foster positive attitudes and respect for diverse cultures. When children find themselves in a school setting that is too unlike their home setting and cultural background, they lose their sense of comfort that comes from familiar surroundings. An effective multicultural curriculum helps children feel comfortable in another cultural setting (Phillips, 1988).

As they help children learn about other cultures in relation to their own, teachers need to be aware of the different ways people *respond* to diversity. The response to differences, not the differences themselves, causes racism and bias. Carol Brunson Phillips writes: "The child who speaks Spanish has difficulty in school, not because he speaks Spanish, but because he's *responded* to as uneducable" (Phillips, 1988, p. 44).

Although preschool children enjoy activities that focus on different countries and customs, they do not understand the concept of "country" nor can they differentiate among different groups within the same country (Ramsey, 1982). Without such an understanding, teachers must take a subtle yet proactive position on helping children perceive and respect cultural differences and recognize similarities among people.

Multicultural activities should be interwoven throughout the curriculum (Jones & Derman-Sparks, 1992). The classroom environment and all materials—including pictures, activities, and books—should reflect a multicultural perspective. Teachers should take every opportunity to stress what people from different cultural backgrounds share in common, but also to point out how differences contribute to and strengthen society as a whole (Jones & Derman-Sparks, 1992). Such an approach helps children understand that even though people may dress, look, or speak differently, all people share common needs and feelings.

The multicultural curriculum celebrates the traditions and everyday life of diverse cultures. These four-year-olds are enjoying a Spanish circle dance.

To effectively implement a multicultural curriculum, teachers should avoid creating an artificial "culture corner." Rather, discussions about various cultures should evolve naturally throughout the daily curriculum. In addition to planned and incidental activities, teachers should know that children of all races, religions, and economic and cultural backgrounds directly and indirectly share aspects of their own backgrounds just by working and playing together (Brenner, 1989). For example, in a preschool program serving three ethnic groups—Navajo, Hispanic, and Anglo—an activity such as building a house can take on a multicultural flavor. Children can enjoy and learn about similarities and differences by constructing a cardboard hogan (traditional Navajo home) or an adobe home made out of cardboard "adobe blocks."

Discussions will develop as children play with classroom materials or observe one another. For example, if a mother wears an Indian sari or has a kumkum painted on the center of her forehead (red or black dot considered in the Indian culture to be a mark of beauty) when she drops off her child, another child may notice and make a comment. If a father wears a yarmulke (type of skullcap worn by Jewish men and boys during prayer but also worn by some Jewish males all the time), a child who has never seen a yarmulke may point and laugh. Addressing children's questions and remarks in a simple, matter-of-fact manner will help dispel misconceptions quickly.

The teacher may use this opportunity to talk about how people dress differently and how climate and cultural beliefs affect what they wear. However, the teacher should also emphasize the reasons why all people wear clothes—for example, to keep them warm—to focus on similarities as well as differences. If the children's interest in different types of clothing is strong, the teacher might incorporate this interest into activities and materials, such as displaying pictures of traditional clothing worn by various cultures, both in the United States and around the world. If practical, families might contribute or loan basic traditional clothing for the dramatic play area so that the children can dress in different types of clothing.

Another way the teacher can introduce multicultural elements into the curriculum is to invite parents of children from various cultural backgrounds to visit the classroom. They might cook a simple ethnic dish with the children, talk about their home countries or why their clothing is designed in a particular way, or teach the children a few simple words, such as hello and good-bye, in their native languages. By creating curriculum activities where children and their families can share experiences and talk about cultural diversity in the context of everyday life, teachers will also be helping children feel good about their own and others' heritage (Brenner, 1989). Parents and the curriculum are discussed in detail in Chapter 6.

Preschool children will grow up to become members of an increasingly global society, and their future success may well depend on their understanding of and respect for other cultures. Under such circumstances, a multicultural perspective at the preschool level is even more relevant. Jones and Derman-Sparks write: "The curriculum that does nothing to counter the biases that dominant-culture children absorb as they go about their daily lives ill-equips them to live effectively and fairly with diversity" (Jones & Derman-Sparks, 1992, p. 14). See Chapter 9 for a more comprehensive discussion of the multicultural curriculum.

Applications

As teachers use the building blocks of curriculum to construct their programs, it is important for them to become aware of how their own personality, biases, and subjectivity affect the child's preschool experience. This section discusses how your own attitudes and behavior, and how you choose to present the activities and materials in your curriculum, can help shape positive or negative attitudes in the children in your classroom. These attitudes will affect not only children's formation of self-concept and how they feel and act toward others, but also their interest in and attention toward building skills and acquiring knowledge.

As a teacher, you have a great deal of influence on how young children develop attitudes about themselves and about other people, including those from various cultures. For example, by choosing certain activities or highlighting particular cultural traits in an anti-bias or multicultural curriculum, you show by example that you consider those activities or traits to be desirable (Hanline, 1985). How children interpret what you say and do as a teacher will affect how they feel about themselves and about people with social, cultural, and economic backgrounds that are different from their own.

By stressing similarities among children and deemphasizing differences, you can foster positive feelings among children from different backgrounds or those with disabilities. For example, Ms. Garcia can explain that while the

The teacher's own attitude and behavior can greatly influence how children feel about themselves and others. A positive, inclusive attitude sets an important example for young children.

children might have to walk more slowly when playing with Beth or wait for her to catch up, she enjoys playing the same games they do. As a child care professional, your own attitude must be one of open and honest acceptance of all children, demonstrating that children are appreciated for both their strengths and their differences (Hanline, 1985).

Although the preschool director or parent-teacher committee decides the educational philosophy and curriculum approach of the program, the teacher gives it form and substance. Children will be influenced most strongly by your attitudes, as you are the person with whom they spend most of the day. You contribute in important ways to children's developing self-concepts, dispositions, and attitudes about others. The following are some suggestions to help you become more aware of your own actions and comments in the classroom. Also, see the "Focus on Cultural Diversity" feature in this chapter for tips on recognizing your own biases.

- In conversations with children, eliminate phrases or comments such as "Girls don't do somersaults on the grass" or "Pink is for girls."
- Don't assign activities on the basis of gender, race, or disability. By selecting only boys to gather leaves and sticks for a collage project or girls to prepare snacks, you indirectly convey that boys have adventures and girls work at home.
- Model cross-gender behaviors for children. For example, if you are female, be sure to demonstrate and participate with the children in such activities as woodworking, block play, and play with cars and trucks. If you are male, make a consistent effort to demonstrate such activities as cooking, pretend play with babies, and changing diapers.
- When you use gender pronouns, use *he* and *she* interchangeably. Sometimes use *he*, sometimes use *she*.

- You can empower children by your actions. Ask the child in the wheelchair to do the same tasks as other children—for example, pass out the straws or collect the pencils. This empowerment will encourage that child to participate in other class activities.

- By looking to the cultures represented by the children in the classroom for activities, songs, props, materials, dress-up clothes, even snacks, you encourage pride in their heritage and provide a broadening experience for all the children.

- Try to give examples that are inclusive of many cultures, especially those represented by the children in the school.

CHAPTER 3   **REVIEW**

SUMMARY

- The content of preschool curriculum directs the skills, knowledge, and attitudes acquired and developed during the preschool years.

- When developing the curriculum, teachers consider a variety of factors, including the educational philosophy of the school; the needs of the community, parents, and children; and the talents of the teachers.

- It is important for young children to develop a positive self-concept during the preschool years.

- To help build a strong self-concept, the curriculum should provide opportunities for children to feel successful—for example, the opportunity to master a variety of developmentally appropriate tasks.

- Preschoolers develop skills in five main categories: physical, emotional, social, cognitive, and creative.

- Activities and materials should be concrete and relevant to the children and should provide opportunities to practice various skills simultaneously.

- Knowledge is the information that children acquire and process through experiences and direct teaching techniques.

- Preschools differ in how they help children acquire knowledge. Teacher-directed programs usually focus on using information chosen by the teacher to construct activities that relate to academic subjects in elementary school. Child-initiated programs typically use the children's interests as the framework for activities that will expand children's knowledge.

- Children's attitudes about themselves and others are formed early in life and largely reflect those expressed by the adults in their lives. The curriculum should include opportunities, materials, and activities to foster unbiased, inclusive attitudes.

- Children develop dispositions—personality traits and tendencies to respond to situations or experiences in a certain way—by watching and listening to the people around them.

- The preschool curriculum should be designed to foster qualities such as curiosity and creativity. These qualities will become part of the child's healthy dispositions toward school and other people.

- An anti-bias curriculum fosters positive attitudes about gender, race, disabilities, and culture.

- By example and discussion, and by being aware of their own biases and behavior, teachers help children develop unbiased attitudes, challenge stereotypes, and confront misconceptions.

- All classroom materials—including pictures, activities, and books—should reflect a multicultural perspective. As teachers implement the curriculum, they should stress what people share in common and how differences contribute to and strengthen society as a whole.

ACQUIRING KNOWLEDGE

1. What are the four main "building blocks" of the preschool curriculum?
2. How can the preschool curriculum foster the development of a child's positive self-concept?
3. How can child care professionals support children's autonomy?
4. What are the five main categories of skills that children develop during preschool years?
5. What types of activities require the use of large muscle skills? What activities require small muscle skills?
6. Explain the difference between emotional skills and social skills.
7. Give two examples of cognitive skills that the preschool curriculum should address with young children.
8. What is meant by *knowledge* when the term is applied to a preschool curriculum?
9. How does the method by which children acquire knowledge differ between teacher-directed and child-initiated curricula?
10. What factors influence the development of children's attitudes?
11. Define *disposition* and describe the traits of a positive disposition in preschoolers.
12. What is the goal of an anti-bias curriculum? How does the teacher affect the successful implementation of this type of curriculum?
13. What is the most effective way to incorporate multicultural elements into the preschool curriculum?
14. Why do early childhood educators believe that learning about diversity is not enough—that the child's response to diversity is most important?

15. How can a teacher foster positive feelings among children from different backgrounds?
16. What are the long-term advantages of a preschool curriculum with a multicultural perspective?

THINKING CRITICALLY

1. A child's self-concept can be greatly influenced by the preschool experience. How does a developmentally appropriate curriculum help to foster a positive self-concept? How might an activity that is not developmentally appropriate damage a child's self-concept?
2. Many activities develop a wide variety of skills, some more obvious than others. What skills can you think of that might be developed by children by playing a game of "Follow the Leader"?
3. Gender biases in a classroom can be very subtle. Small, unperceived biases can contribute to children's negative attitudes toward themselves. What are some basic strategies a preschool teacher can use to avoid gender bias?
4. It might seem logical to set up a special classroom area for the study of cultures and traditions. However, these "culture corners" are not considered by early education experts to be the most effective way to create a multicultural curriculum. Why do you think "culture corners" might be less effective than other methods?
5. Opportunities to learn about different cultures can be planned by the teacher within the curriculum, but they also can occur spontaneously. What incidents might occur in a preschool setting that would create an opportunity to discuss some aspect of cultural diversity?

OBSERVATIONS AND APPLICATIONS

1. Observe two or more children playing together in the block area. Make notes about what parts of their bodies they are using and any aspects of the activity you think relate to the development of motor skills. Then make note of any dialogue or cooperative efforts among the children, as well as any other aspects of their play you think relate to the development of social skills. Do the same for cognitive and creative skills.
2. Ideally, multicultural elements should be interwoven throughout the preschool curriculum to foster positive attitudes among young children. Visit a preschool classroom, and look carefully at the classroom environment, including artwork on the walls, storybooks, and props and clothes in the dramatic play area. In what ways are different cultures, races, or ethnic groups depicted or represented in these areas? What are the different cultures? Is there a "culture corner," or are cultural materials evident throughout the classroom? Estimate how many different cultures and races are represented among the children in the classroom. Can you find each of their distinct cultures represented in some way in the classroom materials or decor? If so, how are they represented?

3. A new child in your school, four-year-old Tanya, is not adjusting well. She rarely plays with the other children, claiming that they do not like her. She does not like to participate in games because she does not do well. Tanya also tells you that she feels different from the other children because she is African American and they are white. What steps can you take to improve Tanya's self-concept?

4. In reviewing your plans for discussions and activities at group time for the coming month, you decide that you would like to use group time to help foster positive dispositions in the children. Specifically, you decide to focus on two objectives: encouraging the children to be open to new ideas and to be curious. Give some examples of how you might plan group time to meet these objectives.

FOR FURTHER INFORMATION

Beardsley, L. (1990). *Good day, bad day: The child's experience of child care*. New York: Teachers College Press.

Curry, N. E., & Johnson, C. N. (1990). *Beyond self-esteem: Developing a genuine sense of human value*. Washington, DC: National Association for the Education of Young Children.

Elkind, D. (1987). *Miseducation: Preschoolers at risk*. New York: Knopf.

Hanline, M. F. (1985). Integrating disabled children. *Young Children, 40*(2), 45–48.

Hohmann, M., Banet, B., & Weikart, D. P. (1979). *Young children in action: A manual for preschool educators*. Ypsilanti, MI: High/Scope Press.

Jones, E. & Derman-Sparks, L. (1992). Meeting the challenge of diversity. *Young Children, 47*(2), 12–18.

Marshall, H. (1989). The development of self-concept. *Young Children, 44*(5), 44–51.

Phillips, C. (1988). Nuturing diversity for today's children and tomorrow's leaders. *Young Children, 43*(2), 42–47.

Ramsey, P. G. (1987). *Teaching and learning in a diverse world*. New York: Teachers College Press.

Workman, S., & Anziano, M. (1993). Curriculum webs: Weaving connections from children to teachers. *Young Children, 48*(2), 4–9.

Play and the Curriculum

OBJECTIVES

Studying this chapter
will enable you to

- Describe the basic characteristics
  of young children's play
- Explain how play influences the
  physical, emotional, social,
  cognitive, and creative
  development of young children
- Discuss various levels or stages of
  play
- Compare and contrast different
  types of play
- Discuss ways that preschool
  teachers can guide and enhance
  the play experiences of young
  children

CHAPTER TERMS

associative play
constructive play
cooperative play
dramatic play
dramatist
functional play
guided play
meta communications
object substitution
parallel play
patterner
pretend communications
sensorimotor play
solitary play
symbolic distancing
symbolic play

A GROUP of four-year-olds in Yolanda Jefferson's class at the Creative Play Preschool rushed to the housekeeping corner. Josh immediately took charge of the other children.

"I'll be the daddy, and Maggie is the mom. Ben is the big brother, and Nina can be the baby. I'm a firefighter, and I have to wear this helmet 'cause I put out fires."

Ms. Jefferson observed this assignment of roles with amusement. For over a week, the same group had been making a beeline for this play area. Josh was always both the daddy and the assigner of roles.

Today, as the play family began their day, Maggie threw her pan down and yelled, "I don't want to be the mommy anymore. Josh, you always say I have to be the mommy."

Ms. Jefferson walked over and sat down in the rocking chair. She waited quietly to see if the children could resolve the conflict.

"I'm going to be the firefighter today," announced Maggie, defiantly putting her pan back in the kitchen cupboard.

"No, you're not," said Josh hotly. "That's my job."

"It can be my job, too, you big dummy."

At this point, Ms. Jefferson felt that she should intervene, as the children appeared to be getting only angrier. "Josh, Maggie, each of you has different ideas, and they're all good ideas. Let's think together of all the different ways you could have a family with firefighters in it."

The group talked about how mommies could also have a job. "My mom goes to work," said Nina matter-of-factly. "Hey, Maggie, what if you and Josh work on the same fire truck? And I'll still be the baby."

Ben said, "Well, I still want to be the big brother, and I'll read you a book and take you to the park."

As Josh and Maggie donned fire hats and looked for something to make a fire hose out of, Ms. Jefferson quietly slipped away and turned her attention to another group of children.

Play is a vital component of the preschool curriculum. Just as eating proper foods and getting adequate sleep are vital to a young child's physical well-being, play contributes significantly to a child's physical, emotional, social, cognitive, and creative development. Play helps children learn about themselves, about others, and about the world around them. It allows them to express their feelings and to experiment. For example, when Josh assigns roles to the other children, he is learning about leadership. When he lets others take a turn at modifying those roles, he is learning about the give-and-take that characterizes mature social relationships.

This chapter discusses the nature of play and its relationship to the development of young children. It also examines how an understanding of children's play can enable early childhood educators to provide varied and stimulating opportunities for play in the curriculum. The chapter concludes with strategies for guiding and extending the play experiences of preschoolers.

What Is Play?

There are various definitions of play. One classic definition is Maria Montessori's idea that play is child's work (Montessori, 1912). Anthropologist Irenäus Eibl-Eibesfeldt, who compared play behavior in animals and humans, wrote that "Children's play is a kind of dialogue with their environment" (Garvey, 1977). Despite differing definitions, most early education experts agree that play contains certain distinguishing characteristics. One characteristic of play is that it is voluntary, and children are free to choose what and how they wish to play. Another characteristic of play is that it is motivated by children from within and not from external direction (Johnson & Erschler, 1982). That is, children engage in play because it is somehow satisfying to them.

A third characteristic of play is that it is an activity in which the process itself is more important than any end product. Catherine Garvey, a researcher who has studied play extensively, identified another characteristic of play.

She noted that, during play, children are actively engaged in an activity, which differentiates play from daydreaming or lounging (Garvey, 1977).

Play also is both meaningful and symbolic. It allows children to connect their own real-life experiences to "pretend" situations, which help them better understand the world around them. Finally, play is pleasurable—children pursue play for the pure joy of it.

Play and Development

Although early education experts generally agree on these basic characteristics of play, there is less agreement on play's purpose or function. Leading theorists have focused on the influence of play on different aspects of development. Piaget, for example, emphasized the importance of play in children's cognitive development. He believed that play is the primary medium through which children gather and process information about their environment and practice what they have learned. Children use play to integrate their experiences into a meaningful whole.

Erikson, on the other hand, emphasizes the importance of play to emotional development. He believes that play is important because it allows children to explore and express strong emotions. He also believes that children gain self-confidence and competence through play, which helps them learn throughout their lives.

Vygotsky stressed the importance of play in terms of social development. He viewed play as a way for children to experiment with adult roles, such as Josh's playing the father and firefighter and Maggie's playing the mother and firefighter. Vygotsky emphasized that as children play they learn how to

Play helps children develop physical skills and discover how their bodies can move. These two-year-olds are practicing balance and strengthening the large muscle groups in their arms and legs.

get along with others, and they experiment with compromise, cooperation, negotiation, and turn taking. Vygotsky also believed that play fosters cognitive development, including language (Vygotsky, 1967).

Play and Physical Development

Movement is an integral part of young children's play. During play, children explore and challenge their gross motor skills while running, hopping, climbing, hoisting a suitcase into a "car" for a make-believe trip, or jumping like a kangaroo. They develop their fine motor skills as they wash a doll, hold a pencil to make a sign for their "store," or decorate a mud "birthday cake" with pebbles. They test their skills in movement and coordination.

Physical play helps children discover what their bodies can do and helps build self-confidence. When a child perseveres for several days and finally opens the closed end of an empty can with a handheld can opener, she gains an important sense of accomplishment. When another child catches a ball without dropping it for the first time, he is rewarded by that wonderful sense of satisfaction that proclaims, "I can do it myself!" Children's play with motion is discussed in more detail later in this chapter.

An important point with respect to teacher involvement in physical play is safety. Children will experiment and take risks with their bodies as they play. They will want to climb a little higher, run faster, or balance on one foot like an older child. Teachers need to develop a sharp eye to tell the difference between activity that is challenging to the child and activity that is dangerous. In general, children should be allowed to experiment physically during play. However, any behavior that is clearly dangerous to the child or to other children in the area should be stopped immediately. For example, a three-year-old who is walking behind the swings or trying to push an older child on the swings so that he can be like the "big" kids is in danger of being hit by a swing. Teachers need to develop a keen eye for activity that really poses danger. Too many teachers stifle children's play in the name of "safety," when in fact the play is simply active or noisy. Chapter 5 discusses play supervision in more detail.

Play and Emotional Development

Play provides children with a wealth of opportunities to express their emotions. While playing alone or with others, they can freely express joy, hurt, anger, fear, frustration, and other feelings. Erikson and other child development experts have noted that play provides a safe, risk-free environment in which children can escape the constraints of the real world and explore or express emotions that might otherwise be considered unacceptable, such as anger or aggression. During play, children become active masters, or directors, of recreated situations. They can control and negotiate who the characters are as well as the plot and the outcome.

Piaget observed that when children play they simplify events and situations, making them easier to manage in both practical and emotional terms.

FOCUS ON Communicating with Children

Helping a Shy Child Join a Group in Dramatic Play

In dramatic play, children use their imaginations as they assume adult roles, act out everyday events, or play out stressful or fearful experiences. The best course for the teacher to follow is to encourage dramatic play in indirect ways, such as giving children the time and props they need to play. At times, however, the teacher should take a more active role. One such instance is when a shy child wants to join a group of children but is too timid to do so.

Ms. Stevens noticed that four-year-old Mara was standing outside the block corner, fingering her new red truck. She looked very interested in the elaborate structure José and Annie were building.

Ms. STEVENS: Is that a new car you have, Mara?

MARA: Uh-huh. It's a truck. I got it from my grandpa for my birthday.

Ms. STEVENS: It's really shiny. Why don't we find out what they're building, OK? (Mara nods and Ms. Stevens takes her hand.) Hi!

Mara and I were admiring your building.

ANNIE: We're making a super new gas station.

Ms. STEVENS: What happens at your gas station?

JOSÉ: Cars come, and we give them gas or fix broken parts.

Ms. STEVENS: It looks like your gas station is almost ready for a customer. Mara, does your truck need gas?

MARA: Yeah. And it's got a flat tire, too. (Mara kneels on the floor and wheels her truck up a ramp.)

ANNIE: Wow! That's a great truck. Come and fill 'er up! (As the children assume the roles of mechanics and customers, Ms. Stevens leaves.)

What other tactics might Ms. Stevens have used to introduce Mara into the group? Do you think that Mara will be less shy the next time she wants to join a group? Why or why not?

A child who is afraid of dogs, for example, can simply announce, "No dogs in this house!" A child who is angry at or jealous of a sibling can chastise her "child," the doll she is playing with. A child can defy parental authority by announcing that he is going on a trip and packing a boxful of pretend "candy bars."

Repetition is an important aspect of play, both in practicing skills and in exploring emotions. For example, when children play out fearful events over and over again, they gradually resolve and overcome their fears and learn to cope with their emotions.

Through play, children can also anticipate and prepare for events about which they are feeling anxious. For example, a child who feels anxious about going to the doctor may play with stuffed animals, such as a teddy bear, and make the teddy bear go to the doctor in a play scenario.

By transforming reality into play situations, children make unmanageable situations manageable. This process helps children work through strong emotions and reduce stress (Elkind, 1983). The fact that children can

regulate their own activity during play, so that it is not too difficult, also reduces stress. In fact, play is such an effective way for young children to deal
with negative emotions, events, and stress that it often is used as a therapeu-
tic tool by psychologists and counselors working with troubled children.

In addition to helping children master their emotions, play helps them
develop their self-concept (self-concept was discussed in Chapter 3). As a
child plays, her experiences and ideas are integrated into her concept of
"self," and they help shape her personality. Play also involves making
choices and decisions, thereby helping children gain a sense of competence
and contributing to a positive self-concept and emotional well-being.

Play and Social Development

When young children play together, they learn social skills that will influence their relationships with others throughout their lives. During play, children learn about getting along with others, making and keeping friends,
making compromises, and cooperating. They learn about sharing and negotiating with others, and dealing with rejection or acceptance from a group.
Another skill children learn while playing is the ability to empathize with
others and to be sensitive to others' needs and feelings. Children also practice leading and following others during play, and, according to some child
development experts, the ability of children to both lead and follow others is
a mark of social competence and adjustment (Stone & Church, 1984; White
& Watts, 1973). All these skills are crucial to the social development of children, and, as discussed in Chapter 1, many parents place their young children in preschool specifically to foster social skills.

Children also have the opportunity to explore different social roles during play—parent, teacher, sibling, baby, and different occupations such as
firefighter and doctor. As they experiment with such roles, children model
and reflect the adult behavior they observe around them. In doing so, they
explore the behaviors and actions characteristic of the adult society in which
they live. Children also experiment with morality during play—the concept
of right and wrong—and the values they learn are practiced over and over
again until they are completely internalized. In some cases, such as with excessive violent behavior in play, the teacher may need to intervene to discuss
issues about violence with the children.

Communication is another aspect of social development that is influenced by play. Through play, children learn to extend and enhance both verbal and nonverbal communication skills. They learn by negotiating with
other children, acting out roles, and empathizing with the feelings or needs
of others. As children play together, for example, the teacher commonly will
hear such exchanges as "You play with this and I'll play with that," or "You
be the mommy and I'll be the daddy." When another child is pretending to
be hurt, the other children playing often will attempt to soothe the child verbally or with hugs, pats, or other forms of nonverbal communication. During play, children also learn the vital social skill of communicating their own
feelings through words rather than actions. A younger preschooler, for

example, simply may grab a toy from another when he wants it. An older preschooler learns to say, "It's my turn to wear the firefighter's helmet," or "Can I play with that truck?" A young child may hit another to express anger. An older child learns to express that anger verbally, as when she scolds her doll or tells another child or the teacher that she is angry.

Play and Cognitive Development

Through play, children learn information and acquire skills that are crucial to their cognitive development. The child who is playing at the water table, the child who is swinging on a swing, and the child who is building a tower out of colored blocks are all involved in discovery and learning. The child at the water table may be discovering that some objects sink while others float. The one on the swing is exploring motion, gravity, and safety. The child who is playing with blocks is learning about colors, balance, depth, and volume.

Play contributes to cognitive development in a number of ways. Play, for example, helps children develop the ability to use imagery and memory, which are essential for thinking about the past, the present, and the future (Singer, 1973). In thinking about the past, children need memory skills, and in thinking about the future, they must be able to engage their imaginations. The "as if" nature of pretend play allows children to remove themselves from the "here and now" and to create new meanings children use later in other, more serious real-life contexts (Sutton-Smith, 1967).

Play gives children an opportunity to practice problem-solving and decision-making skills, two important elements of cognitive development. Research has shown that preschoolers' problem-solving abilities are

Play challenges children's cognitive skills as they explore the properties of objects, experiment with how things work, and observe the outcome of their own actions.

FOCUS ON   Cultural Diversity

Research on Play in Different Countries

The way children play differs from one country to another, as well as from one socioeconomic level to another within the same country. According to researchers, these differences can be attributed to the different parenting styles; the home and community environment; and the social values, everyday life, and customs of different cultures. Here are some findings from cross-cultural studies of children's play, including classic studies on play by Catherine Garvey and Susan Smilansky from the 1960s and '70s, which are still referenced today.

Types of play are sometimes shaped by a child's community and family structure. Among the !Kung of Botswana, for example, girls and boys of various ages are raised together by family members, relatives, or friends. The children tend to engage in physically active play, such as chasing and roughhousing. All the children play together, and any child who is playing alone is encouraged to join the group. Researchers also found that girls in these societies often engage in rough play. Cooperative play appears sooner among these children than in children in Western cultures (Garvey, 1977).

Socioeconomic status may affect the incidence or frequency of dramatic play among children. Research conducted in the United States (Freyberg, 1973) and in Israel (Eifermann, 1971; Smilansky, 1968) showed that children of lower socioeconomic groups in these countries engage in little make-believe play. Freyberg attributed this finding to a lack of parental involvement or support of children's play. Eifermann concluded that pretend play appears at a somewhat later age in children from families with low incomes.

The developmental sequence of play has been found to be similar among children from Western and Asian industrialized countries. Studies comparing children from the Netherlands, Germany, and Norway (Kooij, 1989) and studies comparing children from the United States and Japan (Seagoe & Murakami, 1961) reported similar findings in the frequency and types of play at various ages. Preschool teachers should be aware that although the children in their classroom may come from diverse cultural backgrounds, including Asia and Europe, play can serve as a common ground for them, where they can learn to communicate with and discover similarities about one another.

enhanced when the task involves playing with objects (Sylva, 1977). Research also has shown that play helps children try combinations of behavior that they can transfer to other problem-solving situations (Bruner, 1972). This flexibility in thinking is an important part of cognitive development.

Another area of cognitive development in which play is important is the development of language skills. Children consistently use language in their play. They talk to themselves, they talk to other children, and they talk to the adults who are supervising or participating in their play. Language itself may even be the subject of play, as when children play with sounds and make up nonsense words or novel word combinations. Children practice language skills during play, including expressing their ideas, communicating with others, and experimenting with reading and writing.

Play and Creative Development

Play can have a significant role in the development of a child's creative abilities. Research has shown that play contributes to the development of creativity by providing children with experiences that stimulate their curiosity and challenge them to explore new ways of acting (Singer & Singer, 1985). As children play, they also invent original thoughts and words, try out new activities and actions, and discover new uses for objects, toys, and materials. According to Vygotsky, play signals the beginning of imagination and the ability to think creatively (Vygotsky, 1967). A three-year-old who takes a wooden block and pushes it back and forth across the floor, saying, "Vroom, vroom," is acting creatively. Through her imagination, she temporarily transforms the block into a car. During play, children also use their imaginations to transform, or change, who they are and where they are.

The development of creativity also is related to cognitive development because creative thinking skills contribute to problem solving. Research has shown that children who play imaginatively are better able to make connections, communicate verbally, develop a problem-solving approach to learning, and often perform better at school tasks (Freyberg, 1973).

Levels of Play

Like many other aspects of development, play changes in nature and complexity as children grow older. Some theorists have described different stages of play that occur in a developmental sequence and reflect a child's physical, social, and cognitive development. An awareness of these theories helps preschool teachers plan activities that are developmentally appropriate for the children in their care.

As children develop and learn new skills, their play gradually becomes more elaborate and complex. For young infants, play consists of repetitive motor behaviors, such as banging the hands on a table. As a child gains manual dexterity, play shifts to repetitious actions with objects, such as shaking a rattle or dropping a spoon on the floor over and over again. Children's use of objects gradually becomes more complex, and they combine objects in an increasingly complex sequence of actions. By age three, for example, a child will pour "tea" into a cup, stir the cup with a spoon, and feed the "tea" to a doll.

By the time children reach preschool age, the fascination with playing with objects for their own sake gives way to an interest in playing with other children, playing games, and creating pretend-play situations. Objects remain an important part of play but are used in an abstract, symbolic way, for a specific purpose. Whereas a toddler might be interested in the shape and feel of a tubular block, Maggie and Josh in Ms. Jefferson's class, for example, might use that same block as a tool to open the "fire hydrant." Preschool children continue to integrate into their play new experiences they have had. These experiences might include meeting new people, engaging in new activities, and visiting new places.

These three-year-olds are engaged in parallel play. They are working independently but are participating in the same type of activity.

Parten's Stages of Play

One classic categorization of play was created in 1932 by psychologist Mildred Parten (Parten, 1932). Parten's categories focus on the social aspects of play, especially how much or how little children interact with other children. Based on her observations and research, Parten identified six stages of play. The first five stages are typically exhibited by preschoolers. The stages represent a developmental progression, but while new stages are added, children still go back and forth to earlier stages.

Parten's first stage, called unoccupied behavior, refers to the behavior of a child who demonstrates no involvement or interaction with other children. A child in this stage may wander around and watch the activities of other children, but he is not involved with any specific activity himself. In the next stage, onlooker behavior, the child is aware of other children, watches their play, and may talk with them. However, the child does not participate in their play.

In Parten's third stage, *solitary play*, a child plays with toys alone and independently and is not involved in any way with other children. *Parallel play*, the fourth stage, occurs when a child plays independently but is engaged in the same activity as other children near or beside her. For example, two children may each be sitting on the floor next to each other and playing with a puzzle, yet neither is interacting with the other. This type of play often is seen in two- to three-year-olds.

Parten's fifth stage, *associative play*, refers to children playing together in a similar but loosely organized manner. In this stage of play, a child plays with others but does not subordinate his own interests to any common goal. Some degree of verbal interaction normally takes place in associative play, and toys are shared. Conversation frequently involves asking questions. Sometimes, conversation grows out of suggestions made by children. Associative play is typically seen in 3½- to 4½-year-olds.

The sixth stage of play in Parten's classification, *cooperative play*, involves structured play within a group with a common purpose. The activity may be organized for the purpose of building or making something, dramatizing a situation, or playing a formal game such as hide-and-seek. This final stage is further characterized by taking turns and by a division of labor among the children taking part in the activity. Cooperative play is not typical for many preschoolers. One is most apt to see it in children ages five through eight.

Parten assumed that these stages of play occurred at specific ages, reflecting the social development of children. Most researchers today, however, consider Parten's stages to be descriptive of a "style" of play rather than a level of social maturity. Researchers have found that, as children grow older, they move back and forth between the different stages. Also, Parten's earlier stages can include sophisticated aspects. For example, solitary play can be very complex. In playing bedtime, a child might undress and bathe a doll, "brush" the doll's teeth, put on a nightgown, "read" her a story, tuck her in, and "turn out the light." She might use many props, such as a pencil for a toothbrush, a basket for a bathtub, and an enclosure of blocks for a bed. Moreover, a child may engage in different combinations of these stages during the course of a day or under varying circumstances throughout childhood (Rubin, 1977).

Knowledge of Parten's stages can be very helpful to teachers. For example, an older preschooler who continually engages only in solitary or parallel play may simply be shy or unable to approach a group engaged in cooperative play. A skilled teacher creates opportunities to encourage that child's movement into the next stage, such as suggesting a role for the child to play near or within a group, and encouraging the others to include the child in their play.

Piaget's Stages of Play

Whereas Parten emphasized the social aspects of play, Piaget focused on the relationship of play to cognitive development. Piaget believed that different forms of play are closely associated with a child's cognitive functioning.

Piaget recognized three major stages of play, each of which corresponds roughly to sensorimotor, preoperational, and concrete operational stages of cognitive development. Piaget's first stage of play is sensorimotor play, which is also known as *functional play* or practice play. *Sensorimotor play* is characterized by simple, repeated movements. Infants and young toddlers shake rattles, throw balls or objects randomly, run around and around a room, repeat words or phrases, and perform other repetitive actions. Sensorimotor play is focused on action for action's sake, rather than for a particular goal. Piaget believed that children derive pleasure from this type of play because they are able to practice and master different behaviors or skills. With this mastery, the child gains a sense of control over herself and her environment.

Piaget's second stage of play is *symbolic play*, which is sometimes referred to as *constructive play*. This stage of play is characterized by the manipulation of objects to either represent or construct something. A child may construct an igloo from pillows or use blocks to build a train. According to Piaget, this stage of play marks children's ability to engage in representational thought. They can construct mental symbols and images of objects from the real world (Piaget, 1962). The way children explore play with objects is discussed in more detail later in the chapter.

Piaget's final stage of play is known as games-with-rules. At this stage of play, children recognize, accept, and conform to predetermined rules imposed on a play activity. These games are generally goal-oriented and competitive. Simple board games and outdoor games such as kickball are examples of games-with-rules. This level of play requires complex behaviors and logical thinking. It sometimes involves following a predetermined sequence of steps, exploring different strategies, and responding to situations as they occur. Therefore, children can rarely sustain this type of play without adult supervision until they reach the concrete operational stage of cognitive development, at about age seven.

It is important to note that the developmental stages of play are not mutually exclusive. That is, young children may play in one stage one day and at an earlier stage another day or even within the same day. Also, the cognitive aspects of play, reflected in Piaget's stages, develop concurrently with the social aspects of play, represented in Parten's stages. Therefore, the preschool curriculum needs to provide opportunities for a variety of play experiences.

Types of Play

Providing a variety of play experiences in the preschool setting not only supports play in the different developmental stages, but it also fosters different types of play. Before the preschool years, children have already participated in a variety of play experiences. As infants, they are rocked, tickled, and bounced, and they reach for toys and other objects. As they grow older, they play with different objects and begin to construct things with these objects. They also enjoy running and jumping and other activities that involve movement. Children enjoy pretending and role playing, either by themselves or with other children. Children also enjoy playing games with others, ranging from a simple game of peekaboo while they are very young to more complex games as they get older. This section discusses four basic types of play: play with motion, play with objects, dramatic play, and games. The curriculum should allow time for these different types of play.

Play with Motion

The type of activity that most clearly captures the joy and free spirit of children at play is motion. Children at play often are bouncing, running, jumping, hopping, or skipping. Motion is enjoyed for its own sake, with no goal or purpose in mind.

Motion is generally the first type of play activity that children experience. Parents play with their infants by bouncing them up and down, lifting them up in the air, tickling them, and circling around with them in their arms. Babies show their enjoyment of these motions by smiling and laughing. As infants grow older, motion also is the first type of play that they experiment with themselves. A baby lying in a crib, for example, may discover that kicking her feet in the air feels pleasurable. The baby begins to repeat this motion both to increase her enjoyment and to explore the consequences of the action. As children develop motor skills, the range of repetitive motions increases. The child may bang her hands on the table, strike pots and pans with a spoon, or play patty-cake with a parent or caregiver.

Preschoolers' play with motion enables them both to use objects in more diverse ways and to begin interacting with their peers. They gain physical mastery over their environment and discover new things their bodies can do. Children learn, for example, how to rhythmically pump their legs back and forth to gain height on a swing. Motion for its own sake continues to bring pleasure, such as rolling down a hill, twirling like a top, or dancing freely to music.

Play with motion as an end in itself generally is confined to early childhood. Older children continue to utilize motion in their play, such as playing tag or jumping rope. The motion involved in this play, however, has become part of a more complex activity and is no longer pleasurable by itself. By the time children reach the teenage years, motion has become incorporated into very complex play activities, such as competitive sports or dance.

Play with Objects

From early infancy, children play with objects around them. They are fascinated by the properties of these objects and use all their senses to determine how objects look, feel, smell, sound, or taste. They move gradually from an understanding of the physical properties of objects to an appreciation of

During play, children learn about symbols as they substitute one object for another. With a little imagination, a plastic spoon can become a "telephone."

their more abstract and symbolic qualities. By the third year, children not only are able to play with objects in realistic ways but also can transform, or substitute, one object for another in imaginative ways. A child might, for example, use a mop to "shovel snow," a piece of clay as a "sandwich," or a box as a "car." This kind of creative transformation is called *object substitution* and indicates children's developing cognitive abilities (Nourot & Van Hoorn, 1991).

Research has shown individual differences in the way children respond to properties of objects (Shotwell, Wolf, & Gardner, 1979). Some children, called *patterners*, respond more to the realistic qualities of objects, such as color, texture, and shape. Others, called *dramatists*, respond more readily to the symbolic potential of objects. For example, a patterner may arrange trucks by color and size, while a dramatist is content to play with any one truck as he pretends to make deliveries or pick up garbage. It is helpful for preschool teachers to understand this difference in play styles. For example, a teacher may take one truck away from the patterner to give to the dramatist and not realize that this action would disrupt the patterner's play. Through play with objects, in both realistic and symbolic ways, children begin to formulate many of the ideas and strategies that provide the foundations of future learning.

Over time, children progress through a developmental sequence called *symbolic distancing*, in which the need for realism in objects diminishes (Nourot and Van Hoorn, 1991). Younger children need props that are very realistic, such as plastic "food" if they are pretending to go on a picnic. Older preschoolers begin to show an interest in more unstructured objects for props, such as blocks and sticks. A toddler needs play pots and pans to pretend to cook, whereas a group of four-year-olds will play house using a big empty box for a dishwasher and blocks for dishes. Teachers should be aware of this transformation, as less realistic props may enhance imaginative play in older preschoolers (Pulaski, 1973).

Dramatic Play

Dramatic play, sometimes called fantasy play or sociodramatic play if it involves more than one child, engages all aspects of the child—physical, cognitive, social, and emotional. In *dramatic play*, children use their imaginations to play different roles, transforming themselves and objects to play out various real or imagined scenarios. They pretend to be mommies, daddies, and other people; they make sounds for animals or engines; they create imaginary homes, offices, and schools; they ride in imaginary cars or on make-believe horses; they eat imaginary foods; and they perform different kinds of "work" or other activities.

The importance of dramatic play lies in its effect on the emotional, social, cognitive, and creative development of children. As children explore different roles and dramatize situations, they learn about planning, making decisions, solving problems, and communicating effectively, all of which are important aspects of cognitive development.

FOCUS ON Activities

Setting Up a Supermarket in the Dramatic Play Area

You can encourage different types of dramatic play by introducing new props and asking open-ended questions to stimulate children's ideas and creativity. A familiar activity most preschoolers enjoy acting out is grocery shopping.

About a week before you plan to set up a supermarket in your classroom, introduce the theme during group time. Encourage children to talk about when they go to the grocery store with their parents. You might ask, "What do you buy in the supermarket? Who works there? Can you buy items that are not food in the supermarket? Like what?" Discuss what props you'll need to make the supermarket in the classroom. These objects might include a toy shopping cart or a canvas bag with handles, a toy cash register, a scale, play money, grocery bags, and a variety of empty, clean food containers, such as cereal boxes, milk and egg cartons, plastic ketchup bottles, and detergent containers. You might send home a note with the children asking parents to contribute

materials. If you do, be sure to include a safety note about not including glass bottles and sharp metal cans.

Once your supermarket is set up, discuss the different roles the children might play: cashier, customer, stock clerk, and delivery person. To expand children's play, you might ask an open-ended question, or model how to do something. For example, you might say, "Kim, look at all the food in your basket. What are you cooking for dinner?" or "I see you're buying apples, Scott. May I weigh them for you?"

Extend the Experience

- Provide art materials for children to make their own money, labels for foods, or price signs.
- At group time, create a list of every child's favorite foods. Then make a big "On Sale" sign with pictures of each food for the supermarket play area.

Children use two main forms of communication during play (Garvey & Berndt, 1977). *Meta communications* are communications about the play, such as "You be the patient with a broken leg." Meta communications occur when children provide directions to each other or negotiate who will play what role. This type of communication can be thought of as occurring "outside" the play scenario. *Pretend communications* refer to dialogue within the play situation itself, such as when a child pretends to go to the emergency room and says, "Hey, Doctor Dan, please fix my broken leg." Children often will assume a different voice than their normal voice or use a different tone or inflection in pretend communications, to distinguish their "character" from their "real" self. Pretend communications can be thought of as occurring "inside" the play scenario.

In terms of social development, dramatic play requires the ability to respond to the imagination of another person (Fein, 1986). It also helps children learn how to share, take turns, assume another person's point of view, and cooperate within a group. Emotional development is enhanced during dramatic play as children express their happiness, anger, fear, or other emotions. Dramatic play fosters creative development as it stimulates curiosity and allows children to explore alternative solutions and novel combinations (Singer & Singer, 1985).

Games

A fourth type of play is games. Games are play activities structured by a set of rules and often a specific goal. Games are primarily a social activity involving two or more people at a time. At the simplest level, games may involve merely taking turns, as when toddlers play peekaboo with a parent. For older children, games become more complex. Games might involve a central person and taking turns, such as "Duck, Duck, Goose," or they might involve chance (board games with dice), skill or teams (football), or strategy (chess) (Kostelnik, Stein, Whiren, & Soderman, 1993).

As with dramatic play, games involve several areas of development. To play a game, children must be able to understand and follow rules, plan and carry out sequences of actions, interact cooperatively or competitively with other children, exercise self-control, and submit voluntarily to the rules of the game. Such capabilities are dependent on the child's cognitive, social, and emotional development. This type of game playing does not usually occur until between the ages of five and eight.

Applications

Although research has supported the many benefits of play, it also has shown that adults can enrich the complexity and diversity of young children's play experiences (Smilansky, 1968). As a preschool teacher, you should become familiar with the different levels and types of play so that you can provide appropriate, interesting, and challenging play settings for the children in your care. In addition, it is important to become familiar with the different teaching strategies you can use to guide and encourage play, both indirectly and directly. While much play is spontaneous, you can help facilitate play and ensure that children get the most benefit from their play activities.

Guiding Play

Your role in guiding play can vary from indirect to direct, depending on the nature of the activity. In some instances, you may assume an indirect role, observing children at play or facilitating play in a number of "behind-the-scenes" ways, such as providing new props or scheduling adequate time for play. At other times, you may take a more direct role, becoming actively involved with children in their play activities.

The level of your involvement in play may depend on the nature of the activity. For example, many outdoor play activities, such as sliding down the slide or playing on swings, might require only minimal involvement.

Children may need to be monitored only for purposes of safety, or to resolve any conflicts that erupt, or to be lifted onto a swing. More structured activities, such as musical chairs, may also require a greater level of teacher involvement, both to ensure safety and to facilitate the activity.

With both indirect and direct guidance, you should maintain a friendly, open, and spontaneous attitude toward the children in your care. Recognize the value and the fun of play. Watch children at play carefully so that you are ready to intervene and facilitate play when necessary or to stand back and let children play on their own.

Indirect Guidance. It is important to encourage children's play indirectly in many ways. Indirect guidance includes making sure that children are rested and well fed and physically comfortable in the preschool setting. It includes organizing the classroom environment in a logical, creative, and stimulating manner; providing a variety of high-quality toys, interesting props, and other materials and storing them for easy access by the children; structuring the schedule and curriculum so that children have ample opportunities to engage in a variety of play activities; and providing curriculum activities that support play and creativity, such as story reading and class trips. This type of "behind-the-scenes" involvement allows children to develop their own ideas during play, pursue their own interests, participate at their own level of comfort, and utilize their social skills and creative abilities free from interference.

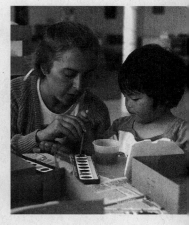

Demonstrating how materials can be used is a form of direct guidance in children's play. This teacher is showing a three-year-old how to use watercolor paints.

Direct Guidance. Children's play in which adults are directly involved is sometimes referred to as *guided play*. Certain occasions are more appropriate for direct guidance than others. These occasions might include times when a particular child is left out of group play activities, when a child seems shy or uninvolved (see the "Focus on Communicating" feature in this chapter), or when play activities are stalled. You might intervene directly to bring a child into group play by suggesting a role for her. You might suggest something to use for a particular prop, such as an upside-down plastic pitcher and a wooden spoon for a drum and a drumstick, or you might even participate in the play itself. Research has shown that such intervention can significantly enhance children's learning and extend their play (Saracho, 1991).

When a child seems hesitant to use materials, you can help by sitting down and playing with the same materials yourself in an open-ended way. Set up a piece of paper next to the child, and begin a finger painting. Be verbal and make comments about your play, such as "I love the way this squishy paint feels," or "I like the way the colors all run into each other on my paper." At other times, a child might need you to demonstrate a particular movement, such as twisting a sponge under water to help rinse out a color or holding scissors to cut paper for a sign.

Direct guidance also can help children who are having difficulty getting started on an activity or who are stuck or off the track. You might extend a child's play with clay by first imitating what the child is already doing and then varying it a bit. If the child is pounding the clay flat, you might pound it flat and then press cookie cutters into it, or poke bumpy holes in it with a toothpick, or press a piece of sandpaper into it to make an interesting pattern. In the scenario at the beginning of the chapter, for example, the children's play became stagnated when Maggie protested about not wanting to be the mommy anymore. Ms. Jefferson's well-timed, appropriate intervention helped move the children's dramatic play in a new direction.

Another form of direct guidance is questioning. For example, to encourage a child to begin a play activity, you might ask, "How could we make a swimming pool outside for these dolls?" To extend the waning dramatic play of a group, you might ask, "What would happen if the lights went out in your house and you couldn't see?" When asking questions, try to avoid leading the child. Such questions as "Why don't you finger paint now?" or "Why don't you build a house with those blocks?" do not allow a child to act on his own feelings or interests, and they limit the child's creativity.

It is important to choose direct guidance carefully. When you do, think of your involvement as being a minor actor on a stage, slipping away quietly when the play "takes off" again. Use direct guidance to revitalize or expand play, but do not become a "manager" or "director" (Saracho, 1991).

Techniques for Encouraging Play

As stated earlier, the primary task of the preschool teacher is to create an environment that encourages children to play and that supports their play. This section describes several specific strategies you can use to foster the play of children. The more you use indirect guidance techniques, such as setting up the environment, the less you will need to employ direct intervention in children's play. Children need to know that they are free to be themselves and to play in ways that are appropriate to their own level of physical, emotional, social, and cognitive development, as long as their play does not infringe on others' rights. The following strategies can help you create a positive play environment in the preschool setting.

Make Time for Play.   Time is an important factor in creating a productive play environment. Leave ample room in the curriculum for free, spontaneous play. (Sometimes, teachers need to discuss the value and purpose of preschoolers' play with parents. The "Focus on Communicating" feature in Chapter 2 addresses this issue.) Also, leave enough time during a play period for children to fully explore materials, carry out their ideas, and bring their activities to a suitable conclusion. An adequate length of time is necessary, for example, for a child to paint a picture or build a castle out of blocks or for a group of children to carry out a dramatic play scenario. Research has shown, for example, that a minimum of 30 minutes is required for young children to develop a dramatic play scenario (Christie, Johnsen, & Peckover, 1988).

In addition to allowing enough time for children to become involved in and to complete activities, teachers should allow time for children to participate in a variety of play activities. Children need time to play alone, to play

Teachers can set the stage for play by providing a variety of toys and materials arranged invitingly on low shelves and in milk crates or baskets. Creating distinct areas in the classroom encourages children to explore and engage in different types of play.

in groups, and to engage in both teacher-directed and free-play activities. See Chapter 6 for a discussion of balancing the curriculum to provide alternate periods of quiet time, active time, individual play time, and group play time. The way these types of activities are structured during the day also affects children's play experiences. Interesting group activities, such as singing or story time, occur best right before free play in order to stimulate play. A "circle time" activity at the end of the day in which children are encouraged to talk about their play shows them that you value play.

Set the Stage for Play. In addition to providing adequate time for children's play, teachers should set the stage for play, based on children's interests. Create interesting and stimulating play areas, and include a variety of toys and props. Provide snacks when children are hungry, create comfortable areas where they can rest or sleep when they are tired, and intervene to resolve conflicts quickly to ensure a stimulating but stress-free environment conducive to play.

Child development experts recommend establishing indoor and outdoor play settings that provide both adequate space and distinct areas for different kinds of play activities (Frost & Klein, 1983; Spodek, Saracho, & Davis, 1991). Indoor areas, for example, should include shelves for toys, games, books, and art materials. They often include a block area, a game area, an art area, and a housekeeping area. There should also be areas for quiet, solitary activities such as reading. Some of these areas, such as the block area and the housekeeping area, are especially conducive to dramatic play. The location of these different areas must be considered when setting up the play environment. Research has shown, for example, that more imaginative play and social interaction occur when play areas are partitioned off from each other (Field, 1980). Outdoor play settings should also be arranged in separate

TABLE 4.1
Prop box ideas

Idea	Items Needed
Cooking Dinner	Pots and pans, spatulas, mixing spoons, measuring cups and spoons, dish towels, sponges, empty food and beverage containers, pot holders, play food, cookbook
Toy Workshop	Safety goggles, toolboxes, table, pieces of wood, hammers, measuring tapes, rulers, pencils, screwdrivers, large nails and screws, toy catalog or book of designs, broken toys (for example, old toys with parts missing)
Rescue 911	White coats, stethoscopes, sheets, pillows, thermometers, gauze pads and bandages, rolls of tape, cotton balls, flashlights, play walkie-talkies, clipboard, first aid kits/cases, blood pressure cuff, first aid book
Farmer in the Dell	Straw hats, overalls, toy hoes, shovels, rakes, wheelbarrow, empty seed packets, plastic vegetables, gloves, boots, plastic (milking) pails, *Farmer's Almanac*
Time for New Shoes	Different types of shoes, shoe boxes, low stools, foot measuring device or ruler, shoehorns, full-length mirror, play cash register, play money, shopping bags or grocery bags

areas, with a sand area, a jungle gym area, and an open area for running, jumping, and other types of active play. Chapter 5 discusses the physical environment of the preschool setting in detail.

Another aspect of setting the stage for play is providing age-appropriate toys and props. These items need not be expensive. "Found objects," such as old clothes, pots and pans, boxes, old suitcases, shopping bags, baskets, and magazines are especially useful in dramatic play and help stimulate the children's creativity and imagination. Create thematic prop boxes, with each containing props for a different dramatic play scenario, such as a kitchen, an office, a hospital, a garage, and a garden. For example, an office prop box might include pads of paper, different-sized envelopes, paper clips, a tape dispenser, magnets, hole punchers, pens and pencils, stamps, a stapler, file folders, an old telephone, and an old typewriter. See Table 4.1 for more prop box ideas.

Prop boxes provide opportunities both for play and for discussions and related activities. A veterinarian prop box, for example, can be used to stimulate a discussion about taking care of animals, differences among animals (such as those that swim, those that fly, and those that walk on land), and children's own pets or favorite animals. Related activities might include drawing animals, reading stories about animals, and a trip to an animal hospital or a petting zoo. Research has shown that theme-related play materials increase the imaginative play of children (Stacker, 1978).

When choosing toys and props for play, consider the age, size, and developmental level of the children who will be playing with them. Certain games and toys, for example, are too sophisticated for very young children. Instead of giving the child enjoyment, they might only produce frustration and stress. For example, old clothes used for dressing up should be suitable to the size of the children using them. Although adult-size hats, purses, and other accessories might be all right, most adult clothing is too big for young children, and they will become frustrated if they cannot put on a big shirt or if they trip over pants that are much too long. Clothes that are sized for 11- or 12-year-olds are a better choice for preschoolers.

Encourage Anti-Bias Play.   When encouraging play, remember to be aware of social or cultural diversity among the children in your care. Preschool classrooms today often include children from diverse cultural, ethnic, and socioeconomic backgrounds. Although this diversity creates a richer social environment for all the children, it also can create a greater challenge for the teacher. Studies have shown that social class or cultural background can affect a child's level of play as well as the ways in which he approaches a play activity (Fein & Stork, 1981; Griffing, 1980). Provide play activities and materials that are relevant to the particular backgrounds of the children in your class. Create an environment that accepts and celebrates diversity, and encourage children to engage in anti-bias play.

Include props relevant to different cultures, such as chopsticks, saris, kimonos, Native American blankets, and magazines with pictures of people from diverse cultures. These kinds of props are important both for groups in which the children represent many diverse backgrounds and for groups that are more similar in nature. Encourage children of different language backgrounds to play together. Play can often overcome language barriers, as children build a block tower together or push toy cars around a play parking lot.

Another aspect of anti-bias play is encouraging non-sex-stereotyped play. Many preschoolers already have distinct ideas about what girls and boys should do, wear, or play with—as discussed in Chapter 3. Teachers should guard against conveying sex-stereotyped messages about what girls and boys can or cannot do. Teachers can help reduce gender bias by encouraging girls and boys to participate in all activities and to play with all types of toys—such as boys washing babies and girls playing in the block or woodworking areas. Chapter 14 includes a discussion of the nonsexist curriculum and teaching strategies to foster positive attitudes about gender.

Observe Children at Play.   As an early childhood educator, you should be a good observer of children's play, whether or not you are participating. As you observe children at play, stand or sit at a comfortable distance from them. Observe individual differences in skill levels, language, interests, and play styles among children. Look for clues about how different children feel toward others and toward themselves, or how confident or hesitant they are.

Observing dramatic play can be especially helpful in learning more about the children in your group. For example, a child who frequently expresses anger and aggression or always tries to dominate may be struggling with negative feelings and emotions. You might help a child who is afraid of cars by encouraging him to build a street scene in the block area with toy cars and dolls or stuffed animals. Then encourage him to help the dolls or stuffed animals practice crossing the "street."

Rotate Materials.   Keep props and other play materials "fresh" by rotating them periodically. Change and variety help maintain children's interest and create new opportunities for imaginative play. Put away some toys and introduce them again the next week. Mix unusual combinations of toys, props, or materials together. For example, put stuffed animals in the block area, bring play dough or housekeeping props outside, or put blocks in the housekeeping area. Mixing unrelated materials helps stimulate children's creativity and encourages them to think and play in innovative ways. Rotating materials, recycling old materials, or introducing new props will help ensure that the classroom or play environment will be a stimulating and exciting place for young children. Make sure, however, that your ideas for rotating materials come from your observations of children in various activities and areas of the classroom.

CHAPTER 4   REVIEW

SUMMARY

- The basic characteristics of play are that it is voluntary, intrinsically motivated, process-oriented, meaningful, symbolic, and pleasurable.
- Play fosters the cognitive, creative, emotional, and social development of young children.
- Play is crucial to cognitive development. It helps children develop language, memory, and imagery skills and learn and practice problem-solving and decision-making skills.
- Children develop their creative abilities through play as they invent original thoughts and words, explore new activities, and discover new uses for objects, toys, and materials.
- Through play, children can safely explore and express a broad range of emotions. Play also contributes to emotional development by helping children develop a positive self-concept.
- Play fosters social skills, including learning how to compromise, cooperate, share, make and keep friends, and work with others. Play also allows children to experiment with different social roles in adult society.
- Mildred Parten categorized six stages of play: unoccupied behavior, onlooker behavior, solitary play, parallel play, associative play, and cooperative play.
- Piaget focused on the cognitive aspects of play and identified three phases of play: sensorimotor play, symbolic play, and games-with-rules.
- Four basic types of play are play with motion, play with objects, dramatic play, and games. Although preschoolers typically enage in all these types of play, the nature of each type changes as children develop and mature.

- Early childhood educators can guide play indirectly or directly. Indirect guidance refers to "behind-the-scenes" activity, such as organizing the play environment; leaving ample time in the schedule for play; observing children to note their individual needs, interests, and play styles; and rotating materials to provide novelty and stimulation. In direct guidance, the teacher becomes actively involved in children's play by making specific suggestions, introducing new props, modeling or demonstrating, or participating in the play.

ACQUIRING KNOWLEDGE

1. What characteristics define all types of play?
2. Describe how Piaget, Erikson, and Vygotsky interpreted the importance of play.
3. How does play encourage physical development?
4. How does dramatic play help children deal with real-life situations?
5. Why is repetition important in physical play? In dramatic play?
6. What social skills are developed through play?
7. Give three examples of cognitive skills that play can help a child develop.
8. Describe the six stages of play Parten developed.
9. How do most early childhood education professionals today view Parten's stages?
10. Describe Piaget's stages of play.
11. What are four basic types of play?
12. How does play with motion differ between preschoolers and older children?
13. How is play with objects different for a one-year-old and a four-year-old?
14. What does a child demonstrate by using object substitution?
15. How are patterners different from dramatists?
16. How can the theory of symbolic distancing help a teacher decide what props to place in a dramatic play area for two-year-olds or five-year-olds?
17. Describe the two common forms of communication children use during dramatic play.
18. Why is dramatic play important to the growth and development of young children?
19. When might a teacher use the technique of guided play?
20. Describe how modeling and question asking can be used by the preschool teacher to enhance play.
21. What is indirect guidance as it relates to a teacher's involvement in play?
22. How much time is typically needed for children to develop a dramatic play scenario?
23. How can the arrangement of the preschool setting encourage play?
24. What steps can a teacher take to encourage anti-bias play?

25. What kind of information might a teacher obtain by observing children during dramatic play?
26. How can rotating materials in the classroom encourage play?

THINKING CRITICALLY

1. Because play is unstructured and does not directly involve the teacher, some parents may not be familiar with the many ways in which it can encourage a child's development. Imagine that a parent is surprised to find a large period of time reserved for play in a daily schedule. How can a teacher explain the importance of play to this parent?
2. Mildred Parten believed that an observer could determine the maturity of a child by observing that child's play. Do you agree or disagree? Why?
3. Young children can be said to respond to objects either as patterners or dramatists. How might a teacher select toys and props for both types of children?
4. Note-taking is a useful tool for keeping track of observations. What kind of notes might a teacher take while observing children during dramatic play? How might these notes be organized so that they are most helpful?
5. One fundamental aspect of play is that it is motivated by children on their own and not from external direction. Do you think that guiding play violates this aspect and makes play into a school activity? Explain your response.

OBSERVATIONS AND APPLICATIONS

1. During an observation period in a preschool classroom, take some time to explore how the teachers have set up the room to encourage play. Do you see distinct areas set up for play activities? Describe each area in detail, listing some of the materials that you see. Are there any "found" objects, such as old clothes, pots and pans, boxes, or magazines? Do you see any items relevant to different cultures, such as ethnic clothing, Native American rugs or blankets, chopsticks, or posters or magazines depicting people from diverse cultures? How are materials set up or displayed—for example, are materials placed on low shelves within easy reach of the children?
2. Observe preschool children in a dramatic play situation inside the classroom or outdoors. Describe the scenario and "plot." Can you identify a "leader"? What is the leader doing and saying? Describe the roles and actions of each child in the scene. Do you see any children using object substitution? If so, describe how props are used. During any time does the teacher intervene in the play process? What does he or she say or do specifically? What kind of outcome does this intervention have on the play scenario?
3. Monica is a very shy four-year-old in your preschool. She almost never joins in group games, apparently feeling more comfortable sitting against the wall and watching. During free-play time each day, Monica finds a solitary activity, such as looking at a book or working on a puzzle,

instead of playing with the other children. Today, you are determined to engage Monica in a group activity. There is a group of children involved in dramatic play in a play supermarket and another group finger painting at a table. How might you encourage Monica in either of these situations? What might you do if she still does not want to play with the other children?

4. Jonathan, a three-year-old boy in your preschool group, recently was involved in a car accident although he was not seriously injured. Ever since the accident, he has been fearful of all vehicles, but especially cars. His mother told you that Jonathan is seeing a counselor to work out these feelings. However, she hoped that the preschool could help as well. In addition to activities you may initiate to help Jonathan, what types of materials would you make available in different areas of the classroom?

FOR FURTHER INFORMATION

Bordner, G. A., Berkley, M. T. (1992). Educational play: Meeting everyone's needs in mainstreamed classrooms. *Childhood Education, 61*(1), 38–42.

Brokering, L. (1989). *Resources for Dramatic Play.* Carthage, IL: Fearon Teacher Aids.

Carlsson-Paige, N., & Levin, D. E. (1992). Making peace in violent times: A constructivist approach to conflict resolution. *Young Children, 48*(1), 4–28.

Christie, J. F., & Wardle, F. (1992). How much time is needed for play? *Young Children, 47*(3), 28–32.

Derman-Sparks, L., & the A. B. C. Task Force. (1989). *Anti-bias curriculum; Tools for empowering young children.* Washington, DC: National Association for the Education of Young Children.

Goldhaber, J. (1992). Sticky to dry; red to purple: Exploring transformation with play dough. *Young Children, 48*(1), 4–28.

Greenman, J. (1993). Just wondering: Building wonder into the environment. *Child Care Information Exchange, 89*, 32–36.

Jones, E. (1993). The play's the thing: styles of playfulness. *Child Care Information Exchange, 89*, 28–31.

Oken-Wright, P. (1992). From tug of war to "Let's Make a Deal": The teacher's role. *Young Children, 48*(1), 4–28.

Sawyers, J. K., & Rogers, C. S. (1988). *Helping young children develop through play: A practical guide for parents, caregivers, and teachers.* Washington, DC: National Association for the Education of Young Children.

Singer, J. L., & Singer, D. G. (1985). *Make-believe: Games and activities to foster imaginative play in young children.* Glenview, IL: Scott, Foresman.

Smilansky, S., & Shefatya, L. (1990). *Facilitating play: A medium for promoting cognitive, socioemotional, and academic development in young children.* Gaithersburg, MD: Psychological and Educational Publications.

Stangl, J. (1986). *Magic mixtures: Creative fun for little ones, preschool–grade 3.* Carthage, IL: Fearon Teacher Aids.

Van Hoorn, J., Nourot, P., Scales, B., & Alward, K. (1993). *Play at the center of the curriculum.* New York: Macmillan.

Preschool Environment: Elements and Opportunities

OBJECTIVES

Studying this chapter
will enable you to

- Discuss how the physical
  environment of preschools
  contributes to the growth and
  development of young children
- Describe the major components of
  the indoor environment
- Explain how outdoor play spaces
  and equipment contribute to the
  development of physical and
  social skills
- List several ways preschool
  teachers can create a safe physical
  environment for children
- Discuss how preschool teachers
  can rearrange and add to the
  physical environment to stimulate
  new types of play and create new
  learning experiences

CHAPTER TERMS

activity area
adventure playground
aesthetics
complex play unit
contemporary playground
global quality-assessment instrument
hardness-softness factor
learning center
physical environment
play structure
simple play unit
super-complex play unit
traditional playground
unit blocks

WHEN Ricky and Bonnie went outside to play at the Roosevelt Community Child Care Center, they headed straight for their favorite spot, a collection of cardboard and wooden boxes, boards, wooden spools, and old tires located in a far corner of the play yard under a large tree.

"Let's play hospital," said Bonnie. "We'll be doctors in the operating room."

"Okay. We'll make this our operating table," said Ricky as he placed a board across two large wooden spools.

"And these boxes will be our waiting room," said Bonnie, arranging several small wooden boxes into a seating area. She placed several plastic cups on one box. "We can have coffee for the patients."

"Can I play?" asked Sherman, running up to the two.

"I want to play, too," said Amanda, joining the group.

"You can be our patients," Bonnie said. "You just wait here in the waiting room, and we'll call you when we're ready," she told them.

"What's wrong with you?" Amanda asked Sherman.

"I've got a broken arm," he replied, giggling and dangling an arm crookedly.

"Well, I've got a broken leg," Amanda said, getting up and limping around the "waiting room" to demonstrate.

"First patient, please," Bonnie announced, leading Sherman over to the "operating table" where Ricky waited.

"Don't worry, sir," Ricky said. "We'll have you all fixed up soon."

The *physical environment* of a preschool or child care center comprises all the surroundings, including the walls and shape of the room, the furniture, the materials, the toys, and the equipment. The physical environment is the stage on which the curriculum is played out and where children and teachers interact. *Aesthetics*, elements that contribute to the appearance and atmosphere of the physical environment, include artwork, lighting, and the colors and textures of the floors, walls, furniture, and materials. In addition to these components, the physical environment includes other less obvious elements, such as traffic patterns, noise levels, safety measures, and the room arrangement. The design of the indoor and outdoor spaces and the choices of materials and equipment enhance or restrict the children's experiences and affect their behavior and even their emotions.

At Ricky and Bonnie's preschool, the staff has furnished the play yard with an assortment of boxes and boards and other objects that the children can use to engage in dramatic play. These objects are part of the planned physical environment. The shady tree that shelters the children from the hot sun and the out-of-the-way corner that gives them the privacy to carry out their play without interruption also are planned components. This chapter discusses the elements that make up the physical environment of the typical preschool or child care center. In addition, it examines how teachers can use these elements to enhance the learning and developmental experiences of young children.

Setting the Stage for Learning

Stimulating, challenging preschool environments do not just happen; they must be carefully planned and designed. The way a room or a play yard is arranged affects both children and adults in many subtle ways. Without planning, the preschool setting will become disorganized and will fail to challenge children. Effective planning, however, can help teachers achieve curriculum goals, foster development, and minimize behavioral problems (Prescott, 1984). For example, storing books and materials on low shelves where children can reach them tells the children that they are trusted to choose their own activities. A family of gerbils kept in a cage on a low table where children can readily observe them encourages the children to discover independently how animals behave and take care of their young. See Figure 5.1 for a sample layout of a preschool setting.

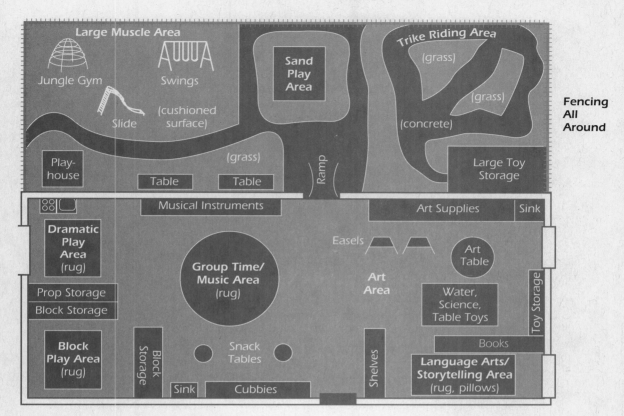

FIGURE 5.1   Layout of a Preschool Setting. This layout of a typical preschool shows various activity areas indoors and outdoors. Teachers should make any necessary adjustments to the environment to accommodate children with special needs. For example, to address the needs of children in wheelchairs, teachers might check that shelves, tables, and coat hooks are an appropriate height and that pathways between learning centers are wide enough. Teachers need to make other adaptations that will facilitate independent use of equipment and materials.

One of the important goals of designing the preschool environment is to encourage children to engage in increasingly complex levels of play. Another is to use materials that encourage them to interact with one another. The choice of materials and equipment that a preschool provides strongly influences the students' play. Preschoolers play with different materials in different ways. For example, research conducted with children from middle and low socioeconomic groups found that these children tended to engage in solitary play or parallel play with sand, water, and art materials, such as play dough or paint, more than in associative play or cooperative play (Rubin, 1977). When they did engage in associative play or cooperative play, they did so most often with dramatic play materials, such as housekeeping props, and with vehicle play.

Complex play materials with many parts that can be combined into different structures can promote dramatic play among children. Kritchevsky,

Prescott, and Walling have classified play units into simple, complex, and super-complex. *Simple play units*, such as swings or tricycles, have one obvious use. *Complex play units* have two types of materials or parts that can be manipulated or used in different ways, such as a playhouse with furniture or a water table with water toys. *Super-complex play units* combine three or more types of materials or parts, such as water and measuring equipment in the sandbox (Kritchevsky, Prescott, & Walling, 1969). Ricky and Bonnie's dramatic play area with boxes and boards and wooden spools, for example, offers many more opportunities for improvisation and manipulation than a slide that can be used by only one child at a time for one activity.

Organizing room arrangements and materials also may require accommodating children who are handicapped or disabled. The preschool may need to build ramps and asphalt pathways, widen corridors, and install bars in bathrooms to provide access for children in wheelchairs. Special furniture and playground equipment also can be designed, purchased, or constructed for wheelchair-bound children. This equipment includes wheelchair swings, and water tables and sand tables that allow wheelchairs to roll underneath them. The Americans with Disabilities Act of 1990 requires that all new construction of public accommodations, including preschools and child care centers, provide easy access for handicapped individuals. Other accommodations may include providing flashing lights instead of alarms on smoke detectors for the hearing impaired. Preschool teachers and child care providers should familiarize themselves with the ADA requirements and review them every time a new child with a disability joins the preschool or center.

Setting the Stage Indoors

Adequate space is a major consideration when planning indoor play areas. Research has shown that children in overcrowded classrooms demonstrate less social interaction and also are more likely to exhibit aggressive behavior—such as hitting, arguing, and taking toys—than children who have more space (Smith & Connolly, 1980). The National Association for the Education of Young Children (NAEYC) recommends 35 square feet of floor space per child and says that 45 to 50 square feet per child is preferable. Preschools and child care centers in very cold climates, where children spend more time indoors, require additional indoor play space. A large area should be dedicated to indoor climbing equipment, running and jumping activities, riding toys, and other activities that develop large motor skills.

Furniture

Furniture needs to be sturdy enough to withstand hard use by large groups of children year after year. Chairs and tables also should be appropriately sized. Children should be able to sit comfortably on chairs with their feet touching the floor. Tables should be an appropriate height so that small children can sit or stand at them comfortably.

Preschools commonly use furniture—such as low bookcases, tables, and chairs—to subdivide large indoor spaces into separate activity areas or learning centers. Keeping the partitions low enables teachers to monitor the activity areas and enables children to see out into the rest of the room. Sometimes, higher partitions are used to create spaces that give children a sense of personal space. In a classroom where activity areas are well-defined, children initiate more activities, become more involved in activities, and play together more often (Moore, 1983).

The arrangement and the type of furniture within each area tell children what specific activities occur there. The art center, for example, may include several easels and a large table where children can spread out crayons and drawing paper or work with clay. A book corner, on the other hand, may be furnished only with bookshelves, carpeting, and large soft pillows or bean-bag chairs. Children can nestle and relax on the floor while listening to teachers read books or tell stories or while looking at books by themselves.

A well-planned physical environment helps children feel excited about exploring and learning. Notice this classroom's distinct areas for art, dramatic play, block play, language arts, and cognitive activities.

Traffic Patterns

In order to plan an efficient indoor space, the child care provider has to visualize how children will move around in the facility. Bathrooms should be near the exit to the play yard, and hand-washing facilities should be close to eating and art areas. Pathways between activity areas should be clearly delineated and unimpeded. For example, teachers should watch for chairs that obstruct pathways. Children should not have to walk through one activity area to access another. This rule applies to the outdoors also. Ricky and Bonnie's "hospital" play was not disturbed by children riding tricycles or running because the outdoor play areas and traffic patterns were well planned. When planning traffic patterns, the overall goal is to create a smooth flow from one area to another with a minimum of disruption and confusion.

Bright colors, warm lighting, cozy furniture, and carpeting contribute to the aesthetics of the preschool environment. The physical setting should help children feel physically comfortable and welcome.

Noise Levels

Noise levels naturally vary from activity to activity. Music, dramatic play, block play, and group games can be very noisy, whereas, for example, art activities, reading, and play with manipulatives such as puzzles are much quieter. Noisy activities distract and disturb children engaged in quiet pursuits. Noise level can be controlled to some extent by using carpeting, acoustic tile, and soundproofing materials to absorb sounds in the noisy areas. Another way to reduce distraction and promote concentration in quiet areas is to place them as far apart as possible from noisy activity areas.

Aesthetics

Emotions and moods are strongly affected by the preschool's or center's appearance. Bright colors and warm, natural lighting create a cheerful environment, whereas dark colors and dim lighting have the opposite effect. Color, light, and texture can be used to create a friendly, warm, and inviting atmosphere. The *hardness-softness factor*, developed by Elizabeth Jones, refers to the balance of hard and soft surfaces in a classroom (Jones, 1977). Hard surfaces, such as linoleum floors and metal cabinets, are more dangerous and less appealing or inviting to children than soft surfaces, which create a homey, comfortable atmosphere. According to Jones, softness can be achieved indoors by using carpeting, soft pillows, and cozy furniture. Rocking chairs, furry animals, soft materials such as felt fabric and play dough, and furniture with curves instead of straight edges also impart feelings of softness. Sandboxes and grassy areas instead of concrete contribute to the softness factor outdoors.

Varying the textures within the classroom also adds aesthetic interest and stimulates the senses. The environment should include contrasting features,

Cultural Diversity

The Classroom Wall: A Multicultural Canvas

The physical environment should play a part in a multicultural curriculum, reflecting the children's ethnic backgrounds, customs, and interests. Consider the classroom walls as a multicultural canvas. Letting preschoolers see familiar materials and pictures of people like themselves hanging in the classroom helps them feel at home.

The following tips can help you plan how to most effectively choose and display materials.

- **Familiarize yourself with the ethnic background of each child.** The more you know about the children in your program, the better you will be able to reflect their background on the classroom walls. Through group-time discussions and communication with parents, encourage children and their families to share information and stories about their home life, customs, and values.

- **Select materials that depict everyday life in the United States.** In order for preschoolers to learn that the United States is made up of a diverse population, they need to see people at work and at play in places that look familiar. Choose pictures, for example, that depict Asian Americans, Native Americans, and Mexican Americans in everyday settings—in the kitchen, getting ready for bed, eating dinner, and riding a bike, for instance.

- **Create wall displays that are inviting and exciting.** Hang materials at children's eye level. Change the wall hangings frequently so that children are exposed to a variety of cultures throughout the year. Choose items that reflect the current interests of the children in your classroom.

- **Invite children to draw pictures or make collages of themselves and their families.** Supply a variety of different-colored paints and crayons so that children can choose colors similar to their skin tones. Consider giving children hand mirrors so that they can see themselves before they begin drawing.

- **Present positive role models.** Many early childhood education resource catalogs offer posters that depict men and women of multiethnic backgrounds in nontraditional roles as well as in everyday settings. Look in consumer and business magazines for pictures of people from diverse ethnic or cultural backgrounds who are prominent in their fields, such as actors, musicians, athletes, politicians, and businesspeople.

such as soft and hard, wet and dry, glossy and matte, square and round shapes, and materials with warm and cold temperatures (Rho & Drury, (1978). For more information on textures, see Chapter 10.

Aesthetics also include the artwork that decorates the classroom walls. Wall decorations should be hung at the children's eye level. Letters of the alphabet, signs, and printed notices help children become familiar with words and letters. Pictures of children from other ethnic groups, races, and cultures—combined with instruction to actually promote understanding—raise children's multicultural awareness. See the feature in this chapter, "Focus on Cultural Diversity—The Classroom Wall: A Multicultural Canvas."

Activity Areas and Learning Centers

The physical environment reflects the preschool's curriculum approach and its educational values. Preschools that follow an academic curriculum approach may arrange the furniture in different patterns from those of a developmental preschool, and materials also may be used in a different manner. These differences can most readily be seen in the sections of the classroom where specific activities are carried out. *Learning centers* is the term used most often in academically oriented preschools, and *activity areas* is the term used most often in developmentally oriented preschools. These defined areas are common to both kinds of curriculum approaches, but they are likely to be used quite differently, and materials are likely to be used differently.

Suppose, for example, that a teacher in an academically oriented preschool plans to teach a lesson about the names of animals. She might sit at the head of a table with the children and show them a chart listing the names of several animals next to pictures of the animals. She would ask the children to repeat each animal's name in unison as she points to it on the chart. Then, she might direct them to copy the names onto cards or trace them on a worksheet. In a developmentally oriented preschool, the teacher might introduce small plastic animals or stuffed animals into the block area and encourage the children to construct a zoo for them. With the teacher's assistance, the children might make signs for the cages naming each kind of animal they contain, or signs such as "Do not feed the tigers." In both instances, the children would be participating in a language skills-building activity, but the teachers would be using different materials, different furniture, different areas of the classroom, and distinct teaching styles to carry out the activity.

Regardless of the curriculum approach, the design and use of activity or learning areas allows children many opportunities for problem solving, decision making, and social interaction. Although many of these areas are discussed in other chapters, the following are the basic elements for each area that preschools consider most important.

The Block Area.   The block area requires a clear area of flooring or a large low table where the children can play with blocks of various sizes and shapes. Tightly woven carpeting helps absorb the noise of falling blocks and general clatter, while still providing a flat surface. The most common kind of blocks are *unit blocks*, solid hardwood blocks that come in various shapes—squares, oblongs, columns, triangles, wedges, and half circles. Some preschool settings also have large hollow blocks—cardboard or wooden—that are about 12 inches long and 6 inches wide. Research has shown that children are more likely to engage in cooperative group play when using the large hollow blocks and in solitary play or parallel play when working with unit blocks (Rogers, 1985). Another type of blocks are table blocks, small wooden blocks that can be manipulated on a tabletop.

Blocks should be displayed on low, open shelving. Some preschool teachers line the shelves with brown paper, then trace the shape of each block to

Building in the block area helps children explore spatial relations, problem solving, and their own creativity. This three-year-old is using hollow blocks to create a home for her stuffed animals and toys.

help children match blocks to their proper place when they put them away.

Building with blocks promotes the development of gross and fine motor skills, as well as language and social skills. Children often combine blocks with cars, dolls, and other toys. Younger children explore the texture, shape, and weight of the blocks, whereas older preschoolers learn about the size, proportions, and relationships of the blocks. Chapter 10 discusses the use of blocks in greater depth.

The Language Arts/Storytelling Area. This area provides a setting and materials that focus on all areas of language arts: reading, writing, listening, and speaking. It is a quiet, comfortable area with carpeting, large pillows, and stuffed animals, where children can look at books, pretend to read books to each other, or listen to teachers read stories. Low shelves display a wide array of age-appropriate books, with the cover, not the spine, facing the children.

The area usually includes a table where children can work with writing materials and play matching and sorting games designed to stimulate language development, prereading, prewriting, and listening skills. There also might be a tape player for children to listen to stories on cassette tapes. Flannel boards and puppets allow children to practice telling and retelling stories.

In an academic preschool, this area is sometimes called the library/language learning center. See Chapter 11 for a discussion of language arts planning and activities.

The Dramatic Play Area. This area is sometimes called the housekeeping area because it is usually furnished with play appliances, dishes, utensils, dolls, and housekeeping props such as brooms or mops. Dramatic play areas typically include a trunk or box full of clothes, hats, and other accessories for dress-up.

In addition, the dramatic play area often contains a variety of occupational props, such as tool kits (for a carpenter), a briefcase and a newspaper (for a businessperson), and a mail bag and letters (for a mail carrier). A thematic play center for a doctor's office, for example, might contain a stethoscope, a first aid kit, a clipboard, a laboratory coat, a nurse's cap and uniform, magazines (for patients in the waiting room), and health brochures. Other props for the dramatic play area were discussed in Chapter 4.

Through dramatic play, children explore emotions, practice problem solving, reenact situations from real life with different outcomes, and practice cooperation and communication with peers.

The Art/Manipulative Area.   Art activities, such as drawing and painting, stimulate the imagination, promote creativity and self-expression, and develop fine motor skills. Manipulative activities, such as stringing beads or molding play dough, also may be set up in this or an adjacent area. Manipulative activities develop fine motor skills and eye-hand coordination and provide enjoyable sensory experiences for young children.

The art/manipulative area usually features several easels as well as a large low table where children can work with finger paints, clay, scissors and glue, and other materials. A well-equipped art area is stocked with a wide variety of supplies, including paper, brushes, paints, crayons, markers, chalk, and clay. Preschool teachers are always on the lookout for various kinds of recycled or miscellaneous materials to use in art projects as well. These materials can include feathers, beads, buttons, fabric and leather scraps, newsprint, cardboard tubes, egg cartons, and any number of other items. Manipulative materials may include puzzles, peg boards, sewing cards, beads for stringing, blocks, play dough, and similar materials. However, teachers should be aware that small objects in the manipulative area, such as beads and buttons, are not safe for two-year-olds. A large, low sink in the art/manipulative area allows for easy cleaning of paintbrushes and spills.

In an academically oriented school, art materials are stored out of reach of the children; the teacher hands out the materials she wants the children to use each day and may model or demonstrate how to use the materials or what to make. In a developmental classroom, the art materials are stored on open, low shelves so that the children can choose the materials they want to work with themselves. Art, manipulative, and other creative activities are discussed in Chapter 13.

The Group Time/Music Area.   In this area, children can listen to music, sing, play musical instruments, dance, and play group games. Typically, the group time/music area is a large unfurnished space, but it may be carpeted to reduce the noise level. If the floor is uncarpeted, teachers may give students individual carpet squares or throw pillows so that they will have a soft place to sit.

The music center is equipped with a record or tape player, and simple percussion and rhythm instruments, such as tambourines and maracas. If

FOCUS ON / **Activities**

Extending the Preschool Environment: Field Trips

Field trips provide preschoolers with an active and concrete way to learn about people, places, and things outside the immediate world of the classroom or home and to broaden children's sense of their surroundings and community. Here is how you might plan a visit to your local bagel shop. Beforehand, ask the person in charge if you may bring some children into the shop for a visit; if he or she will give a demonstration of making bagels, and perhaps let each child shape some dough into a bagel; and how many children the shop can accommodate. Explain that the children will have many questions. Also, be sure to get permission slips from the parents, and arrange for parent volunteers to help out on the day of the trip.

Next, talk with the children about bagels and bagel stores, asking open-ended questions to discover what they know and what they would like to find out. Questions might include the following: What are bagels made of? How many different flavors of bagels can you think of? If you could make up a flavor, what

would it be? How are bagels different from sandwich bread or donuts?

At the bagel shop, visit the back of the store, where the children can watch a demonstration of how bagels are shaped from dough, topped with sesame seeds or salt, or flavored with egg or onion, and baked. In the front of the store, encourage children to look at all the different types of bagels. Watch as a customer chooses bagels and pays for them. Point out any printed items, such as the hours or "Open" sign on the door or a menu with prices.

Extend the Experience

- Write thank-you notes to the owner or manager of the store. Children may wish to draw pictures or dictate stories.
- Provide space for children who might want to set up a "bagel store" or other type of "shop" in the classroom. Ask children what props they will need.

the area has a tape recorder, teachers can tape children's own performances. The area also may include a piano and special props for creative dance and movement.

Music, song, and dance are important outlets for creativity, self-expression, and emotions and for developing social skills. They also promote large motor development and language skills. Group time is important to the development of language and social skills and is discussed in more detail in Chapter 9; music and movement are covered in Chapter 13.

Children's Belongings and the Daily Routine

Cubbyholes, coatracks, or shelving store children's personal belongings each day. Some preschools require that each child have a change of clothing and a blanket or sleeping bag for nap times. Children also need space to keep drawings, paintings, and other creations that they intend to take home. Personal storage spaces should be labeled with each child's picture and

name. They should be located near the door where children arrive and de-
part so that they can be checked daily by parents or guardians.

The room plan also should reflect such practical considerations as where
snacks and lunch will be served, where toilets and hand-washing facilities
will be located, and where children will take naps. If the children are required to set their own places for snacks and lunch and to clean up afterward, dishes and utensils should be stored on low shelves so that they can
be reached, and trash cans should be provided for cleanup. In addition, if
cots or sleeping bags are used for nap times, they may need to be stored out
of the way when they are not in use so that the rest area can be used for
other purposes.

Setting the Stage Outdoors

The design of the outdoor playground should reflect the needs, interests,
and desires of young children. Just as the indoor space is subdivided into activity areas, the outdoor space also should be subdivided into a variety of
play spaces. These spaces may include an area for large, stationary equipment—such as swings and slides—an area for riding toys, a sandbox, and an
area for dramatic play. Ideally, the play yard should provide about 75 square
feet of open space per child. It should have an adequate quantity of toys and
equipment—such as sand toys, tricycles, and swings—to minimize monop-
olizing and arguing over toys. Some experts recommend one large toy, such
as a tricycle, for every two children. The equipment should be developmentally appropriate for the age of the children using it. Toddlers cannot play
safely on standard playground equipment such as slides, but they like low
climbing equipment and small, portable toys, such as buckets, shovels, cars,
and dolls. Four- and five-year-olds prefer more challenging equipment, such
as slides, swings, jungle gyms, and tricycles.

A primary function of the outdoor area is to provide opportunities for the
development of gross motor skills, but playgrounds serve other needs as
well. The playground is a place where children can release pent-up energy
and tensions and express their emotions loudly and freely. Challenging
equipment allows children to build their feelings of self-confidence and
competence. Finally, a well-designed playground also stimulates the social
and intellectual development of children in a variety of ways. Research has
shown that boys engage in more fantasy play outdoors than they do inside
(Sanders & Harper, 1976). Research also has shown that boys use more complex language on the playground than in the classroom, indicating that outdoor play may have an important impact on their language development
(Tizard, Philps, & Plewis, 1976).

Areas to Develop Gross Motor Skills

The outdoor space in the preschool setting creates many opportunities for
young children to develop gross motor skills. Climbing equipment and jungle gyms, slides, tricycles, and wide, open spaces to run and jump freely

FOCUS ON / Communicating with Parents

Asking Parents about Free Materials

Families can be valuable resources when it comes to collecting free materials for your art, block, science, or dramatic play areas. "Unnecessary" items in the home can become treasures in your classroom. Also, many parents have access to materials that are commonly discarded at the workplace, such as magazines, computer paper, and calendars. To enlist parents' help, explain how you will use the materials and how their support will enhance their child's preschool experience.

MS. MILLER: Hi, Mrs. Arnaud. Susan is just saying good-bye to her friends and getting her coat from her cubby. How was your day?

Mrs. Arnaud: Busy. We have a project deadline next week. And the baby woke up too early this morning. I'm exhausted.

MS. MILLER: I'm sorry to hear you've had such a rough day. If you have a minute, though, I wanted to ask if you might help us with a new environmental project. I've been trying to talk to every parent individually.

MRS. ARNAUD: Oh, no, something else to do. I'm sorry—but it sounds interesting. OK, what's it all about?

MS. MILLER: We've been talking about recycling, and the children decided they wanted to build a park for our stuffed animals and dolls out of recycled materials. During group time, we came up with a list of everyday household items we might be able to use. I typed it up and made copies for each family. I know you and Susan take the bus to get here, so skip over the big or bulky items. There are lots of small items we need.

MRS. ARNAUD: How about old sponges in different colors like green and blue? Maybe the children can use them to make flowers or grass. Or empty juice boxes for little cars or something.

MS. MILLER: Exactly! Those are great ideas! The children are really excited about building the park. We couldn't do it without the help and support of parents.

Even though Susan's mother said that she was exhausted, Ms. Miller was able to capture her attention and to get her interested in participating in the recycling project. What are some other ways Ms. Miller could have made Mrs. Arnaud's involvement sound as easy as possible? What might be some other questions Ms. Miller could have asked to encourage ideas for additional items from Susan's mother?

make the playground an ideal place for children to test, challenge, and exercise the large muscle groups.

Playgrounds can be divided into three main types (Naylor, 1985). The *traditional playground* consists of separate large, fixed pieces of equipment, such as slides, swings, and teeter-totters. These kinds of apparatus are very beneficial in developing gross motor skills, such as running, jumping, climbing, balancing, throwing, catching, pedaling, pushing, and pulling.

The *contemporary playground* consists of one or more multiuse play structures. A *play structure* is a large wooden or metal apparatus that combines separate areas for slides, ramps, poles, steps, ladders, tires, jungle gyms, and swings into one large piece of equipment. With a combination of enclosed and open areas, play structures offer more complex play areas than traditional playgrounds. Play structures also promote the development of gross motor skills and encourage dramatic play and social interaction.

The third type of playground, the *adventure playground*, is equipped with several large boxes, large wooden spools, tires, barrels, boards, and crates that the children can lift, pull, push, carry, and climb into. These objects can be rearranged in countless ways and used for many kinds of muscle-building activities. A short board suspended across two low boxes can become a balance beam, or several large objects can be arranged into an obstacle course for a game of Follow the Leader. In addition to building gross motor skills, adventure playgrounds foster cognitive skills and present opportunities for dramatic play.

Other playground areas also promote gross motor development. A large, flat paved area or a paved pathway is a great place for children to ride tricycles and scooters and to play with wagons. Preschools also should provide a grassy play area for outdoor games, running, and tumbling.

No matter what kind of playground is provided, the equipment needs to be extremely safe, durable, and well-maintained. The kinds of outdoor play equipment parents and guardians purchase for home use in the yard are not adequately durable or safe for use by preschools.

Areas to Develop Fine Motor Skills

Many outdoor activities promote the development of fine motor skills. A playhouse with housekeeping materials, sand tables and water tables, and sandboxes are all places where children can hold tea parties, make mud pies, and build sand castles. All these activities involve manipulating small objects and developing eye-hand coordination. Some preschools also maintain garden areas where children can dig, plant, and weed using their hands and small tools.

Indoor activities, such as painting or building with blocks, can be set up outdoors in good weather. In addition, children can enjoy certain activities outdoors that are too messy to be conducted inside. For example, they can wash dolls and doll clothes in a wading pool or "paint" the playhouse with a bucket of water and a paintbrush.

Activities that build fine motor skills also tend to promote dramatic play and socialization. Once a group of children has constructed a road in the sandbox, the children can then use the road to drive their toy cars while pretending to be truck drivers, firefighters, and police officers.

Traffic Patterns and Use of Space

Outdoor play areas should be placed far enough apart to avoid congestion and should be attractively designed to encourage the use of all outdoor areas. Spaces can be defined by the use of pathways, vegetation, and various textures of ground cover. Depending on the activity, one area may be grassy, another sandy, and a third paved with concrete or asphalt. Trees and bushes also can be used to separate play spaces.

The traffic pattern of the play yard should be observed to make sure that one activity does not interfere with another. If tricycle riders are riding through the spaces where children are swinging or engaging in dramatic play, the traffic pattern needs to be redesigned. The preschool staff also should study the pattern of sun and shade throughout the day and place some activities in predominantly shady spots. Water tables and wading pools should be near a convenient source of water.

Many outdoor toys, such as large wooden blocks and riding toys, need to be stored out of the weather when they are not in use. Storage sheds should be placed near the play area where the equipment is used. Teachers may wish that storage facilities be constructed so that children can take out and return equipment themselves.

Keeping the Physical Environment Safe

A basic responsibility of child care providers is to keep the children in their charge safe. Providing a safe environment requires careful thought, meticulous planning, and regular maintenance of equipment. It also requires close supervision of children at all times. This section covers steps that adults can take to make the physical environment safe for young children.

Indoor Safety

Cleaning materials, flammable liquids, and medications must be stored in locked cabinets out of children's reach, and the number of the local poison control center must be posted close to or on all telephones. At least one adult should be trained in first aid procedures and child cardiopulmonary resuscitation (CPR), and a well-stocked first aid kit should be kept on hand. In addition, all parents should be asked to fill out a form listing emergency numbers for their pediatricians and giving the school permission to seek medical treatment for their children in the event of an emergency.

The school building should be equipped with an adequate number of working smoke detectors and fire extinguishers. Teachers should stage fire drills periodically to familiarize children with fire exit routes. Unused electrical outlets should be capped. In some states, extension cords are against licensing rules; if they are allowed, it is important that they be checked for fraying as well as placement to avoid tripping accidents. Water heaters set at 120° F (49° C) prevent children from scalding themselves with hot water.

Furniture should be smooth with rounded edges. Tall furniture, such as lockers and bookcases, can be anchored to the wall to avoid having them tip over. Nonslip pads under area rugs prevent bunching and slipping. Floors and furniture should be cleaned daily so that they are not sticky or dirty. Toys also should be cleaned and disinfected daily, especially in infant and toddler rooms.

A safety checklist should include making sure that all unused electrical outlets are capped. Because young children explore with their hands and mouths, the preschool setting must be checked daily for hazards.

Safety Checklist for the Preschool Setting

✔ Are cleaning materials, flammable liquids, and medications stored in locked cabinets?

✔ Is the telephone number of the local poison control center posted close to or on all telephones?

✔ Is at least one adult on the staff trained in first aid procedures?

✔ Is there a well-stocked first aid kit on hand?

✔ Is there a form for each child listing emergency numbers for the family doctor/pediatrician as well as permission to seek medical treatment in the event of an emergency?

✔ Is there an adequate number of working smoke detectors and fire extinguishers?

✔ Have unused electrical outlets been capped, and have extension cords been checked for fraying and also for placement so as to avoid tripping hazards?

✔ Have hot water heaters been set at not more than 120° F (49° C) to prevent scalding?

✔ Have furniture and toys been checked for sharp edges?

✔ Have lockers, bookcases, and other tall furniture been anchored to the wall to avoid their being tipped over?

✔ Have nonslip pads been placed under area rugs to prevent bunching and slipping?

✔ Do outdoor playground areas have proper cushioning material underneath swings, slides, jungle gyms, and other similar play equipment?

✔ Is stationary play equipment firmly anchored in the ground?

✔ Is there adequate fencing (at least 4 feet high with securely attached gates) around the playground that will keep children from wandering away?

✔ Is the playground area free of poisonous plants?

✔ Have indoor and outdoor furniture and equipment been checked for safety— e.g., rust or loose screws, bolts, or ladder rungs?

FIGURE 5.2   Safety Checklist for the Preschool Setting.

Outdoor Safety

According to studies conducted by the U.S. Consumer Product Safety Commission, approximately three-fourths of playground injuries are caused by falls from play equipment (Tinsworth & Kramer, 1990). Other studies reported by the Centers for Disease Control found that a 1-foot fall on the head directly onto concrete or asphalt or a 4-foot fall onto packed earth can be fatal. Yet, more than 48 percent of child care playground equipment is not installed over impact-absorbing surfaces (Centers for Disease Control, 1988).

Sand, small-grain gravel, wood chips, pulverized rubber, or other soft, resilient materials under swings, slides, and jungle gyms cushion falls and help minimize injuries. Several playground surveys in recent years show that most schools and public playgrounds fail to provide cushioning material at sufficient depth to prevent injuries. Research has shown that cushioning material should be 9 to 12 inches thick to provide the best protection against fall injuries (Ramsey & Preston, 1990).

Large play equipment, such as swings and slides, needs to be placed in a large open area away from buildings, fences, and other structures so that there is sufficient unimpeded space for the activity. Individual swings should be constructed 2 to 3 feet apart. They should be equipped with cloth or lightweight plastic strap-type seats instead of rigid wooden or metal seats, so that children will not be injured if they are struck by a swing. Bars and rungs on play equipment need to be spaced so that children cannot trap their heads between them. The space between bars should be at least 9 inches but no more than 3½ feet.

Playground equipment should be securely anchored in the ground so that it will not tip, and all concrete footings should be below ground level. Any playground equipment with moving parts that can pinch or crush fingers or hands, such as teeter-totter boards, are not recommended for early childhood playgrounds. The preschool or center director should obtain a copy of the standards for outdoor play equipment from the Consumer Product Safety Commission and should make certain that all equipment conforms to those standards.

Proper fencing around the playground keeps children from wandering into woods or traffic. Fencing also keeps out animals and visitors who have not been cleared through the main office. The fence should be at least 4 feet high with securely latched gates. Teachers should form the habit of visually inspecting the play area daily to spot any unsafe conditions, such as broken glass. The playground must also be kept free of poisonous plants. Many common plants—such as rhubarb, poinsettia, castor bean, rhododendron, and sweet pea—can cause vomiting, convulsions, and death if ingested. Teachers also should keep in mind these dangers when planning plants for decoration indoors or for children's gardening activities. Figure 5.2 shows one type of safety checklist.

Supervision of Play

The preschool or center should always have a sufficient ratio of staff to children to ensure adequate supervision. The ideal ratio is one adult for every eight preschoolers. Infants and toddlers require even smaller ratios—one adult for every three to six youngsters (NAEYC, 1991). Providing separate play areas or separate play schedules for toddlers and preschoolers helps prevent knockdown accidents and reduces aggression and tendencies to dominate or control possession of equipment by older children. Whenever possible, at least two adults should supervise each group of children, so that if one has to leave the area temporarily, the other will be on hand. The most

Outdoors, it is important to have two or more teachers supervising the children in case one has to leave temporarily. The teachers' attention should be on the children at all times.

fundamental rule of child care is never to leave children unattended, indoors or out, for even a few minutes.

Teachers should sit, stand, or move around so that they can see every child in every part of the room or yard. For safety's sake, teachers should avoid the tendency to socialize during outdoor time so that their full attention remains on the children. Teachers should always be ready to step in and halt an activity if it looks unsafe. For example, if children are deliberately bumping into one another on the swings, throwing sand at one another, or putting small objects into their mouths, the caregiver should stop them and explain to them why their actions are dangerous.

Children should not be lifted onto any piece of equipment—with the exception of swings—that they cannot get on by themselves. Having to lift children is a good indication that the equipment is developmentally inappropriate for them.

Activities involving water require the closest supervision. Toddlers have been known to drown in wading pools, toilets, and even buckets of water. Children must never be left alone when they are playing in a pool or wading pool or at the water table. Pools and water tables should be emptied or drained when not in use.

Teachers need to show children how to use play equipment safely and correctly. With simple rules for using toys and equipment, stated in positive form, children will have a clear idea of what they are expected to do. For example, a teacher might say to the children, "Always sit on the swings," or

"We let the person in front of us go all the way down the slide before we climb up for our turn." Teachers should always be on the alert for danger signals, such as show-offs who take dangerous chances, or one child's daring another to climb too high. When children are acting inappropriately, they should be taken aside and spoken to individually rather than shouted at from across the room or playground. Teachers also can look for opportunities to recognize and positively reinforce a child's abilities or suggest new and interesting ways to use materials and equipment. By offering encouragement and making suggestions, teachers help children learn to use play equipment more safely.

Equipment Maintenance

Maintaining furniture and equipment is an important safety practice. The preschool staff should regularly check and tighten screws and bolts on furniture and play equipment. Any equipment that has become rusty or corroded or has developed splinters or sharp edges needs to be replaced or sanded and painted. Missing, broken, or warped parts should be replaced immediately, and loose rungs, handrails, and ladders should be tightened or replaced. Periodic inspections of tricycles, scooters, and wagons may reveal loose bolts or moving parts that need tightening or lubricating. Sand or wood chips under play equipment tend to become hard and compacted over time and need to be raked or replaced. Swings, jungle gyms, and other equipment should be inspected often for jagged edges, jutting bolts, protruding nails, loose stitching on strap-type swing seats, rusted chains, and loose or broken bars. Children can help with maintenance chores by reporting broken equipment and picking up trash and debris.

Applications

The physical environment of the preschool is important because preschoolers learn so much about themselves and the world through their interaction with the objects and people in their environment. The equipment, furniture, and materials used for each activity—music, art, storytelling, dress-up, playing on the jungle gym—create opportunities for growth and development. For example, building with blocks provides the opportunity for children to practice several premathematics skills and concepts; thinking skills, such as carrying out a plan and problem solving; motor skills (eye-hand coordination, balancing blocks); language skills (construction terms, such as bridge, tower, ramp, and the names of shapes); and social skills (communicating with others, planning and working together, and sharing blocks). When children play with blocks, they are learning information about themselves as well. As they figure out a way to reinforce a wall or to make a uniquely shaped garage, they feel competent and creative, and this feeling in turn builds their confidence to try new approaches in other areas, too. All these attributes contribute to the development of a positive self-concept.

Private time is important, too. Finding a cozy space creates an opportunity for this four-year-old to enjoy a tape recording of his favorite book.

Creating Opportunities for Growth

The physical environment of each activity area should be designed and equipped to encourage opportunities for growth, development, and learning. Adding variety to the different activity areas also helps create opportunities for growth. For example, in the block area, you might tape up photos of different kinds of constructions, such as towers, buildings, and bridges, to encourage building ideas. Adding toy cars and trucks, small plastic animals or human figures, dolls, doll furniture, dishes, utensils, and writing props turns the area into a combination block/dramatic play/language space.

Pay attention to the needs of individual children as well when you are designing or redesigning the block area or other activity area. Some children may want a well-marked floor space in which to work alone. Or they may want individual work space on the table where they can keep their materials separate from those of other children but still be near others while they play. Some children may be bothered by the noise level in nearby activity areas or may be distracted by activities going on around them. Use portable dividers and small tables to create individual play spaces and to address individual learning styles, so as to improve each child's preschool experience.

Since teachers and children typically spend between 4 and 10 hours a day in a preschool setting, the environment also should be attractive and comfortable. One way to make the environment more appealing to children is to include a variety of differently sized spaces, such as small cozy spaces for private time and larger spaces for group activities. Just as adults need time and space to themselves, children need opportunities to withdraw from contact with others from time to time during the day. Studies have shown that many children like child-size, enclosed refuges with canopies or ceilings where they can hide away but still look out and see others. Turn a large packing crate on its side and furnish it with pillows, place a cushiony chair or sofa in a secluded corner, or install a hammock in a shady spot in the play yard to create inviting retreats for a child in search of peace and quiet.

Taking a Fresh Look

Although you are likely to work in a physical environment that is already designed and arranged, you can still take a fresh look and make small changes that can add a new twist to familiar activities, encourage creativity, or make better use of a space. For instance, as Ricky and Bonnie's teachers found, setting up a typical indoor activity such as dramatic play outdoors can inspire the use of play materials in new ways. Keep in mind that children can get bored with materials and equipment that have become too familiar. Add props to the dramatic play area to make it into a supermarket or a travel agency. Add new materials to the art, music, and manipulative areas, and put away old and tired materials for a few months. Changing the arrangement and aesthetics of the room also stimulates new interest in it. You might make an activity area with objects and materials all of the same color, or experiment with temporary dividers to rearrange the space.

Checklist for Evaluating the Physical Environment
✔ Are activity areas or learning centers well-defined?
✔ Are incompatible activities separated: messy-clean, noisy-quiet, active-passive?
✔ Are there too many large, open spaces?
✔ Are traffic patterns planned carefully? Do the activities in one area interfere with those in nearby areas?
✔ Are materials stored near the space where they are used? In a developmental preschool, are they stored on low, open shelving with visual cues for placement?
✔ Do adults and children appear to be physically comfortable in each of the play areas?
✔ Are there private spaces where children can retreat when they want a break from contact with others?
✔ Does the environment encourage children to make choices among a variety of activities?

FIGURE 5.3   Checklist for Evaluating the Physical Environment.

One way for teachers to take a fresh look at the physical environment is to make a checklist itemizing the elements discussed in this chapter—aesthetics, traffic patterns, noise levels—and analyze each of those elements. See Figure 5.3 for a suggested checklist. Some experts suggest that child care providers "tour" the facilities on their knees so that they can examine the room from the perspective of small children (Miller, 1984).

Teachers also can evaluate the preschool environment with *global quality-assessment instruments*. These instruments are sets of standards formulated to help preschool directors evaluate their programs, curricula, and facilities. The Early Childhood Classroom Observation, used in NAEYC accreditation, and the Early Childhood Environment Rating Scale (ECERS) (Harms & Clifford, 1980) are two assessment instruments that include a section on the physical environment. Physical settings that rate highly on these evaluations contribute to the overall high-quality care and early educational opportunities for young children.

The Early Childhood Classroom Observation rates the following elements of the preschool environment:

- Interaction among staff and children
- Curriculum
- Physical environment
- Health and safety
- Nutrition

The Early Childhood Environment Rating Scale assesses:

- Personal care routines
- Furnishings and displays for children
- Language-reasoning experiences
- Fine and gross motor activities
- Creative activities
- Social development
- Adult needs

Observe the Environment.   Begin by looking at how children use the equipment and materials, activity areas, and playground. Look for and make a note of equipment or materials that the children argue over, or that are rarely used. Pay particular attention to the kinds of play experiences children are having, such as group play, one-on-one play, and solitary play. Ask yourself if you see a good mix of these kinds of play experiences.

Rearrange the Physical Space.   Draw a floor plan to help you picture how a rearrangement might affect the traffic patterns, noise level, and aesthetics in the room, as well as skill-building opportunities. At some preschools, the teachers rearrange their classrooms at the end of each year in an effort to correct any problems encountered during that year and to give the room a fresh look and feel for the coming year.

Encourage Ideas from Children.   Children have many feelings and thoughts about their own environment and can contribute helpful ideas. Ask children what they like and dislike about each activity area and what would they do to change it. They may tell you that a learning center is too noisy or that they do not like the materials. Let children know that you value their ideas. Try dedicating one group time a month to talking about some area of the classroom or playground. Children are the ones who will benefit in countless ways from a well-designed environment.

CHAPTER 5   **REVIEW**

SUMMARY

- The physical environment of a preschool affects children's behavior, development, and play.
- Creating a stimulating environment requires careful planning of many elements, including meeting the needs of children with disabilities.

- When planning the indoor space, teachers should consider furniture, traffic patterns, noise levels, and aesthetics.
- Activity areas include a block area, a reading area or language learning center, a dramatic play area, an art and manipulative area, a music or group time area, and areas for personal belongings, eating, and napping.
- Playground equipment helps develop large and fine motor skills, promotes social interaction, and encourages dramatic play.
- The indoor and outdoor environments need to be designed for maximum safety.
- Children need to be carefully supervised to ensure safety.
- Well-maintained equipment promotes safety. Equipment should be checked frequently and broken and loose parts replaced or repaired.
- The physical environment should be designed to provide as many opportunities for growth, development, and learning as possible.
- Teachers should take a fresh look at the physical environment periodically to determine whether rearranging the space and adding or deleting equipment and materials can enhance play and learning.

ACQUIRING KNOWLEDGE

1. What are the basic elements of the physical environment of a preschool?
2. What types of materials encourage solitary play? Cooperative play?
3. Give two examples of design elements that allow a preschool to accommodate the special needs of children who are disabled.
4. How does a crowded preschool setting affect children's social behavior? What is the recommended minimum space per child indoors?
5. What factors should be considered to determine whether or not furniture is suitable for preschool use?
6. How should the traffic patterns in a preschool classroom affect the placement of furniture and the design of activity areas?
7. What factors help control the noise levels in a preschool?
8. What elements can help increase a preschool's "softness factor"?
9. How can the walls of a classroom be used to improve the aesthetic effect of the room?
10. How does a learning center in an academically oriented preschool differ from an activity area in a developmentally oriented preschool?
11. What materials are usually found in the block area?
12. What activities commonly take place in the language arts/storytelling area? In the group time/music area?
13. What types of props and materials might be found in a dramatic play area?
14. Describe how materials in the art area in a teacher-directed preschool are stored and used differently than in a child-initiated preschool.
15. How are personal storage spaces used to keep track of children's belongings?
16. What physical and emotional needs are met through outdoor play?

17. What type of playground activities develop fine motor skills?
18. Describe the three main types of playgrounds.
19. Describe three classifications for playground units.
20. Describe several measures preschool teachers can take to ensure children's safety indoors.
21. What is the most common type of playground injury? What can be done to prevent this type of injury?
22. What safety factors should preschool teachers check in their daily playground inspection?
23. Should children be lifted onto outdoor equipment that they cannot reach by themselves? Explain your answer.
24. How can a teacher keep children interested in a particular activity area?
25. What are some factors to observe when evaluating the physical environment of a preschool setting?
26. Why should child care professionals encourage children's ideas about the design of the classroom or playground?

THINKING CRITICALLY

1. In a child-initiated curriculum, children select their own activities. How can the physical environment of a preschool classroom encourage children to select a wide variety of activities, rather than return again and again to their favorite area?
2. Few preschools and child care centers use walls to separate activity areas because the areas would feel cramped and teachers would not be able to scan the classroom easily. How can caregivers use simple elements to define each area as a separate place?
3. Many playgrounds combine more than one type of ground covering—for example, a sandy area, asphalt areas, and a grassy area. How might ground coverings be used to help control traffic patterns and to define play spaces in the playground?
4. Children's safety is a primary focus for any caregiver. How would you work with a partner to supervise eight children in an outdoor play area?

OBSERVATIONS AND APPLICATIONS

1. Observe a group of preschoolers in a preschool playground. Is the playground space subdivided into different types of play areas? If so, describe them. List and describe the playground equipment (for example, the number and type of swings, slides, jungle gyms, and movable equipment). Does the playground seem to have enough equipment for the number of children in the group? Are children waiting to use equipment? Which areas and what types of equipment or toys seem most popular? How many children are playing in pairs or small groups? What types of games are these groups playing, or what types of equipment are they using? How many children are playing alone? What equipment, if any, are these children using alone?

2. Observe a group of three- or four-year-olds in a preschool who are engaged in an art activity. Are all children working on the same type of project, or do they have a variety of options from which they can choose? Where are the art materials stored—on low shelves within easy reach of the children, or high above their heads to prevent access? Do the children readily take materials from the shelves on their own, or does the teacher distribute them? Make note of the different types of materials available for the children's use. Describe the area, paying special attention to aesthetics. Is the sink positioned so that preschoolers can reach it easily when cleaning up without adult assistance? Do the children need to walk to another part of the classroom to reach the sink?

3. In one developmentally oriented preschool, the children cannot stop talking about dinosaurs. To build on their interest, the teacher decides to incorporate dinosaurs in both classroom and outdoor activities. Consider the five types of activity areas described in this chapter. What types of activities related to dinosaurs might the teacher include in each of these areas? What activities could he or she plan for outdoors or on the playground? What props or special materials might the teacher need for the activities?

4. A teacher at the Happy Days Preschool notices that the children are getting bored with an activity area focused on shapes. On a low table, the teacher had set up trays with a variety of brightly colored plastic and wood shapes, photographs of buildings with interesting shapes, shape puzzles, and a shape game. How might the teacher create new interest in this activity area? Should he or she ask the children for their ideas?

FOR FURTHER INFORMATION

Books and Journal Articles

Bredekamp, S. (Ed.) (1984). *Accreditation criteria and procedures of the National Academy of Early Childhood Programs.* Washington, DC: National Association for the Education of Young Children.

Brewer, J. A. (1992). *Creating an environment for learning: Introduction to early childhood education: Preschool through primary grades.* Boston: Allyn & Bacon.

Catron, C. E., & Allen, J. (1993). *Classroom design and organization: Early childhood curriculum.* New York: Macmillan.

Dodge, D. T. (1988). The physical environment. In D. T. Dodge, *A guide for supervisors and trainers on implementing the creative curriculum for early childhood* (pp. 89–96). Washington, DC: Teaching Strategies.

Greenman, J. (1988). *Caring spaces, learning spaces: Children's environments that work.* Redmond, WA: Exchange Press.

Videotapes

Dodge, D. T. (1991). The new room arrangement as a teaching strategy. Washington, D C: Teaching Strategies.

Implementing Curriculum: Objectives and Plans

OBJECTIVES

Studying this chapter
will enable you to

- Explain why daily and long-range
  planning is important and describe
  the process of preparing plans
- Compare and contrast four types
  of objectives: academic,
  behavioral, developmental, and
  individual
- Identify factors that influence daily
  plans
- Explain how parents can influence
  the curriculum and participate in
  classroom activities
- Discuss the process and
  importance of evaluating plans
  and activities
- Compare and contrast half-day
  and full-day preschool programs

CHAPTER TERMS

academic objectives
behavioral objectives
daily plan
developmental objectives
goals
individual objectives
long-term plan
objectives
rapport
sequencing
teachable moments
themes
transitions

LOOK, Richard, the sun's shining!"
exclaimed four-year-old Avery, as he
raced to the window with the other
children.

Richard Harper, a teacher at the Child's
World Preschool, smiled. It had been
raining for four straight days. He looked at
the afternoon's schedule—first music, then
naptime, and then outdoor play. "Let's all
sit in the music time circle," he said, as he
handed out tambourines.

The children drifted away from the
window to their positions on the floor.

"We all know 'Row, Row, Row Your
Boat,' but today we're going to sing it as a
round," Richard said. "Does anyone know
what a round is?" Nobody responded.

"We'll split into two groups," Richard
explained. "After the first group sings one
line, the second group starts in. Watch my
hands, and I'll help get everyone started at
the right time."

Avery stared out the window. "Let's try
it," Richard prompted.

As the first group started singing, Avery
asked, "Can I get a drink of water?"

The second group started, but soon
both groups were singing in unison.

"Let's try again," Richard urged. By now, several children were fidgeting, and two children were poking each other.

Richard thought that the children might be tired and ready for their nap, so he concluded the music time quickly. "Let's line up to use the bathroom. Then we'll get ready for naps. Before you know it, it will be time to go outside."

As Richard found, following a predetermined schedule may not always be possible. Had he thought about the children's actions from a different perspective, Richard might have realized that their need to play outdoors after so many days of rain was more compelling than their desire to sing or to take a nap.

This chapter explores the role of the daily plan as a guide to what takes place in the classroom. It discusses the features of a daily plan, the setting of objectives, and the importance of flexibility in planning and attending to the needs of individual children and the group. The chapter explores how parents can become involved in the curriculum and classroom activities. It also examines the need to evaluate activities to improve future planning and implementation. A teacher's plan for daily instruction has a direct impact on the quality of the child's preschool experience.

Preparing a Daily Plan: Getting Started

Even though curriculum approaches vary from preschool to preschool, careful planning always is needed. Planning ensures that a classroom runs smoothly and that the children are learning (Lay-Dopyera & Dopyera, 1992). Planning helps the teacher chart a course for the children to encourage them to develop new skills and participate in new experiences. Effective planning and basic routines also provide the structure, repetition, and predictability necessary to help children feel secure and enjoy their preschool experience (Crosser, 1992).

To prepare plans and use them effectively, preschool teachers and child care providers need to understand and think about how young children grow and develop. Plans reflect teachers' knowledge of the areas of growth to be accomplished by the children throughout the course of the year. To facilitate this process, teachers must design activities that help children develop new skills and provide them with enjoyable early educational experiences.

Teachers typically prepare daily plans as well as weekly or monthly plans. Even teachers who follow a child-initiated approach need to prepare activities and materials in order to offer multiple opportunities for learning. A *daily plan* organizes and provides a structure for each day from the moment children arrive at the preschool or child care center to the moment they leave. The day typically is divided into small blocks of time. The teacher identifies what activities the children will engage in or choose from and why they will be carrying out the activities (see the next section on setting objectives). In the plan, the teacher should include the steps or materials necessary to carry out each activity.

A *long-term plan* maps out activities for a longer period of time, such as a week or a month, and it may center on a theme or particular skills. A teacher may choose a theme with the children, such as water, and construct various activities related to that theme over several days or weeks. Or he or she may wish to work for a period of time on a particular skill with one child or a group of children, such as walking along a low balance beam. Themes and topics are covered in more detail later in the chapter.

Setting Objectives

Goals, sometimes referred to as broad objectives, provide the framework for the preschool's curriculum approach. Goals typically identify the physical, intellectual, social, and emotional skills and behaviors the preschool teachers believe children should develop within a certain broad time period, such as six months or a year. For example, a goal might be for children to master self-care skills. Within these goals, setting specific objectives along the way helps preschool teachers decide which skills and behaviors are most important in early childhood (Robison & Schwartz, 1982).

Objectives are specific ways or steps to move toward goals. Objectives typically refer to skills, behaviors, or abilities that the teacher wants a group of children or individual children to master or learn. Objectives may be open-ended or specific. For example, an open-ended objective related to the goal "Children will master self-care skills" might be "Children will learn about hygiene." A specific objective might be "Children will learn when and how to wash their hands properly."

Objectives can take many forms. "Learning to share" can be categorized as a behavioral objective for a group or as an individual objective for a particular child.

The idea of setting written objectives at the preschool level has been criticized by many early childhood educators. Some believe that written objectives can stifle teacher and child creativity, flexibility, and a curriculum that responds to children's interests (Eisner, 1985).

Despite these criticisms, many educators agree that objectives help teachers decide what and how to teach. Of equal importance, objectives help teachers track children's growth and development. See the discussion in Chapter 15 of ongoing informal assessment of young children, which also plays an important role in tracking growth. By including objectives in daily or monthly plans, the teacher indicates that the skill or ability that the objective reflects is important to the development of the children at that time.

Types of Objectives.   Objectives fall into four categories or types: academic, behavioral, developmental, and individual. *Academic objectives* focus on mastering skills, such as recognizing letters or remembering words in a sequence, which will help children learn academic subjects in grade school.

Behavioral objectives are considered by most early childhood educators to refer to behavior that can be observed (Bloom, 1956). For example, "recognizing letters" stated as a behavioral objective might read, "Says letter names of capital letters out loud" and "Matches one letter to an identical letter." The behaviorist philosophy states that one cannot "see" learning occur in the mind, so learning must be exhibited through an observable, specific behavior. (Objectives also can fall into more than one category. For example, some teachers consider separating rods into groups of two an academic objective, but it also could be a behavioral objective.)

Developmental objectives relate to the various areas of development—physical, emotional, social, cognitive, or creative. The teacher considers the child's present level of development and builds an objective to help the child reach the next level. For example, if a child has mastered recognition of circles, squares, and triangles, he is now ready to learn rectangles and diamonds. Developmental objectives might focus on improving eye-hand coordination, or increasing attention span, or naming facial features after having learned the main body parts. See Chapter 2 and Appendix A for more detail on stages of development.

Individual objectives are set for individual children in the class. These objectives may be academic, behavioral, or developmental. They are designed by the teacher to foster growth in emotional and social areas as well as in academic areas. For example, an individual objective might be written to help a child overcome or handle a specific problem behavior, such as knocking down other children's block structures or not being able to feel secure with adults. For an especially shy child, the teacher might set an objective such as "Karen will interact with one or two other children at least twice a day." (Note that this objective also could be considered a behavioral objective.) Then the teacher will capitalize on situations that require cooperative efforts, such as asking Karen to help another child set out spoons and napkins at the table for snack time.

Stating Objectives.   Some early childhood educators, such as behaviorists, believe that objectives should be stated very specifically. They believe that teachers should identify the behavior, skill, or ability the children are expected to exhibit, the conditions under which it will be exhibited, and a way to measure the objective's success. All objectives need not be stated in this complex format. However, they should provide enough information for the teacher to identify what he or she expects the children to do, and they should specify a way to evaluate children's progress. For example, if a teacher wishes to increase a child's attention span, the objective might state that the child will finish a puzzle two out of three times instead of abandoning it in the middle, or work on a painting for five or more minutes.

Objectives should be written in simple sentences using action-oriented language. The terms that are used also are important. Objectives using words such as "tell," "demonstrate," and "build" explain what behaviors, skills, or abilities the children are expected to exhibit or achieve. An example is "The children will demonstrate the difference between high and low." In contrast, using "thinking" words—such as "understand," "know," or "be aware"—does not work in objectives because the objectives cannot be evaluated or tested. "The children will understand the difference between high and low" is an example of an objective that cannot easily be evaluated.

Objectives should reflect expectations that realistically can be met. The words "always" and "never" reflect standards of perfection that are impossible to attain. Although classroom harmony would improve if preschoolers always shared toys, a child care provider cannot realistically expect children to share all the time. Having realistic expectations helps reduce frustration and increases feelings of competence and self-esteem in both children and teachers.

Also, objectives should not contradict one another. An objective that states that children will improve verbal communication skills contradicts an objective that states that children will not interrupt with questions and will talk less during story reading.

Choosing Themes

A *theme* provides a focus for planning interrelated learning activities. Themes, also called topics or units, should be based on subject matter that interests the children. Activities based on the theme should provide information and experiences related to what the children already know or have experienced in their daily lives, and then extend that knowledge. Generally speaking, the younger the children, the more important it is to include information relevant to their daily lives.

One way to find out about children's interests is to listen to their conversations. Children talk about what interests them. The toys, books, and other personal items children bring to school provide ideas for topics. Most children are eager to see what other children bring from home, whether it be a bird's nest, seashells, a new doll or toy, or pictures of a new litter of puppies.

Choosing a theme is an important first step in developing a curriculum plan. This teacher knows that her group of three-year-olds is interested in animals. Today, she is showing them how to hold a guinea pig.

In addition, children's artwork provides insight into their interests. Even if children do not draw or paint representational pictures, the teacher may pick up on favorite colors, shapes, or textures and turn that information into a topic, such as things that are blue or objects that are round. Topic ideas also may come from observing children's play. If they have been pretending to be alligators, for instance, the teacher could develop a unit on alligators.

Common Themes.   A number of themes are universally appealing to preschool children. Preschoolers are fascinated by their own family lives and the family lives of others, and why some families celebrate different holidays or speak different languages. They also are curious about their bodies, and about foods people eat.

Most children love animals, especially pets. They want to know about caring for and feeding pets, about differences among pets, and about classmates' pets. They also are curious about plant names, how to care for plants, why some plants have flowers, and why some plants are food. In addition, children are interested in their immediate surroundings. They want to know more about people in the community, people's names, what people do, and where people live. Preschoolers are interested in why the weather can be so different each day, and in modes of transportation, such as cars, trains, airplanes, and ships. See Appendix B for more ideas about themes.

Screening Themes.   Although children are curious about many things, not all themes are appropriate or realistic. The following questions can help teachers decide whether to pursue a topic in the preschool setting.

- Is the theme appropriate for the developmental level of the children? For example, a discussion of comets and meteors is far past a four-year-old group's ability to understand. This group would be more interested in a unit on the sun's effects, such as light and shadows. Teachers should save themes that are outside a child's immediate world for six-year-olds because children in that age group are able to grasp concepts from symbols and do not require hands-on experiences to understand concepts.
- Is the theme adaptable to several age groups in multi-age classrooms? Some topics—for example, the details of a serious automobile accident—are not appropriate for all age groups, even if the children are interested. Car safety, however, would be an appropriate theme.
- Do the children have the appropriate background to relate to or understand the theme? For example, if the teacher plans to discuss whales, the children should have an understanding of lungs and breathing.
- Are materials readily available? The teacher must have or be able to locate a variety of appropriate materials related to the theme.
- Is the theme too broad? For example, "animals" is too broad a theme. Narrowing the theme to "circus animals" creates a manageable focus.
- Does the theme allow for hands-on activities? The children should be able to explore and experience the theme with materials they can touch and

FOCUS ON Cultural Diversity

Screening a Lesson Plan or Theme for Cultural Bias

Often, a dominant culture remains the focus in the preschool curriculum, causing plans and themes to be biased. Children from minority cultures may feel inadequate or unimportant in a classroom with such a curriculum. By taking a few minutes to evaluate your lesson plans, you can reduce cultural bias in your curriculum. Ask yourself the following questions as you review plans.

What cultures are represented? Whenever possible, try to represent the cultures of the children in the class. For example, for a food unit on breakfast, plan to include breakfast foods of various groups, such as Japanese and Indian foods, as well as traditional American fare. If you are planning a unit on holidays, include information about lesser-known holidays from a variety of cultures. For a unit on jobs in the community, discuss jobs that you know generate different levels of income, and include role models from both genders and from several races and cultures.

Are there stereotypical images in any of the materials that you plan to use? Be careful that your materials do not reinforce misconceptions about ethnic or racial groups or characterize them by one or two generalities. It is important to avoid a "tourist curriculum"— that is, one that misrepresents a culture by focusing on superficial aspects of it.

Are your plans and materials inclusive of diverse cultures? Art materials in a project entitled "The People in Our Class" should include paints, paper, and crayons in a variety of skin-tone shades (ivories, peaches, olives, browns, and blacks). For a unit on "The Clothes We Wear," talk about and display a variety of examples of dress from different cultures. Try to find parent volunteers or people in the community from different cultures who will participate.

How will you present the activity? Consider reading a story or teaching the children a simple song in Spanish or French as well as in English, for example, when possible. Try using a variety of ethnic music, such as Asian and Mexican music, to accompany a creative-movement activity.

manipulate. For example, children can explore the way the sun dries and hardens objects by making clay shapes and leaving them outside in the afternoon sun.

- Does the theme have a multicultural element? Whenever possible, the teacher should include examples of how other cultures relate to the theme. For example, learning about bread can include sampling and talking about bread products from different cultures, such as pita, Irish soda bread, tortillas, and matzos. See the "Focus on Cultural Diversity" feature above for a discussion of screening lesson plans for cultural bias.

Translating Themes into Activities.   As stated earlier in the chapter, many classroom activities begin as an interest expressed by a child or as an outgrowth of play. To capitalize on children's interests, teachers should be well-prepared to follow up with curriculum activities and related topics that are appealing to preschoolers (Pitcher, Feinburg, & Alexander, 1989). In the scenario at the beginning of the chapter, while it rained for so many days, Richard might have discussed with the children why they could not see the sun. He might have helped the children create "rain" over the water table by making "clouds" using water-filled balloons with pinpricks. Also, if a group of children spent several mornings building an elaborate house with blocks, the teacher might develop a unit entitled "Places Where We Live."

How does a theme get translated into activities? To develop the unit "Places Where We Live," the teacher might provide magazines that show different kinds of houses and apartments. The teacher might read stories about homes in different parts of the country or the world, or take the children on a walk around the school neighborhood to look at different houses, if feasible. The children could build models of their own homes and explore what homes have in common (roof, rooms), and how and why they are different (size, shape, height, location and climate, available building materials, the number of people that live in them). A parent or a community member who is involved in some aspect of construction might bring in samples of construction materials. He or she would explain how the materials are used to build houses or apartment buildings and would let the children handle the materials. He or she might help the children with a simple woodworking or construction project. Children might build houses in the block area, or build a variety of structures over time. The teacher might plan a field trip to a house construction site. See Chapter 2 for a discussion of using themes, or concepts, to develop curriculum webs.

By combining these activities, the teacher capitalizes on the children's interest and provides opportunities to develop several skills: literacy (books about homes), verbal (discussions about where people live), cognitive (comparing house features from pictures), fine motor and creative (drawing houses), and large motor (handling building materials). See Table 6.1 for an example of how to translate a theme into activities.

Sequencing

The ways in which teachers present new information and activities in the daily plan should reflect the children's prior experience, knowledge, and developmental level, as well as the teacher's or preschool's own approach to curriculum. In addition, teachers need to consider *sequencing*, the order in which activities and lessons will be presented over time. Effective sequencing helps children grasp new concepts readily and also absorb information. A teacher who believes that learning is memorizing facts will arrange activities in a different order from one who sees learning as acquiring key concepts (Robison & Schwartz, 1982). Teachers should make a conscious effort to consider sequencing strategies as they prepare their plans.

There are several ways to sequence activities that reflect how children learn. One approach is to help children use information they already know or experiences they already have had to learn something new. When children

TABLE 6.1
A Theme in Action: Babies

	Day 1	Day 2	Day 3
Pretend Play	Nursery: Boy and girl dolls, cribs, high chairs, playpen, stroller	Baby Role Play: Child-size high chairs, cribs, toddler bed, blankets, dishes, playpen, stroller	Baby Food Kitchen: Play stove, sink, refrigerator, dishes, table, chairs, high chair, baby dolls, mortar and pestles, play food, toy blender, potato masher, play dough
Language	Film—"All About Babies"	Experience story, "When You Were a Baby"	Books/Flannel board— "Peter's Chair," "No One Asked Me If I Wanted a Baby Sister"
Math/Cognitive	Sorting baby, children's, and adult clothing	Matching numbers with candles on a cake, 1–10 number recognition	Seriation—Baby to older child, boys/girls, members of a family
Fine Motor	Stringing beads	Dressing babies, snapping, zipping, and buttoning	Peeling carrots and celery for snack
Art/Music/ Aesthetic	Finger painting to music	Finger painting to music	Looking at different artists' paintings of babies
Perception/ Science	Feeling hard and soft baby items	Comparing baby foods to original foods	Pouring ice into containers with different-sized openings
Social	Candyland	Group collage—babies and their families	Group decisions— comparing baby foods to original foods
Gross Motor	Hot potato to music	Exercises—walking, crawling, creeping, scooting, slithering (focus on trunk, arms, and leg support)	Exercises—walking, crawling, creeping, scooting, slithering (focus on trunk, arms, and leg support)
Construction	Woodworking bench (two hammers, one saw)	Large hollow blocks	Small wooden blocks with family figures

Source: Marjorie Kostelnik, Professor and Acting Chairperson, Department of Family and Child Ecology, Michigan State University.

feel themselves pushed by a strong gust of wind, they can better understand how the wind is used to move a sailboat or to turn a windmill. Similarly, a teacher who has already taught a child about shapes can teach her to recognize the letter *C* by telling her that *C* is like a broken circle.

Another form of sequencing is to move from the concrete to the abstract. A concrete experience uses hands-on materials that children can see or touch, taste or smell. By holding a rock and a cotton ball in their hands, children can feel and experience the difference between hardness and softness. Later, the children will understand the more abstract concept of "soft" when the word is used in conversation without having a soft item present. Children also will be able to talk about or think of other "soft" objects without having the objects there.

Sequencing also can progress from the simple to the complex. For example, children can first handle one variable (balance) by walking along a low wide board before they can handle two variables (balance and side-to-side movement) when stepping along a zigzag line of tires. The complexity increases as more variables are included.

A fourth manner of sequencing is to begin with facts and move to concepts. That bicycles travel on wheels is a fact. As children learn about and have experiences with other forms of transportation, they notice that many forms of transportation have wheels (even airplanes use wheels when they take off). As they acquire additional facts and have new experiences, children develop a concept of transportation. In this case, they might conclude that wheels, in some form, often are used in transportation that allows people to travel from one place to the next, except on water.

Sequencing, as stated earlier, reflects the progressions children move through as they learn. For example, children first explore a new material to identify familiar features, then experiment and test hypotheses to learn more about its unfamiliar features, and finally use the newly acquired information for problem solving (Robison & Schwartz, 1982).

What happens if the teacher uses one of these sequencing strategies and finds the children still having trouble or losing attention or becoming frustrated? The teacher may try to determine whether the children were simply not interested in the topic, whether they lacked the appropriate background knowledge, or whether they were not developmentally ready for the activity. The teacher might provide more background information, redesign the activity or lesson, or wait until later in the year when the children may be at a more advanced developmental level and therefore better equipped cognitively to understand the concepts and ideas under discussion (Robison & Schwartz, 1982).

Teachers need to sequence instruction carefully to help children grow, develop, and learn, regardless of curriculum approach or content. Failure to sequence the topic carefully can hamper the learning process.

Factors That Influence the Daily Plan

A variety of factors can affect the daily plan when it is put into action. Some factors, such as choice of theme, can be controlled by the teacher. Others, such as a child's sleeping poorly the night before or the weather, are beyond the teacher's control. But every teacher should "expect the unexpected." Careful planning helps teachers compensate for many of the factors beyond their control. This section looks at several of the factors that influence daily plans: balance, transition activities, timing, flexibility, individual needs, and

Alternating vigorous activities with quiet activities helps teachers achieve balance in the curriculum and gives children a chance to recharge.

weather. By balancing activities, providing plenty of variety, planning transitions from one activity to the next, and, above all, remaining flexible, teachers create the structure that allows each day to progress more smoothly.

The Importance of Balance

Preschool children need a balance of activities during the day that will provide variety and accommodate the ebb and flow of their energy levels. Children need quiet, indoor activities to offset noisier, physical activities (Bredekamp, 1987). Not all children require the same amounts of physical activity, for example, and activities should be provided with these differences in mind. Indoor activities requiring concentration should be balanced by more free-flowing outdoor activities. Large-muscle activities should be balanced with small-muscle activities. Routine activities, such as meals, snacks, naps, and toileting, should be scheduled at natural intervals throughout the day.

A balanced schedule also provides a combination of structured activities in which children participate as a group and activities the children may choose themselves. Children need to have the opportunity to make choices if they are to develop feelings of responsibility and control (Kelman, 1990).

FOCUS ON   Activities

Holding a Brainstorming Session with Fellow Teachers

When planning the curriculum, all teachers benefit from sharing and discussing one anothers' ideas. Working in a group often produces a collection of great ideas that any one teacher might not discover alone.

Among preschool teachers, brainstorming sessions typically focus on generating ideas for themes, activities, and materials (such as "Animals Who Live in the Ocean"). Brainstorming works well with a group of at least three, but no more than ten, people. Schedule the session when teachers will be alert and energetic. Meetings before school are ideal. Meetings during the children's nap time may be more practical. Find a private, quiet, comfortable room in which to hold the session. If possible, meet at the home of one of the teachers.

Let one person start the brainstorming by summarizing the theme. Then ask for suggestions for activities. Discuss some of your own ideas, and encourage others to present theirs. Ask thought-starter questions, such as "What materials might we use? . . . What does this theme make you think of? . . . What outdoor activities relate to this theme?" Generate ideas

for activities that apply the theme to all areas of the curriculum as well as different areas of development.

The most important rule to remember in a brainstorming session is that every idea is a good one. All ideas are accepted; none are criticized, no matter how unusual or impractical (you can weed out unworkable ideas later, if necessary). Designate one person to keep track of the ideas by listing them for all to see on a chart or a blackboard. This visual record also will help you see how activities relate to each other. You might try creating a curriculum web. Write the key theme or concept in a circle, and then draw branches out to related concepts or activities. For example, the brainstorming might start with "Ocean" in the circle, and teachers might link that concept to related concepts such as songs about ocean animals, colors of the ocean, and ocean animals that we eat.

After the brainstorming session, take time to evaluate the ideas, and choose those which will work for you. Remember to provide positive feedback to the colleagues who helped you.

The balance between structured and free-choice activities may be determined by the preschool's overall curriculum approach—for example, teacher-directed or child-initiated. See Chapter 2 for a discussion of these and other curriculum approaches. Children also will learn the rules that apply to different parts of the day. Adults follow different rules at a football game and at a theater performance. Similarly, children learn that rules vary for free play and for story time.

Balance also refers to content. Children benefit from activities that combine the familiar and the unknown, and from access to a variety of experiences and materials. A unit on transportation might include activities about cars and buses, but it also might include a story about snowshoes or riding horses or building futuristic "cars" with unusual art materials. Walking is a form of transportation, too, and activities might include having the children walk backward or like different animals, or seeing how fast they can walk without running.

In terms of materials for activities, the younger the child, the more comfortable the child will be if materials are familiar. A teacher of two-year-olds may find it important to make play dough available every day, for example, whereas a teacher of four-year-olds will notice that the children want a change every day.

Transition Activities

Preschool children need time to shift from one activity to another. These shifts or *transitions*—times in between activities—begin the moment children arrive at the preschool. They occur each time the children change activities, have a snack, eat lunch, take a nap, and go home. Every transition requires special attention (Baker, 1986).

Planning for transition ensures that the process of moving from one activity to another remains calm and casual. One way to alert children to a transition is to use a verbal warning. The warning can be in the form of a request to complete an activity in the next few minutes and a hint about the upcoming activity: "Please finish up with the blocks. We will be going outside in five minutes."

Poor transition planning can lead to disruptions or even chaos. Five to 15 minutes is an appropriate amount of time between activities. Children might clean up after the completed activity, use the bathroom, sing songs, or put coats on during these periods.

Not all children finish activities at the same time. For example, as children finish playing with clay, they individually might go to the sink and wash their hands and then join the teacher in a circle. When children do complete an activity at the same time—for example, singing songs in a group—the teacher can maintain control of the transition by directing small groups to move. The teacher might say that everybody wearing blue pants can go sit at the lunch table, then everybody wearing green pants, and so on.

Educators differ in their attitudes toward having young children wait in line during transition times. Supporters of "waiting in line" say that it leads to a more orderly transition. Those opposed to waiting in line see it either as a waste of children's time or as an opportunity that encourages inappropriate behavior. Restless children may accidentally bump others who, in turn, may shove and misbehave (Crosser, 1992). Some educators believe that expecting preschoolers to wait in line is premature, despite the fact that they can be taught to do it—just as teaching a 10-year-old to drive a car is premature even though he may be physically capable of driving.

Creative planning can eliminate many "waiting" situations in the preschool setting. Some successful techniques include having an adult already on the playground so that those children who dress more quickly can go out immediately; having enough materials for each child; or presetting materials on the table before the children begin the activity.

Timing

The pace the teacher sets for the day affects the children's behavior. A hurried, frantic pace will make children tense and more prone to misbehave. A relaxed and unhurried pace allows children the opportunity to become engrossed in and explore various aspects of an activity or provides time to practice a new skill. Good planning before the day begins leads to a calm atmosphere that encourages children to develop concentration skills and a sense of competence in being able to complete a task successfully.

The key to timing is to allow sufficient opportunity for children to complete an activity before beginning the transition to the next. The amount of time needed for various activities depends on, among other variables, the season of the year; the time of the day; the different ages of the children; individual children's needs, interests, and abilities; the dynamics of the group; the weather; and the teacher's preparation and motivation.

In general, two- and three-year-olds will require longer periods of time to complete tasks than will four- and five-year-olds. For example, a group of two-year-olds might require 10 to 15 minutes to put on coats, hats, and mittens whereas a group of four-year-olds might need only 5 minutes. See Table 6.2 for suggested time lengths for various activities.

The level of interest and excitement the teacher generates with each activity also will affect the children's motivation and how long they will want to

TABLE 6.2
Time Recommendations for Typical Preschool Activities

Activity	Two-year-olds	Four-year-olds
Group Time	5–10 minutes	15–20 minutes
Reading Stories	Best done individually or with a few children at a time until attention wanders	10–20 minutes
Snack	5–15 minutes	5–15 minutes
Outside Play	30–60 minutes	30–90 minutes
Free Play (depends on variety of materials and teacher involvement)	30–90 minutes	30–90 minutes
Cleanup	5–10 minutes	5–10 minutes
Putting On Coats	10–15 minutes	5–10 minutes
Handwashing	5–10 minutes	2 minutes
Premathematics or Reading Games	5–10 minutes	15–25 minutes

participate. Children's behavior and reactions provide the teacher with clues about their attention span. Children who are engrossed in an activity will have deeper concentration, participate in discussions, generally appear to be interested, and ask and respond to questions. With respect to question asking, preschool teachers should be aware that three-year-olds tend to stop their activity while they answer a teacher's question and then go back to it. Four-year-olds are better able to "talk and do" at the same time.

In contrast, as Richard found in the scenario at the beginning of the chapter, children who have reached their saturation point will squirm or fidget, stare into space, ask to get a drink of water or a snack, ask to use the bathroom, or ask inappropriate questions or respond inappropriately. When children exhibit such behaviors, the teacher is wise to move on to the next activity rather than attempt to prolong the current one.

Another aspect of timing the teacher might consider is the order in which activities are scheduled. Scheduling quiet activities just before nap time will help the children relax and rest more easily. Conversely, children who are eager to play outdoors will not want to sit quietly for story time. Thus, story time might better be scheduled following outdoor play to help the children make the transition back to the classroom setting.

Flexibility

Flexibility is an important feature of any lesson plan. Plans should remain flexible enough that teachers can accommodate the needs and interests of the children. If children become deeply involved in an activity and show no signs of losing interest, the teacher should feel free to extend the activity time. Likewise, if the children lose interest in an activity quickly, as did the children in Richard's class, or if an interruption breaks the flow of the activity, the teacher should be able to conclude the activity smoothly and move on to something else if necessary.

The daily plan needs to accommodate the unexpected—such as one or two children arriving at school late and needing breakfast, a guest arriving unexpectedly, or an activity taking longer than anticipated. If Richard had realized that the children were eager to go outside, he might have decided to hold music time outdoors, or to switch outdoor play and music time, or to save the music activity until the next day.

Also, teachers need to have a plan that can be used during emergencies or disruptions (Davidson, 1982). For example, if lunch is 10 minutes late, and the children are already seated at tables, the teacher could put on a puppet show of "The Three Little Pigs," or engage the children in finger plays or some other short activity. Teachers plan in advance for birthdays, holidays, or special programs, but an unexpected opportunity should not be ignored just because it is "not on the schedule." As is true with all classroom activities, the most effective activities for special times are age- and developmentally appropriate. These activities should also reflect the teacher's best judgment about the capabilities and interests of the children in the group.

FOCUS ON   Communicating with Children

Talking with a Child Who Won't Clean Up

Patti Rogers watched her class of four-year-olds as they put away the art materials. She saw that one child in the corner, Tyrone, was busily playing with his paints and seemed unaware that it was time to clean up for lunch. Patti had been teaching at the ABC Learning Center for five years and was used to encountering situations that disrupted the flow of the daily schedule.

MS. ROGERS: Tyrone, did you know that it's time to clean up?

TYRONE: Uh huh.

MS. ROGERS: Then, why you aren't you putting away your paints like the rest of the children?

TYRONE: Don't want to.

MS. ROGERS: I see. I'm glad that you're having fun with the paint, but it's time for lunch. That means that you will have to clean up now. You'll be able to finish your picture tomorrow.

TYRONE: I'm almost done.

MS. ROGERS: Tyrone, do you remember the class rule about listening to the teacher?

TYRONE: Uh huh. Always listen to the teacher.

MS. ROGERS: We need you to clean up the paint now, but we can hang your picture up on the painting clothesline, and you can finish it tomorrow, OK?

TYRONE: Go away.

MS. ROGERS: Tyrone, look over at the lunch table. Everyone's waiting to start lunch. It's time to clean up.

TYRONE: Well, OK, but I'm not going to do a good job.

Who do you think had control of the situation— Tyrone or Ms. Rogers? How might Ms. Rogers have been more flexible with her schedule? For example, should she have let Tyrone continue to paint during the transition time or even while the others ate lunch? Why or why not? What other types of situations can you think of that might disrupt a classroom routine?

Flexibility also means capitalizing on spontaneous opportunities for learning, sometimes called *teachable moments*. For example, if a child unexpectedly brings in a pet frog in a big box, group time might then be spent talking about frogs, where they live, what they eat, what they feel like, and noises they make, even if some other topic had been planned for that day.

Accommodating Individual Needs.   Planning should remain flexible enough to accommodate the needs of individual children, including those with disabilities. Children who are the same chronological age may vary greatly in their abilities, skills, and interests. They may require different amounts of rest, practice, and play and react differently to changes in their environments. For example, a restless child may need some private time in the block area while others are at the art table. Teachers must become shrewd observers of children to identify and, whenever possible, accommodate these differences within their classroom plans. See the "Focus on Communicating with Children" feature in this chapter.

When addressing individual needs, teachers also should look for ways to build on children's strengths or unique experiences. Experiences such as living in a multigenerational family that includes grandparents under the same roof, skills such as speaking another language, or strong interests such as space travel or dinosaurs are valuable resources for the teacher and the other children. Children who are classroom contributors enjoy a boost of self-esteem.

Bad Weather. A meticulously constructed weekly plan can be disrupted by a bout of stormy weather—but only if the teacher allows this disturbance to happen. Effective planning also means making a "rainy day" schedule to keep on hand. During bad weather, children lose their outdoor playtime. The unstructured nature of outdoor play helps children release stored up tensions and energy and develop large-motor skills. The "rainy day" plan needs to include indoor activities that provide the same goals. With sufficient indoor space and appropriate equipment and soft surfaces, children can engage in large-motor activities—such as climbing, jumping, playing catch, and running safely—in order to release some of their energy (Davidson, 1982). The teacher also can plan music and movement activities or group games as a supplement.

Another typical teaching strategy is to stretch out the previous activities so that they use up much of the time that is typically spent outdoors. For instance, if art, free play, and story time usually occur before one hour of outside play, the teacher can spend more time with art, free play, and story time, so that only 20 minutes is left for the usual outside-play time block. Then an indoor large-motor activity can be added to the schedule for that rainy day.

Parents and the Curriculum

Early childhood education begins at home with parents, guardians, or other primary caregivers. They are a child's first teachers. The preschool teacher introduces parents and their children to the formal school experience and should encourage parents to participate in their children's education. Many parents look to the preschool teacher for information not only about their children's progress but also about how children develop and learn. The teacher also can provide information about the school and explain how parents can become involved in curriculum activities.

Research provides support for the benefits of parental involvement. Preschools are more successful when parents are involved and participate in the program (Brenner, 1989). Involving parents or other outside caregivers in the preschool's activities helps build important relationships among family members, school staff, and the children. These relationships in turn also support parents in their roles as caregivers.

Parents have a strong effect on their children's attitudes and values. Understanding parents' beliefs and feelings can help teachers work more effectively with the children in their care.

The link between school, home, and the community has proven to be so important to children's preschool experience that some programs, such as Head Start, continue to require such involvement. Becoming involved helps parents gain a better understanding of what happens during the preschool day. Involvement refers not only to the parents' attendance at school functions but also to their acceptance of the preschool's educational philosophy. This type of support helps establish an important home-school continuum. At the same time, parental involvement enables the teacher to better understand the children's home environment. A sense of mutual respect develops between the teacher and the parents. Moreover, parental involvement in the preschool experience helps the children feel that preschool is important and may encourage their success (Stevens, Hough, & Nurss, 1993). In fact, one of the best predictors of children's success in the primary grades and later schooling is the degree to which parents are involved in early schooling.

Parental Attitudes and Values

The attitudes and values of parents affect children's emotional, social, and cognitive development. Children's development, in turn, affects how children respond to the preschool experience and to teachers (Stevens et al., 1993). One challenge for preschool teachers is dealing with parents whose attitudes and values differ from their own. For example, preschool teachers are likely to encounter parents with many types of parenting styles. Parents may include ones who are nurturing, responsive, and firm, ones who are harsh and unresponsive, and ones who fail to set limits. Culture and families define what is or is not "appropriate," so teachers need to be sensitive to these differences. They also need to help parents and children understand what is considered "appropriate" in the preschool setting.

Also, parents' attitudes toward school can affect their relationship with the teacher and the school. For the most part, parents want their children to be happy in school. Typically, parents work just as hard as teachers to communicate well and to be supportive of and interested in the activities of the school.

Sometimes, however, parents can be "difficult" or critical for a number of reasons. Some may think that they are being ignored or that their opinions do not count. Gloria Boutte and her associates suggest some positive ways of dealing with parent dissatisfaction (Boutte, Keepler, Tyler, & Terry, 1992). The teacher should invite the parents to meet at school. The teacher should begin by stating the purpose of the meeting and then allow the parents to talk without interruption. By paraphrasing their comments, the teacher will acknowledge without apology or agreement what the parents are saying. See the section entitled "Communicating with Parents" later in this chapter.

If the parents have been unable to identify the reason for their criticism or displeasure, the teacher should prompt them by asking specific questions. If parents offer suggestions, the teacher should try to include their suggestions wherever feasible, modifying their ideas if necessary. Parents will be less likely to complain if the teacher tries to incorporate their ideas. The teacher also can describe how the school and the teacher have resolved similar problems successfully in the past.

Again, ongoing communication can do much to prevent parental discomfort or dissatisfaction. If, for example, several parents question why preschoolers play so much, the teacher might either duplicate a published article (with permission from the publisher) in the parent newsletter or write a short description of how children learn through play. Such information offered early in the school year might head off criticisms before they become a problem. Newsletters also can pass along timely information about schedule changes, conferences, suggestions for age-appropriate books and games, or vacation activities.

Parents as Resources

Parents can be invaluable resources to preschool teachers and child care providers. Some parents may have access to free materials, such as excess fabric from a fabric shop or big boxes from an appliance store. See the "Focus on Communicating" feature in Chapter 5 for a discussion of asking parents for free materials. Other parents may know of an unusual and interesting place to visit, such as a dairy or a puppet maker's shop. Some parents work in places that children would enjoy visiting, such as a fire station or a pizza restaurant.

Parents also serve as resources by providing important information about their children's family life, which may affect the behavior or mood of the children in the preschool setting. Family life-styles vary dramatically, and they serve as a major influence on how children view the world, as well as

Parents can become involved in the curriculum in many ways. A father who is a police officer can talk to the children about safety. He also can explain the many ways police officers can help people.

on children's abilities, likes and dislikes, strengths, and attitudes. Information volunteered by the parent about a child's lack of sleep, for example, or the death of a family pet also is useful for the preschool teacher. Such information about a child's individual needs allows the teacher to adjust the curriculum and his or her interaction with the child to suit the circumstances, helping to make the child's preschool experience more successful.

Parents in the Classroom

Parents with expertise in areas of interest to preschoolers may contribute to curriculum activities. Parents who have free time during the school day may help out in the classroom, read stories, accompany the class on a field trip, or create a project related to their work. A parent who is a pilot, for example, might entertain the children with stories about flying airplanes. The teacher can capitalize on the children's interest in flying by constructing a "curriculum web" of activities about flying. Chapter 2 included a discussion of curriculum webs. The children might build paper airplanes, visit the airport that the parent flies from, sit in an airplane cockpit, build a cockpit from blocks, and engage in other related activities. A parent who is a police officer might discuss with the children the many ways that police officers can help people. Such parent contacts help preschool children see the relationship between the people and their community and recognize that community helpers are often also someone's mother or father.

Communicating with Parents

Effective communications between parents and the preschool or child care center should be a priority for child care professionals. Teachers should learn and use parents' names and share with parents anecdotes about their children.

It is important for teachers to communicate to parents that the school values their opinions concerning their children (Herrera & Wooden, 1988). In some situations, especially when parents and teachers come from different cultural backgrounds, teachers should take extra care to avoid miscommunication or misinterpretation of information. Teachers are responsible for establishing *rapport*—a warm, positive, and open relationship—with each child's parent or guardian. It is important for teachers to develop a general rapport with parents—for example, through friendly conversation about the weather, health, and school activities—before approaching sensitive subject areas such as discipline problems with a child.

Teachers can use several strategies for nurturing rapport. One technique is to listen carefully to the parents' concerns during conversations or conferences and to periodically rephrase the parents' comments. This technique gives the parent an opportunity to correct something if he or she feels that the teacher does not understand or is misinterpreting. For example, a parent might say that his son complains that other children don't want to play with him. The teacher might then respond, "Are you concerned that Brian feels left out, or are you concerned that Brian isn't fitting in with the other children?" During any discussion, the teacher should stress the child's positive traits and suggest several alternatives to address areas that may need extra attention. It is important for parents to know that the teacher likes and cares for the child. They can then consider the teacher as part of their "team" and can hear negative information without feeling threatened.

Once rapport and trust are established, parents also will feel more comfortable bringing up issues or incidents that cause them concern. Parents and teachers who talk openly can usually resolve issues before these issues become problems and reduce the possibility of confrontations (Morgan, 1989). If good rapport exists, teachers can interpret parents' negative comments or hostility as frustration at their inability to resolve their child's problem, not as an attack on the teacher or the curriculum. Likewise, parents are less likely to view the teachers' suggestions as criticism of their parenting skills.

Parents also may have different expectations of what constitutes normal behavior. Good two-way communication will help parents understand what is developmentally appropriate behavior. They may then encourage their children to change behaviors without feeling threatened (Morgan, 1989). Or, if the parent views a developmentally appropriate behavior as inappropriate, the teacher can reassure the parent that such behavior is typical of children in that age group.

Informal communications with parents can include posting weekly plans in a highly visible place, such as on the door, on a bulletin board, or near the children's cubbies. Parents also need written reports of minor injuries, such as a scraped knee. After a busy day at school, young children often are confused about how an injury occurred. More formal communications also should be scheduled regularly during the year. A parent conference gives the teacher an opportunity to tell the parent or the primary caregiver about the child's overall progress, including areas in which the child is doing well and areas that need extra attention. See the "Focus on Communicating with Parents" feature in Chapter 3 for more information on parent conferences.

Evaluating Plans

Teachers have a tendency to repeat without change an activity that works well or a schedule that resulted in an enjoyable day. By the same token, teachers too often avoid repeating an activity that did not run smoothly or caused agitation or frustration in the children. Analyzing why the day or a particular activity was successful is just as important as determining why it was not. Evaluating what happened during the day, week, month, or year is an important step in helping teachers improve their planning and their ability to carry out their plans more effectively in the future.

Activity/Daily Evaluation

It is important for preschool teachers to take the time to reflect on the day's plans and activities, either by themselves or with the other teachers. A good time for this review is right after the children have left for the day. This type of evaluation should include recording the children's reactions to each activity, how long the activity actually lasted, and how well it held the children's attention. Notes about any remarks or questions from the children or other staff members can lead to a follow-up or a related activity on another day.

The progress of individual children should be recorded, as well as whether any of the children achieved a particular objective or reached a developmental milestone—such as finally being able to hop on one foot or to finish a favorite puzzle without help. Although logging the progress of all children on a daily basis is not practical, each child's progress should be assessed regularly. Some preschools require extremely detailed records, others do not. Chapter 15 includes a discussion of assessment. In any event, the teacher should talk with each parent or guardian on a regular basis to discuss the child's progress.

The following are questions to consider when evaluating daily plans or individual activities.

- What were the strongest aspects of the day/activity?
- How did the activity achieve its objective(s)?
- What were the weakest aspects of the day/activity? What difficulties did you have?
- What are some specific changes (materials, procedure, location, number of children in group) you would make if you were to repeat the activity?

Evaluating the curriculum with other teachers helps spur new curriculum ideas and creates an opportunity for teachers to compare problem areas and discuss solutions.

Evaluation throughout the Year

In addition to evaluating each day's activities, teachers also should evaluate the broader program several times a year. Children mature during the year, and activities that were appropriate in October may no longer be challenging in March. Likewise, objectives stated at the beginning of the school year may no longer be relevant in the spring. For example, if all the children in the class can group objects based on one feature, such as color or shape, using that feature in stating an objective is no longer appropriate.

In some instances, factors unrelated to the preschool or child care center may have caused changes in the behavior of one or more children and may warrant a change in individual objectives. Such factors might include, but are not limited to, parents divorcing, death of a parent or guardian, birth of a sibling, serious illness, or even a move to a new neighborhood in the same town. Although preschool children may not talk about these incidents, a sudden change of a child's behavior in the classroom may signal adjustment or emotional problems. By modifying objectives, teachers often can help individual children adjust to or accept changes.

Periodically through the year, the teacher also might evaluate broad goals. For example, to evaluate the goal of fostering independence in the children, the teacher should first be clear how he or she is defining independence. That definition will provide insight into what specific objectives the children will need to meet in order to move toward independence. The teacher might consider whether the curriculum is providing opportunities every day for children to make choices. If not, the teacher must decide how to create more free-choice opportunities that are appropriate for the children.

It may be useful for the teacher to meet with other teachers who work with or supervise children of the same age. Professional peers provide a fresh eye that may help identify the areas where long-range goals have not been met. Peers also can offer insight into and ideas about how they have achieved the same or similar objectives.

The following questions may be used in evaluating plans and activities during the year.

- Are the children experiencing success? If not, what can you do to help them be more successful?
- Are the activities still developmentally appropriate?
- Are the children sufficiently motivated to get involved in the activities? If not, what can you do to motivate the children?
- Have you been able to adapt to unusual or unforeseen situations?
- What activities or topics did the children find most interesting?
- Did you bring in special materials for the program?
- What themes or units did parents mention most?
- What themes or units would you do/not do next year?
- What new materials or changes would improve the program?
- Focusing on one child for whom you think your plans were particularly successful, why do you think that they were?
- Focusing on one child whose needs you think you did not meet, why do you think that you did not meet them? What can you do to meet that child's needs?

Applications

Preschools and child care centers today usually are designed as half-day or full-day, part-week or five-days-a-week programs. Scheduling varies according to the number of hours the children are in day care. The written plans for these programs will reflect different time frames. This section contrasts full-day and half-day programs and provides some tips for creating and posting written plans.

Full-Day/Half-Day Programs

Children in full-day preschool programs have different caretaking needs from those in half-day programs. In addition to the obvious need for lunch, morning and afternoon snacks, and nap time, children in full-day programs have different emotional requirements. Because they are separated all day from their parents, these children tend to require more nurturing and support from their teachers than children in half-day programs.

Child care providers in full-day programs also need to allow more flexibility in the curriculum for children who find it difficult to be in a highly routinized, strict schedule for eight to nine hours a day. Perhaps some children need longer naps than others or require a longer time for eating. Remember, if a child were at home, her parent or other caregiver probably would, for example, let her go outside whenever she wished, play with her blocks whenever and for as long as she wished, and spend a little extra time at the lunch table talking about her day. The child care provider should try to emulate the flexibility of a home environment to some extent.

Sample Schedule for a Half-Day Program for Three- to Five-Year-Olds	
Time Block	Activity
8:30–9:00	Arrival time and free play. As children arrive and are greeted by a teacher, other children are free to explore dramatic play, blocks, library corner, some simple art projects (e.g., markers or easel painting), water table, play dough, dolls, trucks, manipulatives).
9:00–9:05	Cleanup
9:05–9:25	Group time. All children sit on a rug in front of teacher where he or she leads group in music, calendar time (marking special dates like birthdays on a big calendar), information about day, and so on.
9:25–10:10	Free-choice activity time. Teacher has prepared several special activities for children to choose from, such as an art activity, an activity to challenge cognitive skills, and perhaps a table toy, water table, or other sensory material activity.
10:10–10:15	Cleanup
10:15–10:25	Story time. Teacher reads children a storybook or tells a flannel-board story. Finger plays or discussions may be included.
10:25–10:30	Handwashing and setup for snack time.
10:30–10:40	Snack time.
10:40–10:45	Cleanup of snack tables and handwashing.
10:45–10:50	Preparation for going outside. This activity may take more or less time, depending on weather and garments worn.
10:50–11:30	Outside play. Children use climbing equipment, sandbox, tricycles, swings, balls, and so on.
11:30–12:00	Preparation for going home and pickup by parent or guardian.

FIGURE 6.1   **Sample Schedule for a Half-Day Program for Three- to Five-Year-Olds.** *Source: Jane Billman, University of Illinois at Urbana-Champaign.*

In addition, teachers who work with children up to 40 hours a week find that they must learn how to pace themselves during the day so that all of their own physical and emotional energy is not depleted by lunchtime.

Half-day programs may have a faster pace, compared to the necessarily more relaxed pace of the full-day program (see Figure 6.1). Children arrive with more intensity in half-day programs and have a higher energy level, since, to them, preschool is the most exciting part of their week. Time blocks need to be carefully organized. If longer time blocks are preferred, fewer total time blocks will be available, and some activities may not be scheduled every day. For example, painting activities may be scheduled for Monday, Tuesday, and Friday, and music time may be scheduled in that same time block on Wednesday and Thursday. You should reserve more time in a half-day program for talking to parents as they drop off or pick up their children.

Sample Weekly Plan with Water Theme

Time Block	Monday	Tuesday	Wednesday	Thursday	Friday
8:30–9:00 Greeting and Free Play	CG 1*—greeting; CG 2—floating	CG 1—greeting; CG 2—floating	CG 1—greeting; CG 2—floating	CG 1—greeting; CG 2—floating	CG 1—greeting; CG 2—floating
9:05–9:25 Group Time and Music Time (CG 1 and CG 2)	What is an Ocean? / Songs about ocean	Aquatic animals / Songs about fish	Kinds of boats / Songs about boats	Salt water / Songs about water	Beaches / Songs about ocean
9:25–10:10 Art (CG 2)	Watercolor on construction paper	Sponge paint on fish shapes	Eye dropper paint on coffee filters	Watercolor and crayon painting	Sand painting—colored sand collage
Cognitive (CG 1)	Playing "Go Fish" card game	Fishing for aquatic animals with magnets	Making names with magnetic letters	Floating in saltwater vs. freshwater experiment	Writing names in sand and salt
Table Toys (Independent)	Plastic interlocking toys	Interlocking toys and boats; building a harbor	Interlocking toys and fish; building an aquarium	Plastic whales and whale poster	In trays: sand, seashells and magnifiers
Water Table (Independent)	Water and plastic seaweed and whales	Coloring water blue	Boats and blue water	Dry sand and seashells	Sand, water, and plastic fish and nets
10:50–11:30 Outside Play (CG 1 and CG 2)	Tricycles, sand buckets and water, soccer balls, "painting" with water	Washing tricycles	Washing doll clothes and hanging on line	Making lake in sandbox with plastic liner and water	Continuing lake; boats on lake

*CG 1 and CG 2 refers to Caregiver 1 and Caregiver 2

FIGURE 6.2   Sample Weekly Plan with Water Theme. *Source: Jane Billman, University of Illinois at Urbana-Champaign.*

As these parents may have more available time and higher expectations from the program, they may demand more of the teacher's time.

Sample Plans

Write daily or weekly plans in a simple and easy-to-read format. Figure 6.2 provides one example. Post plans for all staff members to review so that they are aware of everyone's activities and responsibilities. Posting plans in a place where parents also can see them serves as a form of school/parent communication. Try posting the weekly curriculum plans on the door of the classroom or on a bulletin board near the children's cubbies. Many parents do not realize the amount of time and effort a preschool teacher puts into planning the day. Posting curriculum plans lets parents see the preparatory efforts of the teacher, as well as providing information about the children's day. If you can make copies of the plan, you may wish to send them home with each child ahead of time. If the plan includes simple diagrams or pictures of the activities, children may be able to "read" them with their parents or guardians. See Appendix B for a comparison of daily plans from different curriculum approaches and Appendix D for more ideas about how to set up activity plans.

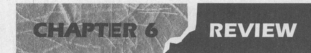

CHAPTER 6   REVIEW

SUMMARY

- Effective planning and daily routines provide the structure, repetition, and predictability necessary to help children feel secure and enjoy their preschool experience.

- Daily plans lay out the activities for each day. Long-term plans ensure that activities follow a logical order to foster children's growth and development.

- Goals are skills or behaviors teachers wish children to achieve or exhibit. Objectives break down the long-range goals into specific ways to reach the goal.

- Four types of objectives are academic, behavioral, developmental, and individual.

- Several themes are universally appealing to preschool children. These themes include family, baby animals, plants, food, and community helpers.

- Sequencing helps teachers decide what to teach next and how to order the activities effectively over time, so that the children will remain interested and experience success.

- Preschool children need a balance of activities during the day that will provide variety and accommodate the ebb and flow of their energy levels.

- Preschool children require smooth transitions to help them shift from one activity to another.

- The key to timing is to leave ample time for children to get involved in and complete an activity. This will help children develop concentration skills and a sense of competence more readily.

- Flexibility is an important feature of any written plan—to accommodate unexpected events, special occasions, individual needs of children, activities that take longer than expected, and even bad weather.

- Preschools are more successful when parents are involved and participate in the program. Parents are invaluable sources of information about their children. They also provide ideas for resources and materials from the community and can serve as volunteers in the classroom.

- Effective communication between the school and the home benefits the parent, the teacher, and the child.

- Plans should be evaluated at the end of each day—to note ways to improve activities, to record individual children's progress, and to identify ideas for follow-up activities.

- Teachers should evaluate their programs several times a year to assess long-term goals and to accommodate changes in children's development.

- Full-day programs have different scheduling requirements than half-day programs. Lunch, snacks, and nap time must be included, and the pace may be more relaxed than in a half-day program.

ACQUIRING KNOWLEDGE

1. What is the main purpose of a daily plan?
2. Why are daily plans necessary in child-initiated preschools?
3. Describe four categories of objectives.
4. What are some recommendations for developing and writing effective objectives?
5. How can teachers find out about children's interests in order to incorporate those interests into the curriculum?
6. What are some common topics that interest most preschoolers?
7. Give three examples of factors that may affect the daily plan and that cannot be controlled by a teacher.
8. What types of activities should be balanced throughout a daily plan?
9. How can a teacher help ensure smooth transitions between activities?
10. Describe two differing points of view on having preschool children wait in line during transition time.
11. How can the pace of activities affect children in a preschool setting?
12. How should the timing of activities in a daily plan for two- and three-year-olds differ from that in one for four- and five-year olds?
13. How might teachers use the order of activities to prepare children for a nap, or to help them make the transition from outdoor play to indoor activities?
14. Explain why flexibility is an important aspect of any daily plan.
15. What is the difference between making a daily plan and sequencing activities?
16. List four approaches to sequencing activities.
17. What is the difference between a concrete and an abstract experience? Give one example of each type of experience.

18. What are some strategies that a teacher might use if children are losing their attention or becoming frustrated with an activity?
19. How do teachable moments help a teacher accommodate individual children's needs?
20. What strategies can help a teacher cope with bad weather?
21. Give three examples of how parents serve as resources to teachers.
22. What are some strategies preschool teachers can use to establish rapport with parents?
23. What are some ways caregivers can keep parents informed about their children's daily activities in the preschool or child care center?
24. What strategies does Boutte recommend to help a preschool teacher deal with parents who are upset or dissatisfied?
25. How might a father's or a mother's employment be used to involve him or her in the classroom?
26. How can parents who do not have unique talents contribute to the preschool classroom?
27. Why is evaluation of activities an important part of curriculum development?
28. What type of evaluation should take place every day?
29. How is the curriculum reviewed differently during a monthly or quarterly evaluation than in a daily evaluation of activities?
30. Describe some factors that are unrelated to the preschool curriculum that might affect a child's behavior.
31. What are some differences between daily plans for full-day and for half-day programs?
32. What are the advantages of creating and posting a written daily plan?

THINKING CRITICALLY

1. The subject of written objectives can serve as a good basis for discussions with teachers. What questions might you ask a teacher about how he or she develops objectives?
2. A very broad topic can result in an unfocused, almost random series of activities. If the children in your class want to explore "food," give some examples of more narrowly focused topics related to food.
3. Activities in a preschool curriculum need to be balanced in order to help children develop. How might a teacher evaluate whether or not the activities in a daily plan are balanced?
4. Some preschools that utilize the child-initiated approach reduce the number of group transitions in a daily plan by allowing children to make their own decisions about when to stop one activity and begin another. What do you think are the advantages and disadvantages of this type of transition management?
5. Preschool children feel secure when they follow a regular schedule. However, unavoidable changes will occur almost every day in a preschool classroom. What do you think are some good ways to help children handle changes to their routine or unexpected situations?

OBSERVATIONS AND APPLICATIONS

1. Spend a morning or afternoon at a preschool observing the activities in which the children are engaged. Look for evidence of balance in how the day's activities are planned. Describe what you see as quiet activities and what you see as noisy activities. Try to determine over the course of the morning or afternoon if there are more quiet activities scheduled or more noisy activities, or if there is a balance between the two kinds. Take note of activities that require gross motor skills and fine motor skills, and describe them. Also, record activities children participate in as a group and those they engage in alone.

2. Observe a group of two- or three-year-olds at a preschool during a series of activities and transitions. How long do the activities generally last? Do you notice any child in the group squirming, fidgeting, or staring into space at any time during an activity? How long do the transitions generally last? How are they carried out or directed by the teacher? At the same preschool, observe a group of four- or five-year-olds. How do the length of activities and transitions differ from those with the younger group of children?

3. You have carefully planned an hour-long creative activity where the children will make their own nature collages. Three parent volunteers are on hand to help take the children on a walk in a nearby park to gather collage materials. However, just as the group leaves for the walk, a bright red fire truck pulls up across the street. The firefighters proceed to try to rescue a kitten from a large oak tree. The kitten is meowing loudly and the children begin talking about the kitten. Do you continue on your walk in order to keep the children focused on the planned activity, or do you take the group over to see the rescue? How might you handle this change in the daily plan today and in the following day or days?

4. As a preschool teacher of four-year-olds, one of your objectives is to help the children learn about responsibility. Toward this goal, you have planned several activities focusing on different aspects of responsibility (including a group discussion about what being responsible means, reading books about children who act responsibly, and using puppets to act out different scenarios). In addition, you have assigned each child a responsibility in the classroom and changed those responsibilities every few days. You have also included an article about children's responsibility in the parent newsletter. Now you want to evaluate the children's progress toward the goal. How can you do so?

5. As head teacher in a preschool, you encourage parents to participate in classroom activities whenever possible. After sending a note home with the children, you receive indications of interest from three parents. After speaking with each parent, you find out that one is a gourmet chef, another is a banker who is willing to volunteer during his lunch hour, and the third is a stay-at-home mother. What types of activities might you suggest to these volunteers?

FOR FURTHER INFORMATION

Books and Journal Articles

Boutte, G. S., Keepler, D. L., Tyler, V. S., & Terry, B. Z. (1992). Effective techniques for involving "difficult" parents. *Young Children, 47*(3), 19–22.

Bredekamp, S. (1984). *Accreditation criteria and procedures of the National Academy of Early Childhood Programs*. Washington, DC: National Association for the Education of Young Children.

Bredekamp, S. (Ed.). (1987). *Developmentally appropriate practice in early childhood programs serving children from birth through age 8*. Washington, DC: National Association for the Education of Young Children.

Brown, J. (Ed.) (1982). *Curriculum planning for young children*. Washington, DC: National Association for the Education of Young Children.

Dodge, D., Goldhammer, M., & Colker, L. (1992). *The creative curriculum for early childhood* (3rd ed.). Washington, DC: Teaching Strategies.

Herrera, J. F., & Wooden, S. L. (1988). Some thoughts about effective parent-school communication. *Young Children, 14*(6), 78–80.

Hildebrand, V. (1991). *Introduction to early childhood education* (5th ed.). New York: Macmillan.

Morgan, E. L. (1989). Talking with parents when concerns come up. *Young Children, 44*(2), 52–56.

Parent-Child Early Education Program. (1980). *Shaping a curriculum for fours and fives*. Florissant, MO: Ferguson-Florissant School District.

Curriculum and Resource Guides

David, A., & Mitchell, J. (Eds.). (1992). *Explorations with young children*. Mt. Rainier, MD: Gryphon House.

Day, B. (1988). *Early childhood education: Creative learning activities* (3rd ed.). New York: Macmillan.

The giant encyclopedia of theme activities for children 2 to 5: Over 600 favorite activities created by teachers for teachers. (1993). Mt. Rainier, MD: Gryphon House.

Hamilton, D., Flemming, B., & Hicks, J. (1990). *Resources for creative teaching in early childhood education* (2nd ed.). New York: Harcourt Brace.

PART 2

Curriculum and the Developing Child

OBJECTIVES

Studying this chapter
will enable you to

- Discuss the elements that
  constitute physical development in
  young children
- Examine the relationship between
  exercise and physical development
- Explain why a positive body image
  is essential for sound physical
  development
- Describe the components of a
  curriculum to promote physical
  development
- Discuss several ways preschool
  teachers can incorporate nutrition,
  hygiene, and safety into the
  curriculum

CHAPTER TERMS

body management/non-locomotor
   skills
cephalocaudal principle
developmental motor patterns
fundamental motor skills
hygiene
locomotor skills
manipulative/object control skills
mature motor patterns
ossification
proficiency barrier
proximodistal principle
rough-and-tumble play

WHEN student teacher Carrie Spencer arrived at the Kids' Place Child Care Center one morning, she found Ellen Sanchez, head teacher of the four-year-old class, busily arranging various objects in the school's play yard. Ms. Sanchez had already lined up a row of tires leading to a sturdy picnic table. On the other side of the table was a barrel lying on its side with both ends removed.

"Help me move this railroad tie so it leads from the barrel to the jungle gym," Ms. Sanchez called when she saw Carrie.

"OK, but what are you doing?" Carrie asked.

"I'm building an obstacle course," Ms. Sanchez replied. "During outdoor play this morning, we'll start a game of 'Follow-the-Leader' through it."

"It looks like fun," Carrie said.

"The children love obstacle courses, and we make a different one every month or so and leave it up for a few days. It helps them practice different gross motor skills like jumping, crawling, climbing, and balancing," said Ms. Sanchez.

"First, I'll have them walk zigzag from tire to tire," she continued. "Then, they'll climb over the picnic table and crawl through the barrel. Then, they'll walk along the railroad tie, which is good for learning balance, and climb across the jungle gym, good for upper body strength.

"After the children go through the obstacle course a few times, I'll tell the leader to do things like twirl, hop like a frog, bend down low, and walk on tiptoes."

"This obstacle course is a great idea!" exclaimed Carrie. "They'll be practicing all of those motor skills, and they won't even know it."

"No," smiled Ms. Sanchez, "but we will."

By the time children have reached preschool age, they already have learned the rudiments of walking, running, grasping, and climbing, but they still are mastering many other gross and fine motor skills. The continuing physical development of preschoolers depends on several factors, including their individual genetic makeup, the quality of the nutrition they receive, and the amount and kinds of exercise they participate in. Other elements that affect physical development include children's overall health, the body image children create, and the hygiene and safety practices they learn. These factors can contribute significantly to children's physical development with positive or negative effects.

In planning their curriculum, preschool teachers need to pay as much attention to physical development as to cognitive or social development, and to how these areas interrelate. As David Gallahue writes, "The motor and perceptual development of young children should not be left to chance" (Gallahue, 1993, p. 24). Preschool teachers play an important role in helping children master motor skills by modeling, guiding, and providing opportunities for children to practice those skills. This chapter explores how physical development can be addressed in the curriculum and discusses the reasons for including the subjects of hygiene, safety, and nutrition within this facet of the curriculum.

Elements of Physical Development

As children grow and develop, their bodies undergo many distinct changes. By the age of three, the average child has doubled in height, gained 20 to 30 pounds in weight, and grown a first set of teeth. During the years two to five, the child's head—which at birth is about one-fourth of the child's body length—approaches the adult ratio of about one to eight. The child's brain and nervous system also are maturing, making it possible for him or her to coordinate hand and eye movements and small muscle groups. This coordination helps the child master fine motor skills. The child's torso, arms, and legs lengthen, cartilage hardens into bones (*ossification*) and body fat decreases. Because of the increasing growth of muscle tissue, the child's strength increases by 65 percent during the third to sixth years. The child begins to master gross motor skills, such as running, jumping, balancing, and

The physical curriculum should include activities not only to foster the development of gross motor skills but also fine motor skills. Activities such as threading wooden beads also help children develop eye-hand coordination.

developing flexibility. It is important for early childhood professionals to know that, in the preschool years, the difference between boys and girls in physical strength and ability is slight.

Motor skills develop according to a set pattern known as the *cephalocaudal principle.* Children learn to control the movements of their heads, shoulders, and trunk before they can control their arms, legs, hands, and feet. For example, virtually the first movements an infant learns is to lift the head and to move it from side to side. Next, children learn to roll over. In addition, children learn motor skills according to the *proximodistal principle.* That is, they acquire physical mastery from the center of the trunk outward to the hands and feet, and they learn to perform gross motor movements before they gain control over fine motor movements. Infants learn to sit up before they learn to stand or walk, and toddlers learn to catch a ball in their outstretched arms before they can catch it with their hands.

Gesell's Theory of Physical Development

As discussed in Chapter 2, Arnold Gesell and his colleagues at the Gesell Institute were proponents of the maturationist theory of child development in the 1940s. They believed that children are born with certain innate characteristics and abilities—physical, cognitive, and social—which emerge in a predictable sequence as children grow and mature. Gesell and his associates established a set of developmental schedules, which they named the Gesell

Developmental Scales, to determine at what age these traits and abilities usually emerge. However, he emphasized again and again that each child is an individual with his or her own specific biological timetable. It is important for preschool teachers to remember that, although the sequence in which a child learns specific physical skills is more or less constant, the timetable can vary widely and still be within the normal range. Gesell believed that, with a nurturing environment and the normal process of maturation, most children who are lagging will catch up to other children and will naturally progress to the next level of development.

Wickstrom's Theory of Physical Development

Physical development researcher Ralph L. Wickstrom observed that children master motor skills by progressing through a series of specific substages (Wickstrom, 1983). First, they learn basic movements, which he called *fundamental motor skills*. These skills include running, jumping, throwing, catching, kicking, and climbing. Next, children learn *developmental motor patterns*, interim patterns combining a number of fundamental motor skills. Finally, they master the highest level of motor skill development, or *mature motor patterns*. Once children have mastered a mature pattern, they can adapt it to specific activities, such as batting a baseball or hitting a tennis ball.

The three stages in Wickstrom's theory can be illustrated by the motions involved in throwing a ball. Three-year-olds throw a ball primarily by extending their forearms—a fundamental motor skill. Five-year-olds add torso rotation, and six-year-olds take a forward step with the leg that is on the same side of the body as the throwing arm—developmental motor patterns. Older children take a step backward and then forward, shifting their weight as they bring their arm forward—a mature motor pattern.

According to Wickstrom, children generally learn the fundamental motor skills within the first five years of life. Left to themselves, they naturally build on what they have learned previously at each stage until they achieve a certain level of skill. However, Wickstrom found that by creating early opportunities to learn motor skills, adults can ensure that children practice and achieve the key skills by age five.

Physical development researchers Vern Seefeldt and John Haubenstricker, in an ongoing study at Michigan State University, have concluded that, if children do not master the fundamental motor skills by age five on their own or with a teacher's guidance, they may never achieve the highest level of skill (Haubenstricker & Seefeldt, 1986). Seefeldt and Haubenstricker developed a list of fundamental motor skills, similar to those identified by Wickstrom, that are mastered in early childhood (see Figure 7.1). These skills fall under a *proficiency barrier*. Children who have not mastered the skills below the proficiency barrier by age five will have difficulty later on with the physical skills required in elementary school. Caregivers can play a crucial role in the physical development of children by providing opportunities for learning fundamental motor skills in the preschool years.

Selected Motor Skills to be Learned in Early Childhood

LOCOMOTOR SKILLS

Walk	Slide	Start
Run	Hop	Bounce
Leap	Skip	Fall
Jump	Roll	Dodge
Gallop	Stop	

NON-LOCOMOTOR SKILLS

Swing	Curl	Push
Sway	Twist	Lift
Rock	Turn	Pull
Stretch	Bend	Hang

PROJECTION AND RECEPTION OF OBJECTS

Catch	Punt	Dribble
Throw	Strike	Roll
Kick	Trap	

FIGURE 7.1　**Selected Motor Skills to be Learned in Early Childhood.**
Source: Seefeldt (1980).

The Importance of Exercise

In the preschool curriculum, exercise refers to the free, joyful, and creative physical movements of young children playing indoors or outdoors. Exercise comes naturally to most children and provides them with great pleasure. As they explore, discover, and play, they gradually master a broad spectrum of gross and fine motor skills—running, jumping, climbing, hopping, and many other kinds of body motions. Children learn the movements involved in motor skills naturally, a step at a time, with many repetitions over a period of time.

It is impossible to overstate the benefits of physical exercise to growing and developing bodies. Exercise helps all the systems and processes of the body—respiration, digestion, circulation, and elimination—to develop and function more fully. Exercise also provides young children with the opportunities they need to practice and master specific motor skills. For preschoolers, exercise and physical activity also contribute to their positive self-concept (discussed in Chapter 3), building feelings of competence and self-confidence in their physical abilities. According to psychologist Albert Bandura, children who are confident in their physical abilities are motivated to try new experiences and to seek challenges (Bandura, 1986).

Children who do not develop physical skills quickly give up trying and, in a vicious circle, lose the opportunities to gain competence. Children who are physically competent are easy for preschool teachers to recognize. They are the ones who push themselves to climb higher, run faster, and pedal harder. Children who are less physically competent sometimes stand on the

FOCUS ON / Communicating with Children

Encouraging Less Active Children to Become Involved in Physical Activity

Just as some children may need encouragement with certain cognitive tasks or social skills, other children need guidance and support to feel comfortable with physical activity, particularly gross motor skills.

Julie Anderson watched her class of three- and four-year-olds as they played outside. She saw that Katya was sitting alone at the end of the playground blacktop. Ms. Anderson felt strongly that Katya was missing out on the opportunity to build motor skills and to enjoy playing with others.

Ms. ANDERSON: Katya, why aren't you playing with the other children?

KATYA: I dunno.

Ms. ANDERSON: Doesn't that game look like fun?

KATYA: No. The bikes are fun.

Ms. ANDERSON: Yes, I know. Everybody seems to have a lot of fun riding the tricycles. Why don't we join them? I'll go with you.

KATYA: But . . . but no more trikes.

Ms. ANDERSON: Oh . . . I see. I didn't notice before that they were all being used. Is that why you're sitting alone here? (No response from Katya.) See those children over there? They've invented their own game under the jungle gym. I bet we'd have fun if we played with them.

KATYA: Don't want to play with them . . . want a trike.

Ms. ANDERSON: Can you think of something else we can do that is like a tricycle . . . something where we go fast?

KATYA: Like horses?

Ms. ANDERSON: Great idea, Katya! We can travel like horses. Do you know how to gallop?

KATYA: Uh huh. Do you want to see?

Ms. ANDERSON: Yes, and I would love to gallop with you. Let's go!

Knowing that Katya liked the trikes, how else might Ms. Anderson have interested Katya in physical play? Do you think that Ms. Anderson's active participation in Katya's play had an influence on her behavior? Why or why not?

sidelines, afraid to try anything for fear that they will fail and embarrass themselves. It is important that preschool teachers spend time one-on-one with these children to provide guidance and practice with specific gross motor skills, (Kutner, 1993). The teacher should be actively involved so that the child sees the adult enjoying physical activity. See the "Focus on Communicating" feature in this chapter for tips on encouraging children who are physically inactive.

According to physical development researchers Seefeldt & Vogel, (1986), one of the most important long-term benefits of regular exercise is that it leads to lifelong competence in such leisure activities as sports, outdoor games, and dancing. Seefeldt and Vogel list many other benefits of regular exercise, including promoting brain function and cognitive development; improving perception, balance, and sense of touch; preventing obesity and coronary and stress diseases; enhancing self-concept and self-esteem; promoting social, problem-solving, creative, and moral reasoning skills; and preventing mental illness.

Exercise also is important for overall physical fitness and health. The American Academy of Pediatrics reports that as many as 50 percent of American children are not getting enough exercise to develop healthy hearts and lungs (Javernick, 1988). In addition, as many as 40 percent of children ages five to eight already are developing risk factors for heart disease, such as high blood pressure, high cholesterol, and a sedentary life-style. These facts underscore the importance of addressing physical development in the preschool curriculum. Young children should be encouraged to enjoy physical activity and exercise well before they reach school age.

Developing a Positive Body Image

As stated earlier, the image that children form of their bodies contributes to their self-concept and their feelings of self-worth. Preschoolers commonly define themselves in terms of physical attributes and abilities—for example, "I'm this tall," or "I can ride a tricycle." If the body image they have formed is negative ("I'm fat," or "I can't swing myself"), then they have feelings of low self-worth. Children who develop a positive body image are adventurous. They use their bodies freely, enthusiastically, and energetically on the playground. Children who have a poor body image hang back during physical activities and are afraid of embarrassing themselves. As a result, they miss out on much of the fun of being a child and an important opportunity to develop feelings of competence.

Early childhood professionals can assist children in developing a positive body image by including activities that help them appreciate their bodies. For example, one way to teach children to appreciate their bodies is to talk about the good things that bodies help people do, such as walking to the park, swinging on a swing, climbing a tree, lying down to sleep, and buttoning up coats. In addition, caregivers can help children by modeling and demonstrating specific skills. For instance, children may need to be shown how to modify their movements in order to throw a ball straight. Guidance also can help children move to the next level of proficiency—such as catching a ball with two hands instead of both arms. Additionally, creative movement exercises can help children become more comfortable with their bodies and gain a greater understanding of what their bodies can do. Creative movement is discussed in more detail in Chapter 13.

At all costs, early childhood professionals should avoid labeling children according to their physical attributes because labeling can harm a child's body image. Labels such as "fat," "skinny," "shrimp," and "clumsy" can be extremely hurtful to young children, and teachers should address immediately any such name-calling in the preschool setting. It is important for caregivers to remember that preschoolers form their body image in part according to how they believe others see them. Once formed, a negative body image is difficult to change.

Preschool teachers also should avoid stereotyping based on gender, physical features, or handicaps. Not all boys are fast runners, not all fat people are jolly, and not all tall people are good basketball players. Children are individuals who should be encouraged to develop motor skills within the context of their own interests and abilities. They should not be forced to conform to other people's ideas or preconceptions of what they can or cannot do.

Components of a Physical Curriculum

It is not enough to simply turn children loose in a playground or classroom and expect them to master gross and fine motor skills on their own. Preschool teachers should gently guide children's physical development. Preschoolers need a stimulating environment and a curriculum of carefully planned activities to ensure that they receive the necessary practice and repetition to learn fundamental motor skills such as those defined by Haubenstricker. This section discusses aspects of the physical curriculum, including indoor and outdoor play, and strategies for integrating physical activities into the daily plan.

Physical Play Outdoors

Outdoor play periods must be more than an occasion to let children run around and release pent-up energy. They should provide an opportunity for children to practice a wide variety of motor skills. Teachers can plan structured activities and leave time for unstructured play. Ms. Sanchez's obstacle course, described at the beginning of this chapter, is a good example of a structured outdoor activity that promotes the development of motor skills. It is a noncompetitive game designed to be fun and also to give the children opportunities to practice several motor skills. See the "Focus on Activities" feature in this chapter for information on how to set up an obstacle course.

Structured outdoor activities need to reflect the developmental levels of individual children. Preschool teachers should be aware that, while some preschoolers can catch a ball, others are still learning to go down steps with alternating feet. Activities can focus on jumping, climbing, rolling and tumbling, and circle games. Jumping strengthens the legs; a jumping activity can involve jumping over chalk lines, between tires or hula hoops, or off a low beam onto a soft surface. Climbing helps children learn coordination of the arms and legs. A climbing activity may explore different ways of getting on or off a piece of equipment. Rolling and tumbling help children explore wide open spaces and how they can move their bodies in space—either down a low grassy slope or in different directions across a grassy yard. Circle games foster social skills as well as specific motor skills.

In addition, structured outdoor activities can focus on such skills as balancing, throwing, catching, and kicking. See "Applications" later in this chapter for descriptions of activities to promote specific motor skills. The

Physical play outdoors helps children develop large- and small-motor skills and experience the freedom of moving in wide open spaces.

teacher should take an active role in structured activities, so that he or she can offer encouragement, guidance, and specific feedback to children. The teacher also should emphasize language during such activities, so that children begin to learn the vocabulary associated with various types of physical activity, such as far and near, or over, under, and through.

Playground equipment and space are important elements in outdoor play. To move about freely and to practice their motor skills, children need a sufficient number of play spaces and pieces of equipment so that they do not spend most of their outdoor time standing in line or waiting to use a piece of equipment. As discussed in Chapter 5, the playground should include several pieces of large fixed equipment, such as swings, slides, and climbing apparatus, to promote gross muscle development and help build such skills as balance, strength, and flexibility. In addition, wheeled toys—including tricycles, scooters, and wagons—help build pedaling, pushing, pulling, and body coordination skills. To promote the development of fine motor skills, such activities as painting, drawing, and building with blocks can take place outdoors as well as indoors. Dramatic play, gardening, and sand play also involve fine motor skills. Chapter 5 covered the subject of playground equipment in more detail and offered specific recommendations for playground maintenance, supervision, and safety.

Teachers need to allow time for free play in the planning of the daily curriculum. Free play includes play with sand and water toys, free use of playground equipment for climbing and swinging, tricycle riding, and free movement such as running and skipping.

FOCUS ON   **Activities**

Making an Obstacle Course

An obstacle course not only helps preschoolers develop physical skills, it also provides cognitive challenges and practice with social skills—such as following directions, recognizing shapes and patterns, and interacting with peers. In addition, mastering an obstacle course helps build children's self-esteem.

Courses can be set up inside or outside. Outdoor courses present opportunities for running and jumping, whereas indoor courses can focus on developing balance and coordination. Although you can purchase equipment from a catalog, you also can set up a course from materials at home or in the classroom. The number one concern is the use of safe equipment. It should be sturdy and well-anchored so that children cannot knock it over easily. It should not have sharp or pointed edges or present any other potential dangers.

Here are some ideas for an indoor course. Arrange carpet squares in a hopscotch pattern leading to a chair with wide legs or a low table that children can scramble underneath. Place hula hoops on the floor, and have children jump or hop in them. Or suspend the hoops se-

curely from the ceiling so that they almost touch the floor, and have the children crawl through them. Place pillows along the course that children can jump over or onto.

Another idea for making a simple obstacle course is to tie yarn or rope to various objects in the room, creating a spiderweb effect. The children can crawl under, over, or around the string. Use arrows made from masking tape to guide the way. To adapt this idea for the outdoors, tie the string or rope from trees to various pieces of playground equipment.

Be sure to space children appropriately at the start of the course—the second child should not start on the course until the first child has left the area. Be careful not to place difficult tasks too close together, or the result may be a bottleneck. Remember that, generally, an oval-shaped course is easiest for preschoolers to handle. Most important, set up the course so that all children will feel successful at the end.

Ideas for the obstacle courses from Tina Cate, University of Michigan.

An important example of free outdoor play is *rough-and-tumble play*, which involves chasing, wrestling, and pretend fighting. Teachers should make sure that this type of activity takes place on soft, grassy areas of the playground. Teachers often mistake rough-and-tumble play for aggressive behavior, but researchers have found that it is a positive form of play that differs from aggression in several ways (Pellegrini & Permutter, 1988). In rough-and-tumble play, children use open hands (as opposed to closed fists), they take turns being aggressor and victim, and the expressions on their faces express pleasure and enjoyment rather than anger.

In addition to fostering motor skills, rough-and-tumble play promotes social skills and gradually evolves into games-with-rules. Teachers should acknowledge that rough-and-tumble play is a normal, desirable aspect of child development. However, if children's expressions change from joy to fear or anger, when their voices become strident, or when youngsters signal that they do not want to play anymore, the teacher should intervene by redirecting the play to an activity with which all youngsters feel comfortable.

Physical Play Indoors

Many teachers think of indoor play as the time for children to engage in activities that build fine motor skills, such as art, building with blocks, and dramatic play. They usually relegate activities that develop large motor skills to outdoor play and move these activities indoors only in bad weather. However, a well-rounded physical curriculum includes daily indoor activities that foster large muscle skills. Creative movement, circle games, climbing, tumbling, and dancing are all gross motor skill activities that can take place indoors.

Such activities require a large clear space with carpeting and soft pillows or mats where children can move around freely without bumping into one another or hurting themselves if they fall. In some preschool settings, it may be necessary to create an open space temporarily by moving tables and chairs out of the way. Also, preschool teachers should remember that activities that develop large muscle skills often involve singing, shouting, music, and laughter. These high-noise-level activities should not be scheduled for the same time that other children are engaged in quiet or solitary activities, such as listening to an audiotape or story reading.

Integrating Physical Activity into the Daily Plan

Virtually all preschool activities enhance physical development because they involve the use of either gross or fine motor skills or, often, a combination of both. With a little thought and preparation, teachers can incorporate a wide variety of physical activities into the curriculum. These activities should be designed to help children improve their performance and achieve success at their own pace. Teachers also can use physical activities to teach cognitive concepts, such as big/little, up/down, in/out, far/near, and high/low. Here are some strategies and techniques to promote physical development in the preschool curriculum.

Observe Children at Play.   Teachers can learn a lot about how indoor and outdoor activities promote or deter large and fine motor development by watching children at play. Do children avoid certain pieces of play equipment and flock to others? Do certain games, toys, and manipulative activities lie gathering dust on the shelves while others are in constant use? By watching the children play, the teacher will soon realize that some equipment or activities are not appropriate for the children's developmental age. The children either will abandon certain toys or equipment because they are bored with them, or they will avoid others that are difficult to use. Once caregivers can identify these factors, they can adjust their physical activity plans to provide activities that will be developmentally appropriate and enjoyable and that will challenge the gross and fine motor development of young children without being too difficult.

Physical activities should encourage children to feel good about their bodies and their own abilities. An "I can do it" attitude, not a competitive attitude, is the best goal.

Provide Opportunities for Physical Involvement.   Physical activities should be scheduled into the daily plan, and materials and equipment should be prepared in advance. Then children will not have to wait for equipment to be found or set up. When games or activities require such equipment as balls, hoops, ropes, or beanbags, teachers should try to have a piece of equipment for each child or pair of children so that waiting time is minimal. These strategies not only prevent boredom but also enable children to have more time to practice such skills as throwing and catching. In general, games in which everyone is moving most of the time, such as "London Bridge" and a noncompetitive version of "Musical Chairs," are preferable to games in which only one or two youngsters are moving while everyone else sits or stands still.

Vary Physical Activity.   When planning the curriculum, teachers should plan one or two activities daily that involve gross motor skills and another one or two activities that involve fine motor skills. Caregivers might plan an obstacle course one day, like Ms. Sanchez's (see the "Focus on Activities" feature in this chapter), sand play the next, a group tricycle ride on another day, and outdoor painting or doll washing on the fourth day. As with all curriculum activities, these activities should be geared to the abilities and interests of the children so that the children will find them challenging and fun but not too difficult.

Encourage Self-Efficacy, Not Competition.   Young children should have opportunities to feel successful, not to compare themselves with others. Preschoolers should be encouraged to play cooperative rather than competitive games. For example, a teacher might provide a group of four or five youngsters with a balloon and demonstrate for them how to bat the balloon back and forth among themselves, keeping it in the air as long as possible. Another technique for encouraging cooperative play and avoiding competitiveness is to group together children who have the same level of skill at a specific activity, such as balancing on a low beam. With such grouping, no one stands out either as being a star or as being incompetent.

In order to encourage self-efficacy, preschool teachers also should avoid hurrying children through physical play. Young children need plenty of time to practice new skills. Teachers always should be on the lookout for children who hang back or refuse to participate. Often, these children just need encouragement to try the activity, time to practice the skill on their own, and a patient teacher who is willing to act as a model or practice partner. Once children have the necessary guidance and feel competent at performing a skill, they will eagerly join other children in activities involving the skill.

Teachers also should avoid reinforcing gender stereotypes about physical abilities. As stated earlier, at the preschool level, girls and boys do not differ markedly in their physical abilities. However, girls often are taught from an early age to be quiet and cooperative. Preschool girls should not be discouraged from participating in vigorous physical activities or from being as loud and boisterous as the boys. Nor should they be treated as if they were less physically competent than boys. On the contrary, girls may need extra encouragement to participate, so that they can have the opportunities to practice that they need to become physically competent.

Demonstrate, Model, and Guide.   Preschool teachers should understand that young children often need guidance in learning new physical skills. As Wickstrom points out in his theory of physical development, many physical skills require a combination of movements in sequence or simultaneous with one another. It is usually easier and more effective for the teacher to demonstrate each of the motions required to carry out a particular skill than to try to describe them. For example, the long jump involves pumping the arms, leaping into the air, drawing the legs together, landing with both feet together in front of the body, and then pulling the body forward. Once the teacher has demonstrated the individual motions, the children can imitate the teacher's actions while the teacher observes and makes suggestions for increased success.

When teaching such physical skills as throwing, catching, or hitting a ball, preschool teachers should try to focus on the correct movements or process rather than the outcome. When a youngster learns the fundamental motor skills necessary to throw a ball, his or her distance, accuracy, and speed will improve with practice. Children should gain feelings of competence during the process of learning and should not attach "being successful" only to a completed outcome.

Modeling physical activity means that caregivers participate in physical activities themselves and that they emphasize the benefits of those activities to the children. Preschoolers need to see that adults routinely incorporate physical activity into their own lives. Teachers can talk to children about their own physical activities and explain how those activities help keep them healthy and energetic.

Guidance includes providing encouragement to children who are learning new skills. Teachers should provide specific, positive feedback when they see children making an effort to master a skill or to improve their abilities. Such comments as "I've never seen you climb so high" and "You ran much faster today than you did last week" help children measure their progress against their own past efforts rather than comparing it with someone else's.

Teachers also should be specific when making suggestions about how children can improve their skills. Saying "If you bend your knees a little before you kick the ball, it will help you keep your balance" is more helpful than the offhand remark "Keep trying and you'll improve."

Physical Development from the Inside Out

The physical curriculum needs to address more than the development of gross and fine motor skills. It also should include activities that help preschoolers learn about the importance of good nutrition. The curriculum should focus on such subjects as healthy eating habits; avoiding illness and disease by practicing good hygiene; and learning how to protect oneself from physical danger. Caregivers, along with parents, play important roles in teaching children about these elements of physical growth and development.

The Benefits of Nutrition Education

An important element of the physical curriculum is nutrition education. More and more preschools are incorporating units and activities to help children learn about food and start healthy eating habits early in life. Head Start has emphasized nutrition education and cultural food patterns in its curriculum since 1965.

Sound nutrition is especially important to young children whose bodies are growing and developing at a rapid rate, adding new bone, muscle, and tissue almost daily. Good nutrition is crucial to maintaining good health and promoting optimal physical development. The body must receive an adequate amount of certain nutrients—vitamins, minerals, proteins, carbohydrates, fats, and water—in order to function efficiently, to grow, and to repair damaged cells and tissues. Proper nutrition also helps children stay alert and enhances their ability to learn (Herr & Morse, 1982).

Teaching young children about nutrition has some additional benefits. When children learn about the nutritional value of various foods, they are more likely to accept new foods (Lamb, 1969) and more likely to accept foods that they previously would not eat (Harrill, Smith, & Gangever, 1972). Further, when children learn and practice sound nutrition early in life, they may reduce their risk of chronic diseases later in life (Ahrnes & Connor,

FOCUS ON Cultural Diversity

Snacks Inspired by the Backgrounds of Children

Food and nutrition activities, including snack time, can help preschoolers learn about typical foods from various cultures. Teachers can easily implement a cultural snack program as part of the curriculum. The first step is to make a survey of the backgrounds of the children. If the class is fairly homogeneous, the teacher could select various cultures to serve as inspiration for snacks throughout the year.

Recipe ideas may come from children's parents or from international cookbooks in the public library. Recipes that are mild-flavored are best, and teachers should remember that young children like bite-size pieces they can pick up with their hands.

The teacher might choose a common food item, such as bread. Children could sample challah, Jewish American braided egg bread; croissants, buttery, flaky French rolls; tortillas, thin, corn Mexican pancakes; and pita, round, flattened Middle Eastern bread. They also could try white or wheat bread, two American classics. The teacher might put out one or two different spreads, such as peanut butter or jelly, for the children to put on the bread pieces.

By sampling different examples of the same type of food, children will have the opportunity to see cultural differences firsthand. The teacher can help the children compare and contrast by asking such questions as "Which breads are soft?," "Which breads have a hard crust?," and "Which breads are flat like a pancake?"

It is also important for preschool teachers to point out to young children that even though tortillas are traditional in Mexico, for example, most Mexican Americans eat other types of bread as well. The teacher might ask about what the children themselves eat—for instance, "Do you eat only hamburgers every day? Of course not." This type of discussion helps children understand that everyone can make and enjoy foods from different cultures.

1979). Suggestions for including nutrition education activities in the curriculum appear later in this chapter.

Preschool teachers should be aware that malnutrition in the United States usually does not result from a lack of food. It results from too much of the wrong kind of food or too few nutrient-rich foods. In the United States, the two most common effects of malnutrition are tooth decay, caused by eating too much sugar, and iron-deficiency anemia, resulting from a lack of iron-rich foods. Early childhood professionals should include dental health activities in the curriculum and should learn to recognize the most obvious symptoms of iron deficiency—lethargy, a pale complexion, and low resistance to colds and other common illnesses.

Caregivers should be aware of other signs of dietary deficiencies as well. These signs include irritability, fatigue, chronic illness, an inability to concentrate, and a craving for sweets. When caregivers detect these symptoms in a child, they should discuss the situation with the child's parents and suggest a medical examination.

The physical curriculum includes health topics that are meaningful and relevant to the children's age group, needs, and interests. These three-year-olds are learning about the importance of handwashing.

The Importance of Hygiene

Learning good hygiene habits is another important part of the physical curriculum. *Hygiene* is the science of preventing the spread of diseases. It is very important for both adults and children to practice good hygiene in preschool settings because of the potential for spreading communicable diseases to large numbers of people. Caregivers should explain to young children the reasons for such good hygiene habits as washing hands after using the toilet and before handling food, keeping the hands away from the mouth and nose, sneezing or coughing into one's elbow (instead of into the hand to keep germs from being transferred from hands), dressing appropriately for the weather, and brushing the teeth after eating.

Teaching hygiene to children can include planned activities, group discussions, field trips to a dentist's office or a hospital, and visits from various health professionals. A wide variety of materials and props related to health education is available from public health agencies and school suppliers. Teachers can address healthy habits with young children through puppet shows, storytelling, and dramatic play. For example, after a classroom visit by a dentist, the teacher might provide simple props—such as a flashlight, lab coat, "X-ray" apron, and a chair—for the dramatic play area so that the children can play "dentist's office."

One of the best ways to teach hygiene is by example. For instance, if a teacher is about to conduct a cooking project, he or she should first lead the children in washing their hands while discussing the importance of hand-washing for killing germs. In addition, caregivers must be scrupulous about washing their own hands thoroughly after diapering each child, assisting a child with toileting, or helping children wipe runny noses or blowing their own noses.

Preschools' policy statements always should require that children be fully immunized against the common childhood diseases. In addition, the director and teachers should enforce a policy of sending sick children home or isolating them from other children.

Learning about Physical Safety

Physical safety is another important part of the physical curriculum. Although the teacher's role in safeguarding the preschool environment and supervising children was discussed in Chapter 5, an important aspect of physical safety is teaching children to watch out for their own safety. Teachers must train them to follow safety rules, explaining why these rules are important, and preparing them to anticipate danger in a wide variety of situations. Curriculum activities should include teaching children about fire safety, playground safety, traffic safety, water safety, poison safety, and personal safety, such as avoiding strangers.

Teachers enforce the preschool's set of safety rules for children at all times. Rules for the playground cover safe practices, such as allowing only one child on the slide at a time, having children use both hands to climb on climbing equipment, and having them stay away from moving swings.

Preschool teachers also need to provide safety guidelines for children regarding everyday life situations that can pose danger. Examples of such guidelines include instructions for crossing streets with an adult, interpreting traffic signals, leaving the building in the event of a fire, and recognizing poisonous plants indoors and outdoors. Children need to understand how these rules and guidelines keep them safe, and they also require opportunities to practice safe behavior. Preschools should hold fire drills at unexpected times. Teachers should make room in the curriculum for safety activities, inviting classroom visitors such as firefighters, and field trips such as a tour of a local firehouse. In addition, art activities, storytelling, and dramatic play can all be tailored to teach specific safety rules.

Applications

Preschool teachers need to be actively involved in guiding and fostering the physical development of the children in their program. They should provide appropriate equipment and materials and organize activities that offer practice in specific gross and fine motor skills. Effective teachers also demonstrate or model specific movements or techniques. Such guidance includes encouraging shy or physically inactive youngsters to participate in physical activities in which they can experience success.

Developing Physical Competence

In their ongoing study of physical development, Vern Seefeldt and John Haubenstricker have studied three main types of physical skills in young children (Seefeldt, 1980). *Body management skills* (sometimes called *non-locomotor skills*) are those in which children must handle or control the body but do not travel anywhere—such as balancing, twisting, turning, or bending. *Locomotor skills* move the body from one place to another—such as walking, running, or jumping in various directions. *Manipulative skills* (sometimes called *object control skills*) involve throwing or catching an item such as a ball, a beanbag, or a sponge shape. In planning your physical curriculum, it is important to make sure that activities address these skills.

Look for creative ways to use the classroom and playground equipment to teach specific skills. For example, draw a *V* in the dirt or on a soft surface, and have the children practice the long jump across the two lines. Letting the children choose for themselves where to jump across increases their feelings of self-efficacy and discourages competition (Hildebrand, 1991). To teach another specific skill, set up a zigzag line of hollow blocks or tires as "stepping stones" for children to practice balancing while walking.

Always look for ways to give specific guidance. For example, when throwing a ball, young children often step off with the leg on the same side of the body as the arm they are throwing with, and the ball goes off sharply to one side. Show them the helpfulness of stepping off with the opposite leg. Also, remember that young children throw best using relatively small objects but catch best using large ones (Arnheim & Sinclair, 1979). As the children improve each motor skill, increase the difficulty of the activity progressively.

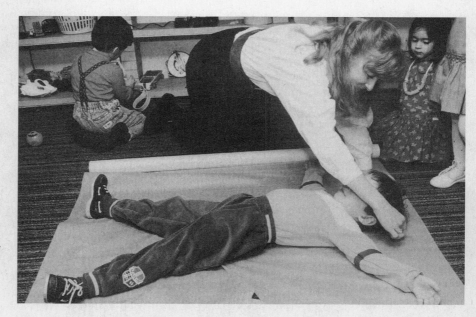

A common curriculum activity involves helping children draw outlines of their bodies on paper and letting them draw on facial features, hair, and other features. This activity helps children learn to respect the human body and feel proud of their own bodies.

Too often, preschool teachers forget that developing fine motor skills is an essential part of the physical curriculum as well. Be sure to include activities every day that develop fine motor skills, especially eye-hand coordination. Puzzles, stringing beads, peg boards, dressing dolls, blocks, drawing, coloring, picking up food or other items with tongs, using scissors and pencils, and other manipulative activities and objects all help develop fine motor skills and provide practice in eye-hand coordination.

Preschoolers need lots of practice with prewriting and scissor skills in particular. They tend to use the whole arm and shoulder and thus experience tension and fatigue—instead of using just the hand and fingers. Gripping practice, first with large writing objects, then gradually with smaller ones, will help preschoolers begin the task of handwriting. Although preschoolers benefit from teachers' showing them the correct form for gripping writing implements, they are too young to be directed into a writing mode. See "For Further Information" for sourcebooks that describe games, songs, and activities to teach various gross and fine motor skills.

Respecting the Human Body

Preschoolers are still learning about their bodies and the names of body parts. In addition, they are developing body awareness, including learning respect for the human body. Preschool teachers should take advantage of young children's great interest in what they look like and in how their bodies function to foster respect for the body. Toilet training is an important first step in learning body awareness. Preschoolers are generally fascinated with skin color, hair texture, and heartbeats. They also are very interested in physical processes, such as how cuts and bruises heal and how babies are born.

Your curricular activities should reflect the fact that preschoolers are beginning to coordinate two perspectives about their own bodies: how others see them outwardly—that is, how they look, feel, sound, and smell—and how the body works inside (Smith, 1982). Many games and creative movement exercises can teach children about their body parts and body processes. For example, one common activity that children enjoy involves drawing each other's outlines on large sheets of paper or newsprint, then painting or coloring in their own features and skin color within their outline. It is important to remember that when you teach children about nutrition, hygiene, and personal safety, you also are teaching them to respect their bodies.

Learning about Health and Safety

It is best to choose health and safety topics for preschoolers that are based on their immediate needs and interests. For example, three- and four-year-olds can learn about the importance of sneezing or coughing into the elbow instead of the hand, but they will not be able to understand how antibiotics fight infection. Preschoolers enjoy learning about dental health; safety in the home, car, and playground; fire and poison prevention; cleanliness; good

Learning about nutritious foods is easy when you get to eat the results! This group of four-year-olds is making oatmeal cookies for a snack.

posture; the role of sleep; and dressing appropriately for the weather (Marotz, Rush, & Cross, 1989).

Remember that hands-on experiences help reinforce concepts. Look for opportunities to incorporate health and safety education into dramatic play. For example, create "streets" with masking tape on which children can practice being pedestrians or drivers. Role-playing can include learning about "strangers" and "safe touching." The curriculum also can address health and safety in art activities—for example, learning the symbol for poison, or making traffic lights out of colored paper—and doll play—such as giving dolls a bath. Classroom visitors might include a nutritionist or a dance instructor. Activities such as growing vegetable seeds and caring for animals also contribute to learning about health and safety topics. See "For Further Information" for curriculum guides and resource books on teaching health and safety concepts to preschoolers.

Integrating Food into the Curriculum

One of the most effective ways to educate preschoolers about nutrition is to serve them nutritious snacks and meals rich in vitamins, minerals, proteins, and carbohydrates. Preschool menus should avoid foods that are high in fat, sugar, salt, chocolate, and caffeine. Children can develop cravings for the taste of fat, sugar, and salt, but too much of these nutrients contributes to obesity, hypertension (high blood pressure), and heart disease.

Serve children foods that vary in taste, color, and texture. Including a wide variety of foods in the daily diet is the best way to ensure that children receive adequate amounts of the vitamins and minerals they need. Choose foods in accordance with the U. S. Department of Agriculture's Food Guide Pyramid, published in 1992 (see Figure 7.2). Remember that preschoolers

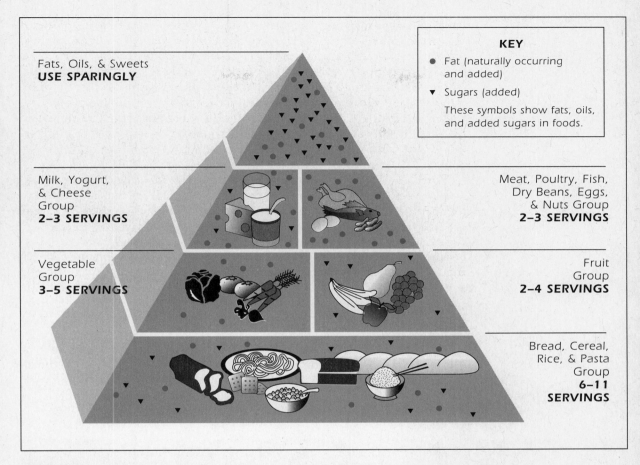

FIGURE 7.2　**Food Guide Pyramid.** A guide to daily food choices. *Source:* U. S. Department of Agriculture, Washington, D. C.

like foods to be served lukewarm, not extremely cold or hot. They especially like bite-size foods they can eat with their fingers (however, watch out for small pieces that young children can choke on). Whenever possible, snacks and meals should reflect various cultures represented by children in the classroom.

Your curriculum should include opportunities for children to make their own snacks and to cook simple dishes. These activities can introduce new foods and create opportunities to talk about where foods come from. If you use eggs in a recipe, for example, you could describe how hens lay eggs. Or if you use apples, you can talk about how apples grow on trees and the many varieties of apples. Cooking provides an opportunity for children to practice fine motor skills, such as measuring, chopping, peeling, sifting, mixing, pouring, dividing, and cutting. It also creates opportunities to practice several important cognitive and perceptual skills—such as following a sequence of steps, counting, learning about quantities, differentiating between sweet and sour tastes and various textures of food, and experiencing cause and effect by mixing and cooking ingredients. In addition, cooking fosters social skills, such as working together and taking turns.

Look for recipes that involve several different tasks, and make sure that everyone in the group has a chance to help with one or more of the steps involved. Make sure that the recipe will make a sufficient amount for all children to sample. Children love to taste test their recipes as they go along and to eat the results once the food has been cooked. See "For Further Information" for a sampling of nutrition curriculum guides and cooking activity books.

Nutrition education in the preschool curriculum does not have to be limited to snack making and cooking projects. Preschool teachers should strive to incorporate nutrition activities into all curriculum areas (Herr & Morse, 1982). For example, to foster sensory development, have children compare the scents and textures of different fruits, such as apples, oranges, and peaches. Language arts activities can include making name/picture cards of common foods or picking out foods in different storybooks. Food-oriented activities to practice premathematics and other cognitive skills can include sorting and matching vegetables, or weighing or arranging them from smallest to largest. To practice social skills, turn the dramatic play area into a lemonade stand or a restaurant.

As you put together your daily or weekly curriculum, think about how health, safety, and nutrition topics relate to the various areas of child development and how they can be incorporated in all activity areas, indoors and out. Such a strategy is much more effective than addressing these topics only in weeklong themes or isolated projects.

CHAPTER 7   REVIEW

SUMMARY

- Children's bodies undergo many physical changes that help them master gross motor skills (such as running, jumping, and balance) and fine motor skills (such as grasping and eye-hand coordination).
- In planning their curriculum, preschool teachers need to pay as much attention to physical development as to other areas such as cognitive and social development.
- Arnold Gesell believed that motor skills evolve in an orderly sequence as children's bodies mature. Ralph L. Wickstrom theorized that children master motor skills by progressing through a series of substages.
- Exercise helps growing bodies develop and function effectively while providing opportunities to practice motor skills. Exercise also is important for overall health and fitness.
- Activities to promote the development of large motor skills can take place

indoors as well as outdoors. Likewise, fine motor skill activities can take place outdoors as well as indoors.

- To integrate physical activity into the preschool curriculum, teachers provide developmentally appropriate equipment and toys to encourage children to practice motor skills during free play, organize games and activities daily that utilize large and small motor skills, and vary activities to maintain interest.
- Teachers seek out and provide guidance and encouragement to children who are reluctant to participate in physical activities.
- Caregivers avoid reinforcing gender stereotypes as they relate to physical abilities.
- Caregivers demonstrate motor skills, act as role models by participating in physical activities themselves, and provide guidance and positive feedback to children struggling to master new skills.
- During physical activities, teachers encourage cooperative play and deemphasize competition. They do not compare children with one another and measure children's progress only against their own past efforts.
- Components of a physical curriculum include learning about nutrition and a variety of foods, good hygiene habits, and safety rules.
- Nutrition education activities can be integrated into the curriculum through snacks and in cooking projects.
- Early childhood professionals choose health and safety topics for preschoolers based on the children's immediate needs and interests.
- Food, health, and safety topics also are incorporated into language arts, science, art, and dramatic play activities and not relegated to weeklong themes or individual projects.

ACQUIRING KNOWLEDGE

1. How does the size of a child's head reflect maturation?
2. Why does a child's strength increase during the third to sixth years?
3. How do the physical skills of boys and girls differ in the preschool years?
4. What patterns of development are described by the cephalocaudal and the proximodistal principles?
5. Give an example of how the proximodistal principle can be observed.
6. What is the main focus of Gesell's work?
7. Describe Wickstrom's theory of physical development.
8. Why is it essential for the preschool curriculum to include activities that help young children master fundamental motor skills?
9. What are some of the benefits of physical exercise for preschoolers?
10. What are some signs that can help a teacher recognize children who are developing physical competence on their own and children who may need guidance or encouragement?
11. How can a teacher help a child who is less physically active?

12. How are a child's body image and self-concept related?
13. What are some strategies that a teacher can use to help children develop a positive body image?
14. What kinds of fundamental motor skills can be developed through structured outdoor play activities?
15. Give some examples of activities that might occur during free outdoor play.
16. How does rough-and-tumble play differ from aggressive behavior?
17. Describe some indoor activities that can be used to develop gross motor skills. How can these activities be done safely?
18. How can a teacher encourage self-efficacy rather than competition?
19. What guidelines should a teacher follow when helping preschoolers learn a new physical skill?
20. What are the most common forms of malnutrition in the United States? How can a preschool curriculum address these problems?
21. Describe how hygiene can be taught through planned and unplanned activities.
22. Describe the three categories Haubenstricker uses to classify physical skills.
23. What kinds of activities help children develop fine motor skills?
24. What are some ways teachers can integrate facts about nutrition into the preschool curriculum?

THINKING CRITICALLY

1. Both children and adults benefit from exercise, but exercise means different things where children are concerned. How do you think children's exercise differs from adults' exercise? Give examples of how exercise benefits both children and adults.
2. Observation of children and the environment is an important tool for evaluating any part of a curriculum. What inferences might a teacher make from noticing that one piece of playground equipment is always crowded while another is never used?
3. Dramatic play is a useful activity for helping children explore and process information about health and safety. Suggest several props that could be placed in a dramatic play area that would encourage children to explore health and safety issues. Describe the types of dramatic play that might result.
4. Physical and cognitive skills are developed together by many activities. Suggest an activity that develops both physical and cognitive skills, and describe how it supports a child's physical development.

OBSERVATIONS AND APPLICATIONS

1. Observe children engaged in outdoor play at a preschool. Are the activities structured, such as in an obstacle course or an organized game, or are they unstructured, such as in free play? Describe several of the activities. List the gross and fine motor skills required by each activity. Which

require a combination of skills? In what ways is the teacher involved in the physical activity of the children?

2. Three-year-old Avery has just joined your preschool class. He has refused to play outside in the playground and just sits on the ground. How might you help Avery become more confident and more physically active?

3. Your preschool's playground includes a slide with a ladder, climbing equipment, a "tree house" structure, a tire swing, and a swing set. In preparation for the children's use, you know that it will be important to establish some rules for safety. What rules will you establish? (There are at least 10–15 children playing at any one time.)

FOR FURTHER INFORMATION

Books and Journal Articles

Herr, J., & Morse, W. (1992). Food for thought: Nutrition education for young children. In J. Brown (Ed.), *Curriculum planning for young children*. Washington, DC: National Association for the Education of Young Children.

Javernick, E. (1988). Johnny's not jumping: Can we help obese children? *Young Children, 43*(2), 18–23.

Kostelnik, M. J., Soderman, A. K., & Whiren, A. P. (1993). *Developmentally appropriate programs in early childhood education*. (Chapter 7: The Physical Domain). New York: Macmillan.

McCracken, J. B. (1988). *Keeping healthy: Parents, teachers, and children*. Washington, DC: National Association for the Education of Young Children.

Pellegrini, A. D., & Permutter, J. C. (1988). Rough and tumble play on the elementary school playground. *Young Children, 43*(2), 14–17.

Wickstrom, R. L. (1983). *Fundamental motor patterns* (3rd ed.). Philadelphia: Lea & Febiger.

Curriculum and Resource Guides

Children riding on sidewalks safely. (1987). Washington, DC: National Association for the Education of Young Children.

Ferreira, N. (1982). *Learning through cooking: A cooking program for children from two to ten*.

Increasing safety awareness of preschoolers through a safety education program. (1989). ERIC Document Reproduction Service #310880.

Tharlet, E. (1987). *The little cooks: Recipes from around the world for boys and girls*. New York: UNICEF.

Veitch, B., & Harms, T. (1991). *Cook and learn: Pictorial single portion recipes*. Reading, MA: Addison-Wesley.

Walk in traffic safety. (1990). Washington, DC: National Association for the Education of Young Children.

We love you—Buckle up! (1987). Washington, DC: National Association for the Education of Young Children.

Whitener, C. B., & Keeling, M. H. (1984). Nutrition education for young children: Strategies and activities. Englewood Cliffs, NJ: Prentice Hall.

Emotional Development

OBJECTIVES

Studying this chapter
will enable you to

- Explain the first three stages of
  Erikson's theory of psychosocial
  development
- Describe how teachers can foster
  self-esteem
- Discuss some of the ways that
  caregivers can help children
  express their feelings and handle
  stress constructively
- Explain how teachers can
  encourage young children to
  develop empathy toward others
- List several strategies for creating a
  supportive emotional environment in the preschool setting

CHAPTER TERMS

autonomy versus shame and doubt
bibliotherapy
competence
egocentrism
empathy
encouragement
initiative versus guilt
praise
redirection
self-report
stress
trust versus mistrust
will

FOUR-YEAR-OLD Emily was playing happily by herself in the sandbox with a dump truck and shovel as three-year-old Dennis looked on.

Suddenly, Dennis lunged forward, grabbing the truck out of Emily's hands.

"No!" screamed Emily, snatching the truck back and giving Dennis a push that sent him sprawling backward.

As Dennis burst into tears, the children's teacher, Mrs. Foster, rushed over to the sandbox.

"Emily pushed me!" Dennis told her between sobs.

"He took my truck," Emily responded.

"I think I understand how you feel, Emily. You are very angry because Dennis took the truck away from you, aren't you?"

"Yes," Emily said. "I had it first!"

"And Dennis, you really want the truck, don't you, and you don't want to wait until Emily is done with it?"

Dennis nodded, his sobs subsiding.

"Emily, even though I know you're angry, you are not allowed to hit or push other children here because you could hurt somebody. Do you understand this rule?"

Emily just nodded.

"Let's talk about how you both can work this out. Emily, what do you think we might do?"

After a few moments, Emily said, "I'll let him play with me if he doesn't grab. He can dig the driveway of my new house." She pointed to the place where she was playing in the sandbox.

"How does that sound, Dennis?" asked Mrs. Foster.

Dennis thought silently and then said, "Well, OK, but I want to dig the driveway by myself. Then we can put your truck in it."

Preschoolers experience a full range of emotions—joy, sorrow, love, anger, fear, pride, happiness. Their feelings can be intense, but they do not always know how to express them. In many cases, they keep their feelings bottled up inside, or they act out in negative ways because they have not yet learned how to express themselves appropriately. For example, Dennis may have snatched Emily's truck simply because he does not yet have the language skills to express his own desire for it. Or he may still have been angry because his big sister grabbed something from him that morning before he came to preschool. When Emily pushed Dennis, it was a physical response to feeling angry or threatened. In addition, both Dennis and Emily are still of an age when children think primarily of their own needs and wants and have some difficulty understanding a situation from another's point of view—a characteristic that is referred to as *egocentrism.* This chapter discusses the opportunities teachers have to use the classroom environment and the curriculum to teach children about different emotions, how to express emotions, and how to develop the ability to understand how others feel.

By the time children enter preschool, most are curious, enthusiastic, self-confident beings ready to strike out on their own. As they become more aware of their independence, and as their cognitive and physical skills develop further, they want to do more things for themselves and to make their own decisions. All these changes are part of the normal process of developing self-esteem, the cornerstone of emotional health. This chapter also explains how teachers can use curriculum to help children develop self-esteem and learn how to express emotions in a positive way.

The Development of Self-esteem

First discussed in Chapter 3, self-esteem is a person's perception or judgment of his or her own self worth. People with high self-esteem feel confident of their abilities to learn and to do things. They believe that they are well-liked by others, and they feel that they are valuable contributors to their family, school, community, or society. Preschool teachers need to understand that preschoolers primarily form attitudes about themselves based on the reactions they receive from others, particularly from adults. The opinions and responses of parents, teachers, and other adults greatly influence how children perceive themselves. When parents or caregivers tell children that they are helpful, or loved, or bothersome, or that they "get in the way," children will believe them. It is important, therefore, for child care providers to interact with and respond to children in ways that will increase their feelings of self-esteem. For example, caregivers should provide materials for children that are age-appropriate and should ensure that children are given some tasks that they can master. These strategies will help individual children feel a sense of personal accomplishment. An example is watering their own plants (a common activity in Montessori schools).

Why Is Self-esteem Important?

Self-esteem strongly affects whether children perceive themselves to be successful or inadequate. Children with high self-esteem are likely to explore freely, take risks, confront new challenges, adapt easily to change, and be motivated to learn. Children with low self-esteem are fearful and timid, have little faith in their ability to do things, are easily frustrated, and are intimidated by new situations. In addition, self-esteem colors children's views not only of themselves but of how they perceive the world. Children with high self-esteem generally see their world as an interesting, exciting place full of new experiences, possibilities, and challenges. Children with low self-esteem may often see the world as a threatening place with obstacles and dangers.

A teacher's words of encouragement can help a child feel confident and increase the child's concentration and patience. One-on-one attention from the teacher helps this five-year-old use fine motor skills to manage a sticky project.

Long-term Effects of Low Self-esteem. Once children have formed attitudes and beliefs about themselves, changing those ideas later in life is difficult. Adults need to begin helping children develop a strong sense of self-worth from birth onward, and early childhood educators can contribute to this process through the preschool years. The long-term effects of low self-esteem can be devastating. Research has shown that children with low self-worth focus on failure rather than on success and see new experiences as problems instead of challenges (Smith, 1988). When children come to believe that they are failures, that belief can generate a self-fulfilling prophecy. If a child is told that she is dumb in mathematics, she may believe that she is dumb throughout her school career, and she may give up even trying to master mathematics skills.

The effects of low self-esteem can carry on into adolescence and adulthood. Teenagers with feelings of low self-worth perform poorly in school and often drop out. Because they tend to blame others for their failings, they also develop attitudes of prejudice (Bagley, Verma, Mallick, & Young, 1979). Research shows that they may feel so poorly about themselves that they stop taking care of their health and well-being and may turn to drug and alcohol abuse and crime (Mecca, Smelser, & Vasconcellos, 1989). In addition, this research found that teenage girls with poor self-esteem are more likely to become pregnant than those with high self-esteem.

Competence and Self-esteem. *Competence* is the ability to accomplish tasks and succeed at endeavors. When early childhood educators speak of "competent children," they mean children who exhibit the skills that are

FOCUS ON *Cultural Diversity*

Cultural Influences on a Child's Sense of Self

In the United States, when parents want children to finish their dinners, they are likely to point out that there are starving children in the world who do not have such nice dinners. But in Japan, parents instead tell their children how hard a farmer worked to produce the food and how badly he will feel if it is not eaten.

Most cultures define the self with one of two divergent views: the independent view and the interdependent view. The *independent* view focuses on the individual and his or her accomplishments. This view is generally held by Americans and by many Western Europeans. The *interdependent* view focuses on the "self-in-relation-to-others" and values the group over the individual. Many Asian, African, Latin American, and Southern European cultures emphasize interdependence rather than independence.

How do these different views of the self influence how preschoolers display emotions? In cultures with an independent view, emotions that focus on the individual such as anger, pride, and frustration are displayed frequently.

In cultures with an interdependent view, emotions such as sympathy and shame predominate. These emotions are focused on or involve others as well as the self.

Consider one emotion—anger—from these two perspectives. People often display anger in "independent" cultures, but not in "interdependent" cultures. In "interdependent" cultures, people believe that expressions of anger would disturb the social harmony that is a cultural norm. For example, people in some Eskimo cultures are known for not expressing, or even discussing, anger. When these people observe angry behavior in foreigners, they consider it childish.

It is helpful for caregivers to learn about the different ways cultural backgrounds influence the emotional development of young children. When a child has trouble expressing anger or gets very frustrated when working with others, this behavior may stem from her cultural background as well as other factors.

typical for their age and stage of development. Competence nurtures self-esteem because competent children feel good about themselves and trust in their ability to make choices and do things for themselves. Even more important, when children feel competent, they do not have to depend on others to tell them that they are worthwhile and valued individuals. Every time they complete a task or project, they experience success and they are rewarded with the reinforcement of their own abilities. They carry that knowledge inside themselves—in effect, internalizing their self-esteem. For example, a child may feel that he is a good builder with blocks, not because his teacher has told him so but because he can see for himself, for example, that he can build a two-story doghouse that will not fall down when the dog goes inside.

In a longitudinal study begun in 1973 called the Harvard Preschool Project, Burton White and his associates developed a list of criteria, based on research and observations, of competence for young children. Competent three-year-olds, they concluded, can express both affection and anger to their peers and teachers in acceptable ways. They also can perform a variety of physical, social, and cognitive tasks—including getting and maintaining the attention of adults, conversing, pretending, gaining information, sensing consequences, leading and following peers, planning and carrying out activities with several steps, and perceiving the point of view of others (White, Kaban, Attanucci, & Shapiro, 1973). In the scenario at the beginning of the chapter, three-year-old Dennis was not yet competent in all these areas.

The researchers also developed guidelines for parents and other caregivers to use in helping children achieve competence. These guidelines include providing a safe and stimulating environment for children to explore, offering opportunities for social interaction, responding to children with encouragement, assistance, and enthusiasm, and holding frequent conversations with children to stimulate language development.

External Influences on Self-esteem

While children are developing internal resources for generating self-esteem, these feelings need to be nurtured externally by their parents and caregivers. Preschoolers, just like adults, need ongoing positive reinforcement and encouragement as they develop new skills. What teachers say to children and how they say it directly affect whether or not children perceive themselves as worthy and competent (Kostelnik, Stein, & Whiren, 1988).

Traditionally, preschool teachers have used praise to help children build self-esteem. _Praise_ is a positive statement intended to reward and reinforce what is judged by the person giving the praise as appropriate behavior. However, several studies in the 1970s and 1980s concluded that praise actually can be ineffective or even self-defeating. For example, one study found that, in some cases, excessive praise lowered children's expectations of success (Meyer, 1979), whereas another study found that praise can create anxiety and defensiveness in children (Ginott, 1972). Many early childhood educators now distinguish between praise and encouragement. Praise is characterized by such statements as "Good work," "That's wonderful," and "What a good girl you are." Praise is very general, does not provide children with much useful information, often sounds insincere, and implies unfavorable comparisons. For example, when a teacher says, "Bobby is being so good because he is standing in line quietly," she is implying that everyone else is failing in that task.

Encouragement, also called effective praise, is specific, sincere, direct, and informative. It avoids using such general labels as "good" or "terrific," and such phrases as "You are such a good boy because. . . ." Encouragement avoids comparing one child with another or making judgments about the quality of a child's product. Instead, encouragement focuses on the child's persistence, effort, and increasing competence in performing a task (Hitz & Driscoll, 1988). For example, if a child comes to his teacher with a freshly finished painting, the teacher might say, "You used a lot of pretty colors in that painting," or "I can see how much work you put into this picture." When a child learns to pump herself on the swings, words of encouragement from her teacher might be, "It must make you feel very proud to be able to swing yourself," or "You were able to swing higher than you ever did before." Encouragement also is used to promote social skills. A child who shares a toy can be told, "Maria really appreciated it when you let her play with the bear you brought from home."

In addition to providing encouragement to children, preschool teachers and child care providers can foster initiative and promote self-esteem in other ways. Providing opportunities every day for children to perform tasks for and by themselves and to practice skills helps children perform these tasks well. However, just providing opportunities is not enough. It is important for preschool teachers to understand that different children excel at different activities. The curriculum, therefore, should provide a wide variety of activities to explore. Teachers should help children try many different activities to find those that challenge them and make them feel competent. It is important, too, for teachers to encourage children to try activities that counter gender bias. For example, boys should be encouraged to spend time in the housekeeping area putting baby to bed, or to participate in cooking activities. Girls should be encouraged to play catch and to learn how to throw a ball or climb the jungle gym.

Early childhood educators also should be aware that some teaching practices may lower self-esteem. For example, comparing one child with another can cause low self-esteem in one of the two children. Instead, teachers should compare a child's current (improved) performance only with that child's past performance, focusing on progress achieved. Also, rushing preschoolers into tasks for which they are not yet developmentally ready, such as reading or competing in organized sports, can set children up for failure and low self-esteem. Child care providers should focus primarily on effort and action, not outcome. When a three-year-old makes an enormous effort to help set the table but fails to place a napkin at every plate, the teacher should praise the effort and avoid criticizing the deficiency. Criticizing very young children only promotes feelings of doubt, shame, and guilt and is counterproductive to the development of autonomy and initiative. Criticism also delivers the message to children that they are incompetent and unworthy. Teachers should be aware that ignoring a child's efforts can have a negative effect. When children are criticized, at least they know that they have been noticed.

The Contributions of Erik Erikson

In the 1960s, psychoanalyst Erik Erikson established what he called the "Eight Stages of Man" (Erikson, 1963). These stages describe the process through which children and adults achieve and maintain emotional health over the course of their lives. Knowledge of the first three stages helps early childhood educators understand the emotional needs of young children. It also helps educators interact sensitively and effectively with individual children and ensure that the curriculum responds to children's emotional needs.

Trust versus Mistrust

The first stage, _trust versus mistrust_, occurs in infancy. According to Erikson, when infants are well cared for, they learn to trust that caregivers will satisfy their needs and keep them safe. They learn that the immediate world around them is a predictable and consistent place. They also learn to trust that they can make their needs and wants known. If they cry, they will be fed or have their diapers changed. When they are held, the hands that hold them are gentle but strong and reliable. Conversely, infants who are not well cared for and whose needs are not always met learn to mistrust their world. They perceive that the world is an unpredictable and even chaotic place where they are not safe, or where they may go hungry or be left cold or wet for a long time, or where they may sometimes be hurt by the same hands that cradle and comfort them. Learning to trust is the crucial first step in developing a sense of identity and self-worth (Erikson, 1963).

Erikson was careful to point out that both sides of the conflict in this stage are important for growth. For example, during the trust-versus-mistrust stage, some mistrust is healthy. A baby who is weaned or for whom night feedings are discontinued will learn that some deprivation is possible. He can still trust he will be fed. The point for each stage is that the balance should favor the positive outcome. Also, the success of any stage depends on the resolution of the previous stage.

Autonomy versus Shame and Doubt

Erikson's second stage, called _autonomy versus shame and doubt_, occurs between the ages of one and three, when children begin to assert their "separateness" from their primary caregivers. For example, children begin to want to do things on their own, such as to feed themselves.

Also during this period, children learn the skill of holding on and letting go, literally and figuratively. During this stage, children learn to control their bowels and bladder and begin the process of toilet training. As toddlers begin to differentiate between themselves and others, they begin to assert themselves and develop _will_, the desire to control or direct the events in their lives. They want to make their own choices and decisions and to do things for themselves even though they may not do them very well. For example, two-year-olds want to feed and dress themselves, push their strollers, and open and close doors. On the other hand, they almost never want to do what their parents want them to do, and they say "no" often. This refusal to cooperate is one way that toddlers establish their individuality and test their newfound ability to control events. Saying "no" often is a way for the child to communicate, "I can assert my voice and contradict you."

Although the "terrible twos" can be a trying time for parents and caregivers, this stage is very important in the child's emotional growth. According to Erikson, when adults thwart children's desire for autonomy, the children develop feelings of doubt and shame. Erikson theorizes that children who fail to develop autonomy turn their negative feelings against

Erikson's "autonomy versus shame and doubt" stage can be frustrating for both child and parent. The child's increasing desire for independence can create conflict when parents criticize a child's efforts to do something on his own.

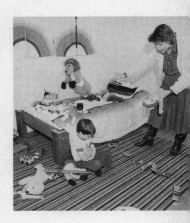

themselves. They doubt their own ability to make choices and to control their environment, and they feel inadequate and self-conscious, even ashamed. To help toddlers develop autonomy, it is important to let them win a "battle of wills" now and then. It also is helpful to give them frequent opportunities throughout the day to make small choices—for example, what they want to wear, what they want to eat for lunch, or whether they want to go outside. They do best when offered a limited range of choices, such as being asked, "Do you want tomato soup or chicken noodle soup for lunch?"

Initiative versus Guilt

The third stage, occurring from approximately age three to age five or six, is the *initiative versus guilt* phase. In this stage, children begin to develop a sense of responsibility and accomplishment. They are learning to plan and undertake tasks on their own. They are enormously energetic and enthusiastic, and, consequently, they forget failures and keep trying to master new skills. However, they often do not follow through and take projects they initiate to completion. Children at this age also are becoming more social and are learning to conform to social roles. They begin to see how their actions affect others. Sometimes, they misbehave purposefully—for example, by disobeying a directive or using bad language—just to see how a caregiver will react or to impress their peers.

One way children at this age show their initiative is to imitate adults. They commonly want to help with household chores and use tools and appliances. Often, children's desire to help and prove that they can accomplish these kinds of tasks by themselves conflicts with the quality standards of the adult. The result may be feelings of guilt in the child. For example, if a child trying to mop a floor merely spreads around a lot of dirty water, the parent may become exasperated. If the parent takes the mop away, the child may interpret that action as disapproval or rejection, and the child may feel guilty. Children of this age also are very inquisitive. If a child asks a question and the adult says, "That's a silly question," the child then may feel not only stupid but also guilty. According to Erikson, the development of some feelings of guilt is normal, as children learn to balance their own desires against the demands of others. The development of too much guilt, however, stifles initiative and causes feelings of low self-esteem.

An understanding of Erikson's psychosocial stages will provide teachers with a perspective for planning activities to help children learn to recognize and express feelings.

Recognizing and Expressing Feelings

Many of the same objects and events that trigger emotional reactions in adults cause similar emotions in children. Research has found that just as adults feel happiness, for instance, at getting a new car or taking a vacation, so children experience similar pleasure at receiving a new toy or getting to eat their favorite food on their birthday (Strayer, 1986). Strayer found that

FOCUS ON — Communicating with Parents

Talking with a Parent Who Is Getting Divorced

Jane Tyler is concerned about Jimmy Robbins. His parents are separated and getting divorced—a difficult situation for a child of any age, but especially stressful for a preschooler. For the last two weeks, Jimmy's father had been negligent in picking him up from school on his designated days. He had either arrived late or sent his girlfriend, with whom Jimmy is not yet comfortable. Jane had requested a conference with Jimmy's mother and father separately.

MS. ROBBINS: Is Jimmy misbehaving in school? I'm afraid he's not adjusting to the divorce very well.

JANE: Well, that will take time. And no, it's nothing that Jimmy has done. Actually, I'd like to see what we can do to help Jimmy during this period of adjustment. For example, often on Mr. Robbins's days to pick him up, a woman comes that Jimmy says is his father's girlfriend.

MS. ROBBINS: Girlfriend? And you've let her take Jimmy?

JANE: Well, yes. We called to verify it with Mr. Robbins. But Jimmy seems to be worried that one or the other parent will leave him. Routine is very important to children, especially in times of stress, and adding an unfamiliar person doesn't help.

MS. ROBBINS: I plan to talk to my husband right away.

JANE: I'm sure you're already doing this, but you also might want to take some extra time with Jimmy to reassure him you won't leave him. Sometimes, children think if one parent leaves, the other will leave, too.

MS. ROBBINS: I am very concerned about Jimmy. I guess I hadn't thought about all these things.

Do you think that Jane handled the situation effectively? Why or why not? Should she have mentioned the father's girlfriend? In what ways did Jane keep the conversation focused on Jimmy's needs?

young children most commonly mention food, material goods, animals, and fantasies as the sources of such emotions as happiness, sadness, anger, fear, and surprise. For example, a cookie for snack can cause surprise and happiness, whereas a neighbor's dog can arouse fear. Interpersonal relations and achievement also can arouse emotions in children, but these causes are more common motives among adolescents and adults. For example, a teenager's quarrel with his girlfriend may generate feelings of anger, whereas a promotion at work can be a source of great happiness for an adult.

Research also has shown that three- to four-year-olds must learn to differentiate between their own emotional reactions and those of other people (Harter, 1983). For example, preschoolers often mimic the emotion that a parent is showing. A child may pout if she sees that her mother looks sad, even though she does not know the cause of that emotion. As children grow older they learn that the causes of other people's emotions are different from

Learning how to express feelings is not always easy. A child who is very upset may just want to be comforted by the teacher before he can talk about what happened.

the causes of their own emotions. In the preschool curriculum, certain activities help young children learn the causes of various emotions and learn how to differentiate between what they are feeling and what others are feeling. These activities include reading books about children who are experiencing different emotions, dramatic play, and play with puppets.

Preschool teachers should be aware that, in many families, children are taught to deny or suppress certain feelings, such as anger, resentment, jealousy, or sadness. For instance, boys often are taught from an early age that crying is not manly, and older siblings are taught not to express jealousy of younger ones. Adults often feel threatened by their children's negative emotions, and they fear that allowing their children to express these emotions will only increase the intensity of feelings. Research has shown, however, that just the opposite is true—that expressing feelings greatly relieves emotional tension, whereas suppressing feelings often leads a child to act out those feelings. Rather than teaching children to deny feelings, parents and teachers should encourage children to express emotions in acceptable ways, either verbally or through creative activities. This section explores techniques that teachers can use to help children express emotions in a variety of situations.

Addressing Anger

Anger is a normal emotion in children, and preschool teachers need to know how to help children deal with anger in socially acceptable ways. A child may become angry for a number of reasons, such as when another child grabs his toy or knocks over his block structure or sits on his favorite pillow during story time. One of the most common ways children express their anger is by crying. Crying is an effective tension reliever. When children become angry, they also may hit or attack one another, and the teacher's first task is to separate them and calm them. Then the teacher needs to encourage them to express their anger verbally, not by acting out—hitting, kicking, or biting. In some cases, it may be necessary to restrain a child who is enraged until she calms down. Very young children, such as Dennis at the beginning of this chapter, do not yet have the skills to express their emotions verbally and may resort to physical expression.

One effective technique for helping young children express their anger verbally is called *self-report*. Each child says how he or she is feeling and then the teacher describes the feelings back to each child, as the other listens. When using self-report, the teacher should use short words that the child understands to describe the emotion and should frame the description in the form of a question or in tentative terms to give the child a chance to correct any misunderstandings. Using such terms as "I wonder if you are feeling . . ." or "Maybe you don't like it when . . ." creates opportunities for children to respond with their own descriptions of how they feel. Teachers should keep in mind, however, that the goal of self-report is for children to learn to describe their feelings themselves.

Mrs. Foster used self-report with Emily and Dennis and was careful to couch the descriptions of their emotions in a way that, if the children felt she was wrong in her assessment, they had the opportunity to correct her. By describing their feelings for them, Mrs. Foster let Emily and Dennis know that she understood how they felt and at the same time provided them with an example of how words, not physical action, could be used to express anger. Once Mrs. Foster allowed the children to express their feelings and engaged their attention, she was able to reinforce the rule about no hitting and encourage the children to propose a peaceful solution. Another technique sometimes used when children cannot resolve a conflict on their own is called *redirection*—steering one child's or both children's attention to another activity. This technique can work well with very young children because they have short interest spans and can easily be influenced to focus on a new activity.

Teachers also can help children dispel their anger through vigorous rhythmic activities, such as hammering, drumming, or pounding play dough. Creative activities, such as drawing, painting, and playing with sand or water, also provide children with outlets to express anger and relieve stress. When one child has done something to hurt another, it is sometimes helpful to suggest that the child do something to make amends, such as drawing a picture and wrapping it up like a present. In this way, that child can communicate the feeling of "being sorry" in a very concrete manner. Role-playing with dolls or puppets is a particularly safe and effective way for children to express their anger toward authority figures whom they are afraid to confront directly. See the "Focus on Activities" feature on puppets in this chapter. A child might not dare tell his mother, "I hate you! I'm going to run away from home!" He can, however, safely express those emotions to the doll he has assigned to play the role of "Mommy."

FOCUS ON / Activities

Making and Using Puppets to Learn about Emotions

Puppets can be a valuable teaching tool because they encourage children to think imaginatively. They are especially effective in teaching children about intangible subjects, including emotions.

You can make puppets from common household items, such as socks, paper bags, and old mittens. You also can create an art activity of making puppets with the children, which will help the children form an early relationship with the puppets.

Write a script that focuses on a particular emotion. For example, you might create a scenario about a shy child on her first day of preschool. The scenario might include one or two other characters, such as a friendly teacher or a bossy child, to create opportunities for a short dialogue. Having a script will ensure that you touch on all relevant points to help the children better understand the emotion.

Encourage the children to interact with the puppets. Ask them questions, such as "How can we make Shy Sharon know we like her?", "Should we ask her what her favorite game is?", "When do you feel shy?", or "What should we have Shy Sharon say to Bossy Billy?" Using puppets gives children a chance to explore emotions objectively—that is, when they themselves are not actually feeling sad, scared, or shy. The question-and-answer aspect of the activity also promotes empathy in children.

Another way that you can use puppets is to present a less structured scenario about an emotion. For example, you might introduce Madame Mean and Queen Scared and act out a scenario based on the children's suggestions. Ask, for example, "Where do they live?", "How is Madame Mean being mean to Queen Scared?", "Why do you think she's being mean?", or "What if she's really scared, too?" This technique allows greater freedom to incorporate the children's responses throughout the role play.

Remember to keep your presentations simple and clear to communicate effectively. Maintain your enthusiasm to keep the interest of the children.

Confronting Fear

Preschoolers typically develop a large number of fears and anxieties because they have not yet reached the point in their cognitive development where they can distinguish between fantasy and reality (Flavell, 1963). Their vivid imaginations enable them to conjure up a great many dangers, in addition to real ones. The same vivid imaginations that let children create "friends" also spurs common fears, such as fear of the dark, monsters, dogs, and water.

Teachers can help children confront their fears in a variety of ways. They can encourage children to talk about their fears using the self-report technique. They can read books out loud about children who were afraid of something and have learned to overcome their fears. This technique, sometimes called *bibliotherapy*, allows children to see how the character in a book deals with a variety of emotions, including fear, anger, sadness, and frustration. As with anger, storytelling and role-playing with dolls or puppets are especially effective techniques to confront fear. Although they may not be fully aware of it, when children tell stories or play roles, they ascribe their emotions to their characters, and they do not have to confront their feelings directly. They can maintain control of the action and can fashion endings in which they triumph over the feared person or object. This success helps give them confidence to confront their fears in real life.

Handling Sadness and Emotional Upset

Children are no more immune to the tragedies and crises of everyday life than adults. Such events as starting preschool, the divorce of parents, the birth of a sibling, moving to a new home, or having to go to the emergency room can cause emotional turmoil in a young child's life. Some children in the grip of sadness, grief, or anxiety react by being excessively aggressive or cranky. Others go into withdrawal. They may crawl under a table or sit in a closet to be alone. Children also deal with sadness and anxiety by regressing to behaviors more appropriate to younger children, such as thumb sucking or bed-wetting. Teachers can help emotionally distressed children by remaining nearby to offer solace and assistance and by being more tolerant than usual of the children's lapses in behavior.

Young children who are emotionally upset need to express their feelings and to be comforted and reassured by trusted and caring adults. When a child is sobbing uncontrollably, the best remedy is to hold and rock the child and to talk softly to him until he calms down. Wiping his tears with a warm cloth and giving him a drink of water can help calm him as well. Once calm is restored, the teacher should try to find out the cause of the upset. Discussing the situation with the child's parents may help identify the cause of the problem. For instance, the teacher may discover that the change in the child's behavior is linked to the child's father having moved out of the house. See the "Focus on Communicating" feature in this chapter.

When the teacher can determine the cause of the upset, he or she can find ways to help the child express feelings. Many of the same techniques used to cope with children's fears can be applied to sadness and emotional upsets. For example, if a child is upset by the birth of a baby sister, the teacher could play dolls with him and encourage him to pretend that a doll is his new sister. Then the child could act out with the doll how he feels about his sister. Teachers also should try to redirect children who are emotionally upset into creative activities involving such materials as water, mud, sand, and finger paints, which are soothing to children. In most cases, children become quickly engrossed in such play.

Stress and the Young Child

Stress is the body's physiological reaction to the demands and strains of daily life that exceed a person's ability to cope (Selye, 1982; Lazarus & Launier, 1978). For adults, stress results from job pressures and deadlines, financial responsibilities, and personal crises, such as a divorce or a death in the

Curriculum activities such as playing with puppets can help children address negative feelings in a constructive way. These three-year-olds gain a sense of control when they use puppets to play out a fictional fight scene.

family. Preschool teachers need to realize that children, too, are subject to stress and should familiarize themselves with the causes and symptoms of stress. Many situations can cause stress in children. Stress can be caused by internal factors—such as illness, fear of abandonment, or listening to parents fight—or external factors—such as a family move, being teased, living in extreme poverty, exposure to violence, the birth of a new sibling, a death in the family, or being hospitalized (Honig, 1986).

Stress in young children also can be caused by pressure from parents, schools, and the media to push or hurry them beyond their developmental level. Adults often hurry children in many ways—even beginning in preschool (Elkind, 1988). For example, some parents enroll three-year-olds in dance class, and others buy computers for four-year-olds.

The results of years of hurrying can be devastating. They include early onset of stress diseases, failure in school, even teenage suicide and crime (Elkind, 1988). Preschool teachers need to recognize and try to counter these kinds of pressures and stresses. Also, an overly academic preschool program can create stress for young children, if they are expected to do and know things that are beyond their developmental level.

Signs of stress in young children include tension, anxiety, withdrawal, irritability, depression, and unexplained stomachaches, headaches, and allergies. If a teacher believes that a child is experiencing stress, he or she can help by creating a sense of security in the classroom as well as by helping the child express emotions.

When a teacher believes that a situation involving the child's home life is causing stress, such as the loss of a parent's job or a death in the family, he or she might suggest to the family how to access community resources, including family therapy. This kind of constructive communication will help parents to not expect too much too soon from their child.

Encouraging Empathy in Young Children

An important step in each child's emotional growth is the development of *empathy*, the ability to understand and relate to the feelings and viewpoints of others. Piaget believed that the ability to empathize is related to cognitive development or, more specifically, to overcoming egocentrism by developing the ability to see another person's point of view. He asserted that preschoolers have not yet reached the level of cognitive development in which they can take the perspective of another. However, some early childhood experts, such as Burton White (see the discussion of the Harvard Preschool Project earlier in this chapter), believe that Piaget underestimated the preschooler's capacity for empathy, at least in familiar situations. Even children as young as three will try to comfort a crying baby. Nonetheless, the ability of preschoolers to empathize is still in an early stage and is not demonstrated consistently.

Preschool teachers and child care providers can begin to foster preschoolers' ability to feel empathy, however, through dramatic play and self-report. When children take on the role of Mommy or Daddy or of someone else in the dramatic play area, or when they listen to other children make self-reports, they begin to understand that other people have feelings and points of view that are different from their own. In a technique sometimes called "remember when," teachers ask children to recall how they felt when an event happened to them and relate that feeling directly to what another

The five-year-old boy on the left is learning empathy as he watches the teacher comforting a hurt child and remembers how he felt in a similar situation.

child is feeling. For example, a teacher might say, "Remember when Martha pushed you down? Remember how you felt? That's how Bryan feels now." or "Remember when your best friend, Kevin, moved away? Genie is feeling sad because her best friend is moving away, too." Parents and teachers often ask children, "How would you feel if Johnny did that to you?" This concept is difficult for young children to grasp. "Remember when" is a more effective and less judgmental technique to help preschoolers learn that other people have the same feelings they do. Also, encouraging dialogue about emotions during group time enables children to hear other children tell, not show, how they feel.

Applications

Preschool teachers discover that many opportunities and situations arise every day in the classroom through which children can learn about emotions. A squabble over a toy, a withdrawn child, the death of a pet, a skinned knee, a joyful birthday party, a parent who is late picking up a child: all of these are occasions that teachers can use to help students explore, define, and express emotions. Here are some strategies that teachers can use to foster emotional growth in preschoolers.

Create an Environment of Acceptance

In order for children to express their emotions freely, they need to feel that they are in a safe, accepting environment in which they will not be ridiculed or belittled. Remember that you are seeking to promote trust, autonomy, and initiative in preschoolers, to build their self-esteem and feelings of competence, and to teach them to express their emotions verbally or nonverbally in socially acceptable ways, or creatively. A teacher can produce an accepting environment by letting children know that he or she likes and respects them and enjoys being with them. Accepting children means that you acknowledge and respect their feelings. It also means giving them your attention and listening carefully to what they are saying without being judgmental. Of course, being accepting does not mean letting children act out in any way they please. When you recognize and acknowledge the feelings of children, you help them learn that having strong emotions is all right. You also must communicate to them, however, that acting on strong negative emotions in a hurtful or destructive manner is not all right.

Leave Your Problems at the Door

Preschoolers are very sensitive to the emotions of others as well as to their own, so it is important that caregivers leave their own personal problems at home. Although everyone has bad days, a teacher who routinely takes out his or her own emotional turmoil by being sharp or curt with the children cannot simultaneously teach them to control themselves or express their emotions in an acceptable manner. Furthermore, if teachers shout or become very irritated on a regular basis, that behavior conveys a message to the children that it is OK to lose control (Honig & Lansburgh, 1991).

This caution does not mean that you can never express your own emotions to children. On the contrary, expressing your emotions in a nonthreatening way helps children learn empathy and improves the closeness of your relationship with them. Statements such as "I'm so happy you were able to bring your turtle to school so we can all enjoy him," or "I really get worried when you climb so high in that tree," let children know that you feel comfortable expressing your feelings to them and provide them with models for verbally expressing their own feelings. Communicating your feelings in "I" statements, rather than saying "You make me feel . . . ," also shows children that you are responsible for your own emotions and are not blaming them for generating those feelings.

One of the most important ways that child care providers teach children how to cope with their emotions is to be a role model for them. Preschoolers need teachers who are warm, reliable, and sincere. They need to see that their teachers treat them in a predictable, calm manner in all emotional situations. This kind of consistency helps children learn to trust their caregivers and to feel safe in their preschool environment.

Creating an environment of acceptance in the classroom encourages children to feel comfortable expressing their emotions because they know that their feelings will not be criticized.

Activities to Encourage Emotional Expression

Activities that help children learn to identify and describe their emotions should be an integral part of the preschool curriculum. For example, you can cut photos of people with various facial expressions out of magazines and ask the children to talk about what the person is feeling, or to group all the sad pictures together. Asking them why they think that the person in the picture is angry, happy, sad, or fearful can lead to a discussion of each kind of emotion. Another activity can be done by using different tempos and types of music—such as a ballad, a polka, and a lullaby—or a variety of sounds—such as a mournful whistle, a person laughing, or a tiger growling—and asking how each sound makes the children feel. Another activity is to paste four pictures of individual people showing emotions (three depicting the same emotion and the fourth a different one) and to ask the children to say which one is different and explain why (Smith, 1982).

Many creative activities help children express their emotions. You might tell a story about a child's experience of feeling a specific positive emotion—such as happiness, joy, affection, or love. Then ask the children to paint a mural about the story together in groups of three or four.

Children also should be given the opportunity to express negative emotions—sadness, anger, fear—through painting, finger painting, and drawing. Storytelling is another creative way to express emotions. You can begin a story such as "Johnny woke up feeling very angry because of what happened the night before . . ." and then let the children add to the story. These activities not only stimulate the imaginations of children but also give them an outlet for expressing their emotions. Creative activities that help children express emotions are described in more detail in Chapter 13.

Dramatic play creates an opportunity for children to explore many emotions and to replay real-life situations with a different outcome. A doll hospital helps these four-year-olds explore the emotions that go along with an illness or an injury.

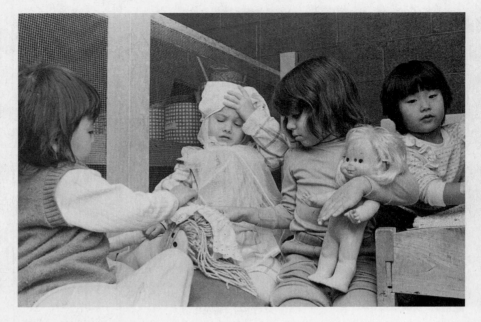

Dramatic play presents another rich opportunity for children to express the full spectrum of their emotions. Puppets, dolls, and props can be employed for children to act out any emotionally charged situation. For example, a child who is facing an operation and a hospital stay can become the "doctor" in a role-playing game using toy doctor's kits, stethoscopes, crutches, and bandages. Usually, dramatic play allows the "victim" to feel more in control by acting out the role of a more powerful character or person. Dramatic play also helps children express their fears or their needs, reverse roles, or create happier endings to certain previously experienced events.

Teachers also can use dramatic play to help children understand the difference between feeling an emotion and acting on it. Suppose that you saw a child using a puppet to "bite" or hit a playmate. This situation is a good opportunity for you to point out that it is OK for him to feel angry at his playmate and to pretend to hit him, but it would not be all right to hit him in real life. Bear in mind that the child may feel that he is not responsible, as the puppet did the biting or hitting. It may be important to explain that the child controls the actions of the puppet.

Activities to Relieve Tension

When children are tense, angry, irritable, or fearful, many simple everyday preschool activities can help relieve their stress and soothe emotional upset. Mud, clay, or finger-painting activities are especially relaxing because young children love absorbing themselves in the medium. Water play and sand play with a wide variety of toys and containers also are engrossing and calming activities. All these activities engage the child's senses without demanding much skill and without requiring the child to produce anything. Vigorous physical exercise is another effective way to dissipate tension—especially activities that promote large motor skills, such as running, jumping, swinging, and pedaling. Inside, rolling on mats or jumping on a small trampoline also can help. When children are upset, music, rhythmic movement, and dancing are other good methods of releasing emotional tension.

CHAPTER 8 REVIEW

SUMMARY

- Self-esteem is an individual's feeling of self-worth. High or low self-esteem affects how children see themselves and the world.
- Competence is the ability to complete or succeed at a task or project.
- Children's self-esteem can be nurtured by the teacher's encouragement and provision of opportunities to practice and master skills.
- From infancy through the preschool years, children progress through the first three stages of Erikson's "Eight Stages of Man."
- Children need to learn to express emotions verbally or nonverbally, and not to act out destructively.
- Using the technique of self-report, a teacher describes how he or she believes that a child is feeling, giving the child the opportunity to agree or modify what the teacher has said. Self-report also presents a model of how a child can verbalize emotions, not act them out in a destructive way.
- Preschoolers develop many fears because of their inability to distinguish between fantasy and reality. Teachers can help children learn to confront their fears through self-report and dramatic play.
- Teachers should first comfort and calm children who are sad or emotionally upset and then try to determine the cause of their distress. Dramatic play, storytelling, and playing with manipulative materials can help children express their emotions.
- Children are subject to stress just as adults are. They can become stressed from the pressure of being hurried or forced to perform beyond their developmental level.
- Preschoolers are capable of feeling empathy and of being able to see another's point of view in familiar situations, but these skills are still in an early stage.
- Teaching strategies to help children learn to express their emotions include creating an accepting environment, being a role model, and acting in consistent, predictable ways.

- Activities that help children learn about emotions should be an integral part of the preschool curriculum. Such activities should include creative activities that help children express their emotions and relieve tension.

ACQUIRING KNOWLEDGE

1. How does a child's sense of self-esteem affect his perception of the world?
2. What are some possible long-term effects of low self-esteem?
3. What factors do researchers in the Harvard Preschool Project use to describe a "competent" three-year-old?
4. Describe the relationship between competence and self-esteem.
5. Why is praise sometimes ineffective for building self-esteem?
6. What are the differences between praise and encouragement?
7. How can the preschool curriculum allow opportunities for all children to succeed?
8. What are some teaching practices that can lower self-esteem?
9. What do Erikson's "Eight Stages of Man" describe?
10. What conflict characterizes the first stage? the second stage?
11. Why are the "terrible twos" an important stage in a child's emotional growth?
12. Describe how a child's desire and an adult's needs often can conflict during the initiative-versus-guilt stage.
13. What are some dangers in not allowing children to express their emotions?
14. Describe the technique of self-report.
15. What are some strategies a teacher can use when a child becomes angry?
16. How can bibliotherapy help children's emotional development?
17. Why is role-playing, such as through the use of puppets, an effective activity to encourage emotional development?
18. What is the best way to help a child who is sobbing uncontrollably?
19. What are some signs that a child is experiencing stress?
20. How can teachers help foster a preschooler's ability to feel empathy?
21. What is the "remember when" technique? When is it useful?
22. Describe some activities that encourage emotional expression.

THINKING CRITICALLY

1. Some young children like to ask a seemingly endless string of questions, or just to repeat the question "why?" again and again. What do you think is the most constructive way to respond to a child who asks many questions? What might this behavior tell you about the child in terms of Erikson's stages of psychosocial development?
2. Activities in a preschool should be devised to foster self-esteem and confidence in young children. What are two key aspects of the curriculum that will help children experience success?

3. Young children are sensitive to whether the teacher's praise or encouragement is vague and disinterested or specific and sincere. What are some comments you would characterize as praise when a teacher was commenting on a child's building with blocks? What are some comments you would categorize as encouragement?

4. Listening to and discussing books can help children explore and express many emotions. What kinds of books would you choose for bibliotherapy? What qualities would you look for in each book?

OBSERVATIONS AND APPLICATIONS

1. Observe a preschool teacher working with four- to five-year-olds during an art activity. Listen to and write down the verbal feedback that the teacher provides to the children. Is the teacher specific or general in addressing the children's activity? For example, does he or she use general words, such as "good" or "terrific"? Or does he or she provide specific thoughts about the child's persistence, effort, and increasing competence, such as "I can see how carefully you are mixing the white into the blue," or "The red in your painting really stands out"?

2. During an observation of a group of three-year-olds, record how many displays of anger you notice. Describe the scenes. What is the child doing? Is the child alone or with other children? What occurs right before the child becomes angry? What does the teacher say to the angry child? How is the situation resolved? For example, does the teacher talk to the child about the situation and/or redirect the child to other activities?

3. Debby Randolph is a three-year-old girl who moved with her mother recently to the city from the suburbs. On the first day of preschool, Debby cried constantly and refused to participate in any of the activities. Mrs. Randolph tells you the next morning that Debby is afraid to go to preschool. She says that Debby was particularly frightened by the loud city noises outside the classroom. What kinds of things might you do with Debby in the classroom to help her feel less fearful of loud noises?

4. You notice a disruption in one corner of the classroom. Only a few minutes ago, Scott and Randy—two four-year-olds in your class—were playing together with the trucks. Now, Scott approaches you with a tear-streaked face. He holds up a broken red fire engine and says, "It's all Randy's fault." Randy says that Scott refused to share, one of the class rules. How might you help Scott and Randy resolve this situation?

FOR FURTHER INFORMATION

Elkind, D. (1988). *The hurried child: Growing up too fast too soon.* Reading, MA: Addison-Wesley.

Erikson, E. (1963). *Childhood and society* (2nd ed.). New York: Norton.

Hitz, R., & Driscoll, A. (1988). Praise or encouragement? New insights into praise: Implications for early childhood teachers. *Young Children, 43*(5), 6–13.

Social Development

Studying this chapter
will enable you to

- Discuss common preschool
  activities that affect social
  development in young children
- Explain how children learn the
  concepts of right and wrong
- List some of the causes of
  aggressive behavior in
  preschoolers and discuss ways
  teachers can control aggressive
  behavior
- Describe how the curriculum can
  affect discipline in the preschool
  setting
- Explain how the teacher can foster
  feelings of acceptance and respect
  among children

CHAPTER TERMS

heterogeneous classroom
homogeneous classroom
hostile aggression
instrumental aggression
monocultural community
negotiation
process of construction
prosocial behavior
time-out

MISS LEE was worried. Two weeks after joining her four-year-old class at the Haverhill Preschool, Marvin still seemed withdrawn. Despite her efforts to involve him during group time and play time, Marvin always stood on the sidelines. Today, she watched as he sat on the floor near Teddy, who was building a block garage. All of a sudden, Marvin walked up to Teddy and gingerly touched Teddy's hair.

"Hey, what are you doing?" said Teddy, as Marvin quickly yanked his hand away. Miss Lee knelt down beside Marvin and said, "Have you ever touched hair like Teddy's before?"

"No," Marvin said. Teddy's hair was soft, blond, and straight. Marvin's hair was very short, wiry, and dark.

"It's all right to be curious about each other," said Miss Lee. "Everyone has hair, but everyone's hair is a different color and feels different. Remember also that it's important to get permission before you touch someone. Marvin, before you touch Teddy's head, you must ask him if it's OK. Then, you might let Teddy touch your hair."

Marvin turned to Teddy. "Can I touch your hair? Then you can feel mine." Marvin waited until Teddy nodded and then touched his hair. "It's soft," he said quietly.

Miss Lee held out a lock of her long, straight, black hair. "Does my hair feel the same as or different from yours, Teddy, or yours, Marvin?"

"Different," the boys said simultaneously. "And your hair is really black," Marvin added.

"Right," Miss Lee said. "As I said, all children have hair on their heads, but look at all the different hair colors we have just in our class!"

Preschool children like Marvin and Teddy are beginning to develop their social skills. They are learning to get along with other children, to make friends, to share, and to help others. They also are learning about how they are similar to and different from one another. Preschool teachers should provide children with opportunities to develop the social skills—such as cooperating, helping, negotiating, and talking through problems (Bredekamp, 1987)—that will help them function well socially during preschool and in the years beyond.

This chapter shows how children develop social skills and how the preschool curriculum affects social development. It also discusses aggressive behavior and describes techniques preschool teachers can use to deal with such behavior. Finally, the chapter discusses cultural diversity and explains how children can learn to respect one another's cultural backgrounds. The chapter concludes with practical suggestions on incorporating multicultural activities in the classroom.

Building Social Skills

Preschools are natural places for young children to build social skills. In the preschool setting, children may meet and play with other children from a variety of backgrounds, races, and cultures. Preschool teachers can help young children learn social skills as the children start to become independent, care for themselves, help others, and play with "best friends."

The roots of social behavior are complex. Psychologists and early childhood educators offer varying opinions about what motivates social behavior. One view is that people are motivated by selfish interests. Another, more altruistic view suggests that people basically respect other people and their property. A third view suggests that people alternate between selfish and compassionate, or charitable, behavior based on their perceptions and reasoning in various social situations (Radke-Yarrow, Zahn-Waxler, & Chapman, 1983).

No single theory explains how children learn social skills. However, early childhood experts generally agree that children learn to get along with others by imitating, or modeling, the behaviors of the significant adults and children in their lives. This theory is sometimes referred to as the social learning theory (Bandura, 1977). The next section discusses how children

Playground equipment that requires two or more children helps develop cooperation and the ability to work with others.

develop positive, or prosocial, behavior and how prosocial behavior can be fostered by preschool teachers and child care providers.

Prosocial Behavior

Positive, constructive social behavior, or *prosocial behavior,* is based on caring and showing concern for others. The person exhibiting prosocial behavior does so without expecting a reward, even if the prosocial behavior requires some cost or sacrifice. Research suggests that all people have the potential for developing prosocial behavior. Such behavior, however, is most likely to be learned from parents and teachers who are models of the behavior, who use reasoning in discipline, who maintain high standards, and who encourage their children to accept responsibilities for others early in life (Mussen & Eisenberg-Berg, 1977).

The cognitive-developmental theory, which asserts that the child constructs an understanding of the world through interaction and exploration, views prosocial development as one aspect of children's emerging understanding of themselves and others. Some experts believe that children's prosocial behavior changes as they mature, based on their increasing cognitive abilities (Eisenberg, 1982). Before children can act in a prosocial manner, they must be able to perceive and understand another person's need, and to decide whether they think that the person can be helped. Furthermore, the child must feel competent to help.

In contrast to the cognitive-developmental view, behaviorists such as B. F. Skinner view prosocial behavior as a behavior learned through positive reinforcement, rather than on emotion or intent (Radke-Yarrow et al., 1983).

A Circle Game to Build Social Skills

Group time is a good time for activities that help children build social skills. Here's a circle game that presents an opportunity for every child to participate. It enhances children's language skills while helping them express their feelings.

After you gather the children in a circle, read a story about friendship. Then start a discussion about how friends can make you feel good. With input from the children, make a chart of "Things We Like About Our Friends."

After the group finishes the chart, introduce the game about friendship with a song to a familiar tune, such as "Here We Go 'Round the Mulberry Bush." Use the name of a child sitting next to you in the song. You might sing, "Steven is a friend of mine, friend of mine, friend of mine. Steven is a friend of mine because he sits next to me at snack time." Then it is Steven's turn to say what he likes about the child seated next to him on the other side. En-

courage all the children to sing along with Steven. Go around the circle until every child has had a turn.

Be aware that you might have to help some of the children think about why they like the child seated next to them. In such cases, go back to your chart. Point to the list and say, "Friends don't hit or push. Friends like to play with me. Friends share toys." Then the child can choose one reason and finish the song.

Extend the Experience

- Send a copy of the chart home to parents, and encourage them to talk about friends with their children. New ideas for the list may result.
- Post the chart "Things We Like About Our Friends" on the wall to help children remember appropriate social behavior.

No single view adequately explains all aspects of prosocial behavior. However, proponents of the leading theories agree that children progress from being essentially egocentric to being gradually more concerned with others. At the same time, the motivation for prosocial behavior shifts from external rewards and punishments, such as parental approval or disapproval, to internal motives or principles, such as making oneself feel good by helping a friend (Mussen & Eisenberg-Berg, 1977).

Most children are interested in helping others, especially other children. Whereas children typically begin to show empathy at about age four, studies show that some children younger than age two are capable of showing concern and a caring attitude for dolls, toy animals, parents, and even themselves (Rheingold & Emery, 1986). They also are capable of demonstrating other positive behaviors—such as empathy, sympathy, cooperation, and compassion—toward other people (Radke-Yarrow, et al., 1983). This research also suggests that the mother's compassion for the child serves as a predictor of whether the child will choose to behave empathetically toward others. Teachers serve as examples of prosocial behavior when they treat children with respect, are helpful and nurturing to all, and have high expectations that the children will do likewise.

Getting Along with Others

The smooth functioning of the preschool relies on young children's getting along with one another. Teachers understand that young children naturally want to get along with others and belong to peer groups but may need practice interacting with others.

As children interact with one another, especially during free play, they receive immediate feedback or information about their behavior by the way other children respond to them. As they play, children test out and explore different words and actions until they discover those that help them get along with others. In addition to responding to feedback, children tend to imitate the behaviors of other children they consider to be socially successful (Rogers & Ross, 1986).

Preschool teachers need to provide time, space, and opportunities for children to play together during the day. However, to make the most of these opportunities, children need to learn several skills. Children who communicate effectively are more likely to get along with others. Teachers can help children learn to communicate more effectively by showing them a variety of ways to ask questions, by helping them talk about their feelings, and by providing opportunities for them to practice their social skills with and without teacher guidance. Dwight L. Rogers and Dorene Doerre Ross (1986) suggest that a teacher may assist a child in joining a group of children already engaged in an activity. The teacher can help that child get a sense of what the group is doing and figure out how he can participate and contribute to the group.

Many preschool activities create opportunities to assist children in learning to work cooperatively. During group projects, for example, the teacher can pair up children who have strong social skills with children who do not. Playground equipment, such as the rocking boat, encourage cooperation because it requires at least two children working together to rock it. Helping to prepare snacks is another opportunity teachers can set up so that children must coordinate their efforts to be successful.

Making Friends. Making and having friends is important to the social development of all children. Friendships contribute to several areas of children's development, including emotional well-being, positive classroom performance and school adjustment, and social skills and competencies (Ladd & Coleman, 1993).

Research has found that children have definite ideas about who their friends are, how friends are supposed to behave, and how friendships begin and end (Smith, 1982). Children as young as two years interact with a "friend" differently from the way they interact with other children both in preschool and in other settings (Ladd & Coleman, 1993).

Young children choose friends based on a number of factors. Typically, children choose friends who are similar to themselves in age and other physical and intellectual traits (Ladd & Coleman, 1993). Children also want their friends to be friendly, not aggressive, and they want them to follow rules. According to Dodge (1983), children who are sought out as friends have good conversational skills, play cooperatively, and are seldom aggressive. Also, children who are rejected as friends tend to be disruptive during play, to display inappropriate behaviors, and to be hostile in conversation—leading to a cycle of further rejection.

As children develop cognitive and communicative skills, the nature of their friendships changes. For example, most young children play with several different children at the beginning of each school year but become more selective and play with fewer children as the year progresses. From this smaller select group of playmates, they may designate a "best friend" and can explain why that child is their best friend (Ladd & Coleman, 1993). However, preschool teachers should plan group activities, such as circle games and cooking projects, to help children learn to get along within larger social groups.

The preschool environment can be arranged to help children develop friendships. The classroom design, the arrangement of play areas, and the types of play equipment selected can all affect the quality of social interactions. Setting up several smaller work and play areas encourages interaction among children. Dramatic play activities encourage cooperative social play. Group activities allow children to become acquainted and foster the development of friendships, as do large outdoor play structures that have smaller play areas within them. On the other hand, overcrowded classrooms encourage behavior problems and discourage the positive social interaction that leads to friendships, as do such solitary activities as sand box play, clay modeling, or painting (Ladd & Coleman, 1993).

Teachers can help keep a play group going and thus support the development of friendships. Chapter 4 discussed techniques for guiding play. For example, if one child in a group harshly rejects another child's suggestion, the teacher can encourage the first child to explain why the suggestion was rejected and encourage the second child to come up with an alternative suggestion.

Shy Children.   Shyness affects most young children at some time during the preschool and elementary years and may be an ongoing personality trait in some children (Honig, 1987). Shy children usually are easy to spot. They tend to avoid another's gaze, are unable to accept friendly social overtures, and feel uncomfortable with unfamiliar people. Although not wrong in themselves, these behaviors can prevent children from growing socially. Because of their shyness, some children may refuse to participate in activities that might be enjoyable and enriching.

The causes of shyness vary among children. Some shy children have a poor self-concept, whereas others just lack social experience and skills

The teacher can play an important role in encouraging shy children to interact with others. This teacher is helping to start up a conversation between two children.

(Sarafino, 1986). Teachers can help children overcome their shyness by encouraging them to learn different ways to approach other children in a group and by building up positive feelings of self-esteem. Alice Sterling Honig (1987) offers the following strategies to the preschool teacher for helping the shy child become more social.

- Teach a shy child phrases or sentences that will help him to join a group or to play with one other child—such as "Can I help you build?" or "Can I play, too?". Also, teach a shy child to say "Good-bye" or "I have to go now" when leaving a group, instead of just walking away.
- Role-play with a shy child to illustrate how other children join others in playing.
- Read to the class stories in which the main character deals with shyness, and make the stories available in the classroom.
- Be tolerant and accepting of a child's shyness. Do not force the child to participate in a social activity or to perform for others. Be supportive without being overwhelming.
- Recognize and compliment the child on making positive gains in social skills, no matter how small the gains. Praise the child's improved social competence.
- Listen attentively when a shy child tells you something. By responding in this way, you convey to the child that she has something interesting to say and people will enjoy listening to her.

Sharing. Sometime between the ages of two and three, children begin to share their own toys and games or those belonging to the classroom with other children. While sharing is considered to be a positive social behavior, children should not be forced to share a toy or a game in their possession if they do not want to. In fact, very young children view their toys as extensions of themselves and are extremely reluctant to allow another child to play with the toy. For these children, sharing is almost like giving away part of themselves.

Because it is not always practical to have the same number of similar toys as there are children in the class, teachers need to develop strategies for helping children share. For example, teachers might place popular toys or more commonly used items in activity areas or learning centers where only a small number of children play at any given time. Also, teachers might keep mental notes of those materials used most often, for when it comes time to buy resources. Teachers should help children learn about different kinds of sharing—such as sharing materials ("I'll give you a little of my play dough") and taking turns ("I'll let you have a turn playing with my dinosaur puzzle"). Teachers need to consider—and set rules about—whether they believe that a child has a right to use a toy or material as long as that child wants to, or whether the child needs to give it up right away when someone else wants it.

Respecting Others' Property.   Children must learn to respect the property of others, whether it belongs to the preschool or to one child. By discussing with the children what toys are available for all to use and what toys require special permission to use, the teacher helps children differentiate between "public" and private property and to respect both.

"Public property" consists of all the toys, games, and materials that belong to the school. By encouraging children to share responsibility for the care of the toys and equipment, teachers help children learn that respecting public property means using it properly and taking care of it so that everyone may enjoy it.

Private property consists of toys, games, stuffed animals, and any other objects or materials children bring to the preschool from home. Teachers need to explain that private property is different from public property. Children must learn that toys brought to school by others are private property, as are all other items stored in a child's personal storage space. Only with the child's permission should another child be allowed to take an item from a private space. If an item that belongs to one child appeals to another, but the owner does not want to share, the teacher can redirect the insistent child's attention to another classroom toy. In this way, a child who does not want to share is not made to feel guilty and learns that the teacher respects her right not to share private property. In turn, the redirected child learns to respect the integrity of private property. To head off this type of situation, many preschools have a policy against children's bringing private toys to school, as these toys can be used by their owners to manipulate others. For example, a child might say to another, "I won't let you play with my toy unless you be my best friend and not play with Mark."

FOCUS ON   Communicating with Children

Talking with a Bossy Child

It is sometimes difficult to tell the difference between a child who is assertive or a natural leader and one who is bossy. One way to determine if a child is bossy is to observe whether that child is dominating other children and making them angry or fearful.

A few children decide to play bakery at the Oliver Twist Preschool. Ms. Kelly notices that Carlos joins the group and immediately begins to tell the others how the store should be set up, who should be bakers and customers, and what the bakery should sell. The other children tell him to go away, that he isn't any fun to play with.

Ms. KELLY: Carlos, I'd appreciate it if you would help me get ready for snack.

CARLOS: OK. They won't let me play with them.

Ms. KELLY: I know that makes you feel bad. Why do you think they don't want to play with you?

CARLOS: I don't know.

Ms. KELLY: Maybe it's because you told Sandy to be a customer and she wanted to bake cookies.

CARLOS: But I wanted to be the baker.

Ms. KELLY: Yes, and you'd be a very good baker. But so would Sandy. How did you feel when Sandy said you should be the customer?

CARLOS: I don't want her telling me what to be.

Ms. KELLY: I know you don't. I think it makes the other children angry when you tell them what to do.

CARLOS: But my brother always tells me what to do.

Ms. KELLY: Well, in our class, we don't boss other kids around. I understand that it's different in your house. Listen, it takes a lot of kids to help run a bakery. I bet we might even need two bakers and two cash register people, maybe two of everything.

Do you think that Ms. Kelly was effective in getting Carlos to talk about his feelings? Why or why not? Do you think that Ms. Kelly should talk to Carlos's parents about his bossiness? Why or why not?

Moral Development and the Young Child

An important aspect of a child's maturing social development is the ability to differentiate between right and wrong (Buzzelli, 1992). As children begin to understand the difference, they begin to develop a conscience. They know what they can and cannot do, what they should and should not do. Often, young children are quick to judge others' actions, but they are less able to see the difference between right and wrong in their own behavior.

Based on his work with young children, Piaget concluded that children move through three successive stages as they learn about rules, moral judgment, and the concept of justice (Piaget, 1948). In the first stage, which is characteristic of preschool children, children view rules as inflexible, determined by adults. To preschoolers, everything is either totally right or totally wrong. Children during this period also evaluate others' actions based on the consequences of the actions and not the intention or motivation. Lastly, because children at this age are still egocentric, they believe that everyone shares their own views and opinions of any given situation.

In the second stage, which begins at about age seven, children no longer see misbehavior as either totally right or wrong. Rather, they believe that punishments should be appropriate to the offense. The third stage begins in adolescence. During this time, children develop a strong sense of equity and justice. They become aware of the importance of considering various circumstances before making judgments (Mussen & Eisenberg-Berg, 1977).

Lawrence Kohlberg's work, based on Piaget's stages, presents another theory of moral development in children and adults (Kohlberg, 1971). Kohlberg believes that moral development progresses through a sequence of six stages grouped into three levels of moral orientation. Most preschool children are in the first, or preconventional, level. They respond to "good and bad" and "right and wrong" in terms of whether they will be rewarded or punished, or in terms of the power of the people who make the rules. In the conventional level, older children and young adults typically behave in a manner that is expected by their families, group, or country regardless of the consequences. They conform to expectations and acknowledge the social order. In the postconventional level, adults begin to define their own moral values apart from those held by authority figures or their peer group.

Research also suggests that moral development may be influenced by gender. Carol Gilligan, a colleague of Kohlberg's at Harvard University, asserts that Piaget's and Kohlberg's concepts of moral development are one-sided because their assumptions are based mainly on observations of boys (Gilligan, 1982). According to Gilligan, boys and girls respond differently to situations where moral judgment is required. For example, she asserts that males tend to reason based on logical consistency, whereas females tend to reason with a more caring approach. Gilligan's work highlights differences in thought and interpretation between the sexes. The care perspective is more inclusive of group needs and consensus. The logical perspective favors individual rights and autonomy. Although Gilligan's case perspective is more likely to be exemplified in children over the age of five, differences in boys and girls with respect to moral development may begin as early as the preschool years. For example, Gilligan's work shows that preschool girls already show evidence of being more inclusive, cooperative, and affiliative than boys.

Contrary to Piaget's belief that individual moral judgment does not begin until about age seven, recent research has found evidence of moral judgment in children as young as two years. These children can evaluate their behavior and the behavior of others against a standard that reflects, among other things, the experiences children have with adults (parents and teachers) and their surroundings (Kagan, 1984). For example, children whose parents provide reasons for good behavior based on how certain behavior affects (or hurts) another person tend to be better able to focus on another person's point of view than are children whose parents set up rule-oriented reasons for good behavior. For example, parents who adopt an other-person-oriented perspective might say, "We don't run indoors because we might bump into something and hurt ourselves." Parents who adopt a rule-oriented perspective might say only, "Don't run indoors."

Teachers can help children's early efforts at moral development. Through conversations, activities, and routines, young children see what rules and behaviors are valued. By recognizing that children's moral development evolves only slowly, as does physical and cognitive development, preschool teachers can be more accepting of the children's efforts and find ways to help in this process. In situations that warrant some type of consequence, the teacher should explain why to the child, in order to encourage the child's moral development. Similarly, if the teacher determines that some type of behavior is inappropriate, even though it may not need to be punished, he or she needs to give an explanation to the child.

Moral development is closely related to whether children behave prosocially or aggressively, as they begin to differentiate for themselves between right and wrong. What they consider "right" relates to the concept of helping others, or prosocial behavior. Behavior they consider "wrong" relates to the concept of hurting others physically or emotionally—that is, aggressive behavior. However, it also can mean behavior that breaks a rule, such as "No running inside" or "No talking to strangers." The next section discusses how teachers can establish a classroom environment that helps control such behavior.

Dealing with Aggressive Behavior

Aggressive behavior in the preschool setting, such as hurting someone or destroying property, interferes with learning and can be physically or emotionally harmful.

Aggressive, or oppositional, behavior is often caused by a child's struggle between establishing independence, or asserting himself, and learning cooperation (Haswell, Hock, & Wenar, 1993). Lorraine B. Wallach (1993) believes that teachers can help control aggressive behavior by establishing an environment that provides consistency, structure, clear expectations, behavior limits, and opportunities for children to express themselves. This type of environment helps children learn self-control. Children with self-control can tolerate a higher level of frustration before they resort to aggressive behavior. They often also have better problem-solving techniques.

One challenge for preschool teachers is to differentiate between a child's natural exuberance and aggressive behavior. Although teachers want to encourage energy and enthusiasm, they cannot permit aggressive behavior— that is, behavior that hurts or destroys the work of another child.

Finding the Cause

The first step in finding the cause of aggressive behavior is to understand that children misbehave for a number of reasons. For example, children may misbehave because their needs are not being met; they are unaware that the

Children who are still learning about self-control often resort to aggressive behavior. This can include grabbing, yelling, or pushing. Teachers first need to find the cause of the aggressive behavior, and then consider appropriate solutions.

behavior is inappropriate; they feel insecure or frustrated; or they want the teacher's attention. Others may misbehave to show their power or to "get back at" someone or something that has annoyed them, whether real or imagined (Dreikurs & Cassel, 1972). Children who are rejected by their peers display significantly more aggressive behavior than popular children and are more threatening to other children (Honig, 1987).

Before taking any action, the teacher should determine why a child is behaving aggressively. Is a child bored or not becoming involved in sufficiently challenging activities? Is he big for his age, and does he not know his own strength? Should he participate in more large-muscle play, outdoor play, creative play, or manipulative play that may help him release excess energy? Might he suffer from attention deficit disorder (ADD)? The teacher also should examine the curriculum and room arrangement, as well as observing and talking to the child, to find reasons for aggression. Although children act out for many reasons, behavior that is stopped but not resolved may be replaced by a different, more aggressive behavior in the future.

Unintentional Aggression.   Not all acts of aggression by young children are intentional. Very young children who lack language skills, for example, may appear to be aggressive. One young child may push another as a way of greeting. Sometimes, preschool children accidentally kick or hit another child if they lack adequate communication or motor skills. Under such circumstances, the teacher must regain control of the situation and protect the hurt child by stopping the aggressive child. The teacher should give attention to the hurt child first. Then, by talking to and comforting the angry child, the teacher can help that child regain self-control with dignity.

Hitting, kicking, spitting, biting, and verbal abuse are the only ways some children know of to meet their needs. In many cases, these children are imitating behaviors displayed by the adults or older children in their family or neighborhood. See the section "Making Peace: Conflict Resolution" later in this chapter for ways preschool teachers can help these children learn acceptable and nonthreatening ways to satisfy their needs.

Intentional Aggression.   Intentional aggression may be either instrumental or hostile. Preschoolers generally engage in *instrumental aggression*, in which they may grab a toy, push, or hit in order to fulfill a specific goal. *Hostile aggression* is purposeful physical or verbal behavior that is intended to hurt another child physically or emotionally or to destroy property. Children who willfully and continually misbehave over an extended period of time, regardless of the teacher's efforts, require the attention and advice of a professional mental health or behavior therapist (Greenberg, 1992).

Even though there are numerous causes of aggressive behavior, most children do not willfully and purposefully misbehave. Teachers can help children learn to redirect their behavior into more constructive behavior and to resolve disputes in a peaceful manner.

Conflicts arise even in a well-planned program. A popular piece of playground equipment, such as this play school bus, requires children to take turns. In this case, the teacher might encourage the children to come up with solutions, such as one child playing driver and one playing passenger.

Making Peace: Conflict Resolution

Teachers need to respond immediately to aggressive behavior in order to defuse a potentially dangerous situation. They also need to develop strategies for preventing future episodes of aggressive behavior.

Social psychology offers insights into how children can learn to resolve their conflicts and disputes peacefully. Children go through a long process of developing an understanding of conflict and how to resolve it, referred to as the *process of construction* (Kohlberg & Lickona, 1990). Children use what they see in their lives as the basis for constructing an understanding of how people treat one another. As children mature, they constantly revise their understanding of conflict (Carlsson-Paige & Levin, 1992).

The process of conflict resolution has evolved to help child care professionals teach children to settle disputes. Nancy Carlsson-Paige and Diane E. Levin suggest a strategy based on defining the problem, brainstorming possible solutions, using negotiation skills, and choosing solutions that satisfy both sides.

Before being able to resolve conflicts on their own, children must be able to understand another's perspective, be concerned about another's rights and feelings, and appreciate the consequences of the conflict. They must have self-control and patience, as well as sufficient emotional, cognitive, social, and language skills (Greenberg, 1992).

How children define a conflict has a great deal to do with how they resolve it. As children mature in their thinking, around ages three to five, they no longer see the problem only in terms of how it affects them. They begin to understand the problem from other perspectives and can evaluate motives, feelings, and intentions (Carlsson-Paige & Levin, 1992). Some research

This teacher is using the technique of self-report to help children in a conflict practice expressing their feelings verbally.

suggests that some children as young as age three are capable of decentering enough to evaluate others' motives, feelings, and views (Kagan, 1984).

By age six or seven, children also learn that most problems have more than one solution. However, some younger children are capable of understanding alternative solutions if presented in a very concrete manner. The key to resolving the problem is finding a solution that satisfies the needs of everyone involved. Some solutions are positive and let everyone feel like a "winner." Children who learn how to resolve their own conflicts feel "empowered." They have a sense of being able to control a part of their lives and to improve the quality of their interactions with peers in social relationships (Carlsson-Paige & Levin, 1992).

Negotiation is an important part of conflict resolution and marks the process of moving from a problem toward a solution. Negotiation requires communication, compromise, the ability to see two or more points of view, and the ability to see how aspects of a conflict are related to one another (Carlsson-Paige & Levin, 1992).

Polly Greenberg (1992) suggests a process for helping children learn negotiation and peaceful ways to resolve conflict. The teacher kneels to be at eye level with the children having the conflict, makes sure that both children are paying attention, and suggests talking over the problem in a quiet corner of the room. The teacher assures both children that each will have an opportunity to tell what happened. The teacher's job in this situation is to help each child explain the cause of the conflict from each point of view. Each child should be encouraged to offer a solution or to decide what to do next.

If the solutions differ, the discussion must continue until a solution that is considered acceptable to both parties is determined.

Preschool teachers need to understand that, before children can learn to resolve their conflicts in a peaceful way, they must possess a certain level of social, emotional, and intellectual maturity. As with learning other skills, children require sufficient opportunities to practice conflict resolution skills in the classroom with the assistance and guidance of the teacher. Teachers can help children who are not yet ready to resolve conflicts on their own by working with them on techniques such as self-report and "remember when."

How the Curriculum Affects Conflict Resolution.   The curriculum should include developmentally appropriate activities that provide opportunities for children to practice conflict resolution skills. For example, during class meetings or group time, children can talk about ways they try to get along with other children, what they think works well, and why they think it works (Carlsson-Paige & Levin, 1992).

The teacher might read books with conflict themes that illustrate how the characters successfully resolved their conflicts. Afterward, children can create their own stories or playact a conflict and experiment with different solutions. Showing children pictures of a conflict situation can stimulate discussion about the conflict. This activity can provide children with the opportunity to define the problem and suggest ways to solve it that might be acceptable to all involved. Puppets also might be useful to role-play a conflict similar to the one the children in the class are experiencing (Carlsson-Paige & Levin, 1992).

To complement these conflict resolution activities, teachers should encourage nonviolent solutions to disputes, should value cooperation, and should provide opportunities that foster cooperation and sharing. Teachers also should consistently ask for and use children's ideas and involve children in the decision-making process (Carlsson-Paige & Levin, 1992).

Teachers can structure the curriculum and the classroom environment in such a way as to make children more likely to behave appropriately. For example, by greeting each child in a welcoming manner at the beginning of each day, teachers can make children feel welcome and happier, and more likely to behave.

Also, a classroom that offers enough activities, toys, and equipment to involve and interest all the children discourages misbehavior (Feeney, 1993). A schedule that provides a balance of activities—for example, active and quiet, indoor and outdoor activities—keeps variety in the day and helps keep children involved in constructive activities. Sufficient indoor space gives children room to work and to walk around without disrupting another's activity or bumping into other children. Likewise, the playground should have sufficient outdoor space for small-group and large-group games.

In addition to being aware of aspects of the environment and curriculum that might cause misbehavior, teachers also can directly guide children toward acceptable behavior. Teachers can establish a set of clear and simple rules, and explain and discuss them with the children in a straightforward manner. Then, the teacher must be consistent in upholding the rules and reminding children to do so, too.

Teachers should discuss with the children such topics as the importance of respecting the rights of others, maintaining self-control, being cooperative, and acting responsibly within the context of the classroom and with other children. But the teacher's actions will speak louder than words. Children who understand the classroom rules and what is expected of them will usually respond by behaving well (Greenberg, 1992). Sometimes, a smile or a simple thank-you is sufficient for the teacher to communicate to children which behaviors are appropriate. More specific feedback may be needed to remind others. For example, a teacher might say, "Jonah, I'm glad you used your words instead of grabbing the truck."

Maintaining Order.   There are several different approaches to maintaining order. If a child disobeys the classroom rules, the teacher can speak with him in a quiet corner of the room. The teacher should discuss the rule that he disobeyed and make sure that he understands the rule and the reason for it. The teacher can then encourage him to suggest how he might behave differently the next time (Greenberg, 1992).

If that child continues to misbehave, the teacher might once again explain the rule he is breaking and tell him that he cannot continue to participate in the activity or must take "time-out" until he is in better control (Greenberg, 1992). *Time-out* literally refers to time out from play or from an activity and is a common form of discipline in the preschool setting. Cheri Sterman Miller (1984) believes that time-out should not be humiliating but should last long enough for the child to regain control.

The amount of the time-out will depend on the child's ability to reflect on his misbehavior and gain enough control to resume the activity from which he was removed. Typically, three to five minutes is sufficient for three- to five-year-olds. Before the time-out is completed, the teacher should always ascertain from the child that he is ready to resume the activity. The teacher should not simply "release" the child from the time-out. Rather, the teacher should obtain the child's verbal assurance that he is ready to participate. The child needs to say that he is now ready to join the group and that he will participate under the classroom rules. Time-out is controversial because it is sometimes used only as a punishment or it is used in a careless and humiliating way.

If a child continues to misbehave after these strategies have been used, the teacher might try to identify the reward or satisfaction he gets from misbehaving. For example, does the child enjoy the extra attention he gets? If so, the teacher might find other, more constructive ways for him to feel included and cared about. Perhaps the teacher needs to help him learn more effective problem-solving strategies, such as techniques for joining a group of children playing without being aggressive (see Chapter 4).

The best way to maintain order is to avoid situations that are likely to cause discipline problems (Soderman, 1985). Jeannette Stone (1992) suggests

Talking about rules directly with children is an important strategy for maintaining order in the classroom. These discussions work best when they take place during or immediately after a classroom conflict.

a number of curriculum factors that boost self-esteem and eliminate opportunities for misbehavior, including allowing plenty of time for activities and transitions during the day. Children sense when the teacher is rushed, tense, or unhappy, and they may, in turn, become tense or unhappy. The daily plan that includes plenty of developmentally appropriate, interesting, and stimulating activities will engage children and hold their interest. The curriculum should reflect a balance of activity levels. Some children require lots of activity, whereas others require quiet activities and more restful periods. Children should be able to participate in a number of activities without adult intervention, so that they will gain a feeling of control and self-esteem.

Even after structuring the curriculum to prevent discipline problems and setting a curriculum goal to help children develop self-discipline, preschool teachers still need to be vigilant and to stop problems before they get out of control. Effective discipline begins before disruptive behavior occurs (Miller, 1984). Teachers should learn to sense when trouble is imminent and to intervene by separating the children involved. Once the children are calm, then conflict resolution techniques can be used.

Some preschool activities provide opportunities for children to substitute acceptable behaviors for aggressive behaviors. Playing with clay or other manipulative materials, climbing on large, sturdy play equipment, dramatic play, and play with puppets or dolls can help calm children or encourage them to verbalize whatever is bothering them. These kinds of activities help release tensions. Such activities should be available to children at all times, and especially on days when tension and excitement are likely to be high—for example, if a holiday or birthday party is planned or if bad weather extends over a number of days.

Helping Children Respect One Another

In addition to learning about prosocial behavior, controlling aggression, and developing moral judgment, the social development of young children involves learning to interact and get along with people from various cultures. In recent years, there has been considerable interest in anti-bias education that confronts discrimination and bias in all areas of the curriculum (Ramsey & Derman-Sparks, 1992). Anna Kelman writes that anti-bias education—which includes reducing bias against people based on gender, disabilities, or cultural background—is important to children's social development because they "learn attitudes much faster than they learn the alphabet" (Kelman, 1990, p. 43). The trend toward anti-bias education is supported by research that shows that racism and bias damage the development of children's identities (Derman-Sparks & the A. B. C. Task Force, 1989). Elizabeth Jones and Louise Derman-Sparks (1992) warn that a curriculum that ignores the existence of bias and discrimination does not prepare children to live effectively and deal fairly with diversity.

Books that portray the everyday lives of children from a variety of racial and cultural backgrounds help preschoolers learn to recognize similarities between themselves and others.

Checklist for Anti-Bias Materials
Materials in the classroom should show:
✔ Contemporary children and adults from major racial/ethnic groups in the community doing everyday activities
✔ Diversity within racial/ethnic groups
✔ Women and men of various groups doing a variety of jobs in the home and outside the home
✔ Elderly people of all groups doing various activities
✔ Differently abled people of various backgrounds in a variety of settings, including at home, at work, and playing
✔ Diverse life-styles
✔ Individuals of all groups contributing to the community's well-being, including movements for justice

FIGURE 9.1 Checklist for Anti-Bias Materials. Adapted from "Meeting the Challenge of Diversity" by E. Jones and L. Derman-Sparks, 1992, *Young Children*, 47(2), p. 16. Copyright © 1992 by the National Association for the Education of Young Children. Adapted by permission.

As stated in Chapter 3, children develop racial and gender awareness and begin to notice physical disabilities between the ages of two and six. By age two, they know gender labels and color names, which they apply to skin color. Derman-Sparks (1989) notes that, between ages three and five, children begin to ask questions about differentiating features, such as "Will I always be a girl?" and "Why are Masashi's eyes different from mine?".

As discussed in Chapter 3, multiculturalism is a kind of subset to the anti-bias curriculum, and it specifically addresses issues related to culture. An individual's cultural identity is based on a number of traits and values related to national or ethnic origin, family, religion, gender, age, occupation, socioeconomic level, language, geographical region, and residence (rural, urban, suburban) (Hernandez, 1989). Culture encompasses customs, beliefs, values, and experiences as well as art, dress, music, and traditions. Culture permeates every aspect of a person's life. Children bring their culture with them when they come to school. Susan Workman (1992) asserts that, by focusing on various cultures within the curriculum, teachers help children learn to take pride in their identities, and to appreciate the similarities and differences among people from different backgrounds.

Fostering Acceptance and Respect

Teachers are the key to fostering mutual acceptance and respect among children in the preschool setting. They create the environment and curriculum that influences children's attitudes toward others. See Figure 9.1, Checklist for Anti-Bias Materials. In classrooms where children are encouraged to ask questions about race, disabilities, and gender, there are likely to be more opportunities to discuss bias issues. Teachers should address questions or

FOCUS ON   Cultural Diversity

Setting Up a Sister School Relationship

If a preschool group is made up of children who share the same racial and ethnic background, how can a teacher integrate multiculturalism into the curriculum? One possibility is to establish a sister school program that will pair two preschools that have different cultural mixes—for example, one in which most of the children are black and one in which most of the children are white. The first step in setting up this type of program is to contact the chief administrator or head teacher of a preschool in another area of town or in a nearby town or city. Consider the following curriculum activities.

Introduce the sister school to the children.   Look on a map to see where the children from the sister school live. If the communities are geographically different, talk with the children in your class about what it might be like to live in a city instead of in a suburb, for example. Exchange class pictures, and learn the children's names.

Focus on similarities.   It is likely that the children in both preschools enjoy many of the same games, stories, songs, and foods. A child also may have the same name as someone in the sister school. Sending outlines of the children's hands or footprints made with finger paint, labeled with each child's name, will help children focus visually on similarities.

Share classroom photographs.   The children in the sister school will be curious to know what your preschool looks like. Where does the class sit during group time? Where do the children play outside? Take some photographs, or, if possible, make a videotape of the children enjoying some typical activities indoors and outdoors.

Make a tape recording.   A tape recording allows children to hear one another's voices and accents. Children can sing a favorite song, tell a story, or send a special message.

Exchange art projects and stories.   By sharing drawings and experiences, the children can get to know one another better. Ask children to make pictures of their families, their pets, and what they do after school to send to their new "friends."

Arrange to visit the sister school, if possible.   Do not plan too many structured activities because, most likely, the children will be happy and excited to meet and play with their new friends.

negative responses to differences immediately. The teacher should explain to the child that negative responses are hurtful. He or she should talk about alternative, constructive ways of asking questions or making comments about other people (Derman-Sparks & the A. B. C. Task Force, 1989).

Teachers who want to foster acceptance and respect among children in the classroom make multicultural experiences a part of the classroom's daily activity, rather than limiting them to a particular area of the room, week of the year, or isolated projects (Workman & Staff, 1992).

The Multicultural Curriculum in the Classroom

Multicultural education is relevant to all preschools and child care centers, whether or not they include minority children. The United States is a multicultural society. Therefore, starting at a young age, all children should begin to learn about various cultures and to interact with children and adults from diverse backgrounds.

The nature of the multicultural curriculum will vary, depending on the cultural makeup of the class. In a *heterogeneous classroom*—that is, one with children of diverse backgrounds—the activities of the multicultural curriculum often are based on the experiences and backgrounds of the children. The primary goal is to help the children understand and appreciate the extent of their similarities and the nature of their differences. Children in a culturally diverse classroom will experience this concept in a concrete way.

Multicultural activities in a heterogeneous classroom may relate to foods, languages, clothing, or customs. Such materials as books, pictures, and dolls selected for classroom use should show people of different cultures and races and differently abled people working in a variety of jobs. Music should reflect a variety of cultures from around the world.

In a *homogeneous classroom,* the children come from a similar background, sometimes called a *monocultural community.* For example, the children may be all white, all black, or all Native American. In this type of classroom, the multicultural curriculum has two goals. It attempts to identify and capitalize on whatever diversity does exist in the community. It also helps children learn about other cultures and ways of life (Ramsey, 1982).

Cultural differences are more difficult to convey in a homogeneous classroom than in a heterogeneous classroom. Children in a homogeneous setting do not have the benefit of seeing children of other cultures in day-to-day play situations. These children also may live in neighborhoods that are made up of families belonging to one cultural group. Differences among the children in a homogeneous classroom may be limited to family size, personal experiences, and physical appearance. Teachers need to look for ways, through activities and materials, to help children learn about other cultures. The fact that people look, eat, work, cook, and speak differently has to be consciously introduced by the teacher into the curriculum. By providing concrete activities to illustrate these differences, teachers help children become more receptive to variations among people. Patricia Ramsey (1982) asserts that these activities help the children become more open to contact with less familiar people and learn to treat others with respect and an open-minded attitude. See the "Focus on Cultural Diversity" feature on sister schools in this chapter for insight into a suggested program for a homogeneous classroom. Books about children from different areas of the United States can help a child learn that people have common needs even if they look and sound different. The goal of such a program is to provide children with images and experiences that support the development of cultural identity and the awareness of diversity (Ramsey, 1982).

Opportunities to learn about diverse cultures can be planned in the curriculum or can occur spontaneously. In this planned musical activity, the teacher talks about the role of drums used by Native Americans. Later, the children will take turns playing the drums.

Applications

Multicultural education can be incorporated effectively into every aspect of the early childhood program. A concrete way to begin making cultural diversity an integral part of the curriculum is by examining the classroom environment. The heterogeneous preschool should reflect the daily home life of the children. By recognizing the foods, clothing, stories, customs, and everyday way of life that are part of the experiences youngsters bring to school, the school says that ethnic identity is valuable. This approach, in turn, enhances children's self-esteem. The very composition of the room conveys a feeling of acceptance for all children, as well as provoking an awareness of diversity (Workman & Staff, 1992). The homogeneous preschool should reflect a variety of cultures through materials, wall displays, and activities.

Photographs are another effective way to reflect cultural diversity. Pictures of children at work in the classroom, at home with families, and with parents and siblings in different places in the community or neighborhood capture the classroom's diversity. These photos can be used in displays, in "big books" made by the children, and for sharing with family. Many important cultural messages can be discussed during a variety of activities. For example, while the children make sand paintings during art time, the teacher might discuss the traditional use of sand painting during Navajo ceremonies. Classroom signs in several languages encourage visual awareness of diversity, even though most of the children will not be able to read them. Putting various kinds of clothes that reflect cultural diversity in the dramatic play area will help children become familiar with the different ways people dress, every day and on special or ceremonial occasions. Susan Workman (1992) suggests that teachers or parents share a part of their lives with the children in school. For example, if a teacher's mother knows how to play some simple Spanish songs on the guitar, she might visit the classroom and teach the children the songs.

Unplanned Opportunities

Opportunities to discuss various cultures often come up spontaneously in the day-to-day goings-on of the classroom. Teachers must be prepared to discuss any aspect of bias, such as bias based on gender or culture, at any time, as Miss Lee was ready to discuss how people have different kinds of hair. Children's offhand comments about a picture of a person in nontraditional clothing, preparations for a holiday, a grandparent visiting from overseas, or a child with a physical disability who is joining the class all become opportunities to foster anti-bias attitudes and respect for others.

When children use stereotypes, such as cultural stereotypes, as part of their play, teachers must respond to their actions. For example, if children play "Cowboys and Indians," the teacher can explain how this game may hurt people's feelings, especially if there are Native American children in the class. In this game, Indians usually are the "bad guys." If they portray Native

Americans as living in tepees or wearing feathers, the teacher needs to explain that Native Americans today live in houses and have jobs and go to school just like the children's own parents and siblings.

Planned Opportunities

Anti-bias and multicultural education are such important aspects of early childhood education that they should not be left to spontaneous moments. Planned activities that focus on anti-bias topics and cultural diversity should be integrated into the daily plan. An important concept to remember is that anti-bias "education embodies a perspective rather than a curriculum" (Ramsey, 1982, p. 134).

Learning about diversity works well using the project approach, which was described in Chapter 2. For example, a teacher may choose to focus a unit on a particular people, such as the Navajo. The following topics, adapted from Workman & Staff (1992), might be included.

- Caring for infants (props may include a cradleboard, Navajo and other types of blankets, baby pictures of children in the classroom)
- Making ethnic foods, such as Kneel Down Bread (find information about and explain the Navajo translation of *Nitsidigo*—September, month of the Big Harvest)
- Storytelling (find a book that focuses on the rich oral tradition of the Navajo "Coyote Tales" told during the winter months)
- Music (discuss how Navajos use drums as musical accompaniment and to draw the group together; use the drum as a signal to children that an activity is about to begin)
- Fine motor skills (stringing "beads" made of turquoise-painted styrofoam and silver foil-covered straws)
- Respect for the environment (take the children outside to participate in the Navajo holiday custom of decorating a tree with food for the animals)

Children's books provide many opportunities to foster respect for diversity. Before choosing books for the classroom, teachers should check to see whether the books include materials that might be offensive, discriminatory, or stereotypical. See the "Focus on Cultural Diversity" feature in Chapter 11 for a discussion on evaluating children's books for bias.

In an increasingly diverse society, the preschool curriculum needs to adopt an anti-bias and multicultural perspective on the social development of young children. As children grow up, they will meet and interact with people with differing abilities and people from a wide variety of backgrounds. A curriculum with an anti-bias focus will help children recognize similarities and respect differences in their expanding social world. Tolerance, understanding, and respect for people with differing abilities and people from different backgrounds than their own will help children establish rapport and friendships with others. These feelings will also help children communicate and work with others successfully throughout their lives.

Parents can inspire many multicultural learning experiences. A child's question about a mother's sari sparks an unplanned opportunity to talk about Indian clothes. If this mother is invited to teach the children about Holi, an Indian festival in which people tint their faces with colored powder to celebrate the advent of spring, that would be a planned opportunity.

SUMMARY

- Young children are learning social skills, such as getting along with others, making friends, sharing, helping others, and assuming small responsibilities.

- Preschools are natural places for young children to build social skills because they generally include individuals from a variety of backgrounds, races, and cultures.

- Although no one explanation describes how children learn social skills, it is commonly accepted that children learn by imitating the behaviors of the significant adults and children in their lives.

- Prosocial behavior is based on caring and concern for others, with the benefactor acting without expecting a reward.

- Friendships contribute to several areas of children's development, including emotional well-being, social skills, and competencies.

- Children who make friends easily can communicate clearly, find things they share in common, and resolve conflicts satisfactorily.

- Although sharing is considered constructive social behavior, children should not be forced to share a toy or a game in their possession if they do not want to.

- Children must learn to differentiate between "public" and private property and understand and follow the rules that apply to each.

- Piaget concluded that children and adolescents move through three stages as they learn about rules, moral judgment, and the concept of justice.

- Aggressive behavior interferes with the preschool setting and the children's experience, can be physically or emotionally harmful, and can result in damaged or destroyed property.

- Before taking any action, the teacher should determine why the child is displaying aggressive behavior and should help the child learn nonaggressive ways to solve problems.

- The curriculum should include developmentally appropriate activities that provide opportunities for children to practice conflict resolution skills.

- Teachers maintain order by making sure that the children know the rules, identifying alternative behaviors, and redirecting children to more constructive activities.

- Teachers are the key to fostering acceptance and mutual respect among children. The materials and activities the teacher selects create the setting that influences children's attitudes toward others.

- Anti-bias and multicultural experiences must be integrated into the classroom's daily activities rather than being relegated to a particular area of the room or week of the year.

ACQUIRING KNOWLEDGE

1. Describe three views about what motivates social behavior.
2. How can you tell if a child is exhibiting prosocial behavior?
3. How do the cognitive-developmental and behaviorist theories differ in their view of prosocial development?
4. How can a teacher's actions and attitudes encourage the development of prosocial behavior?
5. How do friendships contribute to the ongoing social and cognitive development of young children?
6. What factors affect the friends that young children choose?
7. In what ways can the classroom design help promote or discourage the development of friendships?
8. What strategies does Honig suggest for helping shy children develop social skills?
9. Why is it important for preschool children to understand the difference between "public" and private property?
10. How did Piaget view the moral development of children?
11. How do Kohlberg and Gilligan's theories of moral development differ from Piaget's?
12. How can teachers help promote a child's moral development?
13. What are some common causes of aggressive behavior in young children?
14. What factors in the preschool environment help children develop self-control?
15. What is the difference between intentional and unintentional aggression?
16. Define the process of construction, and discuss how it promotes social development.
17. Describe some strategies teachers can use to help children resolve conflicts with others.
18. What are some curriculum activities that help children develop conflict resolution skills?
19. How can a teacher make sure that a curriculum and the classroom environment do not promote misbehavior?
20. What strategies should a teacher use when a child deliberately misbehaves?
21. Describe some activities that help children substitute acceptable behaviors for aggressive behaviors.
22. How do the multicultural elements of a preschool curriculum relate to children's social development?
23. What types of classroom materials contribute to a multicultural curriculum?
24. How does a multicultural curriculum differ in heterogeneous and in homogeneous classrooms?
25. How can a multicultural curriculum use both planned and unplanned opportunities to foster social development?

THINKING CRITICALLY

1. Preschool teachers should keep parents informed about children's social development. Describe some observations that a teacher might share with parents to keep them informed about a child's developing social skills.

2. Forcing children to share an item can create conflict and aggressive behavior. What kinds of activities do you think might help children develop the ability to share on their own?

3. Carol Gilligan has studied the ways in which males and females respond to situations that require moral judgment. Do you think that there is a significant difference in the ways that males and females respond to these situations? Explain your answer.

4. Even in a well-planned curriculum, aggressive behavior will occur. What steps do you think a teacher might follow to discover the reasons for the behavior?

5. Parents do not always understand the necessity for a multicultural curriculum. For example, the parent of a child attending an entirely Asian American preschool might feel that posters showing people of other ethnic backgrounds are unnecessary and do not promote a positive self-image. How might a teacher respond to this parent?

OBSERVATIONS AND APPLICATIONS

1. Observe a group of three- or four-year-olds at play together in a preschool setting. Do you notice any of the children showing concern, cooperation or empathy toward other children with whom they are playing? Record some specific examples. Write down the children's actions and dialogue, and the materials, props, or toys they are using. Are they sharing toys or other items? Does the teacher interact with the children? If so, how? What are the children's reactions?

2. Visit a preschool setting in your area to observe how multiculturalism is integrated into the environment. Do photographs and posters of children and/or their families on the walls portray people from diverse races and cultures? Which races and cultures do you see represented? Do the books, materials, clothes, and props for dramatic play, and toys in different activity areas, reflect a variety of cultures? If so, how? Describe them.

3. Billy ran into preschool, charged with excitement. As he took off his coat, he knocked several children's jackets off the pegs. Seemingly oblivious, Billy stepped on the coats and skipped over to the block area. He started playing with the blocks but quickly became interested in Andre's elaborate block building. Billy looked back at his own block house, which he thought was horrible. He kicked his foot and toppled Andre's blocks. Andre squealed in protest, catching the teacher's attention. Mrs. Randolph looked over in exasperation. For the past few weeks, Billy consistently exhibited aggressive behavior. What might Mrs. Randolph do to address Billy's negative behavior pattern?

4. Five-year-olds Janet and Kelly are best friends. Ever since they joined the same group at the New Beginnings Preschool, the girls have been inseparable. They play together, eat together, nap together, and even visit the bathroom at the same time. On Janet's birthday, she is asked to choose someone to help hand out the birthday cupcakes to the children during snack time. Surprisingly, Janet chooses Nora, a new girl in the preschool group. At this announcement, Kelly starts to cry. When the teacher asks her what is the matter, Kelly exclaims angrily, "Janet doesn't like me anymore!" How might the teacher help Kelly and Janet resolve this conflict?

FOR FURTHER INFORMATION

Allen, J., McNeill, E., & Schmidt, V. (1992). *Cultural awareness for children.* New York: Addison-Wesley.

Axline, V. M. (1967). *Dibs in search of self.* New York: Ballantine.

Banks, J. A. (1988). *Multiethnic education: Theory and practice* (2nd ed.). Boston: Allyn & Bacon.

Buzzelli, C. (1992). Young children's moral understanding: Learning about right and wrong. *Young Children, 47*(6), 47–53.

Child choice—Another way to individualize—another form of discipline. (1987, November). *Young Children, 43*(1), 48–54.

Derman-Sparks, L., & the A. B. C. Task Force (1989). *Anti-bias curriculum: Tools for empowering young children.* Washington, DC: National Association for the Education of Young Children.

Greenberg, P. (1992). How to institute some simple democratic practices pertaining to respect, rights, roots, and responsiblities in any classroom (without losing your leadership position). *Young Children, 47*(5), 10–17.

Honig, A. S. (1987). The shy child. *Young Children, 42*(4), 51–64.

Thompson, B. (1993). *Words can hurt you: Beginning a program of anti-bias education.* New York: Addison-Wesley.

York, S. (1992). *Developing roots and wings: A trainer's guide to affirming culture in early childhood programs.* St. Paul, MN: Redleaf Press (distributed by Gryphon House, Mt. Rainier, MD).

10 Cognitive Development: Perception

OBJECTIVES

Studying this chapter
will enable you to

- Explain how young children learn by using their senses
- List the primary perceptual skills and discuss the role they play in the development of young children
- Name two types of perceptual problems and suggest ways of addressing each
- Give examples of activities and materials that encourage children to use perceptual skills

CHAPTER TERMS

amblyopia
auditory discrimination
bimodal perception
conservation
eye-hand coordination
multisensory environment
perception
perceptual development
phonemes
sensory integration
spatial relations
strabismus
visual discrimination
visual perception
visual perceptual disorder

THE group of three-year-olds had just returned from playing outdoors. They washed their hands and sat down on the carpet for circle time. Their teacher, Mrs. Banik, held up a big glass bowl filled with small yellow pieces—corn kernels. As they gathered around her, Mrs. Banik asked, "Does anyone know what these are?" None of the children answered.

"I'm going to give each of you three of these," Mrs. Banik said. "Let's see if you can guess what they are. What do they feel like?" she asked. Each child rolled the kernels in their hands and squeezed them.

"They're smooth and hard. Like marbles," said Veneice.

"What do they smell like?" Mrs. Banik probed. The children sniffed, but no one made any response.

"Not much smell, right? Let's see what happens if we put a bag of these in a microwave," Mrs. Banik said, placing a bag of microwave popcorn in the oven and turning it on. In a few minutes, Mrs. Banik asked, "What do you hear?"

"It's going pop-pop-pop," said Alex.

"It's popcorn!" several children shouted.

"Right," said Mrs. Banik with a smile. She gave each child some popped kernels and asked, "Do these smell different from the unpopped kernels in your hand? Let's smell them each again."

"The popped ones smell yummy," said Veneice, "They look different, too."

"Yeah, this one is hard and yellow," said Alex, holding up the unpopped kernel. "The other is white and squishy. And it tastes good!" The children laughed as he put it into his mouth.

"It sure does! Enjoy your snack," said Mrs. Banik.

Young children first experience the world through their senses. Through seeing, hearing, smelling, tasting, and touching, they begin to explore and understand their surroundings. It is through *perception*, the organization of sensory information, that they develop and modify their concepts about the world.

As children mature, they learn to coordinate information from their senses with physical motions and activities. This process is called *perceptual development* or perceptual-motor development. As children's muscles develop, for example, they gain increasing control over their actions, learning first to control the large muscle groups in their arms and legs and then the small muscle groups of their hands and fingers. This coordination, for example, enabled the children in Mrs. Banik's class to pick up and manipulate the corn kernels to look at them closely, feel their texture, and detect their smell and taste. Virtually all activities in the preschool setting involve children's perception skills, and these activities play an important role in perceptual development.

This chapter discusses how perceptual development relates to the cognitive development of preschoolers and how young children learn to integrate information through their senses. It also illustrates many ways that preschool teachers can help children refine perceptual skills.

Perception and Cognitive Development

Early childhood experts agree that perception and cognitive development are closely related. They have disagreed, however, on the nature of this relationship. Some have argued that perception is dependent on the development of cognitive processes. According to this view, perception matures with increasing cognitive development (Pick, 1983). Another view, reflected in the work of Piaget, is that perception is the primary process on which cognition is based. According to Piaget, perception acts to either inform or mislead intellectual processes. Thus, the earliest stage of Piaget's theory of cognitive development is the sensorimotor stage, in which infants learn about objects through acting on objects using all their senses.

Early childhood educators today believe that very young children learn about their world by interacting with it (Biber, 1984; Fein, 1979; Forman &

Kuschner, 1983). Children use their senses to explore and manipulate objects and materials. Long before children can speak, they learn about their environment through their perceptual experiences. They discover the properties of objects, how things work, and the characteristics of people, such as what their mothers look like and how they smell. Research has shown, for example, that infants as young as five months old can distinguish faces on the basis of general traits, such as age and sex. As they grow older, children begin to differentiate on the basis of more specific features, such as hair color and facial characteristics (Fagan & Singer, 1979).

During the preschool years, children continue to use the information acquired through perception to identify relationships among objects and people. They develop concepts and ideas that explain and categorize these relationships. This ability is vital to the learning process. By providing developmentally appropriate activities and materials for preschool children, teachers can help foster the development of keen perceptual skills that will remain with children throughout elementary school and, in fact, throughout all of life.

Perceptual Skills and the Young Child

Because young children gain information through all their senses, it is important that preschool settings provide a *multisensory* environment. The school environment should offer a variety of activities and materials that stimulate children's senses. It might include cloth-covered books; differently textured clothes in the dramatic play area; collage materials, such as feathers, uncooked noodles, and sequins; colorful stickers; a basket of pinecones, shells, or rocks and pebbles; all types of music; and a variety of food experiences, such as exploring the touch, taste, and smell of fruit. A multisensory environment with easily accessible materials encourages children to use all their senses.

Before learning how to create such an enriched multisensory environment, however, preschool teachers need to understand the different types of perception and how children learn through each of their senses. This knowledge is essential for devising curriculum activities that help children strengthen their sensory acuity and learn through combining sensory information. See the "Applications" section later in this chapter for a description of several activities designed to foster specific perceptual skills.

Young children develop visual perceptual skills as they observe and examine objects and materials during play. This three-year-old is fascinated by the swirling patterns made by sunlight on his bubble.

Visual Perception

Visual perception is the ability to use the sense of sight to recognize, differentiate, and recall objects. Children use visual perception skills when they try to copy a shape, draw an object from memory, or line up a group of sticks from shortest to longest. Children also use visual perception skills to watch a rabbit eat, or for "scientific observations," such as watching snow melt when brought inside or the bubbling of vinegar mixed with soda. Visual perception skills develop gradually during the first few years of life. By age two,

FOCUS ON Cultural Diversity

Gender Differences in Block Play

Block play helps children explore visual-spatial relationships, fosters creative expression, and provides opportunities for cooperative play.

However, some classic studies that are still referenced today (Clark, Wyon, & Richards, 1969; Coates, Lord, & Jakabovics, 1975) show that boys play with blocks more frequently than girls do. Girls who play only with dolls, housekeeping props, and toys other than blocks may receive a more limited preschool experience than boys. What can preschool teachers do to reduce gender differences in block play?

One way to encourage mixed gender play with blocks is to combine props in different areas of the classroom. For example, the teacher could move some of the blocks into the housekeeping area and ask the children how they might use the blocks to create furniture for a house. The teacher might move some housekeeping props into the block area and see how the children use them in that setting.

The teacher also might talk with individual girls to identify some specific interest and then add relevant props to the block area. If the girls say that they like horses or baby animals, for instance, the teacher might encourage them to build a stable for some toy horses. Or the teacher might bring in plastic grass and small sticks and encourage the girls to build a nest with the blocks for a baby bird.

Asking questions along the way lets the girls know that the teacher values their input. The teacher's comments and questions such as "Can the horse fit under the bridge?" also help the girls focus on spatial relations.

for example, children's eyes are fully developed, but their perceptual abilities are not. They may be able to focus on an object, but their ability to perceive motion or depth is not yet fully developed (Payne & Isaacs, 1991; Williams, 1983).

Visual perception plays an important role in the physical development of young children. Ball skills, such as kicking, throwing, and catching, all require highly developed visual perception skills. Good visual skills also are essential for reading and writing. The ability to recognize letters and words is one of the prerequisites of learning to read and write. Studies have shown that children's eye muscles are not adequately developed to move across a series of letters until about age six. Thus, most children are not physically prepared for formal reading instruction until the first grade (Vurpillot, 1968).

Preschool teachers should provide children with ample opportunities to use and practice skills involving visual perception. Such activities as having a child identify all the things in a room that are blue, or describe the new outfit a doll is wearing, or how a leaf looks, help children hone their visual skills as well as language skills. Children who have few experiences to foster visual skills often are less curious and less interested in exploring their environments (Read, Gardner, & Mahler, 1993).

Visual perception activities for preschool children should address three important aspects of visual perception: visual discrimination, eye-hand coordination, and the concept of conservation.

Visual Discrimination.   The ability to identify differences and similarities among shapes, objects, or people—*visual discrimination*—is remarkably accurate from early in life. Studies have shown that even newborn infants have the ability to recognize familiar objects (Werner & Siqueland, 1978). This skill is so well developed in young children that there seems to be little difference between their abilities and those of older children or adults (Olsen, 1976).

Children use visual discrimination when they reach out or run to a parent, teacher, or sibling, grab for a favorite toy, match or sort objects, or put together a puzzle. The children in Mrs. Banik's class used visual discrimination when they examined and compared the unpopped and popped corn kernels.

Visual discrimination is essential to the reading process. As stated earlier, in learning to read and write, children must be able to identify and differentiate among letters and words. Children who have difficulty perceiving likenesses and differences in shapes, patterns, and forms may have trouble recognizing words and letters (Spache, 1976). To some extent, a child's ability to become a good reader is dependent on the ability to discriminate visually. Studies have shown that children who are good readers recognize letter sequences and differentiate between similar letters (for example, *b* and *d*). Likewise, those who have difficulty with these skills are more likely to be poor readers (Wolford & Fowler, 1983).

The curriculum activities used to foster visual discrimination skills will vary according to the approach used by the teacher and the preschool. In an academically oriented preschool, children are likely to use workbooks, skill sheets, and other pencil-and-paper activities to practice visual discrimination. For example, worksheets might require children to draw a circle around the same or different objects or to underline the same or different letters. The teacher also might use activities in which children copy shapes or letters from the chalkboard onto a worksheet.

In a developmentally oriented preschool, the teacher is likely to provide a variety of manipulative materials instead of pencil-and-paper activities. The children might sort or match these materials (for example, pebbles, marbles, coins, beads, or buttons) by common traits or discuss how they are dissimilar. In a developmental program, the teacher acts as a facilitator who helps the children discover how to sort or match the materials.

Eye-Hand Coordination.   Another important aspect of visual perception is *eye-hand coordination*, a fine motor skill that requires coordinating what the hands do with what the eyes see. In other words, the hands are guided by visual cues. Young children demonstrate eye-hand coordination in many activities. For example, working on a puzzle requires a child to see and distinguish the shapes and pictures on puzzle pieces and to manipulate them until they fit together correctly. Preschool activities that require eye-hand coordination include cutting paper, putting pegs in a peg board, stringing beads, drawing pictures, and shaping clay. In fact, most activities involve some degree of eye-hand coordination. Even gross-motor activities—such as building a fort with packing boxes, and climbing—require eye-hand coordination. Each step requires that the eye sees and sends signals to the brain, which, in turn, notifies the hands or fingers to act.

Piaget's Concept of Conservation.   One aspect of young children's cognitive development that is closely linked to visual perception is the concept of conservation. Studied and described by Piaget, the concept of *conservation* refers to the understanding that a given quantity does not change when its appearance changes. For example, a half pound of clay remains the same quantity regardless of its shape—flat like a pancake, round like a ball, molded into a cube, or having some other shape.

Preschool children in Piaget's preoperational stage of development (ages two to about seven) rely heavily on their perceptual skills to interpret their environments. Their visual perception, however, sometimes can mislead them. For example, in the classic Piagetian experiment, a young child is shown two identical glasses filled with equal amounts of water. An adult then pours the water from one glass into a short, wide jar and the water from the second glass into a tall, narrow jar. A child under five years of age usually will say that the tall jar contains more water even though she could see that the amount was equal before the water was poured.

As children move into Piaget's concrete operations stage (ages six or seven to about twelve), they become less egocentric, or decentered, although some children become decentered at younger ages. Thus, they are able to look at the world from different perspectives, enabling them to "conserve," or hold the mental image or properties of an object. They recognize, in a cognitive sense, that the volume or quantity of a substance remains the same even if its appearance changes, as long as nothing is added or taken away.

Auditory Discrimination

The ability to hear sounds and identify them is known as *auditory discrimination*. This skill provides the foundation for the development of language skills, including the ability to pronounce words correctly. Children are exposed to a wide variety of sounds, and they learn to identify and differentiate these sounds. They learn, for example, to identify the honking of a car horn, the ringing of a telephone or doorbell, and the buzz of an alarm clock. These sounds have specific meanings for them. For example, a particular honk is the honk of a parent's car, or the doorbell ringing means that a friend has come to play. Children learn more subtle distinctions, too, such as distinguishing between familiar and strange voices and between voices that are angry or excited. They also learn to distinguish the quality of sounds, such as loudness, and the sources of sounds, such as the outdoors or the kitchen.

Researchers have studied the relationship between auditory discrimination and reading ability. Some have found that auditory discrimination, especially the ability to distinguish phonemes, is an important factor in learning to read. *Phonemes* are small units of sound that distinguish one word from another, such as *m* in *made* and *sh* in *shade*. For example, a child

Learning a new song fosters auditory discrimination skills, as children identify differences in tone and volume.

who is unable to hear the difference between letter sounds, such as the *t* and *p* in *cat* and *cap,* will encounter more difficulty learning to read (Fox & Routh, 1976).

In addition to helping children learn to read, auditory discrimination skills contribute to other factors that lead to success in school. For example, children with poor auditory discrimination skills may have difficulty paying attention to the teacher or concentrating on classroom activities. They cannot focus their auditory attention on one person or area. They may be easily distracted by other sounds in the room. Thus, what they hear is muddled noises, and their ability to learn is hampered. In the preschool setting, teachers can help children develop auditory discrimination skills and thus improve the chances for success in school. For example, they can direct the children's attention to sounds in various activities, as Mrs. Banik did with the popping corn in the scenario at the beginning of the chapter. They also can encourage children to listen to and distinguish common classroom sounds, such as the ticking of a clock or the rustling of papers. Crackling leaves, the trickle of a brook, the movement of swings, and the sound of passing traffic are common outdoor sounds that children like to identify. Older preschoolers like to guess "trickier" sounds on tape, such as the voices of different children in the class or the sounds of different animals, different musical instruments, or different kinds of transportation (a car engine starting or a train chugging along a track, for instance).

The Sense of Touch

Preschoolers acquire a tremendous amount of information through the sense of touch. By providing opportunities for the children to handle a wide variety of objects and materials, teachers help them acquire knowledge of and formulate concepts about the world around them. For example, the children begin to recognize the difference between warm and cool, damp and dry, soft and hard, and smooth and rough. As children's language skills increase, teachers help them associate words—such as smooth, sharp, or furry—with the objects or textures they are touching, and the children's vocabularies expand.

The preschool environment should offer a variety of tactile experiences. In the dramatic play area, for example, differently textured objects—such as stiff, straw hats, furry hats, and silky scarves; rough canvas bags and smooth vinyl pocketbooks; stuffed animals and hard plastic jewelry—allow children to explore a wide variety of textures. Materials or objects for sorting might include beanbags made of different fabrics on one occasion, and different kinds of paper (rough, glossy, tissue, metallic, sandpaper, wallpaper) on another. Even snacks—such as crackers, granola, cheese, or gelatin cubes—provide interesting textures for young hands to touch. Chapter 5 discusses in more detail how materials and the physical environment contribute to children's learning experiences.

Some curriculum approaches focus more than others on the sense of touch as an avenue for learning. As you read in Chapter 2 in the discussion of different curriculum approaches, the Montessori approach makes extensive use of tactile materials to support learning activities. In a Montessori classroom, rods and other objects that children can manipulate are used to reinforce number concepts. For example, children might be asked to arrange a set of rods of different lengths from shortest to longest. They might place one end of each rod along a straight line and then run their fingers along the top, feeling how the rods decrease or increase in length. Geography activities may use map puzzles—in which each piece is a different state—put together by the children.

Additionally, tactile materials—for example, a set of sandpaper letters—are used to help children learn about shapes and letters. Children select a letter, move their fingers over the rough surface, and trace the letter's outline with their fingers. The children then trace the outline of the letter on a piece of paper. They may practice reproducing the shape of the letter from memory by "drawing" it in a pan full of sand or uncooked rice. In addition, the teacher might help the children make pretzels in the shape of different letters or the letters of their names (Montessori, 1975).

The Senses of Taste and Smell

Young children also learn much about their world through taste and smell. Babies use their tongues to explore objects around them and constantly put things into their mouths to test texture, shape, and taste. Most two-year-olds and some three-year-olds continue to explore their environment with their tongues and mouths.

Most preschoolers can offer an opinion about whether something tastes "good" or "bad." With time and experience, they can discriminate among such tastes as salty, sweet, bitter, and sour, and such textures as warm/cold and crunchy/smooth. Through curriculum activities, preschool teachers can help children make these associations and discriminations, and help them learn the language to describe them. Also, snack time and cooking activities

Through such activities as snack time and cooking projects, young children hone their discrimination skills. They differentiate among and categorize a multitude of smells and tastes, such as salty, sweet, bitter, and sour.

present opportunities for children to experience a variety of foods with different tastes and textures.

Throughout the day, at home and in the preschool setting, children are exposed to many kinds of smells—food, soap, flowers, clothes, clay, and paints, for example. Children quickly learn to categorize these smells as pleasant and others as unpleasant, just as they do in tasting food. Children also begin to associate certain odors with places, things, people, and animals.

Teachers can incorporate activities and materials into the preschool curriculum that challenge and stimulate children's sense of smell. For example, the children might grow herbs—such as basil, lemon verbena, and mint—in a science center or a garden. Each herb has a distinctive aroma when its leaves are torn or rubbed between two fingers. During a walk, the children can be encouraged to smell pinecones, flowers, and damp earth. Teachers also can include tins of ground spices—such as cinnamon, thyme, and ginger—in the manipulatives area. Children can be encouraged to match small samples of each spice with the larger containers by smell. Children also can make spice collages, shaking spices onto glue on paper.

Sometimes, teachers design curriculum activities that foster the development of visual perception and visual and audio discrimination by depriving the children of one sense so that the children must rely more on another sense. For example, teachers might blindfold the children and ask them to identify objects using only the sense of touch. Or teachers might play a film or video with the sound off and ask the children to describe the scene.

One note of caution regarding children's exploration through taste. Because of the propensity of young children to put things into their mouths, caregivers need to be concerned about the children's safety. Young children

FOCUS ON Activities

Make Your Own Musical Instruments

Music is a vital part of any preschool curriculum. It not only introduces the concepts of rhythm and sound but also allows children to explore their own creativity. You can enhance the experience by having children make their own musical instruments.

Percussion instruments—which are struck or shaken to make sounds—usually are the simplest to make. Two pot lids become cymbals when struck together. Similarly, you can use two stones, spoons, or sticks to create different sounds. Try filling a can with rice or dried beans. Securely seal the can, and you've created Latin-style rattles known as maracas.

To make a set of bongo drums, use strong tape, such as duct tape, to hold together three empty metal coffee cans of different sizes, each with a plastic lid. The variety of sizes will produce distinct sounds when the children beat the cans. Or tie a clay flower pot upside down with thin rope, and you've made a bell that can be played with a wooden spoon.

Wind instruments create sounds when the air inside them moves. You can make a simple wind instrument by blowing across the top of a bottle. Add several bottles with varied levels of water inside them to produce different tones.

Make a flute by punching holes close together in a rubber pipe. To make a harmonica, take a fine-toothed comb, cover it with plastic wrap, and hold it to your mouth, tooth end up. Hum and listen to the buzzing sound.

String instruments create sounds when their strings move. A simple string instrument can be made by securing a rubber band over a metal bowl. Pluck the band to hear the sound. A more sophisticated instrument can be made by taping strings of different lengths to one side of a box so that they are taut. Then, stroke them with a fine-toothed comb.

Once your instruments are ready, it's time to strike up the band!

---

do not discriminate between safe and unsafe objects or substances. If not watched carefully, a child could easily swallow or choke on a small object. A teacher who is conducting a science experiment with mothballs, for example, may not be aware that a child might put a mothball into his mouth. It is important to teach young children the meaning of such words as *sharp* and *hot*, the names of objects they can touch but should never put into their mouths, and the names of objects they should never touch. Chapter 5 discusses this subject in more depth.

Sensory Integration

Unless they are impaired in some way, people generally utilize two or more senses simultaneously. The ability to use information from two or more senses is called *sensory integration* or *bimodal perception.* For example, digging in the sandbox requires coordination of sight (putting the shovel into the sand until it fills the shovel) with touch (holding the shovel and feeling the pressure of the sand on the shovel). If materials for the spice activity which was mentioned earlier included the stick or root form of some spices, the children could compare cinnamon sticks with powdered cinnamon, or fresh ginger root with powdered ginger, using smell, taste, and sight.

Early childhood experts disagree on the age at which children start using their senses simultaneously and on how many senses children can use at one time. Piaget believed that the primary perceptual abilities—such as sight, hearing, and taste—are uncoordinated at birth and that infants develop bimodal perception only after months of sensory experiences. Other researchers assert that infants are born with bimodal perceptual abilities, such as the ability to integrate information about an object both by tasting and touching it (Gibson, 1979, 1986).

As children mature, they are better able to integrate information from several senses, and they use this information to guide their activities. For example, two children who are playing with cars and trucks in a pretend traffic jam are using their sight as they maneuver their cars, and their hearing as they respond to each other's car-honking noises and "Watch where you're going!" exclamations. If their hands, arms, or bodies bump one another during their play, they also will respond through their sense of touch. They coordinate these senses with their physical actions.

Spatial Relations

Spatial relations refer to the physical dimensions of objects and their position in relation to the environment. For example, objects are defined by their weight, height, depth, and volume. They also are defined by where they are found—*inside* the box, *under* the table, *beside* the truck, or *on top of* the book. Learning to define objects in this way is an important skill that children develop as they explore their surroundings with their senses. In the preschool setting, physical activities—such as creative movement and climbing activities—and block play are two of the most significant types of activities in which children can develop spatial relations.

Physical Activities. Many indoor and outdoor physical activities help children learn such spatial relations as balance, height, and depth (depth perception, however, does not develop fully until about age 12). When children run, hop, jump, or throw or kick a ball, they learn about these types of relationships. They also experiment with spatial relations as they fill baby food jars with sand, work on a puzzle, or cut out a piece of paper to fit inside a cake tin.

As children become more confident about a newly learned physical skill, such as hopping, they begin to explore its variations. They try to hop higher than they did before or compare how fast they can travel by hopping on one foot or two feet. Or perhaps they will try to hop with two feet like a kangaroo while holding onto a big ball. As they experiment with these kinds of activities, they learn how much effort is required to hop different heights, to jump from one point to another, or to throw a ball a certain distance. These experiments contribute to their understanding of spatial relations.

As they grow older, children's physical activities become the basis for developing abstract spatial concepts. For example, when children learn to rollerskate or ride a bike uphill, they experience for themselves a basic principle of physics—a greater force is required to move an object uphill than to push it on flat ground.

Teachers can help children recognize spatial relations by commenting verbally on children's play or pointing out certain relationships in planned activities. For example, a teacher might say, "I see you're packing your stuffed animals for a trip. What can you use to carry all of them? Will they fit in this canvas bag? Will they fit in this big suitcase?" Or the teacher might ask, "How could we arrange these chairs like a train but not go into the art area?" Or he or she might suggest, "Let's take all these ribbons and pieces of yarn and line them up end to end to fit around the whole room."

Block Play.   Block play combines a number of visual and motor skills, helps children learn about spatial relations—such as relative size, balance, and height—in a hands-on fashion, and develops in stages (See Figure 10.1). Block play creates opportunities for children to think through solutions to spatial challenges and problems involving balance, size, and space. For

FIGURE 10.1   Stages of Block Play.

Stage 1: In the *nonconstructive stage*, toddlers carry their blocks around or place them by or near each other.

Stage 2: In the *stacking and rows stage*, children stack blocks in either vertical piles (towers) or horizontal rows.

Stage 3: In the *bridging stage*, typical of three-year-olds, children learn to connect two blocks with a third one.

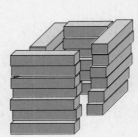

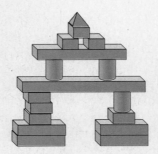

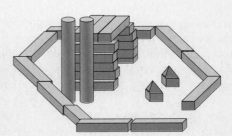

Stage 4: In the *enclosure stage*, children begin to arrange blocks in order to enclose a space or an object, showing that they understand the concepts of inside, outside, and around.

Stage 5: In the *structural stage*, children begin to develop more creative and complex structures, characterized by decorative and often symmetrical block patterns.

Stage 6: In the *functional building stage*, usually reached by age four, children may use blocks to create an environment with a purpose—possibly for dramatic or fantasy play.

Suggestions for Props in Block Play

DRAMATIC PLAY MATERIALS
Animals: small plastic or wooden farm animals
small plastic or wooden zoo animals
dinosaurs
stuffed animals
Small cars, trucks, airplanes, boats
Construction toys
Farm equipment
Small people figures
Occupation figures
Pots, pans, and dishes
Pillows
Sheets or blankets for a roof
Hats (construction worker, firefighter, fancy lady) and purses
Dolls
Long boards for roof, ramps
Plastic trees and flowers
Blue paper or cloth to serve as a lake or ocean
Plastic floor mats
Posters related to themes or units

CREATIVE ACCESSORIES
Miscellaneous cardboard pieces, such as mailer tubes and small boxes
Feathers
Construction paper and tape
Artificial flowers
Egg cartons
Tablecloths
Scarves

OUTSIDE ACCESSORIES
Portable gross motor equipment, such as stairs, bridges, A-frames, boats
Buckets and shovels
Pulleys and ramps
Tires, old steering wheels
Old sheets or blankets
Clothesline, rope

FIGURE 10.2   Suggestions for Props in Block Play.

example, they learn how to build a bridge that will not fall down. Playing with blocks also encourages children to use other skills, including planning ahead and then following a series of steps to carry out the plan. Block play is one of preschoolers' favorite activities. Figure 10.2 offers some ideas for adding variety to block play, indoors and outdoors. Children enjoy building towers, bridges, fences, rocket ships, houses, and structures that are not functional but allow children to experiment with design.

Research has shown that children move through several stages of block play, and that these stages are related to their level of cognitive development (Reifel, 1984). Teachers who observe a child playing with blocks can learn something about that child's cognitive development, as well as about her understanding of spatial relations. In the first stage of block play, the non-constructive stage, toddlers simply carry their blocks from place to place or put them by or near each other. By the end of their second year, children begin either to stack blocks vertically in piles or towers or to line them up in horizontal rows.

Three-year-olds learn to connect two blocks with a third one on top. This third stage, sometimes referred to as bridging, reveals their understanding of simple spatial relations. In the fourth stage, three-year-olds then begin to arrange blocks in a way that encloses a space or an object, revealing their understanding of the concepts of inside, outside, and around. Once children are comfortable manipulating blocks, they begin to develop more complex structures. This fifth stage, called the structural stage, is characterized by decorative and often symmetrical block patterns. The sixth and final stage of block play is functional building. In this stage, usually reached by age four, children use blocks to create an environment with a purpose—for example, a castle, a barn, or a garage—and the structure becomes a part of dramatic or fantasy play.

A preschool classroom for three- and four-year-olds can never have too many blocks. Because of the significance and appeal of blocks, preschools generally offer a variety of types, including table blocks, unit blocks, and hollow blocks. These different types of blocks are described in Chapter 5. Block activities that help develop spatial relations are discussed in the "Applications" section of this chapter.

Assessing Perceptual Problems

Sometimes, children have difficulty with a particular aspect of perception, such as hearing or vision. However, because of their limited experience, they do not realize that they have a problem, and that they should be able to hear or see better than they do. As a result, they may not speak up or complain.

Visual and Hearing Problems

Preschool children with perceptual problems often exhibit symptoms that caregivers can recognize through observation. Some symptoms of visual problems are easy to notice. A lazy or wandering eye is a symptom of *amblyopia*, in which a child has weak eye muscles that make an eye difficult to control. The medical term for crossed eyes is *strabismus*. Other signs of visual problems include fatigue, headaches, squinting, rubbing of the eyes, or eyes that are watery, encrusted, or inflamed. Children who are uncoordinated and clumsy in spatial relations tasks, who show difficulty in sorting and matching, or who have trouble recognizing objects when only a part of the object is visible may have a *visual perceptual disorder* (Deiner, 1993). This is an inability to identify and interpret what the eye perceives.

Other signs of visual problems may be less obvious in young children, but they can still be recognized by careful observers. These signs include a disinterest in learning, avoiding visual activities, ignoring or misinterpreting pictures in books, or holding objects very close or far away from the eyes. Children who perform poorly in ball toss or other activities that require eye-hand coordination also might have vision problems.

Children with hearing problems exhibit a different set of signs. The most noticeable is the inability of a child to hear someone talking unless the speaker is facing her—she will not respond to her name being said by someone behind her. Other, less obvious signs of hearing problems include a level of language and social skills more appropriate for younger children, a lack of interest in classroom conversations, and a tendency to play alone. Some children also may behave inappropriately because they are unable to hear directions. They may run words together, have an unusual voice quality (such as a flat, high pitched monotone), or use volume inappropriately (such as yelling during naptime) (Deiner, 1993).

Identifying Perceptual Problems

Because they work closely with young children, often in a one-on-one situation, preschool teachers often can help identify possible perceptual problems. A child's difficulty in performing a certain task may signal a perceptual problem that needs attention. The problem, however, may or may not be related to a perceptual skill. A child's inability to perform a motor task, such as buttoning buttons, may be caused by a muscular problem rather than a perceptual one. Yet, it might also indicate that something is wrong with the sensory information the muscles are receiving or that triggers a response. One way to determine the source of the problem is to create a situation that focuses on a perceptual skill and does not require a motor response. For example, instead of asking a child to do a puzzle that requires matching geometric shapes by hand, the teacher might ask him to tell whether two shapes are the same or different only by looking at them. The teacher also might ask that child to identify the shape by name (Pitcher, Feinberg, & Alexander, 1989). Such exercises help the teacher identify the source of a child's difficulty and provide appropriate developmental activities or guidance to parents.

Dealing with Perceptual Problems

When a teacher suspects vision or hearing problems, he or she should consult with the child's parents. The teacher might give examples of the problems he or she has seen and ask the parents if they have noticed anything similar. The teacher might suggest that the child be tested by a professional. Teachers should be familiar with local resource and referral agencies. Often, the first contact is the child's pediatrician, who may then refer the child.

Preschool programs may be tailored to address the special needs of children with perceptual problems. For example, a teacher who has a child who is hearing-impaired in his class may provide instruction in American Sign Language to the whole group.

FOCUS ON Communicating with Parents

Talking about a Child's Perceptual Problem

Elaine Kurtz, head teacher of the Morningside Preschool, was fairly certain that five-year-old Brian Sheldon had a perceptual problem. Knowing that Brian would enter kindergarten in the fall, she was especially concerned.

ELAINE: Thank you for coming in today. I know that it's difficult for you to take time off from work.

MR. SHELDON: Well, you said it was important. Is there a problem?

ELAINE: Well, yes, there is. I've been watching Brian, and he seems to be doing things a little differently than many of the other children.

MR. SHELDON: What do you mean?

ELAINE: Well, there are behaviors that indicate Brian may have a perceptual problem. Brian has a lot of difficulty with the matching games we play, in which the children group similar shapes. He also has trouble putting puzzles together. We think it would be a good idea to have him tested before he enters kindergarten.

MR. SHELDON: Brian is a very smart boy. He doesn't have any difficulty with school.

ELAINE: This has nothing to do with his intelligence, Mr. Sheldon. It just means that Brian may perceive things differently than other children. On the other hand, it may be nothing.

MR. SHELDON: I want another opinion. I'm not sure you're qualified to make this judgment.

ELAINE: I understand your concern. That is why we are suggesting that Brian be tested by a certified assessment professional.

MR. SHELDON: I don't know. Teachers always want to give tests. I don't think it's necessary.

Do you think that the examples Elaine gave to illustrate Brian's perceptual problem were adequate to convince his father? Why or why not? What might you do if a parent kept insisting that a child had no problem and you believed that he did?

Public health departments or other government agencies usually offer free preschool screening for vision and hearing.

The most common way of helping children who have some type of mild sensory impairment is through a preschool program operated by specially trained teachers. Such programs provide activities tailored to address particular areas of weakness. These programs also teach alternative strategies for learning to children who are sensory-impaired. For example, children who are hard of hearing may learn sign language while they are receiving speech training. At the same time, they may be encouraged to rely more on their other senses for getting information. Research has shown that the most effective programs are those that provide a coordinated approach focused on both the child's cognitive development (Stedt & Moores, 1987) and the development of communication and independence (Warren, 1984). See the "Focus on Communicating with Parents" feature in this chapter for a discussion of how to talk to parents about perceptual problems.

Individual Differences in Perception

People perceive things in different ways, often because one sense is more fully developed than the others. These differences may affect the way people learn. For example, some people learn more easily by seeing, others by hearing, and others by touching. Consequently, children in the preschool setting may focus on the same activity in different ways. For example, with easel painting, some children may focus more on the color and shading of the paint while others may be more interested in the paint's texture.

Preschool teachers should be on the lookout for individual differences in perception. Then they can think about ways in which they might design activities and modify their interactions with various children to foster perceptual strengths while encouraging the children to use other senses as well. For example, a teacher might ask a child who is visually oriented to identify other objects in the room that are the same color as her paint. However, the teacher also might encourage her to try finger painting—adding a tactile dimension to her interest in color.

In addressing individual differences in perception, the teacher also should attempt to assess whether strength in one area compensates for a deficit in another. For example, the teacher should ask himself or herself whether a tactile learner relies on texture because he has a vision problem, or whether a visual learner relies on sight because she lacks sufficient tactile experiences.

Applications

A multisensory environment with curriculum activities focused on developing the five senses will help children explore, test, and challenge their own perceptual abilities to the fullest. There are many ways of encouraging children to use their senses. This section offers suggestions for activities to develop specific perceptual skills as well as suggestions for creating stimulating, interesting multisensory activities.

Activities to Develop Perceptual Skills

The types of activities that can be used to develop perceptual skills are limited only by the teacher's imagination. Virtually every object in a preschool classroom is a good candidate for developing the senses. This section describe four types of activities that foster the development of perceptual skills. Although each focuses on a specific sense, these activities also provide an opportunity for multisensory experiences.

Sense of Taste.   Snack time or cooking activities are good ways to help children learn through their sense of taste. For snack time, provide margarine, cream cheese, jelly, peanut butter, and other items that children can spread on small pieces of bread, bagels, or crackers using plastic knives. There should be enough knives so that each child will have one. Plastic knives are safe and can be cleaned in the dishwasher. As children butter their bread or spread softened cream cheese on their bagel or peanut butter

Sensory Recipes

Play Dough
Combine: 1 c. flour
          ½ c. salt
          1 c. water
          1 tbsp. vegetable oil
          2 tsp. cream of tartar
Heat in a heavy pan until ingredients form a ball. Take out of pan and knead on a floured surface until smooth. Add food coloring or powdered tempera paint.

Play Dough Variation
Combine: 2½ c. flour
          ½ c. salt
          2 pkgs. unsweetened powdered fruit drink mix
          2 c. boiling water
          2 tbsp. vegetable oil
Follow directions as for regular play dough. The drink mix adds scent and color. Food coloring can be added to brighten colors. Knead as it cools. Add flour if needed.

"Clean Mud"
Materials: 10–12 rolls toilet paper
            4 bars soap
            1 c. borax
            water
            (all measurements approximate)
Have children shred toilet paper and grate soap. Add water and stir until it's a "goopy" mess.

"Play Putty"
Combine: 2 parts white school glue*
          1 part liquid starch*
          food coloring
          *approximate amounts
Mix until the putty achieves the "right" texture. If the "play putty" is too sticky, it has too much glue, so add more starch. If the "play putty" won't stick to itself, it needs more glue. Be sure to have children wear plastic smocks, as "play putty" is very hard to get out of clothing or hair.

Bubbles
Combine: 1 c. liquid dishwashing soap
          10 c. water
          ¼ c. glycerine (makes bubbles last longer, but not absolutely necessary)
Bubble mixture may be saved in plastic jugs.

on their cracker, ask them to describe the color and texture of the different spreads. As they eat their snacks, they can describe and compare the different smells and tastes.

Auditory Discrimination.   You can help children develop auditory discrimination with activities that use musical instruments. You can use real instruments—such as a piano, a tambourine, or a xylophone—or you can have the children create their own instruments. See the "Focus on Activities" feature in this chapter. You might play the children's favorite nursery rhymes or folk songs and ask the children to identify the songs from the melodies. You might play high, medium, and low sounds or loud, normal, and soft sounds and ask children to identify the sounds by calling them Papa Bear, Mama Bear, or Baby Bear. If several instruments are available, you might ask the children to close their eyes and identify each instrument from its sound. Or you might produce simple rhythmic combinations (for example, two quick beats or notes, followed by two short ones) and have the children reproduce the rhythms by clapping their hands.

Eye-Hand Coordination. There are many activities that help children develop eye-hand coordination. For example, have the children hunt for "treasures," such as old pieces of jewelry or small plastic toys, buried in an indoor sand table. If done in the outside sandbox, use balls of aluminum foil for the "treasures."

Spatial Relations. A well-designed block activity fosters the development of spatial relations. One idea is to outline a building or house on the floor and ask children to help build on this "foundation" with blocks (large hollow blocks are best). Once the children have finished building, encourage them to furnish the house with props and to use it in their dramatic play. Or suggest that they build the Three Bears' house, which would need a kitchen, a living room, and a bedroom.

Multisensory Materials and Activities

You can create a multisensory environment by using a variety of materials and changing them often. This strategy helps stimulate children's curiosity and encourages them to explore all aspects of their play environment. Integrate such materials as sand, water, finger paint, play dough, "play putty," cornmeal, flour, and glitter into curriculum activities. Figure 10.3 provides recipes for some of these materials. Find materials with interesting colors, textures, or smells. Have children finger paint with shaving cream. Add glitter to paint. Create an activity center based on one color, and change the color two weeks later.

Vary the temperature of the water at the water table. Add shells to the sandbox. Decorate some blocks with neon tape. Make stars out of aluminum foil by wrapping the foil around a star shape cut out of cardboard. Hang a crystal in the window or a set of chimes outside. Play music softly in the dramatic play or reading areas.

Create an activity to compare sweet foods (jelly beans, raisins), sour ones, (pickles, lemon slices), salty ones (pretzels, soy sauce), and bitter ones (unsweetened chocolate). Integrate foods with different tastes and textures from different cultures—miso soup, crisp tacos, smooth hummus, and curry.

Multisensory materials stimulate children's creativity, curiosity, and exploration of their environment. These four-year-olds are discovering the endless possibilities of play dough with a variety of tools and props.

You can stimulate children's curiosity during multisensory activities by asking a variety of questions. Use questions to encourage children to be descriptive and to make them more aware of how their surroundings look, sound, smell, and feel. For example, the teacher in the scenario at the beginning of the chapter asked questions that prompted the children in her class to explore the kernels in their hands with all their senses. She asked them to say how the kernels felt and smelled, and she asked them to compare the popped and unpopped kernels. She asked them to listen to the popping corn.

You can broaden the use of the water table and provide new sensory-rich experiences by replacing the water with soil or wet sand. Large plastic mixing tubs—the bigger the better—also could be used for these activities. They are sold at building supply stores. Dishpans are too small for a whole class but can be used for one child. Place plastic drop cloths, newspapers, or throw rugs under the pans. The following are ideas for props to use with different materials in the water table or plastic tubs. Also see Figure 10.4 for water activity ideas indoors and outdoors.

- *Soil.* Add farm vehicles and plastic animals; plastic cars and trucks/construction vehicles; cooking utensils; bowls of water and pie pans to make mud pies; or garden hand tools, pots, and plastic flowers.
- *Wet sand, dry coffee grounds, or cornmeal.* At various times, add sifters, cooking utensils, pots and pans, measuring cups and spoons, or cookie cutters; funnels and tubes; plastic animals and dinosaurs; cars and trucks/construction vehicles; or old film canisters.
- *Rice or flour.* Mix uncooked plain white rice or flour with brown rice or wheat germ to create color contrast. For variety, mix food coloring with alcohol, pour it over the rice, and blend. (The alcohol will evaporate.) Color flour with powdered tempera. (Be sure to use smocks.) Add kitchen utensils or sandbox-type props.
- *Shaving cream.* Color shaving cream with food coloring. Add props, such as plastic people or animals, cooking utensils, an eggbeater, and muffin pans. Be sure to have the children wear smocks!

An enjoyable activity that focuses on the senses of sight and touch is making "ooblik." "Ooblik" is a mixture of cornstarch and water that creates a wonderful sensory goo. You'll need several boxes of cornstarch, shallow trays or a water table, water, and, if desired, food color. Have children feel the dry cornstarch, and ask if it feels hard or soft and what color it is. Put cornstarch in the tray or water table, and add a few drops of food coloring (the color will not show until water is added in the next step). Add water slowly until the mixture becomes gooey. Ask children to take some in their hands and roll or squeeze it. (The heat of their hands and rubbing and squeezing will turn the ooblik into a solid. When they stop rubbing and squeezing, it will turn back into a liquid.) (Hine, 1993).

Another multisensory activity that many young children find challenging and enjoyable is making cloth-texture books. Provide children with a variety of textured fabrics or heavy paper cut into rectangles as "pages." Children

FIGURE 10.4   Water Activities. *Compiled by:* Jane Billman and Judy Uebelhoer, University of Chicago at Urbana-Champaign.

Water Activities

INSIDE
Use a water table or multipurpose pan. Props can include:

- Materials that sink and float. Two-year-olds and three-year-olds need a variety of materials to explore the concepts of "sink" and "float." Four-year-olds and five-year-olds may wish to sort items that sink and those that float into different pans and may wish to find their own items to sink and float.

- Seashells, pebbles, stones

- Funnels, plastic bottles of varying sizes with lids, plastic cups

- Turkey basters, ketchup bottles, dishwashing liquid bottles

- Colored water. To mix colored water, prepare gallon milk jugs with red, yellow, and blue water. Pour into small pitchers for the children to mix in yogurt containers, margarine tubs, ice cube trays, or cupcake pans. Children love to mix using turkey basters, scoops, or eyedroppers.

- Magnets and magnetic objects (Magnets work in water!)

- Bubbles (See recipe in Figure 10.3) Add food coloring, if desired. To froth up the bubbles, have children use handheld eggbeaters.

- Ice cubes and tongs

- Doll clothes, dolls, and dishes to wash

- Plastic toys and containers

- Boats made from wood, soap, straws

OUTSIDE
Use a water table, multipurpose pan, or children's swimming pool.

- Most of the ideas for inside water tables also work outside. Experiment!

- "Paint" with water using old paintbrushes.

- Freeze large blocks of ice and put them out in the hot sun.

- Make a lake in the sandbox by having the children dig a hole and then line it with plastic garbage bags.

- "Fish" with magnets.

- Hang wet clothes on a clothesline.

- Wash tricycles and other outside vehicles.

can glue on sand, feathers, macaroni, sequins, or other scraps of material, to create their "book." Discuss with the children such concepts as soft, scratchy, smooth, and fuzzy, based on the materials they choose for their book.

Encourage children to stimulate their senses of sight, hearing, and touch by filling empty coffee cans or film cans with different objects—such as uncooked rice or noodles, sand, paper clips, pebbles, and rubber balls. Children can cover the cans with plastic lids and shake the containers, listening to the sound each makes. Ask them to describe the sound, and ask if they think that the sound would change if the coffee cans were only partially filled. Have them compare the sound of a completely filled can with that of cans filled to different levels. You might fill pairs of film cans with similar amounts of the same material, arrange a group of the cans on a table, and ask the children to match the pairs. Use your imagination—the possibilities are endless.

CHAPTER 10   REVIEW

SUMMARY

- Young children first experience their world through their senses of sight, hearing, smell, taste, and touch.
- As children mature, they learn to coordinate information from their senses with physical motions and activities in a process known as perceptual development.
- Children use their senses to discover the properties of objects, how things work, and the characteristics of people.
- Visual perception is the ability to use the sense of sight to recognize, differentiate, and recall objects. Children use this skill, for example, when they try to copy a shape, line up sticks from longest to shortest, or draw from memory.
- Visual discrimination—the ability to identify differences among shapes, objects, or people—is essential to the reading process, as well as other aspects of learning.
- Eye-hand coordination is a fine-motor activity that requires coordinating what the eyes see with what the hands will do. Most preschool activities involve some eye-hand coordination.
- Auditory discrimination—the ability to hear sounds and to identify them—provides the foundation for developing language skills, including the ability to pronounce words correctly.
- For children, especially very young children, the sense of touch is an important means of exploring and experiencing the world.
- The Montessori curriculum makes extensive use of tactile materials to support learning activities.
- Sensory integration is the ability to use information from two or more senses. Early childhood experts disagree about what age children acquire this skill.
- Spatial relations define an object's physical dimensions and its position in relation to the environment. Learning to define and explore objects using spatial relations is an important skill that helps children learn about volume, balance, height, and depth.

- A child's difficulty in performing a certain task may signal a perception problem that needs attention. Teachers should learn to recognize the symptoms of such problems. They should consult parents and suggest professional help and/or modify the curriculum to provide activities that address areas of weakness.
- Teachers should include a variety of multisensory activities in the curriculum and add multisensory materials to the physical environment to stimulate children's curiosity and challenge them to utilize all their senses.

ACQUIRING KNOWLEDGE

1. How does perceptual development differ from physical development?
2. How do most early childhood educators believe that young children learn about their world?
3. What is a multisensory preschool environment?
4. Give three examples of activities that require visual perception.
5. How are physical development and visual perception related?
6. Why are most children not physically prepared for formal reading instruction before first grade?
7. What are two important aspects of visual perception that should be addressed in the preschool curriculum?
8. How do academic and developmentally oriented preschools differ in the types of activities used to promote visual discrimination?
9. Why is it so important for the preschool curriculum to promote eye-hand coordination?
10. What did Piaget's classic conservation experiment show about young children's visual perception?
11. How are auditory discrimination and reading ability related?
12. Name three activities that promote auditory discrimination.
13. Name several different textures that teachers use when devising or presenting materials to preschool children.
14. How do children's descriptions of tastes and smells change as their perception develops?
15. What is bimodal perception?
16. When did Piaget believe that children develop bimodal perception? Why do some researchers disagree with Piaget?
17. How can physical activities help children develop spatial relations?
18. How does block play contribute to understanding spatial relations?
19. What are the sequential stages of block play?
20. What are some signs that a child has a visual problem?
21. What are some signs that a child has a hearing problem?
22. Describe how a preschool teacher can use activities to explore whether or not a child has a perceptual problem.
23. What should a teacher do if he or she suspects that a child has a perceptual problem?
24. What types of teaching strategies can a teacher use to accommodate individual differences in children's perceptual skills?

25. How can a teacher's questioning enhance or challenge children's perceptual skills during activities?

THINKING CRITICALLY

1. The sense of taste is sometimes overlooked in the preschool curriculum. What are some types of activities that help develop taste perception? Why is special care necessary when conducting activities involving food?

2. Many common children's games require sensory integration. Choose a game such as "Duck Duck Goose" or "Hide and Seek" and describe how the game develops sensory integration.

3. The Montessori approach uses a wide variety of tactile materials, including rods, clay, sand, and sandpaper. Do you think that these materials help a child develop senses other than touch?

4. Piaget used partially filled glasses of water to observe children's abilities related to conservation. Describe an activity a teacher might conduct with another material, such as clay or paper, to explore conservation with children.

5. Preschool children frequently explore such unusual materials as "ooblik," "play putty," and "clean mud." Why is it helpful for children to explore and manipulate these materials, even though they are unlikely to use them later in life?

OBSERVATIONS AND APPLICATIONS

1. Arrange a visit to a local preschool. Look carefully at the materials in the classroom. Record materials with interesting colors, textures, or smells. Does the classroom have any of the following materials: sand, finger paint, play dough, "play putty," cornmeal, flour, shaving cream, or glitter? Is there music playing, or might tapes be available for children to listen to? What kind or variety of tapes or music is offered? If you are observing during snack time, notice whether the children are able to explore different tastes. Describe some ways in which two or three children interact with sensory materials. Does the teacher ask any questions dealing with taste, touch, smell, sight, or hearing?

2. As you observe a preschool group of four- or five-year-olds, describe any activities you see that strengthen visual discrimination skills. For example, do the children use manipulative materials (such as pebbles, marbles, coins, beads, or buttons) to sort or match by common traits? Describe any activities that require eye-hand coordination. For example, are children cutting paper, stringing beads, manipulating pieces for a puzzle, or shaping clay?

3. Dana is a happy, four-year-old girl in your preschool group. She enjoys school and has lots of friends. However, unlike many of her peers, she has not yet mastered some simple tasks, such as buttoning her coat or catching a ball with both arms. She also has difficulty with some of the games, in particular the one that requires the children to match differently colored shapes. What steps might you take to help Dana?

4. Matthew just recently joined your group of five-year-olds at the Haverhill Hills Preschool. Although he seems to be well behaved, he is not a good listener. Often, when you call his name, he ignores you. He usually is the last one to come in from outdoor play. What kind of one-on-one activity might you do with Matthew to help you isolate his listening or auditory discrimination skills from other perceptual skills?

FOR FURTHER INFORMATION

Books and Journal Articles

Baratta-Lorton, M. (1972). *Workjobs: Activity-centered learning for early childhood.* Reading, MA: Addison-Wesley.

Baratta-Lorton, M. (1987). *Workjobs II: Number activities for early childhood.* Reading, MA: Addison-Wesley.

Brown, C. (Ed.). (1984). *The many facets of touch.* Skillman, NJ: Johnson & Johnson Baby Products.

Deiner, P. L. (1993). *Resources for teaching children with diverse abilities: Birth through eight* (2nd ed.). Fort Worth, TX: Harcourt Brace Jovanovich.

Forman, G., & Hill, F. (1984). *Constructive play: Applying Piaget in the preschool* (rev. ed.) Reading, MA: Addison-Wesley.

Goldhaber, J. (1992). Sticky to dry, red to purple: Exploring transformation with play dough. *Young Children, 48*(1), 26–28.

Kamii, C., & DeVries, R. (1993). *Physical knowledge in preschool education: Implications of Piaget's theory.* New York: Teachers College Press.

Nourot, P. M. & Van Hoorn, J. (1991). Symbolic play in preschool and primary settings. *Young Children, 46*(6), 40–49.

Reifel, S. (1984). Block construction: Children's developmental landmarks in representation of space. *Young Children, 40*(1), 61–67.

Williams, C., & Kamii, C. (1986). How do children learn by handling objects? *Young Children, 42*(1), 23–36.

Curriculum and Resource Guides

Granovetter, R., & James, J. (1987). *Sift and shout: Sand play activities for children ages 1–6.* Lewisville, NC: Kaplan.

Hill, D. (1977). *Mud, sand, and water.* Washington, DC: National Association for the Education of Young Children.

James, J., & Granovetter, R. (1987). *Waterworks: Waterplay activities for children ages 1–6.* Lewisville, NC: Kaplan.

Kohl, M. (1980). *Mudworks: Creative clay, dough, and modeling experiences.* Bellingham, WA: Bright Ring.

Skeen, P., Garner, A., & Cartwright, S. (1984). *Woodworking for young children.* Washington, DC: National Association for the Education of Young Children.

Thompson, D. (1981). *Easy woodstuff for kids.* Mt. Rainier, MD: Gryphon House.

OBJECTIVES

Studying this chapter
will enable you to

- Discuss three leading theories of
  language acquisition
- Compare and contrast two curriculum approaches to developing
  early literacy skills
- Discuss the special language
  needs of children for whom
  English is a second language
- Describe several types of
  curriculum activities that promote
  language and literacy skills

CHAPTER TERMS

bilingual
constructivist or process approach
culturally responsive curriculum
early literacy
emergent literacy
interactionist/constructivist
   theory
limited English proficiency
narrative competence
nativist theory
nonstandard English
open-ended questions
print-rich environment
private speech
reading readiness
scaffolding
transmission or skills approach
whole language approach

MRS. SMITH'S class had just
returned from a trip to the zoo.
The children, ages three and
four, were seated on the floor for group
time. Mrs. Smith asked, "What will you tell
your parents about the zoo when you go
home today?"

"I goed to the zoo with my friends," said
three-year-old Max, proudly.

"I saw lots of gatos, except bigger than
my cat at home," said Lisa, a four-year-old
whose native language is Spanish. "I really
like the one with spots."

"What is the cat with spots called?" Mrs.
Smith asked the group.

"Leopard!" responded Stacy and Komiko
simultaneously. Mrs. Smith smiled in
approval.

"The zoo was the best," sighed Mina. "I
wish we had a zoo at school."

"We can make a pretend zoo right
here," said Mrs. Smith enthusiastically.
"What would we need?"

"Animals," replied Mina. "I know, we can
put our pets in the zoo place," she
continued, referring to the classroom's fish,
two hamsters, a white dwarf rabbit, and a
turtle.

"But we need more," said Stacy, "We could draw some in cages. I'll draw a big bear. And we better make a sign saying, 'Do not feed the bear.'"

"Mina and I can draw leopard gatos," added Lisa. "OK, Mina?"

Mrs. Smith then asked the other children which animals they would like to draw.

Mrs. Smith knew that preschoolers can develop a variety of language skills by talking about enjoyable experiences, such as a trip to the zoo. She also knew how valuable it would be to the children's language development to integrate these experiences into different aspects of the curriculum.

Language is the basic form of human communication. Language skills include speaking, listening, reading, and writing. Infants and toddlers learn a language by hearing it spoken by the members of their families and other caregivers and through spontaneous interaction with these people. In time, long before they can engage in formal reading, children begin to draw a connection between the spoken and the written word. For example, when a child sees her grandmother looking at a book and reading her a bedtime story, or when she sees her mother using a telephone book and then making a telephone call, or when she notices her father looking at a newspaper, she is beginning to learn about literacy. That is, she is learning that communication involves reading and writing as well as speaking and listening.

In the preschool setting, young children increase their ability to use language through activities that focus primarily on speaking and listening skills. In addition, the preschool curriculum can help young children develop such skills as visual and auditory discrimination (discussed in Chapter 10) and how to use a pencil. These skills will help prepare them for learning to read and write in elementary school. This chapter explains how children learn to talk and then begin to understand the relationship between oral communication and the written word. It also discusses the leading curriculum approaches used by preschools to help children build language skills.

Learning to Talk

Learning language is a complicated process, yet very young children appear to do it effortlessly. They first begin to babble, concentrating on the cadence of language. Then they move from single words to two-word sentences to more complicated sentences in about the same sequence and at about the same age (Temple, Nathan, & Burris, 1982). Children learn to talk in order to communicate with others and to find out more about the world—or, to be more specific, their world (Smith, 1979). Their early attempts at the spoken word relate to situations that have direct meaning for them, such as pointing to and asking for a food item they want in the grocery store. By age five, children already know the basic structure of language.

There are three leading theories of language acquisition—nativist, behaviorist, and interactionist/constructivist.

FOCUS ON **Cultural Diversity**

Tips for Avoiding Stereotypical Children's Books

In choosing children's books, look out for the following indications of bias.

- Illustrations that depict a person or groups of people in a stereotypical manner. Examples: the naked, savage Native American, or the mammylike large black woman.
- Illustrations that support gender stereotypes. Example: in a story about people at work, teachers or nurses shown as women and police officers or doctors shown as men.
- Story lines that base standards for success on "white" ideals. Examples: stories in which white characters are always smarter and more understanding than nonwhite characters; stories in which minorities are blamed for a problem or mistake, while solutions are found by white people.
- White, middle-class life-styles presented as the norm, or depictions of life-styles of minority cultures that convey false conceptions or a generally negative impression. Examples: a story that shows present-day Native

Americans only in traditional costume or traditional adobe houses; a story in which a single parent home is described in a derogatory way.

- Relationships between people that support gender stereotypes. Examples: stories in which only men are given leadership roles; stories in which women are relegated to minor roles or are not judged on their own abilities.
- Stories in which only white males are heroes; stories in which nonwhite or female characters' accomplishments are not acknowledged in the same positive way as those of white male heroes.
- Words that may be insulting, racist, or sexist. Examples: "wily," "shifty," or "primitive," and job titles such as police*man* and mail*man*.

Adapted from material in *Guidelines for selecting bias-free textbooks and storybooks* (1980). New York: Council on Interracial Books for Children.

Nativist Theory

The *nativist theory* of language acquisition asserts that people are born with the ability to learn language. All cultures develop and use a language to communicate, and children are exposed to the vocabulary and syntax of the language of the particular culture into which they are born. Children learn to talk, in part, by imitating others, and they use the same words and sentence structures as the people with whom they come into contact. Therefore, children in Texas learn Texan English and children in Paris learn Parisian French (Temple et al., 1982).

Noam Chomsky and Eric Lenneberg are two important proponents of the nativist theory. Chomsky believes that children are born with the capacity to produce and understand language, a mechanism he called the "language acquisition device," or LAD. His theory reflects the fact that children all over the world learn language at about the same time (Chomsky, 1965). Also, children learn the unique grammatical rules of their language from their families and friends. Chomsky found that all children acquire language in the same sequence. He describes a "sensitive period," occurring between the ages of 18 months and puberty, as the most productive period in which children learn language. He noted how easily young children can learn a second language and how difficult learning a second language later in life can be.

Lenneberg's research supports Chomsky's assertions that children of all cultures begin using language at about the same age, and that there appears to be a critical period in which children learn language easily (Lenneberg, 1967). He noted that, during the ages of three to five, children refine the complexity and the use of language, as they progress from the babbling stage to using sentences.

The work of D. I. Slobin also supports the nativist theory. Comparing the development of syntax in children in Russian- and English-speaking cultures, Slobin found that children develop syntax in the same sequence (Slobin, 1985). For example, the first three-word sentences children use are typically simple negatives, such as "No more doggie." Also, children tend to overgeneralize new grammatical rules, such as creating the past tense of a verb. Children who are learning English may say "runned" or "sitted," even though they may have used these incorrect forms correctly.

Behaviorist Theory

The behaviorist theory states that, in order for children to learn language, they must have an external stimulus and reinforcement. Children acquire language through imitation in addition to an external stimulus and reinforcement. They repeat or "echo" what they hear, modeling their own attempts at speaking on the examples of their parents and others around them. Their "correct" utterances are reinforced by positive responses from a parent or a teacher. The reward or reinforcement motivates the child to speak with increasing accuracy.

Critics of the behaviorist theory say that it does not account for novel combinations or forms of words children create on their own, as Max did by using "goed" instead of "went." Some adults might call these invented words "mistakes." Yet, these "mistakes" indicate that children can create rules based on their own experiences with language (Genishi, 1992).

Interactionist/Constructivist Theory

The *interactionist/constructivist theory* recognizes that language is learned in social settings. Children construct their own ideas about language as they interact with others in a meaningful context (Barbour, 1992). Three leading proponents of this theory are Lev Vygotsky, Jean Piaget, and Celia Genishi. There are others, too, including Constance Kamii and Lawrence Kohlberg.

Vygotsky focused on the social aspect of language acquisition. First, he said, children experience language skills through interaction with another person. Second, they experience these same aspects of language within and by themselves.

Vygotsky believed that language helps children shape thoughts and construct meaning. For example, children often talk to themselves out loud

Children use private speech to experiment with different sounds and word combinations. This three-year-old is also using private speech to give direction to her solitary play.

while performing a task or solving a problem (Mason & Sinha, 1993; Morrow, 1990). Vygotsky described this type of speech as *private speech*. It helps children integrate their thoughts with their actions. Private speech begins as children and adults talk and play informally—for example, in games such as peekaboo. Children remember and internalize words and comments that adults make. Then they use private speech to experiment with different sounds, words, and word combinations in a playful way. They also use private speech to give direction to their solitary play and to imitate others. An example is when a child says to a doll, "It's bedtime, so you are going to have to put your toys away and brush your teeth." Eventually, the patterns of speech used in private speech are internalized. Then children begin to engage in more social speech—that is, speaking with other children and adults.

In contrast to Vygotsky, Piaget believed that children must learn to think before they can talk. Piaget maintained that children must be able to think symbolically—that is, form mental images and categorize objects and events—to learn a language.

Celia Genishi (1992) presents a slightly different view of language acquisition than Vygotsky or Piaget. She asserts that children learn language as a combination of heredity and environmental factors. Like Chomsky, she believes that human beings are biologically prepared to use language. However, children become more fluent when they interact with other people and objects. Thus, children gradually figure out for themselves the rules of language and communication. Genishi also asserts that children learn to communicate based on the standards within their own communities. Teachers should acknowledge that these standards may vary widely and that none should be considered inferior (Genishi, 1992). This idea has important

A print-rich environment exposes children to the printed word in many different ways.

implications for classrooms with children from diverse backgrounds (Au, 1993). See "Multicultural Influences on Language" later in this chapter.

Curriculum Approaches to Early Literacy

In the preschool setting, curricula that focus on developing literacy skills often are called *early literacy* programs. Early literacy generally refers to the language arts components of curricula that promote early forms of reading and writing by young children—such as listening to stories and drawing pictures. Curriculum approaches to early literacy generally reflect different theories of how children learn. It is important for preschool teachers to become familiar with various approaches to determine the strategies that will be most effective for the children in their classrooms.

There are many curriculum approaches to developing literacy skills in young children. The approaches discussed in this section reflect two different perspectives on what language skills and experiences children need before starting elementary school. These approaches reflect two distinct perspectives—emergent literacy and reading readiness.

Proponents of *emergent literacy* assert that learning to read and write involves a combination of social, linguistic, and psychological aspects and is not just a cognitive skill (Teale & Sulzby, 1989). Emergent literacy is an ongoing process that emphasizes the interconnectedness of speaking, listening, reading, and writing. Preschool teachers who adopt the emergent literacy perspective will focus on providing experiences related to the spoken or written word throughout the classroom, as opposed to having a specific area of the classroom designated as the "language center."

Proponents of *reading readiness* believe that preschool is the time for formal, direct instruction in specific language skills, such as learning letter names and letter-sound relationships. Preschool teachers who adopt the reading readiness perspective act as "transmitters" of information directly related to reading skills.

Constructivist or Process Approach

Developmentally oriented preschools are likely to favor emergent literacy and to use the *constructivist or process approach*. According to the constructivist approach, children construct meaning about language on their own and through interaction with others and the environment (McLane & McNamee, 1990; Strickland, 1990). Teachers who utilize this approach do not teach specific skills in a set sequence, but rather they provide curriculum activities that surround preschoolers with the spoken and written word. These activities are designed to help children learn about the functions of literacy—that is, the important, vital uses of words in society and everyday living, such as street signs, food labels, and newspapers. Constructivists believe that specific skills, such as being able to form individual letters, at this age are not as important as making language meaningful.

Teachers who use the constructivist approach try to provide a *print-rich environment*, with plenty of reading and writing materials throughout all areas of the classroom. These materials may include prominently displayed charts and signs with pictures and words; plenty of books; different kinds of pens, markers, pencils, and paper; magnetic letters and "cookie cutter" letters; and props related to language—such as telephone books, magazines, business forms, and restaurant menus—in the dramatic play area. Teachers plan to provide the opportunity, encouragement, and time to use the materials. They may, for example, encourage experimentation with writing, without correcting mistakes (Fields, Spangler, & Lee, 1991).

The print-rich environment needs to include meaningful examples of print, such as labels with children's names and pictures on their cubbies and displays of children's drawings and writing. Frank Smith (1979) has found that, if language is not meaningful, children will neither learn from it nor respond to it.

This type of learning environment is referred to by many early childhood educators as the *whole language approach*. It combines speaking, listening, reading, and writing into one interrelated process rather than treating them as separate skills to be mastered (Smith, 1979). In the scenario at the beginning of this chapter, Mrs. Smith engaged the children in a whole language experience. They practiced speaking and listening as they talked about their favorite parts of the visit to the zoo. They practiced writing as they drew pictures of their favorite animals and made signs for their pretend zoo in the classroom. The activities were based on a relevant real-life experience of interest to the children.

As children begin to learn, they move from the "whole" to learning about the "parts." Thus, for example, as children begin to write, they may be encouraged to disregard correct spelling in order to write their ideas quickly and without hesitation (the "whole"). Eventually, they formulate rules to help them remember correct spellings and grammar rules (the "parts") (Goodman, Smith, Meredith, & Goodman, 1987).

An important teaching strategy in the constructivist approach is called *scaffolding* (Cazden, 1988). Scaffolding refers to ways in which the teacher provides verbal support and feedback to expand children's language skills. Here is an example of scaffolding, in which a teacher elaborates on what a child says during a conversation.

"I have a new fire truck."

"I see your new fire truck. Where did it come from?"

"My brother gave it to me."

"Tell me what the fire truck can do."

"It's got a big tall ladder that can save people, and a lot of wheels to make it go fast. It has a place to make the water come out."

"Where's the place where the water comes out of the truck to put out the fires?"

"Here."

"That's called a hose, and the water can shoot out of it, right?"

The teacher provides only enough guidance to help children expand their use of language, while the children maintain most of the responsibility for the content of the conversation. Vygotsky believes that scaffolding helps children's cognitive development as they process new information on top of what they have already experienced.

Transmission or Skills Approach

Academically oriented preschools are likely to have reading readiness goals and to utilize a curriculum approach to early literacy based on the behaviorist theory of how children learn. This approach is referred to as the *transmission or skills approach*. Teachers "transmit" meaning about language by breaking down the complex skills of reading and writing into individual steps or components. In direct contrast to the whole language approach discussed earlier, the transmission or skills approach focuses first on the parts, then on the whole. Each skill is a "part." For example, prereading skills include being able to tell letters apart and learning the names and sounds of letters. Prewriting skills include learning to print individual letters.

Instruction in these skills uses a drill and repetition method and progresses in a predetermined order. Language patterns are first modeled by the teacher, imitated by the children, and reinforced by the teacher. Materials generally include workbooks and worksheets with multiple-choice answers or fill-in-the-blank exercises. Children are directed to read a selection from a basal reader instead of having the opportunity to choose a book from the vast collection of children's literature.

In addition to modeling proper speaking patterns, the transmission approach also stresses the development of listening skills. Once a correct pattern or word meaning is learned, the teacher might purposefully use an incorrect pattern or series of words to "fool" the children. The following is an example of this type of lesson.

TEACHER:	(Holding a metal canister marked "flour"). This is a container.
TEACHER:	(Holding the canister). Is this a container?
CHILD:	Yes, this is a container.
TEACHER:	(Holding a book). Is this a container?
CHILD:	No, this is not a container.
TEACHER:	This is a container. (Teacher holds up various containers, such as a box, a cake pan, an ice cube tray, and a canvas bag, and the pattern is repeated with each.)
TEACHER:	Is this box a container?
CHILD:	Yes, this box is a container.
TEACHER:	Is this book a container?
CHILD:	No, this book is not a container.

The teacher then defines *container*, by saying, for example, "A container is something with connecting sides and a bottom used for holding things." The teacher then continues in the following way.

TEACHER:	Is this ball a container?
CHILD:	No, this ball is not a container.

TABLE 11.1	
Key differences between the constructivist and transmission approaches to early literacy	
Constructivist Approach	**Transmission Approach**
Assumes that children can learn early literacy skills through hands-on interaction with props, toys, and materials during a variety of preschool activities	Assumes that children can learn early literacy skills by watching, listening, and modeling the teacher, or "transmitter" of information
Uses activities designed to relate to the real-life experiences and interests of the children, including their families and the community	Teaches skills methodically, following a preset program or sequence of lessons not connected to a particular real-life context
Helps children focus on the functions of literacy, particularly the written word, such as learning that a dictionary helps people look up the meaning and spelling of words they do not know	Focuses on the forms, or skills, involved in literacy, and places little or no emphasis on the uses of literacy
Allows children to pursue early literacy in their own way and at their own pace	Assumes that all children learn to read and write in the same way

Adapted from "Differences Between Instructional Models" from *Literacy Instruction in Multicultural Settings* by Kathryn H. Au. Copyright © 1993 by Holt, Rinehart and Winston, Inc. Reprinted by permission of the publisher.

TEACHER: Does this ball have sides and a bottom?
CHILD: No, this ball does not have sides and a bottom.
TEACHER: Is this ball a container?
CHILD: No, this ball is not a container.

The teacher continues these patterns, focusing on correct speaking and listening skills. Gradually, lessons using similar patterns begin to focus on reading and writing skills, such as learning the letters of the alphabet. For a summary of the key differences between the constructivist and the transmission approaches, see Table 11.1.

Long-term follow-up studies on the effectiveness of this type of curriculum model have shown favorable results, especially in reading achievement. DISTAR, one of these models, is a highly structured and scripted program (see discussion in Chapter 2). Although children in the DISTAR program initially scored higher on IQ tests than children from developmentally oriented programs, the gains tended to disappear over time (Schweinhart, Weikart, & Larner, 1986). In another long-term follow-up study of the DISTAR direct instruction model, Wesley C. Becker and Russell Gersten (1982) noted favorable achievement results in the areas of reading, problem solving, and spelling. However, the children's achievement results declined once they left the program. Preschool teachers should know that the results of these program models are mixed. The results are considered controversial by early childhood education experts, often because the tests used favor the transmission or skills approach. See Chapter 15 for a discussion of more progressive assessment methods for tracking the development of literacy skills in young children.

Researchers have found that both the constructivist and the transmission models are successful in different situations. Teachers should select the approach that supports their goals and understanding of how children learn.

Building Language Skills

In both the transmission and the constructivist approaches, effective language instruction includes daily opportunities for young children to speak, listen, and become familiar with reading and writing. Although some preschools utilize the transmission approach exclusively, many early childhood educators today lean toward a constructivist approach that gives equal emphasis to all the language arts—speaking, listening, reading, and writing (Clark, 1976a; Durkin, 1972). Because this type of program exposes children to the spoken and the printed word through different avenues, or different areas of the curriculum, it may be able to accommodate more children with differing abilities and interests in the same classroom than a formalized, group-instruction approach (Clark, 1976b). To illustrate how this approach can be integrated into the preschool curriculum, this section presents several teaching strategies for a constructivist curriculum.

Language activities in emergent literacy programs encourage children to use what they already know about language and to learn new concepts. Activities should be interesting and developmentally appropriate. They should provide opportunities for children to learn from and help one another, as well as to work through a task from start to finish (Mason & Sinha, 1993; McLane & McNamee, 1990; Schrader, 1990).

As they plan and implement these emergent literacy activities, teachers need to be aware that their own language skills serve as models. They should speak clearly in well-modulated voices, spend about the same amount of time talking to each child, and avoid baby talk, slang, and harsh language.

Encouraging Children to Communicate

Language is an important aspect of social development. Consequently, teachers should encourage children to talk and listen to one another. Teachers can plan activities that involve more than one child. For example, children enjoy the challenge of guessing the sound made by another child or the teacher—such as the sound of a goat, a siren, or a car. They enjoy imitating environmental and nature sounds (for example, the wind or a frog); speaking in different degrees of loudness (for example, saying the word "yes" in a whisper or a shout); and playing with musical instruments. All these activities provide opportunities for informal and enjoyable language interaction.

An important component of encouraging children to talk is helping them become better listeners. In addition to engaging the children in literacy activities, teachers sometimes need to explain to children the importance of listening and not interrupting. It is important for teachers to demonstrate good listening skills when children speak to them. By listening actively to the ideas expressed verbally by children, teachers communicate that they support the children's efforts. Preschool children often struggle to communicate their thoughts. Part of a teacher's active listening to children means allowing them to finish their sentences on their own rather than suggesting words. Encouraging children to think of and use words without pressure builds competence.

Including Language in Every Activity

An emergent literacy approach includes a language component in as many curriculum activities as possible. Interesting activities lead to interesting conversations. Children like to talk about what they are doing as they do it or afterwards. For example, if a child is driving trucks through the sand, the teacher might ask the child to explain or describe what is happening. If children spend a morning working with clay, the teacher can ask children afterwards to talk about how the clay felt, what they liked to do with the clay, and where clay comes from. If the class is putting together a photo display of family pictures, the teacher might ask each child to talk about who is in the picture, where it was taken, and what the people in the picture are doing.

Being an attentive listener is a simple teaching strategy that encourages children to talk. Children need time to formulate and express their thoughts at their own pace, without feeling rushed or pressured.

Children's conversations can lead to ideas for new curriculum activities. For example, if a teacher asks a child about his drawing, he might reply, "This frog is the best jumper in his whole family." The teacher might then capitalize on this interest with a creative movement activity that involves jumping or a science activity about animals that jump. Mrs. Smith initiated a conversation about the zoo trip and picked up on Mina's wishful thinking. She then encouraged the children to plan their own play zoo. The children discussed which animals to include in the zoo and how they could use the classroom pets and pictures of favorite animals. They used writing materials to draw animals and to make signs for the animal cages.

Asking Open-ended Questions

An important technique for encouraging preschool children to talk is asking open-ended questions. *Open-ended questions* do not have just one "right" answer. Instead, they are designed to stimulate children to explore their own ideas and feelings and to present them verbally. Questions that require a yes-or-no or a one-word response—for example, "Where are your feet?"—do not encourage conversation. In contrast, open-ended questions—for instance, "What are all the things your feet can do?"—require description, thought, and consideration. Instead of asking, "Is that doll sad?," the teacher might ask, "What things are making the doll feel sad?" More divergent questioning techniques are described in Chapter 12.

Selecting Appropriate Books

Research has shown that children who are exposed to quality books throughout their early years develop advanced literacy skills (Chomsky, 1972). Books help children learn the relationship between the written and the spoken word. In addition, books help children learn about the uses of language in different situations as well as about language elements, such as story structure, which they may use in their own conversations and storytelling.

The preschool teacher must exercise judgment in selecting books for young children. Good children's books contain interesting, natural language and attractive illustrations and are large enough to be easily seen by a small group of children to whom an adult is reading. Preschoolers are interested in stories about pets, community helpers, and social behavior—such as making friends, dealing with siblings, or defying parental authority. They enjoy stories that reflect familiar aspects of their lives—such as mealtime, visiting a relative, sleeping and dreaming, playing with friends, and going to the doctor. They also like stories in which they can "predict" what will happen.

When teachers select books for young children, they should include stories that present multicultural and anti-bias perspectives by showing people of different backgrounds in the context of everyday life. In a classroom with children from culturally diverse backgrounds, such stories promote cross-cultural understanding and build self-esteem. In a homogeneous classroom, such books help children recognize similarities in people from other cultures. The "Focus on Cultural Diversity" feature in this chapter offers tips on screening books for multicultural and gender bias.

Classifying books according to children's chronological age may be misleading since children's interests are more closely related to their experiences than to their ages. However, in general, children of the same age tend to enjoy similar types of books. The following are some guidelines for choosing books for preschoolers of different ages. All young children respond to stories read aloud with feeling, enthusiasm, and expression.

- Very young children enjoy books with simple illustrations that depict one object, person, or animal. Toddlers have difficulty distinguishing reality and fantasy. They also become confused when animals or objects display human emotions or feelings. Consequently, "here and now" stories that reflect typical events in everyday life are more appropriate. Very young children also enjoy simple nursery rhymes.
- Three-year-olds are interested in stories about the seasons, people at their jobs, and extended family members, such as uncles, aunts, and grandparents. They are beginning to enjoy fairy tales and even scary stories about wolves, bears, and witches, if the children are securely ensconced in a lap

As part of the curriculum planning process, these teachers are looking for books with attractive illustrations and good story lines. The books they choose will relate to planned activities and will reflect the interests of the children in their group.

or in the group time circle. Three-year-olds also enjoy stories with repetitious language.

- Four-year-olds recognize and enjoy humor, dramatic adventures, fantastic tales, and stories with real plots, as they begin to grasp the basic story structure of a beginning, a middle, and an end. Four-year-olds enjoy the cadence, repetition, and wordplay found in nonsense books and rhymes. Children effortlessly memorize their favorite jingles in nonsense books, such as those by Dr. Suess, and often create new verses that follow word and rhythm patterns.
- Five-year-olds appreciate longer stories or books with more elaborate plots. They are no longer confused by stories that portray animals with human characteristics. Five-year-olds are especially entranced by the lyrical quality and sound of poetry. They enjoy fiction and nonfiction books about nature, fish and animals, their communities, and typical aspects of their everyday lives.

Books for very young children should be made of cardboard, plastic, cloth, or other sturdy materials to withstand rough treatment by toddlers. Older preschoolers need to be taught to respect and care for books. They need to learn to store them on shelves when not in use and to take care not to spill on them or tear the pages. Teachers also can teach respect for books by reading and talking about the author; and the dedication page if there is one; by describing how books are made; and by assisting with child-constructed books during a creative language activity. A representative list of books that present a realistic view of different cultures is given in Table 11.2.

Planning Prewriting Activities

Emergent literacy programs not only focus on helping young children make connections among speaking, listening, and reading but also focus on writing. Since many young children are initially attracted to reading through writing, teachers should provide many early opportunities for writing (Durkin, 1972).

Preschoolers are fascinated by the writing activities of adults and attempt to imitate adult writing behavior in a variety of ways—including scribbling on walls, on paper, and in their books. Teachers should display models of writing and print at children's eye level, give them writing implements and materials to write on, and provide reasons for them to write. Teachers can encourage children to explore writing by including prewriting activities in the curriculum. Prewriting activities are discussed later in this chapter.

Teachers need to remember that young children's writing attempts are individual and not necessarily imitations of adult writing. Scribbles illustrate that even very young children are beginning to understand the significance and importance of writing (Dyson, 1989). The talk that often accompanies scribbles indicates children's awareness of symbols. Preschool teachers need to acknowledge and encourage this talk to help children draw the connection between writing and speaking.

TABLE 11.2
Books that realistically represent diverse cultures

Type of Book	Author, Title, Publisher, Description	Ethnic Focus
Picture Books	Dooley, N. (1991). *Everybody cooks rice*. Minneapolis, MN: Carolrhoda. Searching for her brother in the neighborhood, Carrie samples the rice-based evening meals of many cultures.	Multiethnic
	Johnson, A. (1992). *The leaving morning*. New York: Orchard. A young boy and his older sister are both sad and excited about moving from their old apartment to a new house.	African American
	Jones, R. C. (1991). *Matthew and Tilly*. New York: Dutton Children's Books. Good friends Matthew and Tilly have occasional differences, but racial prejudice is not one of them.	Multiethnic
	McKissack, P. (1988). *Mirandy and Brother Wind*. New York: Knopf. Mirandy must live up to her boastful promise that the wind will be her partner at the upcoming cakewalk.	African American
	Oxenbury, H. (1987). *Clap hands*. New York: Macmillan Children's Book Group. A simple board book with delightful illustrations of babies at play.	Multiethnic
	Roe, E. (1991). *Con mi hermano = With my brother*. New York: Macmillan Children's Book Group/ Bradbury. A bilingual (Spanish/English) text describes the things a preschool-aged boy admires about his older brother.	Latino
	Rosen, M. (1992). *Elijah's angel: A story for Chanukah and Christmas*. San Diego, CA: Harcourt. When an elderly African-American artisan gives a young white Jewish boy one of his angel wood carvings, the latter worries about accepting a "graven image."	Multiethnic
	Steptoe, J. (1988). *Baby says*. New York: Lothrop. An ingenious story uses only baby words to describe the playful relationship between an endearing toddler and his long-suffering older brother.	African American
	Wheeler, B. (1986). *Where did you get your moccasins?* Saint Paul, MN: Pemmican. When Jody wears his new moccasins to school, one	Native American

(continued)

TABLE 11.2
Books that realistically represent diverse cultures (continued)

Type of Book	Author, Title, Publisher, Description	Ethnic Focus
	question about them from his classmates leads to another . . . and another!	Native American
	Williams, V. B. (1990). *"More, more, more," said the baby*. New York: Greenwillow. Three brightly illustrated stories about sharing, caring, and unconditional love.	Multiethnic
	Williams, V. B. (1984). *Music, music for everyone*. New York: Greenwillow. Rosa and her friends start a neighborhood band and practice for their first gig at a community event.	Multiethnic
Folklore and Traditional Literature	Begay, S. (1992). *Ma'ii and Cousin Horned Toad: A traditional Navajo story*. New York: Scholastic. Lazy Coyote always seems to show up at his relatives' homes at mealtime—until his Cousin Horned Toad teaches him a lesson.	Native American
	Te Ata. (1989). *Baby rattlesnake* (adapted by L. Moroney). Emeryville, CA: Children's Book Press. A Chicksaw story about a young rattlesnake who begs for a rattle and gets one before he knows how to use it.	Native American
Poetry and Song	Greenfield, E. (1991). *Night on Neighborhood Street*. New York: Dial Books for Young Readers. Seventeen poems offer glimpses into the lives of various families on one particular evening who live on the same city block.	African American
	Hopkins, L. B. (1992). *Through our eyes: Poems and pictures about growing up*. New York: Little. Photos and poems feature the lives and experiences of all kinds of children.	Multiethnic
	Hudson, W. (1993). *Pass it on: African-American poetry for children*. New York: Scholastic. Full-color paintings illustrate an excellent introduction to the richness of African-American experience through poetry.	African American
	Sneve, V. (1989). *Dancing teepees: Poems of American Indian youth*. New York: Holiday. Nineteen poems from diverse traditions celebrate the promise of children from babyhood to adolescence.	Native American

FOCUS ON Communicating with Children

Coping with "Bathroom Language"

The children in Sue Connors's class had been experimenting with "bathroom language." She knew that preschoolers often use such language as a way of experimenting with words. Most of them simply repeat words and phrases that they hear from their parents or older siblings without knowing what the words mean. For several days, Sue had chosen to ignore the language, a strategy that often worked. But she planned to address the problem if it surfaced again. Then she noticed Billy. He was grinning broadly and holding up one of the puppets. The children around him were laughing.

BILLY: Poop head . . . poop head. This puppet's a poop head!

SUE: Billy! I really need to talk to you alone. Please come over here!

BILLY: What?

SUE: Do you know what a poop head is?

BILLY: No.

SUE: Then why were you saying it?

BILLY: Because. (Pause.) Hey, my big brother Tommy always says it. (He laughs loudly.)

SUE: Well, it may sound funny . . . but poop head really is not a nice thing to say about anyone—even a puppet! If you want to use a word like poop head here in our classroom, you can only say it quietly to yourself, not in front of other people.

BILLY: But it's funny . . .

SUE: It's not funny. Would you like it if I called you a poop head?

BILLY: Ummm . . . no.

SUE: Let's talk about the puppets. How about if you tell me how we might create a story with them? Could we make up a story about things we say to friends and things we don't? (They begin to talk about the puppet show.)

Is there anything Sue did that you think might have been handled differently? Explain. What do you think are some advantages of ignoring "bathroom language"? Of confronting it? Do you think that Sue should make Billy's parents aware that he is imitating his older brother's language in school?

Even when they are not directly taught about writing, most children make similar discoveries about writing. When very young children produce squiggles and call them writing, the children know that writing consists of certain shapes that are used over and over again. They also learn that these shapes can be rearranged in different combinations, that print has meaning beyond its shapes, and that it is arranged on the page in a certain way (Temple et al., 1982).

When children see adults and older children writing, they are likely to view writing as a worthwhile activity. Preschoolers especially enjoy such activities as "writing" a few words on a note or bulletin that the teacher will send home to parents. This activity allows children to experience writing in a real situation (Schrader, 1990).

An important aspect of encouraging writing in very young children is to help them develop fine motor skills. See the "Applications" section later in this chapter for activity ideas. Also, Chapter 7 includes a discussion of promoting fine motor skills. As preschoolers learn to use writing implements, their muscles can tire easily, and they soon become frustrated. Therefore, teachers need to keep early writing experiences frequent but short (Lamme, 1982).

Multicultural Influences on Language

It has been predicted that, by the year 2000, approximately 7.7 million children under age 14 in the United States will be from non-English-speaking backgrounds. This number will amount to an increase of about 37 percent since 1976 (Oxford-Carpenter et al., 1984). The majority of these children will live in urban areas and will be Spanish-speaking (Genishi, 1992).

Children who are able to speak and function in two different languages are considered to be *bilingual*. In the United States, many bilingual children speak a language other than English at home and English at school. Bilingual children who do not have a working understanding of English are said to have *limited English proficiency (LEP)*.

Young children who are bilingual exhibit certain language problems (Garcia, 1982). Although most of these children can "switch" back and forth between languages with relative ease and develop grammatical forms independently for each language, they occasionally may carry over words or a particular ordering of words from one language to the other. For example, in the scenario at the beginning of the chapter, Lisa said, "Mina and I can draw leopard gatos," interjecting the Spanish word for "cat" into her English. Test results indicate that bilingual children may lag behind monolingual children during the early years of language acquisition. However, their performance is about equal in elementary school.

In addition, research has noted positive effects of early bilingualism on children's cognitive development (Diaz, Padilla, & Weathersby, 1991). Children who were becoming proficient in two languages better understood the importance of language than monolingual children. They also were more adept at concept formation, creative thinking, and problem solving.

Some children speak a dialect of English, or *nonstandard English*, that has its own structure and vocabulary. Most dialects are strongly influenced by regional and socioeconomic factors. Preschool teachers should respect the structure and intricacies of dialects and should not label in a derogatory way children who use nonstandard English. They should recognize that children who speak nonstandard English need a positive preschool environment that accepts their language, and teachers who use their language to inspire a variety of literacy experiences. Research has shown that, in this type of setting, children will become confident in their abilities to communicate and eventually will learn Standard English (Brooks, 1985).

Preschool teachers should be aware that many of the children for whom English is a second language will have special instructional needs. Yet, early childhood educators do not agree on how to foster early literacy in young children who are bilingual or LEP. Some suggest that programs should include instruction in the children's native language and experiences related to their own culture (Rigg & Enright, 1986). Others suggest that instruction should focus on developing proficiency in English and providing experiences related to the culture of the United States (Wong, Fillmore, 1991). Others have developed curricula for specific groups of children. One example is the ALERTA curriculum, designed to teach bilingual Hispanic children using a theme approach, multicultural activities, and specific planning forms and observation methods (Williams & De Gaetano, 1985). Many school administrators feel that integrating LEP children into the regular classroom is an acceptable approach, and that they will learn English through "immersion" in an English-speaking environment. These administrators also may not have a choice of programs to offer LEP children because of budgetary constraints or because the populations of their schools include relatively few LEP children.

One type of curriculum model focused on teaching children from diverse backgrounds is called a *culturally responsive curriculum* (see Pease-Alvarez, Garcia, & Espinosa, 1991). In this type of curriculum, the teacher devises activities that utilize the languages of the children's cultural background and that reflect various aspects of these particular cultures. Theme ideas for projects come directly from discussions with the children. Much like the project approach described in Chapter 2, children work together in small groups on a wide range of emergent literacy activities.

For example, if the children are interested in caring for babies, projects might include the following activities.

- Comparing and labeling baby pictures
- Talking about specific ways the families of the children provide care for baby sisters and brothers, while the teacher creates a written list
- Discussing what babies are called in different languages and the names of basic baby items, including diaper, bottle, and crib
- Creating a hospital nursery in the dramatic play area, with writing props to make name bracelets for the babies and for filling in hospital records indicating birthdates and weights at birth
- Creating a group story about a baby, as the teacher writes it down or tapes it

An important element in the success of a culturally responsive curriculum is that children form trusting and caring relationships with one another and with the teacher. Lucinda Pease-Alvarez and her associates (1991) have found that children who feel that they are in a safe environment are more open to learning. Further, the teachers using this curriculum approach see their classrooms as small communities or families. This type of curriculum works best in schools that encourage multiculturalism.

The culturally responsive curriculum reflects the constructivist model described earlier in the chapter. Katherine Au (1993) notes that this model works particularly well with children of culturally diverse backgrounds because it purposefully creates language experiences based on the cultural milieu in which the children live. Further, because the constructivist model focuses on the functions of the spoken and the written word, it can familiarize these children with how language is used in the dominant culture.

Successful preschool language programs consider the learning style of each child and reflect the teacher's knowledge of the children's cultural and social background. Most children need a combination of approaches, with some activities that teach specific language skills and others that engage children in their own discovery and exploration (Genishi, 1992).

Applications

To help young children develop the skills necessary to build a foundation for becoming a reader and a writer, language and early literacy activities should emphasize several areas. These areas include visual and auditory discrimination (discussed in Chapter 10), grouping, following directions, and developing eye-hand coordination. Activities also should be designed to help young children practice listening and speaking skills and learn the functions of writing in a context that relates to their interests. Activities, in addition, should be designed to foster the curiosity and imagination that are essential to developing a lifelong love of books. The activities and teaching strategies discussed in this section will show how you can integrate language and early literacy experiences in the daily preschool curriculum.

Reading Aloud

Research suggests that reading to children on a daily basis helps them understand the relationship between oral language and print, as they see that

Even very young children, such as this group of two-year-olds, enjoy and benefit from being read to every day. Including one or two story times in the daily curriculum fosters children's love of books and helps them understand the relationship between spoken language and print.

the reader reproduces the author's story by reading printed words (Temple et al., 1982). Reading aloud to children provides an active experience that supports Vygotsky's view that children develop language skills through social interaction. As you talk with children about the story you are reading—what they think will happen next and how the story may relate to their own experiences—they begin to construct the meaning of words, and to recognize different parts of the story and basic story structure (Morrow & Smith, 1990). They also learn that words in books always stay the same no matter where the book is read or who reads it (McLane & McNamee, 1990).

Research has shown that reading aloud to small groups of about three children at a time is beneficial to children's early literacy experiences and encourages a high level of interaction between the children and the adult reader (Morrow & Smith, 1990). Children who hear stories in small groups tend to ask more questions, make more comments, and, when tested, achieve higher comprehension levels than children who are read to one-on-one or in large groups. Further, in small groups, teachers are better able to encourage responses from quiet children.

Try to read aloud on a variety of topics, especially those that interest the children. To broaden their experience, however, you might occasionally choose a book on an unfamiliar topic. Make sure that the subject matter is still appropriate for the age and developmental level of the children. Periodically, let the children choose the books. Children enjoy the opportunity to hear their favorite stories repeated.

It is also important to remember that a caregiver's reading style can affect how well children understand the story read to them (Morrow & Smith, 1990). Practice reading a new book out loud before reading it to children. You can identify parts of the story that might prompt particular questions, require explanation, or create an opportunity to relate the story to some other activities in the curriculum that day or that week. You also can practice sound effects, special voices for different characters, or complicated rhymes. Practice will improve your reading style and in turn will improve the children's enjoyment of the story. Remember also that nothing breeds enthusiasm like enthusiasm, so keep your energy level high and show the children that you are really enjoying the story, too.

As you read to children, create ways to make the experience more interactive. You might encourage the children to predict what the story is about by looking at the cover, or to predict what might happen next after every two or three pages. You also might ask all the children in the group what they might do in similar circumstances. If a discussion goes on too long, you can keep the flow of the story going by saying, for example, "Let's hear one more idea about what the alligator might do next, and then we'll turn the page to see what really happened."

Storytelling

Letting children tell stories is another interactive early literacy activity—in this case between the teller and the audience. Like story reading, storytelling

Creating a Post Office

A post office helps familiarize children with the printed word and different kinds of communication. Use such materials as junk mail; postcards (from visitor centers and museums or made by the children); unused personal or business stationery (from businesses and parents); envelopes; stamps (used or made by the children); paste; magazines; drawing materials; ink pads and rubber stamps (for putting the "postmark" on letters); and milk cartons for mailboxes. Add dress-up props, such as mail delivery bags, mail carriers' hats, and blue postal shirts.

Talk to the children about mail and what goes on in a real post office. Encourage discussion about letters or cards the children may have received and how mail gets delivered. Ask children how they might create their own card or stamp. Make mailboxes by cutting out one end of each milk carton and taping on a flap that lifts. Write each child's name on the flap, or use a photograph. Encourage children to make and deliver mail for other children in the class. Offer to write a letter, a story, or a special message that a child dictates.

Extend the Experience

- Use postcards as "story starters." At group time, let each child choose one picture and create a story about it.
- Have children create get-well cards, and send them to a local hospital.

provides a link between oral and written language. When children reenact their favorite stories, they know that their stories came from printed words in a book. Reenacting also improves children's comprehension, their ability to use oral language, and their knowledge of story structure, and it fosters their interest in learning to read (Durkin, 1966; Mason, 1992; Morrow, 1985).

Children enjoy telling stories. Leave room in the curriculum for children to participate in storytelling. They may participate either solo or as part of a group—such as when the teacher tells part of the story and the children chime in for the chorus, or repetitive refrain, in the story. Group storytelling helps preschoolers practice listening skills and become familiar with story language and structure.

You might encourage children as a group to create a story to accompany a book of pictures. Or you might allow each child to make up an individual version to describe the same pictures. Another good idea is to collect travel or humorous picture postcards from friends, or museum postcards of different paintings, for use as "story starters." Hold up one card, and ask children to describe the picture and to make up a story about the people, the animals, or the places depicted. Remember that young children also like to tell stories about their homes and families, their pets, a favorite toy, or their artwork. You can help the children "write" and illustrate their story for later retelling.

Puppets are useful props to help children tell an original story or retell a favorite story. Children also love to use puppets to create imaginative stories about a classroom incident or events in their lives. Puppets are especially useful for encouraging shy children to tell stories—the puppets speak for them. See the "Focus on Activities" feature in Chapter 8 for more information about making and using puppets.

Verbal Games

Verbal games give preschoolers the opportunity to both listen and talk. For example, following directions in "Simon Says" helps children learn the names of body parts and directions (up/down, over/under, and so on). Finger plays, such as "Eensy Weensy Spider," combine story, music, verbal repetitions, and the finger motions of the moving "spider." Joke games, such as "Knock, Knock," encourage communication and interaction among children.

Games involving repetition, such as "Grandmother's Trunk," also are fun for young children in a small group. The first child repeats the phrase, "Grandmother came back from her trip and in her trunk was a _____." (List an item such as an "umbrella.") Each child in turn repeats the phrase followed by the list of items created by the other children and then adds a new item.

Another verbal game builds on children's familiarity with grocery shopping. Fill a box with empty food containers and cartons, such as soup cans, pasta and cereal boxes, and egg cartons. Read a shopping list for a group of children or individual children, and ask the children to gather the items. In addition to building verbal skills, this game focuses on the connection between the written and the spoken word, and it illustrates a common function of literacy—labeling items people buy in the store.

Gather a small group of young children and say, "I'm thinking of something _____" (hot, cold, far away, up high, and so on). Children enjoy this verbal guessing game, as they build basic vocabulary. Another game you can play with a small group or individual children is to ask, "What would you do?" questions. You might say, "You are going to visit someone for a weekend. What would you take?", or you might say, "Pretend you have a friend who is feeling sad. How would you make her laugh?", or you might say "Pretend you are planning a picnic for the three little pigs. What would you bring?"

Prewriting and Prereading Activities

The preschool curriculum should include prewriting and prereading activities. These activities are often referred to as emergent writing or emergent reading activities. Regardless of the child's developmental level, these activities help children understand the relationship of writing and reading to meaningful communication. Prewriting activities help preschoolers develop the small-muscle control and eye-hand coordination they will need when they actually learn to write. Chapter 10 includes a more detailed discussion of this topic. Prereading activities help children form important connections between the spoken and the written word, which will lay the groundwork for learning to read.

Creating opportunities in the preschool curriculum for children to experiment freely with writing, without correction, helps them develop the fine motor skills and eye-hand coordination necessary for learning to write.

Children who are unable to hold a pencil properly usually lack small-muscle control. Activities that require manipulating materials help children develop muscle control. For example, to help children practice using their hands, fingers, and grasping technique (which is needed for holding a writing implement), you might encourage play with puzzles that contain few but very large pieces. As children develop greater control and coordination, they can gradually move to more complex puzzles with smaller pieces. Snap beads, molding materials (clay, dough, and putty), dressing activities (zipping, buttoning, and tying shoe laces), and paper activities (cutting, folding, tearing, and coloring) also provide grasping practice.

Activities to develop eye-hand coordination can include balancing objects, pushing buttons, turning knobs, stringing beads, or weaving. Such activities as climbing or jumping rope, games that provide practice with up/down and left/right, and paper tasks—such as coloring, painting, tracing, copying, pasting, and finger painting—also foster eye-hand coordination.

Cooking is a good prereading activity. Cooking illustrates another function of literacy in an everyday context. It is relevant to children and helps children link reading and the printed word. Try creating picture recipes, drawing pictures to portray the ingredients and directions. For example, "stir" would be written below a drawing of someone using a large spoon to stir the batter. "Flour" would be written below a sack or a jar of flour. The pictures will help children "read" and follow the recipe. As you cook with children, remember to use lots of verbal activity to accompany actions—such as saying, "Let's take the big wooden spoon and stir the flour," or "Now we have to add half a cup of grated cheese."

Prewriting activities—such as having children create their own labels to identify their block structures or "write" their own and their friends'

A dramatic play area based on a theme, such as this pretend grocery store, lets children learn the everyday functions of literacy in a context related to their real world.

names—help form a personal connection between the written word and the child. Your feedback and guidance can help familiarize children with the proper shape of each letter in their names, for example. Repetition helps them refine and duplicate the shapes.

Dramatic Play Areas Based on a Theme

Dramatic play centers based on a theme can serve as an important tool in the curriculum to promote language skills. They create opportunities to integrate personal experiences with the spoken and the written word, as well as to hone listening skills. Research has shown that, by choosing a theme, designing the space, and providing literacy-related materials, teachers can create dramatic play areas that encourage play combined with language behavior (Pellegrini, 1986). In a study conducted by Lesley Mandel Morrow (1990), literacy props were added to a "veterinarian's office" dramatic play setting. The following literacy activities were observed: children "reading" to their stuffed animal pets; children drawing with crayons and pencils, "filling out" forms and appointment books; and doctors "making notes" about pet ailments and "writing prescriptions" for medicine. Such settings as post offices, grocery stores, restaurants, airports, offices, and banks make interesting and stimulating theme-based dramatic play areas. See the "Focus on Activities" feature and Table 11.3 in this chapter.

You can help children extend dramatic and literacy play in these areas by providing background experiences with the topic, as Mrs. Smith did with the zoo. Field trips expose children to different roles in a real-life setting and enable children to hear language connected with the different roles (Vukelich, 1991). You also might discuss an experience familiar to the children to get conversation started. For example, if any children in your group have gone camping, you might encourage them to talk about their camping experiences during group time. Talk about and make a list of the items that children took on their camping trips. Then begin to collect items on the list, and set aside an area of the room for "camping." Some of the items may already be available in the classroom. You also might talk to parents and send a note home with the children to let families know what props you are still looking for. Props might include backpacks; assorted plastic food, plates, and eating utensils; water bottles; binoculars; compasses; and flashlights.

Help children label each of the items and arrange them in the "campsite." As the children play in the "camping area," you may discover additional materials that will contribute to a print-rich environment, such as maps of hiking trails or campground sites, outdoor magazines (with pictures of birds, wildlife, and plants), federal or state park posters, and markers and poster board (for signs). You can extend play by asking questions or making suggestions that grow from the children's actions and conversations (see the discussion of encouraging dramatic play in Chapter 4).

Research has shown that theme-based dramatic play for children allows them to create their own "worlds," solve problems, and express ideas verbally (McLane & McNamee, 1990). Anthony D. Pellegrini (1983) has found

TABLE 11.3
Dramatic play areas based on a theme

Name of Area	Needed for Area
Preschool Café	Preschoolers will enjoy "eating out" in their very own café. Needed: tables and chairs, menus (from a real restaurant), order pads, place mats and/or tablecloths, napkins, plastic tableware, paper plates and cups, chef's hat, aprons and/or uniforms for servers, cash register, play money, a chalkboard for specials, plus other signs or pictures for the walls.
Scientific Experiment	Turn your preschoolers into future scientists. Needed: white coats, safety goggles, plastic test tubes, beakers and measuring cups, jars of colored water, rulers and other measuring devices, petri dishes, microscope, small items to be analyzed, such as feathers, leaves, and seeds, disposable gloves, and children's science books.
Picnic at the Beach	Create your own beach scene for those dreary days. Needed: beach scene travel posters, beach umbrella, beach towels, swimsuits, sunglasses, lounge chairs, radio or tape player, air mattresses, blanket, picnic basket, paper plates, cups, and napkins. Use play food or add real food for a memorable experience. Don't forget plenty of books to read on the beach!
Airplane Flight	Make this a flight to remember. Needed: posters of sky/cloud scenes, airliner dashboard (cardboard with fluorescent-painted dials), captain's hat, earphones, wing pins for attendants, serving trays, plastic cups, TV dinner trays, soda cans, in-flight and travel magazines, safety cards.

that this type of play also improves story comprehension and the ability to tell stories and recall details. He also found that children use more imaginative language when props are available. In classrooms with thematic play areas, children tend to assume different roles and are more likely to participate in language-related activities (Morrow, 1990). Even with few literacy props, dramatic play improves children's understanding of the function of the written word—such as when a child pretends to "look up" a number in the phone book or "take down" a phone message. Increasing literacy props in the dramatic play area can be as simple as adding paper, pencils, and various print materials, such as message pads, menus, and used appointment books and calendars. Literacy props stimulate play scenarios as children explore the use of the spoken and written word in a variety of situations.

Theme-based dramatic play also improves *narrative competence*—that is, the ability to create characters and their behaviors and language in the context of a particular situation. An example would be speaking like a doctor in a play hospital scenario (Vukelich, 1991). In dramatic play, children produce narrative "scripts" that show that they have adapted roles and language from everyday experiences.

Children are most likely to develop early literacy skills in classrooms where they are encouraged to participate in listening, speaking, reading, and writing activities. By taking advantage of these opportunities, children can become competent listeners, speakers, readers, and writers (McLane & McNamee, 1990).

CHAPTER 11   REVIEW

SUMMARY

- Language is the basic form of human communication. Language skills necessary to communicate well include speaking, listening, reading, and writing.

- Children begin to develop language skills early in life. Language acquisition is an ongoing process that continues as children develop.

- Proponents of the nativist theory of language acquisition believe that each person has an innate biological ability to learn language.

- Behaviorists believe that language is acquired through imitation and adult reinforcement of the "correct" utterances of children.

- Interactionist/constructivists—such as Piaget, Vygotsky, and Genishi—believe that children acquire language when they interact with adults, other children, and their environment.

- Emergent literacy is an ongoing process in which young children begin to recognize the interconnectedness of speaking, listening, reading, and writing.

- The constructivist approach to developing language skills surrounds children with experiences designed to help them construct meaning about language in an everyday context. This approach focuses on helping preschoolers understand the functions of literacy, not specific skills.

- Proponents of reading readiness believe that preschool is the time for formal, direct instruction in specific language skills such as learning letter names and letter-sound relationships.

- The transmission approach is based on the behaviorist theory of how children learn and focuses on reading readiness. Language and prereading skills are taught through drill, repetition, and reinforcement.

- A print-rich environment includes plenty of reading and writing materials throughout all areas of the classroom.
- Children for whom English is a second language may have special instructional needs.
- The preschool curriculum should include daily opportunities for children to experiment with language. It is important for caregivers to enrich the language component in as many curriculum activities as possible.
- Teachers should provide opportunities that encourage children to talk. Teachers need to give children plenty of time to express their thoughts and should avoid interrupting or hurrying children during conversations.
- Books for preschoolers should be developmentally appropriate, reflect children's interests, encourage discussion, and, where possible, offer anti-bias and multicultural perspectives.
- Curriculum activities especially helpful in developing language and early literacy skills include reading aloud, storytelling, playing verbal games, and creating thematic dramatic play areas.

ACQUIRING KNOWLEDGE

1. How does the nativist theory account for language acquisition?
2. What evidence does Chomsky cite to support the existence of the "language acquisition device"?
3. How does the behaviorist theory of language acquisition differ from the nativist theory?
4. What are the main points emphasized by the interactionist/constructivist theory of language acquisition?
5. According to constructivist theory, how does private speech help a child develop language?
6. How do Vygotsky and Piaget's theories on the interaction of language and thought differ?
7. What are the primary elements of Genishi's theory of language development?
8. How do the goals of the emergent literacy and reading readiness perspectives on literacy skills differ?
9. Why is a print-rich environment essential to a constructivist curriculum?
10. What is the whole language curriculum approach to early literacy?
11. How does scaffolding support a constructivist approach?
12. Why is the skills approach to early literacy also called the transmission approach?
13. Why is transmission not a primary teaching strategy in the constructivist curriculum?
14. What features of the constructivist approach are especially helpful for accommodating children from diverse backgrounds in the same classroom?
15. What factors are important in a teacher's own use of language in the preschool setting?

16. Should a teacher finish children's sentences for them if they are hesitant or unsure? Why or why not?
17. What are open-ended questions, and how do they promote language skills?
18. How can the selection of books for story reading support an anti-bias curriculum?
19. What types of books are most appropriate for three-year-olds? For five-year-olds?
20. What guidelines should a teacher follow during early writing experiences?
21. Do all bilingual children have limited English proficiency? Explain your answer.
22. Describe the varying opinions about how to foster early literacy in preschool children who have limited English proficiency.
23. How does a culturally responsive curriculum accommodate bilingual children?
24. How does the teacher's reading aloud to children help promote their language skills acquisition?
25. What activities can help a child develop the motor skills necessary for writing?

THINKING CRITICALLY

1. The layout of a classroom can provide a lot of information about a preschool's curriculum. What type of curriculum approach to early literacy might be used in a classroom in which all books and writing materials are stored and used only in one large area, clearly labeled "Language Center"?
2. Creating a print-rich environment helps children develop language skills and understand the importance of writing. Do you think that a print-rich environment in a classroom made up of English-speaking and bilingual children should include materials in languages other than English? Why or why not?
3. Most parents and guardians understand the importance of reading stories aloud to young children, but having children tell their own stories may be a less familiar activity. How might you explain to an adult why storytelling can be as important to the process of language acquisition as story reading?
4. Group games and musical games can provide children with an enjoyable method of practicing language skills. Choose a common children's game and describe how it helps children develop language.
5. The dramatic play area can provide children with many opportunities to explore literacy. Imagine that a teacher has created a theme of breakfast foods. What kinds of materials or props might he or she provide in the dramatic play area to encourage the development of various literacy skills? What dramatic play scenarios might occur?

OBSERVATIONS AND APPLICATIONS

1. Spend some time with a group of three- or four-year-olds in a preschool setting to observe prewriting activities. Watch one child in particular. Take note of any scribbling or "writing" on paper. Record any verbalizations that accompany the writing process. What writing implements does that child use? How is she moving her hands and arms? What kind of marks is she making? In what ways do they resemble formal writing?

2. In that same preschool classroom, look for evidence of a print-rich environment. Describe any charts and signs displayed prominently on the walls. Are there literacy-oriented props in the dramatic play area, such as magazines, menus, telephone books, and newspapers? If so, describe how some of the children use these props in their play.

3. Nestor Yepes is a four-year-old boy who recently joined your preschool group. Born in Mexico, Nestor has been raised in a Spanish-speaking household. His family moved to the United States two years ago, and he has learned English from his American-born cousins, extended family, and friends. During preschool, you have noticed that Nestor does not seem to understand everything that is being said. Often, he uses English and Spanish words interchangeably. In what ways might you help Nestor in the classroom?

4. During the summer, you are asked by the head teacher to select the books that you would like to use with your group of four-year-olds. You would like to select books that will be developmentally appropriate for that age group—as well as interesting to the children. What topics or types of books will you look for?

FOR FURTHER INFORMATION

Books and Journal Articles

Clay, M. S. (1991). Introducing a new storybook to young readers. *The Reading Teacher, 45,* 264–273.

Genishi, C. (1988). Children's language: Learning words from experience. *Young Children, 44*(1), 16–23.

Gibson, L. (1989). *Literacy learning in the early years: Through children's eyes.* New York: Teachers College Press.

Mallan, K. (1992). *Children as storytellers.* Portsmouth, NH: Heinemann.

Strickland, D. (1990). Emergent literacy: How young children learn to read and write. *Educational Leadership, 47,* 18–23.

Videotapes

International Reading Association (1992). *Reading and young children: A practical guide for child care providers.* Newark, DE: Author.

Center for the Study of Reading. (1991). Strategies from successful classrooms. *Emergent literacy* (Vol. 1). Newark, DE: International Reading Association.

Cognitive Development:
Thinking and Learning

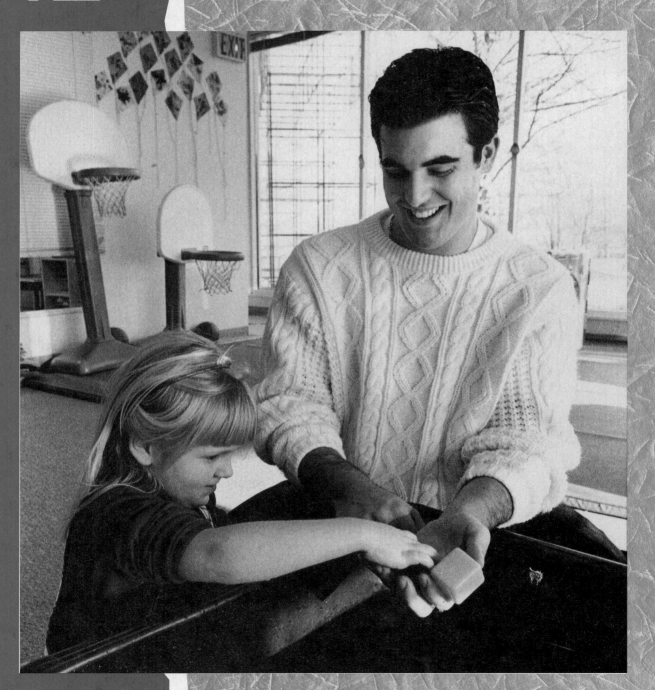

FOUR-YEAR-OLD Amelia had been waiting all morning for a chance to engage in one of her favorite activities—playing at the water table. Now she stood at the edge of the table and reached her hands into the water. Her fingers felt several objects—marbles, a golf ball, and a water-filled hollow plastic block. Lifting them out of the water, she made a pile of the objects on the apron of the water table.

On the water table, Amelia's preschool teacher, Stephen, had erected a miniature sliding board, which extended out over the water. Amelia put a large marble on the top of the slide and watched as it rolled down and hit the water with a small splash and a "kerplop."

Laughing with glee, Amelia picked it out of the water and rolled it down the slide again and again. Tiring of using the marble, Amelia next tried the golf ball. It, too, rolled down the slide, hitting the water with an even bigger splash. After making the golf ball roll into the water a few times, Amelia placed the plastic cube at the top of the slide. But the cube did not move, so she gave it a nudge with her finger. The cube slid down an inch or so and stopped. Amelia had to nudge it again until it finally reached the bottom of the slide and fell into the water.

Stephen, who had been watching Amelia's experiments with interest, came over to her and said, "Amelia, tell me about what you're doing."

"I'm making things go down the slide," she answered.

"Tell me about which things rolled down the slide."

"This," said Amelia, handing him the large marble.

"Anything else?" asked Stephen.

"And this," Amelia said, handing him the golf ball.

"What happened when you tried this?" Stephen asked, picking up the block.

"It got stuck. I had to push it down," Amelia said.

"Round things roll down the slide easily," said Stephen, as he showed her the marble and the golf ball in one hand and the block in the other. "But square things don't. Let's feel in our hands how they're different."

"Yeah," said Amelia with satisfaction, as she reclaimed the objects one at a time from Stephen's hands.

Children in preschool today will grow up in a complicated world full of information and technology. They will need to acquire a vast amount of knowledge as they progress through their years of formal education and into the world of adulthood and work. Fortunately, young children come equipped with a great enthusiasm for learning. This enthusiasm is evident in the "never-ending" questions of preschoolers and the concentration with which they learn to manipulate a stacking toy or to assemble a simple puzzle, for instance.

Since information in the world is always changing and increasing, children need to do more than simply absorb and memorize information in preschool. They also need to learn how to think. The preschool curriculum needs to address the development of cognitive and creative thinking skills that children will need to help them understand complex concepts and solve problems throughout their lives.

For example, while Amelia played at the water table, she was learning—without even being aware of it—about grouping various objects according to a particular characteristic (shape) and according to function (rolling and nonrolling). The ability to group or classify information is a basic cognitive skill that Amelia will need in later years in order to learn mathematics and scientific concepts.

Preschoolers develop cognitive skills through hands-on experience, imitation, and repetition. Teachers help children develop these skills by providing them with the opportunities and materials they need to practice specific skills. Teachers also help by guiding children's thinking process through question-asking techniques, just as Stephen did with Amelia. This chapter explores the ways in which early childhood professionals can create opportunities to develop cognitive skills in the preschool curriculum.

The Role of Cognitive Skills in Young Children

Infants learn about the world first through their senses—sight, hearing, taste, touch, and smell. They learn that this face looks familiar, this one does not . . . this sound is a mother's voice, that sound isn't . . . this food tastes different from that one . . . this object is soft, that one is hard.

As infants and toddlers grow, their brain skills continually evolve and increase in complexity. They acquire the ability to remember information for longer periods of time, and they spend a lot of time observing the actions of people and trying to imitate those actions. They learn about objects in their world by manipulating them and they begin to perceive relationships between specific objects. They learn that some objects are shiny, some are used for eating, some are found only outdoors, and some, like the family dog, can move on their own. Very young children also begin to experience cause and effect. If they cry, someone picks them up. If they bang the cup against the table, it makes a noise. If they spill a cup of juice on themselves, they feel wet.

Preschool activities help children begin to master the cognitive skills that lay the groundwork for future learning. This three-year-old is learning about shapes, matching, and one-to-one correspondence.

Making Sense of the World

Cognitive skills—perception, memory, observation, communication, establishing common relations between objects, and understanding cause and effect—are the basic tools that help young children make sense of their world. For example, Amelia learned through observation that spherical objects will roll but square objects will not. She experienced cause and effect when she placed the golf ball at the top of an incline and it rolled down into the water and made a splash. She was able to solve the problem of making the block move by pushing it with her finger. When Stephen placed the two round objects in his hand, Amelia established a relationship between them.

As discussed in Chapter 11, the cognitive process of acquiring language also enables children to learn much more about their world. Language enables children to assign names and labels to objects and events so that they can sort and group them more efficiently, and language gives children the opportunity to ask questions to increase their knowledge.

Laying the Groundwork for Later Learning

The basic cognitive skills mastered in the preschool years become the groundwork for further intellectual development in the school years. For example, in the preschool setting, children begin to master such cognitive skills and concepts as matching, grouping and classifying, establishing common relations, seriation, and temporal ordering (see Table 12.1). These skills provide the foundation for mastering reading, science, and mathematics in the elementary school years. The ability to match, for example, is critical to literacy. When children can match objects that are identical, they also can distinguish between objects that are not precisely the same. Therefore, they will be able to tell the difference between a Q and an O, for example. The

TABLE 12.1
Cognitive skills and concepts for preschoolers to learn

Skill/Concept	Description/Examples
Matching or One-to-one Correspondence	Identifying objects that are the same, such as matching by color, shape, or function
Number and Counting (does not refer to recognizing numerals)	Rote counting—counting out loud, reciting numbers from memory
	Rational counting—counting objects (requires rote counting and matching abilities—that is, matching number to each object as it is counted)
Symbols (numerals)	Understanding how many the numeral *8* represents, for example
Grouping and Classifying	Identifying or sorting objects with a common attribute, such as color or shape
Establishing Common Relations	Pairing or sorting dissimilar objects, such as shoes and socks, according to a common function
Seriation or Ordering	Arranging objects in a graduated order, such as shortest to longest
	Temporal ordering—identifying events in a chronological order, such as listing all the steps a child takes to get ready for bed
Comparing	Recognizing amount (more/less), size (large/small, long/short), speed (fast/slow), temperature (cold/hot), distance (near/far), age (older/younger), volume (loud/soft), height (higher/lower, tall/short)
Shape	For younger preschoolers: circle, triangle, square
	For older preschoolers and early elementary school children: rectangle, diamond, oval
Space	Position: where? (on, off, over, under, and so on)
	Direction: which way? (up, down, across, away from, and so on)
	Distance: how far? (near, far, and so on)
Parts and Wholes	Necessary for addition, subtraction, and fractions in early elementary school
	Also related to language use (such as "the whole thing," "part of it," "broken," "pieces")

(continued)

TABLE 12.1 Cognitive skills and concepts for preschoolers to learn *(continued)*	
Skill/Concept	**Description/Examples**
Measurement	Using volume, weight, length, temperature, and time
	Using comparison terms or arbitrary units (such as "How many blocks high is that tower?") instead of inches or feet
Problem Solving	Identifying a problem, asking questions, experimenting, devising solutions, and testing the consequences

ability to group objects into distinct classes and to determine cause and effect are the underlying principles of scientific discovery. Similarly, grouping, seriation, common relations, and temporal ordering are all necessary skills for understanding mathematical concepts.

Views of Cognitive Development

Each of the leading views of cognitive development summarized in this section have contributed greatly to our understanding of how children learn and think. Preschool teachers should consider how each theory can influence the development of preschool curriculum and teaching strategies.

Among the leading views of cognitive development are the stage theory of Jean Piaget, the sociohistorical view of Russian psychologist Lev Vygotsky, the multiple intelligences theory of Howard Gardner, and the intuition/reasoning theory, which compares the two sides of the brain.

The Stage Theory of Piaget

As discussed in Chapter 2, the cornerstone of Piaget's theory of cognitive development is the idea that children actively construct knowledge as they interact with their environment. Each time that children play with a toy, explore how a ball rolls when they push it, and flinch when they touch something hot is a learning experience that allows them to construct more efficient mental strategies for processing information.

Piaget theorized that children progress through four stages of cognitive development in an orderly sequence as their brains mature and as they interact with their environment. Preschool teachers should be most familiar with the first two of Piaget's stages, the sensorimotor stage from birth to age two and the preoperational stage from age two to age seven.

In the sensorimotor stage, children learn about their environment by using their senses and by interacting physically with objects. An infant might learn about a spoon, for example, by picking it up, "tasting" it, banging it against the floor, and tossing it in the air.

In the preoperational stage, children still are learning about their environment through exploration and hands-on experiences. They also, however, are beginning to transform physical action into mental images (Piaget, 1963). In the preoperational years, for example, children master the ability to picture objects in their minds, even if the object is not present. They begin to engage in symbolic play, as when one child uses a block as a play telephone to call his grandmother, and another child sits on the floor on a pillow and grabs a plastic plate as a steering wheel to pretend that she is driving a car. In addition, the capacity of children to remember increases greatly. This capacity enables them to use their past experiences to learn new skills or to solve simple problems, such as how to play with a new toy or to remember a new word.

The concrete operations stage follows the preoperational stage and occurs between the ages of seven and eleven. Preschool teachers should be aware of the main achievements of this next stage, as their work with young children lays important groundwork for further intellectual development. In the concrete operations stage, children continue to acquire knowledge through their interaction with the physical environment, but they also master several complex operations and concepts. These include conservation (see Chapter 10) and *reversibility*, the ability to mentally split a whole into two or more parts and put the parts back together again or to mentally retrace one's steps back to the beginning of a sequence. Children in this stage master more complicated kinds of seriation and classification, such as sorting objects according to two or more attributes—for example, size, shape, and function.

Piaget believed that children learn primarily through play and physical interaction with the environment and with peers. He did not believe that they could be or should be taught specific cognitive skills, such as seriation, in order to accelerate them through the stages of development.

The Sociohistorical View of Cognitive Development

The Russian psychologist Lev Vygotsky took a somewhat different approach to cognitive development. His *sociohistorical theory* asserts that people pass knowledge down to younger generations within each culture and society (Vygotsky, 1978). In a primitive society, for example, fathers taught their sons to hunt and make fires, and mothers taught their daughters to gather food and make clothing out of animal skins. Vygotsky believed that all learning occurs in the same way—that it is a social event that usually takes place between two people, the learner and the teacher.

To explain how the learning process occurs, Vygotsky developed the idea of the *zone of proximal development (ZPD)*. The ZPD is the zone of knowledge just slightly more advanced than a child comprehends on her own. For example, Janet has learned to recognize the *J* and the *t* as the first and last letters in her name, but she thinks that all words that start with a *J* are her name. With help from a teacher, Janet can learn to distinguish the name *Jamal* from her name, by pointing out that her name has the *t* at the end and Jamal's name does not.

Another example might be a toddler trying to learn how to put blocks of different shapes into the correct openings in a shape box. He cannot fit the star shape into its hole. His mother may show him how to turn and slide the block over the hole until the shapes match and the block falls in. She may then guide the toddler's hand as he tries to fit the block to the hole. After a few tries, the toddler can then insert the block himself without any further help.

According to Vygotsky, the zone of proximal development is the point at which a child cannot learn anything more about a particular skill or task alone but can take the next step toward mastery with the help of a more knowledgeable teacher. What does the ZPD mean for teachers? It means that the teacher must be sensitive to the child's abilities and know how to "stretch" the child toward a higher level within the child's ZPD. For instance, it is probably within a two-year-old's ZPD to learn to recognize the color blue after he has learned to recognize the color red. Learning how to walk in a line with other children is not within a two-year-old's ZPD but probably is within a kindergartener's ZPD.

The major difference between Piaget's and Vygotsky's theories about intellectual development is as follows: Piaget believed that children construct knowledge from their own experiences. Vygotsky believed that new skills are transferred from an external source through demonstration and explanation and are gradually internalized by children.

The sociohistorical theory of cognitive development suggests that young children learn primarily through social interaction with adults. For example, this four-year-old is learning about how to choose puzzle pieces with the help of his teacher.

The Theory of Multiple Intelligences

Neuropsychologist Howard Gardner developed his theory of multiple intelligences through his work with patients with brain injuries at a Boston hospital and with gifted children at Harvard University's Project Zero. Gardner found that people with brain injuries could perform certain mental functions quite well. For example, they could perform mathematics computations or music composition, but they could not perform other functions, such as speaking or walking. Similarly, he noticed that many gifted children were very talented in certain areas but were only average or even below average in other areas.

Gardner (1993) concluded that there are seven ways to be intelligent (see Figure 12.1). Schools, he said, tend to measure intelligence in only two ways, verbal/linguistic and logical/mathematical ability. For example, the Scholastic Aptitude Tests (SATs) for college entrance have two parts, verbal and mathematics. However, Gardner theorized that, in addition to verbal/ linguistic intelligence and logical/mathematical intelligence, there are at least five other types of intelligence that focus on different strengths or talents. These types include musical intelligence, such as that possessed by a conductor or a concert pianist; visual/spatial, intelligence, such as that possessed by artists and architects; interpersonal intelligence; intrapersonal intelligence; and body/kinesthetic intelligence (see Figure 12.1).

People with interpersonal intelligence have a talent for establishing relationships with other people. Therapists, ministers, and politicians show this

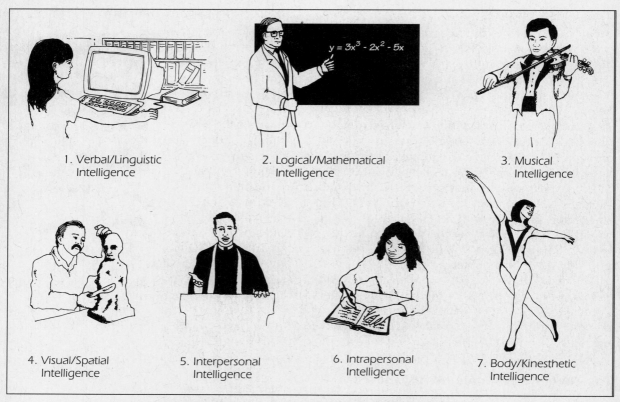

1. Verbal/Linguistic Intelligence

2. Logical/Mathematical Intelligence

3. Musical Intelligence

4. Visual/Spatial Intelligence

5. Interpersonal Intelligence

6. Intrapersonal Intelligence

7. Body/Kinesthetic Intelligence

FIGURE 12.1   **The Theory of Multiple Intelligences.**

kind of intelligence. Those with intrapersonal intelligence are "in tune" with themselves. Poets and philosophers often have intrapersonal intelligence. Body/kinesthetic intelligence refers to skill in using movement or understanding the body. Dancers, athletes, and surgeons possess this type of intelligence.

Gardner theorizes that each kind of intelligence involves its own form of learning, memory, and perception. Each person differs in the extent to which he or she possesses each of the seven kinds of intelligence. One person may be able to remember and recall songs with great ease. Another may be a gifted athlete or dancer but may do poorly on an IQ test measuring language and mathematics skills.

The implication of Gardner's theory for preschool teachers is that, while early linguistic and mathematical abilities may predict which children will do well in elementary school, some young children will exhibit strengths related to Gardner's other types of intelligence. These children should be encouraged to develop their special talents and find their places in society. Therefore, it is important for teachers, as well as parents, to recognize and support the development of each child's unique talents and gifts.

Howard Gardner's theory of multiple intelligences asserts that there are several different ways to be intelligent. Young children may begin to demonstrate "musical intelligence" at a very young age. An example is this five-year-old playing the piano at her preschool.

The Intuition/Reasoning Theory of Cognition

The intuition/reasoning theory of intelligence also recognizes the existence of more than one kind of intelligence. This theory is based on the discovery that each side of the brain—left and right—controls certain mental functions. Research has shown that the right side of the brain controls intuitive, nonlinguistic, and spatial knowledge, whereas the left side controls logic, language, and reasoning (Vander Zanden, 1993). For example, Vakil, Soroker, and Biran (1992), in a study of brain-damaged patients, classified the two hemispheres of the brain. They stated that the right side of the brain controls "automatic" (innate or intuitive) processes, and the left side controls "effortful" learning, such as writing or tasks that require a significant amount of memory.

Typically, the two halves of the brain work together in a highly integrated fashion, passing information back and forth (Best, 1985). For example, when a person forms a mental road map of a familiar geographic area, the right side of the brain is responsible for the overall visual scheme of the map, but the left side is responsible for the route numbers and names of each road and street. Both hemispheres are used to develop cognitive skills, but individuals vary in the extent to which they develop right- or left-brain skills. One person may be a gifted mathematician (using the left side of the brain) and another a talented sculptor (using the right side of the brain). Each person contributes to society in his or her own way.

The implications of the intuition/reasoning theory of cognition for preschool teachers are similar to those of Gardner's theory of multiple intelligences. Schools commonly focus on developing the left-brain activities involved in language skills and analytic thought while neglecting the intuitive, creative right-brain skills. However, since the two halves of the brain normally work together as a kind of intellectual team, children in the preschool setting will benefit from practice with using both intuition and reasoning. For example, a teacher might ask the children to each tell a story (using language/left brain) about a scary storm (using emotional/right brain). Research shows that the more stimulating a person's environment is during early childhood, the stronger his or her neural activity—the connections among the different parts of the brain—becomes (Vander Zanden, 1993).

Two Curriculum Approaches to Learning

How do preschool teachers transform the various views of cognitive development into useful teaching strategies? They begin by making certain assumptions about how children learn. Then they devise a curriculum that most effectively supports those assumptions.

Underlying the construction of most preschool curricula is the basic assumption that cognitive development involves two distinct elements, the acquisition of knowledge and the development of thinking skills. The acquisition of knowledge means learning facts, information, and procedures through exploration, experimentation, and modeling. Developing thinking skills means learning how to reason, understand cause and effect, solve problems, and recognize relationships. This section looks at how two curriculum approaches address the development of thinking skills in preschoolers, using premathematics as an example.

The Constructivist Approach to Curriculum

The constructivist approach to curriculum is based on Piaget's theories of cognitive development. It is grounded on the assumption that children learn on their own and create their own knowledge through experience, without being taught directly by an adult. Children actively construct new concepts by building on simpler concepts they already have learned. One of the leading proponents of using the constructivist approach to curriculum development is early childhood educator Constance Kamii.

Kamii's constructivist approach to mathematics means that children actively construct mathematical knowledge by relating new information or experiences to what they already know or have experienced (Campbell & Casey, 1992). Through their own discovery or through question-asking techniques by the teacher, children do not just collect pieces of information. Rather, they draw connections and learn to think about things in new ways.

The constructivist premathematics curriculum focuses on helping children begin to construct the meaning of numbers by learning relationships during everyday preschool experiences (Kamii, 1985). It also utilizes visible, tangible objects to help children make connections and establish relationships (Resnick, 1983). For example, in the sandbox, children begin to experience volume by filling and emptying containers with sand. They experience the concept of more/less as they see that the bigger of two buckets requires more shovelfuls of sand to fill it. When children place a napkin at each place setting for snack, they experience for themselves the concept of one-to-one correspondence.

Part/whole relationships are considered by some early childhood experts to be the major conceptual task of the early school years (Resnick, 1983). Part/whole construction allows children to think about numbers as parts of other numbers. This skill will lead to understanding of addition, subtraction, multiplication, division, and fractions. However, children usually do not have this ability until about age seven or eight. The concept is related to reversibility, which, as stated earlier, most children master during concrete operations (Kamii, 1985). Preschoolers begin to experience this concept, for example, as they assemble simple puzzles. A child might be working on a puzzle with a white house with a red roof and a green front door. The child sees how many puzzle pieces are needed to "fill up" the red roof or the green door. Similarly, in the block area, children will discover for themselves that two 6-inch blocks cover the same length as one 12-inch block, even though they will not know the actual measurements of the blocks.

Preschool teachers who use the constructivist approach foster premathematics skills by surrounding children with number-oriented experiences and materials in different areas of the curriculum and in different areas of the classroom and playground (Greenberg, 1993). For example, music time provides practice with one-to-one correspondence when children clap their hands to imitate different, simple rhythms created by the teacher on a piano. Outdoor play provides practice with the concept of more/less as children take "giant steps" and then "baby steps" to get across the playground.

Proponents of the constructivist approach to curriculum believe that children create their own knowledge and draw important connections through their own experimentation. This three-year-old is exploring the concepts of volume and weight at the sand table.

The Behaviorist Approach to Curriculum

As discussed in Chapter 2, the behaviorist approach to curriculum draws on the work of B. F. Skinner. It is an academic-oriented approach in which the teacher uses direct instruction or rote learning, demonstration, modeling, and positive reinforcement.

The DISTAR program, developed in the 1960s to teach language, arithmetic, and reading skills to disadvantaged youngsters, is a good example of the behaviorist approach. It requires teachers to follow a prepared script and to use certain teaching materials for each lesson. Each lesson is made up of a series of steps leading to a specific objective. For example, the DISTAR reading program uses phonics in a very systematic manner. When learning to read the word *man*, the entire group of children says the sound of each letter "mmm-a-a-a-n-n-n." Then they say it faster and faster until they say "m-a-n" and are praised by the teacher.

Most preschool teachers today use the constructivist approach to teach premathematics skills. However, behaviorist programs can be very effective with children from disadvantaged backgrounds or children with learning disabilities who respond well to a highly structured learning environment.

A behaviorist premathematics curriculum usually groups children according to ability, and the teacher works with each group individually. The teaching script involves breaking down the components of each mathematics skill into small pieces. For example, certain lessons are designed to teach children the concepts of more/less, and others are designed to teach part/whole. The lesson may involve having the children repeat information verbally back to the teacher or having them give verbal responses to which the teacher responds whether they are right or wrong. The lessons are structured so that the children are correct most of the time, and when they answer correctly, they are rewarded with verbal praise and other forms of positive reinforcement, such as stickers. Teachers enliven each lesson with rhythmic exchanges with the students, sudden changes of pace, broad body language, and other attention-getting devices.

Encouraging Thinking Skills

The preschool curriculum can help children become creative thinkers by providing practice in such skills as choosing among options, proposing alternative ideas, solving simple problems, and developing new ideas. Preschool teachers should recognize that all areas of the curriculum present opportunities for children to practice creative thinking. This section discusses how the preschool curriculum can be constructed to foster children's curiosity and maintain their interest so that they enjoy the process of creative thinking.

Guidelines

In addition to keeping activities developmentally appropriate for the children's ages and abilities, the curriculum should reflect the children's interests. Planning by following the children's interests is called *responsive planning.* When children are interested in a topic, they become more involved in it and more excited about it. If the children are fascinated by the ladybugs on the playground, for example, the teacher can develop activities related to ladybugs. He or she might help the children make a terrarium where they can keep some of the bugs, let them observe the insects through a magnifying glass, and help them discover what the ladybugs eat. The teacher also might look for songs and storybooks about ladybugs to incorporate the interest in ladybugs into different parts of the curriculum.

Children need opportunities to manipulate materials to find out for themselves how things work. When children manipulate objects, the immediate results help them make connections and establish relationships between their actions and objects. Through hands-on manipulation, they also can vary their actions and experience different results. Amelia's experiments with the slide at the water table were much more meaningful to her than observation—sitting quietly and watching her teacher, Stephen, roll objects

Creating activities that focus on children's interests—such as this young boy's interest in birds—helps children become more involved in and excited about learning.

down the slide—would have been. When she put the marble and golf ball at the top of the slide, she saw an immediate reaction—the balls rolled down into the water. When she varied the activity by using a square block, she was able to see immediately that the block behaved differently from the spherical objects. As children learn by manipulating objects, the teacher also can provide the vocabulary that goes along with the experience, just as Stephen did when he talked with Amelia about "round things" and "square things."

Children will be most interested in activities that are related to their everyday lives. Since much of their experience is centered on home and family activities, they usually are interested in cooking, cleaning, outdoor activities, and activities related to daily routines, such as getting dressed and getting ready for bed. Teachers can build activities around special events in children's lives, such as the birth of a sibling, the acquisition of a new puppy, or a move to a new neighborhood. Activities that are relevant to children hold their interest and attention. For example, they are likely to find it more fun to experiment with the concept of more/less with crackers at the snack table than with piles of cards.

Providing children with ongoing opportunities for repetition helps them master such cognitive skills as matching, grouping, and seriation. Using a wide variety of materials adds interest, as children practice the same task with different objects or in different situations. For example, children might practice sorting with seashells one day and with fallen leaves they gathered on a nature walk another day. Through practice, children will increase their competency at various tasks. The teacher should pay close attention to this process and increase the difficulty level gradually so that the activity remains challenging and interesting.

Teachers need to leave some unstructured time for children during the day. Preschoolers need time to register or internalize new concepts. As they acquire new knowledge and master new thinking skills, they need to process the new information into their existing mental framework. This process of reorganizing knowledge enables them to use what they have learned in increasingly complex ways. The unstructured time might be part of what is commonly referred to as free play. The teachers set up activities for the children that are not teacher-directed, such as dramatic play or block play. Outside play also is generally unstructured time.

Question-Asking Techniques

One very effective way for preschool teachers to promote the development of thinking skills in children is to ask them questions. Having to think about answers stimulates and clarifies their thinking, and makes them aware that they possess new knowledge. Effective questions draw information out of children instead of feeding it to them. This section discusses three types of questions—open-ended, analysis, and relationship questions.

Open-Ended Questions.   Open-ended questions, first discussed in Chapter 11, have many answers. Examples are "How many ways can we use these blocks?", "What will we see at the zoo?", and "What kinds of things can we do outside when it snows?" Open-ended questions allow and encourage children to consider different options. They foster *divergent thinking*—that is, thinking that promotes imaginative reflection and the consideration of different options and solutions. Divergent thinking encourages children to engage in their own kind of research that helps them make discoveries and associations on their own (Henninger, 1987).

Many teachers, however, tend to ask *convergent questions*, questions with preconceived right answers—such as "What color is this ball?" and "How many apples do I have in my hands?"

Analysis Questions. *Analysis questions* focus on solving a problem by examining its parts. Some examples are, "What do we have to do to plant these seeds?", "What steps do we follow to make cookies?", and "What would happen if . . . ?" Like open-ended questions, analysis questions can have more than one correct answer. These questions promote creative thinking by requiring children to think about the steps necessary to carry out an activity or solve a problem. They also help children learn about temporal ordering because many problems are solved by performing steps in a sequence.

Relationship Questions. *Relationship questions* require children to focus on the relationship among objects, actions, and events. For example, a teacher might ask, "Which things belong in the bathroom and which go in the kitchen?", "Which objects in this box are for cleaning our teeth and which are for cleaning the house?", or "What are the clothes we wear to go out in the rain?" These questions promote such cognitive skills as matching, grouping, comparing, and seriation.

Tips on Question Asking. Question asking is a skill that teachers must practice in order to encourage thoughtful, creative answers from children. The following are some guidelines that help teachers formulate questions effectively and use questions to carry on a fruitful dialogue with preschoolers.

- With a little thought, it is quite easy to change a convergent question into a question with choices or more than one answer. For example, instead of a teacher's asking, "Should we put a pillow on our backs to pretend we're a camel?", she might ask, "What can we do to pretend we have a hump on our backs like a camel?"
- Children need adequate time to consider all the options or to explore different possibilities before being told the answer to a question. Teachers should avoid rushing children into answers.
- Questions can be used to initiate a dialogue and to generate more questions.
- Teachers need to respect children's responses by listening carefully and responding courteously.
- Teachers should never reprimand a child for giving a wrong answer but should encourage the child to continue to think about alternative answers.

This teacher has created a hands-on matching activity that uses pictures and real objects—in this case fruit—to stimulate the child's senses as well as cognitive development.

- Teachers need to provide positive feedback to children that focuses on the thinking and the answering process, not on the answers themselves.

Applications

A preschool curriculum designed to develop cognitive skills should be balanced between activities that promote information acquisition—such as learning the names of different parts of a tree—and creative thinking skills—such as trying to figure out a way to climb a tree. For example, the High/Scope curriculum model places much emphasis on the integration of information acquisition and fostering creative thinking in young children. Preschool teachers should make a consistent effort to devise activities that combine acquiring knowledge, exploring materials and the environment in a hands-on fashion, and practicing higher-order thinking skills. This section discusses some of the ways preschool teachers can create activities focused on developing specific cognitive skills, activities that combine learning and thinking, and activities that encourage creative problem solving.

Activities That Develop Cognitive Skills

When you are planning the curriculum, think about how you can use materials and activities to promote specific cognitive skills. Look for opportunities for children to practice cognitive skills in all areas of the classroom. Remember that children need practice and repetition as well as variety in materials to master cognitive tasks.

FOCUS ON / **Cultural Diversity**

Learning the Concept of Same/Different

Helping young children recognize similarities and differences is an important aspect of the multicultural curriculum. Same/different also is an important cognitive concept related to sorting and grouping skills and early literacy skills. One way to reinforce the concept of same/different is through cultural diversity.

The teacher might start by encouraging the children to identify similarities among the children in the class. For example, children can observe similarities in hair color, or the color of the clothes they are wearing—such as blue pants or red shirts. Children might also match their own hair color or clothing color with paint, crayons, or clay.

The teacher might help the children create a list entitled "Things We All Do the Same." Items on the list might include eating, sleeping, washing our hands, playing with our friends, wearing shoes, and combing our hair.

Once children focus on similarities, such as hair and clothing color, the teacher might ask

them to identify differences, such as hair texture. For example, they might observe that several children have black hair. They might discover, through the sense of touch, that one child's black hair is soft and straight whereas another child's black hair is thick and wavy.

The concept of same/different can relate to other aspects of cultural diversity. For example, the teacher might address the concept of different by talking about the different ways people carry babies and dress babies, depending on their culture. At the same time, the teacher can address the concept of sameness, by talking about similarities in baby care. He or she might explain that, in all cultures, newborn infants' heads have to be supported at all times and babies have to be kept warm.

In these discussions and activities, open-ended questions will encourage children to contribute their own ideas about sameness and difference.

Matching, Common Relations, and Grouping.   The teacher can devise countless preschool activities that involve these three skills.

- Label shelves or boxes in the block area according to shape. Then ask each child to put away objects with a different shape. Say, "Susan, you can put away all the cylinders, and Matthew, you put away the triangles."
- Set up a table with different-colored buttons, or dried macaroni in various shapes, and egg cartons with each cup painted a different color, or with one type of macaroni glued to the bottom of each cup. Then ask children to sort the buttons or macaroni into the egg-carton cups.
- For younger children, give children sets of four objects, three of which are related or have a common attribute. Then ask the children to find the item that does not "fit." For example, you might use three toy fire engines and one toy sports car, or three hats and one mitten or glove.
- For older preschoolers, pull together a pile of objects that have a common relation, such as shoes and socks, a hat and a coat, a can opener and a can,

a ball and a bat, or a cup and a saucer. Mix them all up, and then ask the children to create pairs of items that go together. To stimulate language and reasoning skills, ask the children why they matched the items as they did. Some children may see relationships the adult had not thought of.

- For younger preschoolers, put out a selection of six to ten pairs of shoes and a corresponding number of shoe boxes. Mix up the shoes, and let the children match them and place them in shoe boxes.
- When children help set the table, or put the dishes away, they learn categorization skills.

Seriation and Temporal Ordering.   Songs, stories, and flannel board activities often involve seriation and temporal ordering, as do many simple toys, games, and puzzles.

- For example, the story of "Goldilocks and the Three Bears" involves both simple seriation and temporal ordering. You can tell the story with the help of a flannel board and let the children put the cutouts of beds, chairs, and bowls of porridge on the board in the correct order. Other stories and songs that lend themselves to practicing seriation and temporal ordering include "The Three Little Pigs," "The Ants Go Marching One by One," and "The Eensy, Weensy Spider." Children also can act out stories such as "Goldilocks" in the housekeeping/dramatic play area.
- When telling or reading children a familiar story, stop frequently and ask, "What happens next?" This challenges children's memory and temporal-ordering skills.
- Assemble a collection of five or six objects, and place the smallest one on one end of the table. Ask one child to choose an item from the pile that is "just a little bit bigger" than the one on the table. Have the children compare the two items to see if the second one really is bigger. Then ask another child to choose an even bigger object, and so on, until all the objects are used.

Cause and Effect.   Cause-and-effect activities can be created in all areas of the classroom, from cooking to art to outdoor play. You can help children explore the relationship of cause and effect during everyday activities by asking them to predict, "What happens if we . . ." or to recall "What do you think made this happen?" The following are four activities designed to address cause and effect.

- On a low table, set out containers of colored water. Use primary colors (red, blue, and yellow). Using eyedroppers, the children will put drops of water into plastic ice-cube trays or other small containers. The children will experiment with mixing different colors. Children will experience cause and effect, while practicing fine motor skills and eye-hand coordination with the eyedroppers.

FOCUS ON **Activities**

Sharpening Children's Powers of Observation at the Water Table

Water presents a natural attraction for preschoolers. Water also is an ideal medium for sharpening children's powers of observation. Water tables are large pans, shallow tubs on table legs, or other similar containers filled with water. Toys and other materials are added to the water.

Fill your water table about half full with water. Make sure that the area around the container is "waterproofed." For example, put down plastic or vinyl sheeting or large, old towels to prevent a slippery, messy floor. Dress the children in plastic aprons so that they will not get their clothes wet.

To focus children's activity on observation skills, you might try incorporating materials that are transformed when they interact with water. Examples include liquid soap (which changes into bubbles), food coloring (which turns the water a different color), and straws (through which the children can blow air to create bubbles). You also might provide different kinds of sponges, so that children can observe and explore how the sponges absorb water. Different-sized colanders can be used to observe different streams of water. Heavy and light objects, some that float and some that sink, give children an opportunity to experiment with weight and buoyancy. Just about anything that is unbreakable and rustproof can be used, but do not try to present too many new items at once. Rotate items on different days.

Observation skills can be honed by asking the children open-ended questions. Look for opportunities, for example, to ask, "I wonder what would happen if . . . ?" and "What do you suppose made it do that?" These questions will help the children to focus more closely on what is happening and allow them to formulate their own answers.

- Also on a low table, set up small glasses of vinegar and a spoon, one for each child, and a larger bowl of baking soda in the center of the table. Experiment with the children to see what happens when they add a small spoonful of baking soda to the vinegar. (It will produce a dramatic carbonation effect.) Let the children perform this experiment over and over again until they are satisfied and until they understand that they are causing the effect with the baking soda.
- Another way to explore cause and effect is to take a bowl of ice cubes and ask children how many ways they can think of to get the ice cubes to melt. (Answers might include melting them in the sun outside or on the windowsill, leaving them at room temperature, holding them in palms of the hands, and using a hair dryer.) Then compare how fast the ice cubes melt under the various conditions.
- On the playground, set out buckets of water with old paintbrushes. Have the children "paint" the playground with water. They will see the effects of water on wood, concrete, and other surfaces, and the effects of sunlight on water.

Activities That Combine Learning and Thinking

Many preschool activities create an opportunity to combine acquiring knowledge—learning facts, information, and procedures as well as hands-on discovery—with practicing thinking skills. These types of activities also provide practice for your own questioning skills.

In a project about farm animals, for example, children might:

- Learn information such as the names of different farm animals, what they eat, where they sleep, and where eggs and milk come from
- Practice observation through watching and petting animals if a trip to a farm or petting zoo is possible
- Practice grouping skills, such as matching pictures of adult animals with their babies or grouping animals in various ways
- Practice discrimination skills by picking out different farm animal sounds from a record or tape
- Practice problem-solving and creative-thinking skills by answering "What if" and "What happens when" questions—such as "What happens after the chicken sits on her eggs?" or "What do you think would happen if the farmer forgot to milk the cows?"

Other activities can involve learning about weather.

- Using simple charts or flannel boards representing the four seasons, you can discuss typical kinds of weather for each season and why the weather changes.
- Ask children to match different symbols on the chart. For example, put up a cloud (children would look for the rain and lightning symbols) or announce "It's summer!" (children would look for the sun symbol).
- You can also use a flannel board to have children match up outdoor clothing with different kinds of weather. Draw attention to outdoor clothing that is used for more than one kind of weather, such as boots for rain and snow.
- Let children run around with streamers to see the effect of air currents.
- Make a rain gauge with a pail, and monitor it with the children.
- Make rain over the water table by filling a balloon with water and pricking it with a pin.

Although weather is a complicated subject, you can keep activities at a developmentally appropriate level. Remember to ask open-ended questions such as "What kinds of things can we do outside in the rain?" (Answers could include jumping in puddles, tasting raindrops, and looking for a rainbow).

All these activities will help increase children's knowledge of weather and weather-related vocabulary. They also will provide practice with common relations, cause and effect, and other cognitive skills.

These four-year-olds are figuring out how to make a parking garage for their toy cars. Creative-thinking skills are challenged by activities that encourage problem solving.

Activities That Encourage Creative Problem Solving

One of the most important cognitive skills to develop in young children is the ability to solve problems. Children need practice with thinking of different solutions, and they also need practice with thinking through the steps required to achieve those solutions. Children naturally begin to learn problem solving as infants and toddlers when they figure out how to get a cupboard door open, how to climb up to a kitchen counter, or how to get a lid off a jar. You can help preschoolers become creative problem solvers by providing activities that require problem solving and by looking for spontaneous opportunities in children's play to pose a problem-solving challenge.

Suppose, for example, that a few children are trying to make a lake in the sandbox. Each time they pour water into a hole in the sand, the water disappears. Ask them where they think the water is going and what might help hold the water in place. The children may offer two or three different solutions. You can then help them find the materials they need for their solutions and let them experiment with each one to see which works best. If they cannot think of any solutions, you might help them out by having them pour water into a large rectangular cake pan, and then into a sieve, to see which holds water. Ask them how the cake pan and the sieve are different. Point out the holes in the sieve, and explain that there are also tiny holes in between the grains of sand. Help the children to push the cake pan down into the sand so that its edges are flush with the sand. Ask the children "What else could we use to hold the water if we didn't have a cake pan?" to prolong the dialogue and the problem-solving task.

Another kind of problem-solving activity could involve a visit to the school by a person in a wheelchair. A day or two before the visit, ask the

FOCUS ON | **Communicating with Parents**

Talking about Learning Disabilities

During the first few weeks of preschool, four-year-old Alexa Randall was the most disruptive child in the class. She was constantly in motion, whether it was free-play time or story time. When Alexa did try to sit quietly, she still jerked her feet, twitched, or rocked back and forth. She often hit other children without being provoked. In addition, she was easily distracted and could not follow directions.

After observing Alexa closely for several weeks, her teacher, Mariel, decided that Alexa's behavior might be related to attention deficit disorder (ADD). ADD, formerly called hyperactivity, is a learning disability with many of these symptoms. She planned a meeting with Alexa's father to discuss her behavior and to suggest that Alexa might need outside evaluation.

MARIEL: Thank you for coming in today. I am concerned about Alexa's behavior.

MR. R.: But you told me on the phone that she hasn't done anything wrong.

MARIEL: Let me explain. I've been watching Alexa closely. She has difficulty sitting still, and she is easily distracted. I've also noticed that she has trouble following simple directions. She has been hitting other children when she is frustrated. Have you noticed any similar behavior at home?

MR. R.: I guess. But isn't that normal behavior for a kid her age? They have all that energy.

MARIEL: Her energy level is actually quite a bit higher than normal. In fact, her symptoms closely follow the pattern of attention deficit disorder, a learning disability. I'd like to suggest . . .

MR. R.: Hold on a minute! What are we talking about here? Symptoms? Disability? Nothing is wrong with Alexa. She's just a high-energy kid.

MARIEL: Mr. Randall, I want to help Alexa. If she has a learning disability, there are concrete ways we can help Alexa focus more and control her energy so that she enjoys her time here and gets the most out of preschool.

MR. R.: It's not possible! Everyone in our family is *very* smart.

MARIEL: The presence of a learning disability does not indicate whether or not a person is smart. It just means that sometimes our bodies interfere with how we gather and process information. In fairness to Alexa, we'd like you to consider this further.

How might Mariel have begun the discussion differently? How might she have let Mr. Randall know how much she liked and respected Alexa? Do you think that Mariel reacted appropriately to Mr. Randall's comments? Explain your answer. In what ways might you have handled Mr. Randall's comments differently?

children to think about what obstacles the wheelchair will meet and how they can overcome those obstacles. The obstacles may include steps, a thick area rug, and a narrow pathway between activity areas. Once the children have talked about some solutions, help them carry out their plans. These plans may include rolling back thick rugs and rearranging pathways. They could use a wagon or tricycle to test their solutions.

You can introduce problem-solving activities throughout the day by simply asking your students, for example, "How can we divide an apple for four people?" "How can we find out what attracts magnets?" "How can we find out how many legs an insect has?" "How can we build a dam or a canal or a bridge?" "How can we make a pebble float in the water table?" "How can we fix this doll's broken leg?" "How can we find out which of these rocks is heavier?" "How can we measure the length of a piece of wood?" Many of these activities also provide practice with simple equipment, such as rulers, scales, magnifying glasses, magnets, and measuring cups and spoons. Be ready to ask questions to stimulate the children's thinking, and give hints about overlooked solutions.

CHAPTER 12 REVIEW

SUMMARY

- The cognitive development of children involves two elements, the acquisition of information and the development of thinking skills.

- Cognitive skills developed during the preschool years include grouping, matching, establishing common relationships, seriation, temporal ordering, and understanding cause and effect. These skills become the foundation for problem solving, as well as for learning reading, writing, science, and mathematics.

- Four leading views of cognitive development include Piaget's ages-and-stages theory, Vygotsky's sociohistorical theory, Gardner's theory of multiple intelligences, and the intuition/reasoning theory of cognition.

- The constructivist approach and the behaviorist approach to curriculum address learning to think differently. The constructivist curriculum exposes preschoolers to number concepts indirectly by surrounding them with number-oriented experiences in various areas of the classroom. The behaviorist approach involves teaching children number concepts directly through rote learning. However, both approaches acknowledge that preschoolers need to understand basic concepts, such as more/less and part/whole, before they can attempt addition and subtraction.

- Teachers can stimulate creative thinking by asking open-ended, analysis, and relationship questions. Open-ended questions have many answers and foster divergent thinking. Analysis questions focus on solving a problem by examining its parts. Relationship questions require children to focus on the relationship among objects, actions, and events.

- Guidelines to help teachers stimulate cognitive development and creative thinking include keeping activities developmentally appropriate and devising activities that reflect children's interests.

- Other guidelines include creating opportunities for children to manipulate materials and enjoy hands-on discovery and exploration, keeping activities relevant to children's lives, providing variety in materials and opportunity for practice and repetition, and leaving time for children to reflect on their work.
- Early childhood professionals also should plan activities that address both aspects of cognitive development—the acquisition of knowledge and the development of thinking skills.

ACQUIRING KNOWLEDGE

1. How do infants first learn about their world?
2. List some examples of cognitive skills acquired by young children during the preschool years.
3. Which two of Piaget's stages of cognitive development are most relevant to preschool teachers? Why?
4. How is the sensorimotor stage different from the preoperational stage?
5. What is the sociohistorical theory of cognitive development?
6. How do Vygotsky's ideas about the acquisition of knowledge differ from Piaget's?
7. Name the seven types of intelligence in Howard Gardner's theory of multiple intelligences.
8. How is interpersonal intelligence different from intrapersonal intelligence.
9. What is meant by right- and left-brain skills?
10. How does the intuition/reasoning theory of cognition reflect the right/left split in brain activities?
11. How is the constructivist approach to curriculum related to Piaget's theory of how children learn?
12. Explain why it is important for children to develop an understanding of part/whole relationships.
13. How does the behaviorist curriculum approach to premathematics differ from the constructivist approach?
14. How does responsive planning help children's cognitive development?
15. Name three types of activities that provide opportunities for hands-on exploration and experimentation.
16. Why are open-ended questions more effective for encouraging cognitive development than convergent questions?
17. What cognitive skills are fostered through analysis questions? Relationship questions?
18. Describe two activities that help children develop matching or grouping skills.
19. What kinds of activities promote the development of seriation and temporal-ordering skills?
20. What cognitive skills do children develop by experimenting with different ways to melt an ice cube?

21. How can preschool teachers help young children become creative thinkers?
22. Give two examples of questions that could be used to initiate a problem-solving activity.

THINKING CRITICALLY

1. Vygotsky identified the zone of proximal development as an important indicator of a child's development level with respect to various skills. What signs might indicate that a child has reached the zone of proximal development in a particular task? How might a teacher help the child reach a more advanced level of understanding?
2. The preschool curriculum provides a balance between activities that stimulate both the left and right brain. Describe left- and right-brain activities a teacher might use to help children explore a specific theme, such as comfortable clothing.
3. Teachers may wish to discuss with parents the value of open-ended questions for young children. What points and advice might a teacher offer about question asking that would be helpful to parents?
4. While outdoor activities often focus on the development of motor skills, they also can help develop cognitive skills. Give an example of an activity that can take place outside, and explain how it might help children develop certain cognitive skills.

OBSERVATIONS AND APPLICATIONS

1. Observe a teacher interacting with a group of preschool children. Listen carefully to the questions that the teacher asks, and take notes on the wording of his or her questions. Write down examples, if any, of open-ended questions. Write down examples, if any, of convergent questions. Does the teacher ask any analysis questions, focusing on solving a problem by examining its parts, or any relationship questions, requiring children to focus on the relationship between objects? Record as many different types of questions as you can, also paying attention to the children's answers to each type of question.
2. During a visit to a preschool classroom, look for examples of activities that may help children develop cognitive skills. Describe the activities, such as those that involve matching, grouping, or common relations. What materials are used? Are the children grouping items based on certain relationships? What are those relationships? Do you see activities that involve seriation or temporal ordering? For example, are the children placing items in order from smallest to largest, or shortest to longest? What activities, if any, involve cause and effect? Describe them.
3. At the water table, a group of preschoolers decides to mimic the boats they saw in the town's recent boat races. Johnny chooses a brightly colored plastic cup to be his boat. While the other two children's boats—a

bar of soap and a plastic soap dish—are floating, Johnny's "boat" keeps tipping over, filling up with water, and sinking. As Johnny's teacher, how might you help Johnny?

4. As the teacher of the four-year-old group at the Great Start Preschool, you are developing activities for a new unit on Native Americans. What types of activities might you include to incorporate the school's philosophy of learning through the direct acquisition of knowledge (such as facts, information, and procedures) and learning through hands-on discovery and problem solving?

FOR FURTHER INFORMATION

Books and Journal Articles

Baroody, A. (1987). *Children's mathematical thinking: A developmental framework for preschool, primary, and special education teachers*. New York: Teachers College Press.

DeVries, R., & Kohlberg, L. (1990). *Constructivist early education: Overview and comparison with other programs*. Washington, DC: National Association for the Education of Young Children.

Greenberg, P. (1993). How and why to teach all aspects of preschool and kindergarten math naturally, democratically, and effectively—Part 1. *Young Children, 48*(4), 75–84.

Kamii, C., with DeClark, G. (1985). *Young children reinvent arithmetic: Implications of Piaget's theory*. New York: Teachers College Press.

Kamii, C., & DeVries, R. (1993). *Physical knowledge in preschool education: Implications of Piaget's theory*. New York: Teachers College Press.

Curriculum and Resource Guides

Althouse, R. (1988). *Investigating science with young children*. New York: Teachers College Press.

Forman, G., & Hill, F. (1984). *Constructive play: Applying Piaget in the preschool* (rev. ed.). Reading, MA: Addison-Wesley.

Holt, B. (1986). *Science with young children*. Washington, DC: National Association for the Education of Young Children.

Kohl, M., & Potter, J. (1993). *ScienceArts: Discovering science through art experiences*. Bellingham, WA: Bright Ring.

Lorton, M. (1972). *Workjobs: Activity-centered learning for early childhood*. Reading, MA: Addison-Wesley.

Rockwell, R., Sherwood, E., & Williams, R. (1986). *Hug a tree and other things to do outdoors with young children*. Mt. Rainier, MD: Gryphon House.

Sherwood, E., Williams, R., & Rockwell, R. (1991). *More mudpies to magnets*. Mt. Rainier, MD: Gryphon House.

Williams, R., Rockwell, R., & Sherwood, E. (1987). *Mudpies to magnets: A preschool science curriculum*. Mt. Rainier, MD: Gryphon House.

OBJECTIVES

Studying this chapter
will enable you to

- Define creativity as it relates to
  preschoolers
- Explain the relationship between
  creativity and physical, emotional,
  social, and cognitive development
- Discuss how the curriculum can
  promote creativity
- Discuss several strategies teachers
  can use to help unlock the creative
  potential in young children
- Describe several types of creative
  activities for young children

CHAPTER TERMS

controlled scribbling

creativity

design stage

early representational stage

exploratory stage

finger plays

kinesthetic

mandala

manipulatives

named scribbling

pictorial stage

placement stage

preschematic or representational
  stage

process orientation

random scribbling

selectivity

shape stage

AS Mrs. Nakamura walked into the art area, she noticed the different ways the children were engaged in painting activities. Four-year-old Kaya was working intently at an easel, painting large red circles with a big paintbrush.

"You are working very hard on that picture," Mrs. Nakamura said. "I know you've been working hard on that painting for two days. You like painting at the easel, don't you?"

"Yep. This is my cat, Max. He's big and red, and he's really fluffy."

"I like big fluffy cats, too," said Mrs. Nakamura.

Mrs. Nakamura moved on to the next easel, where Anthony was dipping a piece of sponge into blue paint and making big sweeping swirls on the paper.

"Can you tell me about your big blue swirls?" Mrs. Nakamura asked. "I like the way they go all over the paper."

"I'm making an ocean," Anthony replied.

"It's a big ocean, isn't it? Is the water deep?"

"Yeah, really deep. I was on a boat with my mommy and daddy, and there was a storm. The waves were really, really big. I didn't like it being very stormy."

"That certainly looks scary," said Mrs. Nakamura.

"Yeah, really scary," said Anthony, as he added more big swirls with another color of paint.

Seated at the table, Kim was using a brush and her fingers to paint a picture. And Danny was cutting up pieces of paper, dipping them in paint, and placing them on his painting.

Mrs. Nakamura made several notes about the different creative ways in which the children were approaching the activity. She liked to keep a log of the materials each of the children liked and how they used them. She used this information to devise new creative activities.

People generally associate creativity with such activities as drawing, painting, dance, music, writing, and storytelling because these activities allow for the greatest exercise of imagination and self-expression. In preschool settings, such as Mrs. Nakamura's class, art and music activities often are the major means of fostering creativity in young children. Creativity, however, is not limited to artistic and musical endeavors, either in children or in adults. Children express their creativity every time they find a new and original way of doing something or of solving a problem. Thus, creativity can be fostered in all curriculum areas, including physical activities, dramatic play, science and health activities, and early literacy activities.

Creative activities are an important part of the preschool curriculum. Children need time and resources to explore materials and to develop ideas. They need to pursue creative activities in an accepting atmosphere in which they feel free to try new experiences without fear of criticism, ridicule, or failure. In addition, preschoolers need encouraging and supportive caregivers who know how to stimulate imagination and thought in young minds. This chapter will discuss the role of creativity in young children's growth and development and examine ways in which the preschool curriculum can be designed to foster creativity.

Definitions of Creativity

Most early childhood educators generally define *creativity* as the ability to be original, to have new ideas, to create something that did not exist before, or to put things together in new ways (Mayesky, Neuman, & Wlodkowski, 1985; Gordon & Browne, 1989). Mayesky wrote, "Creativity is a way of thinking and acting or making something that is original for the individual and valued by that person and others. What this means is that any new way to solve a problem or to produce a new product, such as a song, a poem, or a new machine, is a creative act" (Mayesky et al., 1985, p. 3).

Paul Torrance, a pioneer in the study of creativity, defined creativity as having four characteristics—fluency, flexibility, originality, and elaboration (Torrance, 1970). Fluency refers to the seamless communication between people's imaginations and the medium in which they are working, such as paint or clay. Flexibility refers to the freedom to experiment with the medium, as the children in Mrs. Nakamura's class were doing. Originality refers to the person's own ideas and decisions about how or what to create. Elaboration refers to additions, extensions, or embellishments to the work (Edwards & Nabors, 1993).

Although preschoolers have yet to become very fluent in any medium, they are, nevertheless, creative in many ways and in all areas of the curriculum—art, music, science, health, prereading, and premathematics. Young children use their imaginations to create new images, such as Kaya's cat Max or Anthony's stormy ocean. Building a play spaceship, setting up a hospital in the dramatic play area, figuring out how a frog jumps, or telling a story about a trip to grandmother's house show how children express their own unique and original thoughts every day. Children use their imaginations to defeat the "monster" under the bed, to pretend to be a mommy or a daddy, or to draw an animal that never existed before. Their creativity grows as they dare to take risks and to try new things that they have never experienced before.

Preschool teachers should remember that, although some children may exhibit more creativity and talent than others, all children are creative. All children seek new solutions to problems, reorganize information in new ways or use materials in new ways, and construct original works or express new ideas. The teacher's job is to encourage children to express their own creativity.

Activities such as playing musical instruments not only foster creativity but also promote physical development. This three-year-old is enjoying the sounds she is making on a xylophone and practicing eye-hand coordination, an important skill involving the small muscle groups.

Creativity, Growth, and Development

Throughout this book, the reader has seen how the curriculum helps foster the physical, emotional, social, and cognitive growth and development of young children. Creative activities in the curriculum play an important role in each of these areas of development—alone and in combination. They are essential in helping children achieve optimum growth and development.

Creativity and Physical Development

Creative activities help young children sharpen their senses. For example, their sense of hearing is challenged as they identify or learn new songs and explore different tones, pitches, and volumes in music. Their sense of touch develops as they use new materials that are rough, smooth, soft, hard, hot, and cold.

During the preschool years, creativity is primarily a *kinesthetic*, or movement-oriented, experience. As children paint, draw, pound clay, bang drums, and move their bodies rhythmically to music, they use and develop their large and small muscles, gaining increasing motor control, strength, flexibility, balance, and eye-hand coordination. For instance, when children hop, skip, and spin in response to music, they learn to control the large muscle groups. Movement activities also help children learn about the different parts of their bodies and how those parts work together.

Although most children have already developed basic motor control over their large muscles by the time they get to preschool, they still are a long way from gaining mastery over the fine muscles of the hands, wrists, and fingers. Such activities as drawing with crayons or pencils and cutting with scissors promote small-muscle control and other skills that will be used in creative ways. Because preschoolers are still in the process of developing such motor control, some creative activities may be developmentally inappropriate at certain ages. For example, four-year-olds greatly enjoy cutting pictures and shapes with blunt scissors, but most three-years-olds find this activity too difficult.

Creativity and Emotional-Social Development

Creative activities not only help children develop physically, they also help them develop emotionally and socially. Running their fingers through finger paint or punching a pile of clay provides children with a natural, nonaggressive outlet for emotional release and individual expression.

Creative activities also are important forms of nonverbal communication. Through such activities, young children can express feelings and desires that they may be unable to express otherwise because they lack adequate verbal skills. For example, children often work through traumatic events and situations by drawing or painting them or by acting them out in dramatic play. Anthony's painting of a stormy ocean, for example, may be a way of dealing with the feelings of fear he experienced while on the boat with his parents. Art is a useful form of therapy for emotionally upset children—as well as for adults—because it allows children to express strong emotions that they are not able to describe in words. Some experts warn, however, that adults should not draw too many conclusions about children's emotions from their artwork. A child's drawing of a faceless person, for instance, may not signify an emotional problem, but merely that the child was interrupted before completing the drawing (Brittain, 1979).

Creative activities also provide opportunities for building self-esteem. Kaya's painting of her cat is the product of her own imagination and abilities. She is deriving great satisfaction from the act of creating her picture—from swirling the paint on the paper and seeing the cat take shape, and from feeling her hand and eyes work together smoothly to move the brush around the easel. Sincere words of praise and appreciation from Mrs. Nakamura help increase her feelings of self-esteem.

Creative activities also promote in children a sense of independence, which contributes to a feeling of competence. Teachers who store art materials on low shelves that are easily accessible help the children learn to make their own choices about what materials to use and when to use them. These children learn that adults trust their competence in making decisions.

Creative activities contribute to the development of social skills as well. Social skills are fostered as children interact and work together—for example, to build a train out of chairs, pillows, and blocks. Many creative activities lend themselves to having children share materials or share the same

Creative activities present children a natural outlet for emotional expression. This three-year-old's enjoyment comes simply from feeling the wet paint running through his fingers and observing the designs he can make with his own hand movements.

space, as in creative movement. These experiences help children learn how to cooperate, share, take turns, and follow rules. Working together also provides opportunities for leadership, division of labor, and communication. As with other curriculum activities, preparing for creative activities and cleaning up afterwards build self-management skills and good work habits and foster a sense of responsibility.

Creativity and Cognitive Development

In addition to helping develop physical, emotional, and social skills, the creative activities of preschool children provide countless opportunities for discovery and learning in the area of cognition. For example, when children mix paints together to produce new colors, they are learning new concepts and developing many cognitive skills.

Creative activities help children learn to understand symbols—an important milestone in cognitive development. When a child uses a coffee can lid for a wheel, he is mastering symbolic thinking. This ability is very important, since children's understanding of symbols helps them learn about letters and numbers—part of the emergent literacy process. Art activities such as painting allow children to represent real objects in symbolic form.

An important aspect of activities that promote creativity is that they provide opportunities for divergent thinking and problem solving. Figuring out how to build a race car with blocks, discovering a way to make hair out of yarn or string, and singing notes in rhythm all call on the child to analyze and solve problems of form and structure.

Creative activities also help children learn about the properties and uses of objects, and the ways that objects can be transformed. During open-ended art projects, for example, children can practice on their own such cognitive processes as grouping, matching, and discriminating among objects according to size, shape, color, texture, use, and other properties.

In addition, through creative activities, children can practice using numerous concepts. They may experiment with such ideas as light and dark, shiny and dull, and wet and dry. Through actively participating in a creative project, children reinforce their understanding of spatial relations concepts—for instance, how parts relate to the whole and how three-dimensional objects can be depicted in a two-dimensional space. Through creative music activities, children increase their understanding of concepts of tone (high and low), duration (long songs or short songs), and volume (loud and soft). The concepts mastered during these activities help children make sense of their world and organize their thinking.

Music activities help expand children's memory and sharpen listening skills, as when children learn the words to new songs and discriminate among different sounds or instruments (Bayless, 1990). When children become absorbed in an art project, such as making an illustration for a favorite fairy tale, or listen intently to a story, they develop concentration. Memory and concentration skills are important for all types of learning experiences.

Creativity and the Curriculum

Drawing and painting have been an integral part of the preschool curriculum since the beginnings of early childhood education. Today's preschool curriculum usually includes a wide variety of activities that encourage drawing, painting, collage, music, movement, and working with manipulatives such as clay and play dough. Creative thinking activities can be included in the science, health, and premathematics areas of the curriculum.

During the 1970s, many leading art educators—such as W. Lambert Brittain, Rhoda Kellogg, and Jacqueline Goodnow—conducted research that revealed much new information about the creative development of young children. Their research still greatly influences the curriculum planning of teachers today. It identified certain stages of learning, which are helpful for teachers to know as they plan activities and interact with individual children. Figure 13.1 illustrates Kellogg's stages.

Drawing and Painting

The leading theories about children's art are based primarily on the way children of different ages approach drawing and painting activities. The two most generally accepted theories are the developmental theory—that children's use of art materials progresses through a predictable sequence of stages, as seen in Brittain's theory below—and the cognitive theory—that children's drawings reflect their cognitive development or what they know. Familiarity with these theories will help teachers nurture children's creative expression in a variety of areas.

The Developmental View.   Developmental art theorists assert that children's drawing and painting go through distinct stages of growth and development. These stages are seen as part of a natural pattern of growth as a child ages. Brittain (1979) described five developmental stages. In the first stage, the *exploratory stage,* children intently examine and manipulate the material, employing all their senses in doing so. For example, two- and three-year-olds may spend a long time grasping, rolling, feeling, and smelling a crayon before making any attempt to use it in the conventional way. In terms of drawing during the exploratory stage, toddlers' early attempts are called *random scribbling*—the random creation of lines on paper. From about age two to age three or three and a half, children move into *controlled scribbling*, in which they gain mastery of the drawing tool and create more intricate patterns. *Named scribbling* follows from about age three and a

FIGURE 13.1   Kellogg's Four Stages of Drawing.

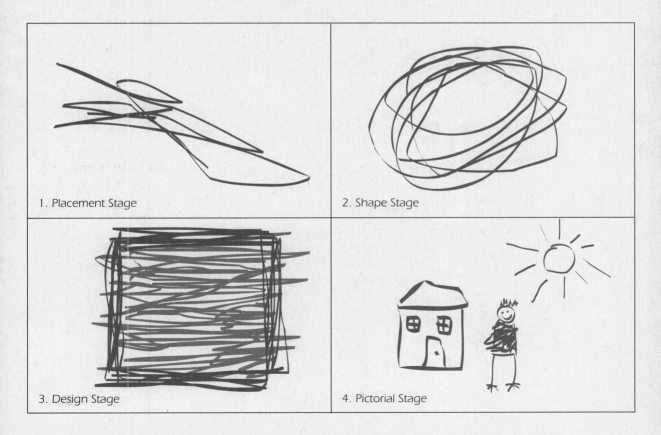

1. Placement Stage

2. Shape Stage

3. Design Stage

4. Pictorial Stage

half to about age four or four and a half, when children identify scribbling as standing for an object in real life.

Once children have fully explored a material, they move on to the *early representational stage*. At this stage, which usually occurs at age four to five, children have gained some skill in manipulating the material and are beginning to use it in a purposeful and creative way. For example, they begin to use paint and brushes to paint a symbolic picture, although the actual content of the artwork is not apparent to others. Thus a young child may identify a drawing as being of himself, his mother, or his dog, but no one else looking at the drawing can recognize any of these in the finished product. In the scenario at the beginning of the chapter, Kaya was creating a painting of her cat, but to adults her painting might only look like large red circles. Sometimes, a child at this stage paints without intending to depict something and is just exploring the medium or making designs. Teachers should avoid asking what a child's picture is during this stage, because the question may diminish the creative process and cause anxiety. See the "Focus on Communicating with Children" feature in this chapter.

In the last stage, called the *preschematic* or *representational stage*, which appears at about age five, children begin to use materials to produce recognizable objects. A drawing of a family appears to be people, for example. In the realm outside of drawing and painting, the child might create a clay object that appears to be a bowl, or a block building that appears to be a house. Children deliberately set out to reproduce or create something recognizable, and they generally are quite successful. Few children achieve this stage during the preschool years, but most attain it during kindergarten. Research has found that children go through these stages in the same sequence no matter what kind of creative materials they are using (Brittain, 1979).

Through her studies of children's art, Kellogg (1970) defined four developmental stages through which children progress in learning to draw. In the *placement stage*, very young children begin scribbling spontaneously in certain places on a sheet of paper. In the *shape stage*, children begin drawing familiar shapes. Kellogg found that children draw in universal shapes, one of the most recognizable of which is the *mandala*, or sunburst, pattern. In the *design stage*, shapes become more elaborate, and the child begins to combine shapes. In the *pictorial stage*, children begin to draw recognizable pictures. As teachers observe children moving into pictorial or representational stages, they should include activities in the curriculum that focus on different shapes and objects—round, square, balls, and cubes, for example. They also should include activities that focus on spatial relations, to heighten children's awareness of form. Table 13.1 summarizes Brittain's and Kellogg's stages.

Another aspect of children's art has been described by art researcher Jacqueline Goodnow. She found that young children tend to fall into two groups: those who finish details in their drawings and paintings as they go along and those who go back to finish details (Goodnow, 1977). Children in the second group often leave something out of their pictures, such as arms or faces on human figures. Goodnow offers two reasons for these omissions.

TABLE 13.1
A comparison of developmental art stages in drawing

Researcher	Age	Stage	Characteristics
Brittain	1–2 or 2½	Random scribbling	Child creates random lines on paper; child holds drawing tool tightly and makes lines with simple arm movements, rarely taking drawing tool from the paper; child enjoys watching movement and appearance of lines as they grow longer or go in different directions.
	2–3 or 3½	Controlled scribbling	Child gains mastery of the drawing tool and creates more intricate patterns.
	3½–4 or 4½	Named scribbling	Child identifies and names the scribble as standing for an object in real life. Lines become symbols—an important step toward abstract thought.
	4–5	Early representational	Child begins to reproduce symbols for objects, although they may not be recognizable to others.
	5	Preschematic drawing	Child begins to draw and paint recognizable objects and to portray relative sizes accurately; child places a line on the page to mark the ground or sky; child knows the concepts of "right side up" and "upside down."
Kellogg	2 and 3	Placement	Child scribbles spontaneously on certain preferred parts of a sheet of paper. (Kellogg identified more than 20 basic types of scribbles that all children make and more than 17 different placement patterns.)
	3–4	Shape	Child draws familiar shapes, such as squares, rectangles, triangles, and crosses. Each shape is self-taught and mastered through much repetition and practice.
	4	Design	Child makes more elaborate shapes; child begins to combine shapes, such as placing a cross in a square. By moving, combining, and juxtaposing shapes, child learns concrete concepts that help later in forming abstract concepts and ideas.
	4 and 5	Pictorial	Child draws recognizable pictures; child synthesizes the skills and knowledge learned in the earlier stages and uses them in drawings. For example, a square may become the side of a house, and rectangles may be used for windows and doors. Child understands figure-ground relationships—for example, animals will be drawn on the ground in front of a barn.

FOCUS ON   **Communicating with Children**

Talking to Children about Their Art

Barry Edwards walked by the easels where the children were making paintings to celebrate the coming of spring. He did not talk to the children because he did not want to interrupt their concentration. Barry noticed that Katelyn was finished. He paused at her easel and looked at her painting before saying anything. He knew that, too often, adults belittle a child's artwork by simply saying that it is good. Although Barry could not tell what the painting was, he wanted to focus on how Katelyn had created the picture and did not want to say anything to diminish her self-esteem.

BARRY: Katelyn, can you tell me about your painting?

KATELYN: This is my house . . . flowers and trees . . . and my dog.

BARRY: Oh, I see. I like those big pink circles.

KATELYN: Those are clouds in the sky. Do you like my picture?

BARRY: I do. I especially like the bright pink colors that you used for the flowers and the clouds. I also like the shapes that you used for the house. I see a triangle and a square. We've

been talking about those shapes a lot. But tell me, Katelyn, do you like your picture?

KATELYN: I guess.

BARRY: Hmm. Is there something else you might like to add to the picture?

KATELYN: I don't know. Maybe more colors.

BARRY: You can add more colors if you like. I can see that you really worked hard on it.

KATELYN: I did.

BARRY: When you are finished, would you like me to hang the painting on the wall with our favorite pictures, or would you rather take it home to show your mommy?

KATELYN: I think my mommy wants to see it. Can I make another picture for the wall?

BARRY: Yes, you can.

Throughout their discussion, was Barry's feedback specific or general? Explain your answer. Suppose Katelyn had not wanted to talk about her artwork. In that case, do you think that Barry should have encouraged her to talk about it? Why or why not?

One reason may be that children who omit certain details use *selectivity*, choosing only those details that are relevant to them at the moment. The second reason is based on Goodnow's findings that young children tend to draw from the top of the paper to the bottom. Therefore, once children reach the bottom of the paper, they may decide that they have finished and forget to go back to add details.

The Cognitive View.   According to the cognitive view, children's art is related to their cognitive development and concept formation. F. L. Goodenough, whose research from the 1920s is still referenced today, believed that children draw what they know rather than what they see. Distortions in children's artwork are, therefore, the result of their lack of knowledge of the world (Harris & Goodenough, 1963). Furthermore, children's art reflects their ability to form concepts by classification and discrimination. Thus, the way in which they use such concepts as color, size, shapes, balance, rhythm, and space in their artwork is directly related to their level of cognitive development. According to Goodenough and others, as children mature intellectually and perceptually, they put more details into their drawings and begin to use more complex artistic concepts, such as perspective, relative size, action, and figure-ground relationships (Harris & Goodenough, 1963).

Cognitive theorist Howard Gardner (1984) presents a somewhat different cognitive view of children's art. He has linked creativity and symbolic development with the idea of multiple intelligences. According to Gardner, seven different domains, or kinds, of intelligence exist: verbal/linguistic, logical/mathematical, musical, visual/spatial, interpersonal, intrapersonal, and body/kinesthetic. For example, a ballet dancer has a highly developed kinesthetic intelligence, a fiction writer excels in linguistic intelligence, and a sculptor has a well-developed spatial intelligence. Chapter 12 discusses Gardner's theory of multiple intelligences in more detail. In addition, Gardner believes that the symbol systems people use to understand and communicate in the world—drawing, writing, language, and gestures—are grounded in the arts. He believes that the learning of these symbol systems through art education is essential to cognitive development.

Manipulatives

Manipulatives include such malleable materials as clay, play dough, Plasticine, and wet sand. These materials can be pounded, squished, flattened, rolled, and molded into different shapes. They are soft and moist, but they can become hard and dry when left out in the air. (In many preschool settings, the term *manipulatives* also refers to materials that promote small-motor skill development, such as peg boards and snap cubes.) Manipulatives such as clay and play dough not only provide sensory experiences, they also stimulate the imaginations of children. Children can use manipulatives to make cars, trucks, animals, people, food, and virtually any object, as well as to express ideas.

An important function of manipulatives is that they allow children to explore shape and texture and to work in three dimensions. Working with manipulatives requires different kinds of fine-muscle control and skills than two-dimensional activities, such as painting and drawing. It enables children to explore the uses of a variety of tools, including plastic knives, spoons, cookie cutters, rolling pins, and molds. Moreover, the three-dimensional aspect of manipulatives presents interesting challenges and technical problems that are different from those encountered in two-dimensional activities. For example, a child playing with wet sand may need to experiment to see how many sand bricks can be piled on top of one another before the combined weight causes the structure to collapse.

Manipulatives serve another function that is related to emotional development. They provide children with opportunities to release tension or to express strong emotions, such as anger or fear, in a nonverbal way. Children can dispel angry feelings by pounding and squeezing clay, perhaps imagining that they are pounding the objects of their anger. Similarly, children who are emotionally upset usually can be distracted and calmed by becoming absorbed in rolling and shaping a manipulative material.

Music

Music is a fundamental and joyous part of a child's world and should be an integral part of the preschool curriculum. Music provides children with enormous pleasure, gives them an outlet to express their individuality, and contributes to their development. It helps children practice language skills, as they learn a new song or the names of instruments. It helps them improve motor skills, as they bang a drum or blow on a kazoo. It also helps them practice social skills, by singing together or playing a musical game. Music helps children develop empathy skills, as they experience the feelings suggested by the music (Kalliopuska & Ruokonen, 1986). A rousing marching band number excites children, whereas a soothing lullaby calms and relaxes the listener. In addition, music can be used to help children learn about other cultures (see the "Focus on Cultural Diversity" feature in this chapter).

Musical activities can take many forms. Children can listen and move to music, learn songs, and play musical instruments. Besides providing enjoyable experiences, these activities can help children learn such basic concepts as rhythm, rhyme, melody, tone, pitch, and tempo. Music also can be combined with other curriculum activities. For example, a teacher might encourage creative expression by having children paint in response to how the music makes them feel. See the "Applications" section later in this chapter for music activity suggestions.

Just as there are certain developmental stages in drawing and painting, there also are some identifiable stages in the development of musical skills (Bayless, 1990). Children normally begin chanting at age two and learn to sing around age three. While three- and four-year-olds sing in a very limited vocal range, their vocal range expands as they get older. By age four, children generally can create their own rhythms, but they have difficulty maintaining a rhythm for any length of time or keeping time with others. As they grow older, their personal sense of timing improves, as does their ability to relate to the timing of others. By age four or five, children also can reproduce the pitch, melody, and rhythm of simple songs with considerable accuracy, and they know a fairly large number of songs.

Making Music Is Learning Music.   Young children learn about music primarily by making music (Peery, 1993). They learn to sing songs, to play simple rhythm instruments, and to dance and clap in rhythm to a song or tune. One way that young children learn about music is by playing out the actions in songs and games, such as "In and Out the Window" and "London Bridge." Action songs combine songs with movements. A popular singing activity that does not require music is *finger plays*—using the hands and

FOCUS ON / **Cultural Diversity**

Using Music to Foster Cultural Understanding

Music helps children learn about rhythm, tone, and volume and fosters auditory discrimination and creativity. Music also presents opportunities to help children learn about diverse cultures. Preschoolers learn best through first-hand experiences, and music creates occasions for direct involvement through singing, playing simple instruments, and listening.

Teachers can easily incorporate music from diverse cultures into games and other areas of the curriculum. For example, during "Musical Chairs," the teacher might choose to use Indonesian music—with its long musical phrases ending with deep gongs.

The teacher, or perhaps a parent or a visiting musician, can teach children easy songs from different cultures. If the words are very simple and repetitive, the teacher might present the song in its original language. Children also can be given the opportunity to experiment with percussion/rhythm instruments, such as drums and bells, from various cultures.

Music from a wide variety of cultures should be represented in these activities, including music from North America, South America, Europe, Asia, Africa, and Australia. Exposure to music of many countries will help children learn to differentiate among various types of music. For example, the unique scales, instruments, and rhythm patterns of Japanese and Chinese music sound distinctly different from American music.

The teacher also can focus on different aspects of the music itself. For example, the teacher can have the children try to clap a beat to the complex rhythms typical of African or Native American music. With tapes or records, the teacher can demonstrate how an instrument such as the piano has a different sound in early American ragtime and in a 19th-century Viennese waltz.

In addition, the teacher can point out a specific purpose for which music is used within a culture. For example, American folk music often tells tales of history and adventures, frequently humorous tales.

fingers to represent characters or movements to accompany songs and nursery rhymes, such as "The Eensy Weensy Spider" and "Three Blind Mice."

Preschool teachers can incorporate music into any number of activities. Children can make their own instruments, such as drums out of coffee cans, tambourines from paper plates stapled together with bottle caps inside, and rattles from dried beans and hollow tubes. See the "Focus on Activities" feature in Chapter 10 for more musical instrument ideas. Teachers can lead children in songs or chants as they clean up and put away equipment, as they march around the playground, or during transition times. Teachers can use tape recorders to record children's singing and play the recordings back during group time. Outdoor activities, such as jumping rope and swinging, can be accompanied by music or songs to help children learn about rhythm. Whatever the activity, music should be made a daily part of the preschool curriculum and should be incorporated into other activities whenever possible (McDonald & Ramsey, 1982). In addition to incorporating many planned

Moving freely to music allows children to explore how their bodies can move. Movement activities also let children express their own creativity and feelings inspired by the music.

music-oriented activities into the curriculum, teachers can give encouragment when children spontaneously hum and sing songs that they have made up themselves.

Music and Movement.   Movement goes naturally with music. Young children enjoy moving their bodies to music. They like to dance, to march, to tap their feet, to clap their hands, or to sway their bodies to the beat of a lively tune. As their experiences with music and movement become more complex, their understanding of music and musical concepts also increases (Reimer, 1989).

Movement games and action songs help children build language skills. For example, "The Hokey-Pokey" teaches language and spatial concepts, such as in/out and around. (Note that, during "The Hokey-Pokey," three- and four-year-olds need to be given ample response time to hear the direction and then to execute the movement.) These types of songs and games also teach children social skills, such as following directions, playing with others, and getting along in a group.

As in other areas of the preschool curriculum, teachers need to consider the developmental level of children when choosing music and movement activities. Young children under the age of five, for example, are not yet ready to learn dance steps or specific dances. They should be allowed to explore movement and rhythm freely in creative ways and to make up their own movements to music. If preschoolers are always required to follow precise directions or duplicate their teacher's movements, their creativity will be stifled and they soon will become bored or frustrated (McDonald & Ramsey, 1982).

Finally, in planning any music and movement activities, teachers should keep in mind that the objectives of the games and activities are twofold. One objective is to provide children with the pleasure of experiencing their own body movements and expressing themselves through rhythm and song. The other objective is to enhance their understanding and appreciation of music and musical concepts.

It is important for teachers to know that, in some instances, art and music activities may not really be creative at all. For example, if a child is merely copying a teacher's picture or imitating a teacher's movements, he is not engaged in a creative activity, although he is engaged in an art activity. The same holds true for any other activity or curriculum area in which no original thinking or problem solving is taking place.

Extending Creativity beyond the Arts

Creativity can be promoted not only through art activities, but also through other areas of the curriculum. Creativity can occur in language arts through storytelling, poetry, finger plays, and guided fantasy play—where the children close their eyes and the teacher talks them through an imaginary experience, such as going to the beach on a hot day. These activities stimulate young minds to use words, images, and ideas in many new ways. Building with blocks is another important activity that provides many opportunities for children to express their individuality and creativity. Figuring out how to build a two-story house, for example, fosters creative thinking. A safety activity might encourage children to figure out how to make a play traffic light to use on the playground. A dramatic play scenario might involve deciding how to rearrange boxes, spools, and boards to make an airplane or a doctor's office. For any of these and a host of other projects, children must draw on their own imaginations to create something new and to think of creative solutions to problems they encounter.

Another way to encourage creative thinking in children is to ask open-ended questions that stimulate divergent thinking. As you may recall from Chapters 11 and 12, open-ended questions have more than one "right" answer. They encourage children to come up with several solutions to a problem or challenge. Examples are "How many ways can you move a ball across the playground without using your feet?" and "What can we use to make a fort?" Divergent thinking and problem solving can be promoted in all areas of the curriculum. They are important aspects of creativity because they create opportunities for children to develop new ideas and use new ways to organize information.

Science activities help children explore their creativity by "playing" with ideas and materials (Mayesky et al., 1985). For example, a teacher might talk with the children about how nests are built and then take them for a walk to look for leaves, twigs, and moss. Then, back in the classroom, he or she might set up a science discovery table with those materials and small boxes, glue, and cotton balls, and ask children how they might make their own nests.

Creativity can be fostered in all areas of the curriculum. Science activities—such as taking care of one's own plant and examining its leaves under a magnifying glass—challenge children's creative thinking skills.

Creative activities also can mix science and dramatic play or movement. A teacher might ask the children to think of activities related to different kinds of weather. Then she might have the children take turns acting them out—shoveling snow, sledding, or trying to walk against the wind. The teacher might ask the children how they could make it "rain" over the water table or what materials they would need to make pretend clouds. An outdoor discovery activity might help children explore where the rainwater goes after it rains.

The teacher also can foster creativity through premathematics activities. For example, a teacher might sit outside with the children in a circle on the grass. She might start off by saying, "I see something small," as she points to a pebble on the ground. Then she might ask, "Who sees something just a little bit bigger?" One child might point to a rock or a stick. In the block area, the teacher might ask, "How can we build a set of stairs for these dolls?" These types of activities focus on the cognitive skill of seriation. Chapter 4 includes a discussion of fostering creativity in play, and Chapter 12 includes a discussion of fostering creative thinking.

The Teacher and the Creative Process

Teachers can play a crucial role in promoting children's creativity by providing opportunities for self-expression. There are several strategies teachers can use, including using creative materials in interesting ways, and communicating acceptance and enthusiasm about children's involvement in creative activities. Teachers should make creative activities inviting and attractive and encourage children to participate in a wide range of creative activities.

The Creative Environment

In addition to providing materials, activities, time, and space for a stimulating, creative environment, teachers should be aware that their own attitude is an element of the creative environment. If children see their teacher enthusiastically pounding clay or spreading finger paint across a sheet of paper, they, too, will think that such activities are fun. Teachers should assume an accepting, supportive, noncritical attitude toward young children and their creative activities. They should let children know that new ideas and new approaches are welcome. For example, if a child wants to make a face with two noses, she should be allowed to express her ideas without criticism or comment. An attitude of acceptance helps children feel secure and self-confident as they pursue their own creative endeavors. Of course, teachers still need to set rules for using certain materials. Children need to understand that tossing glitter all over the room, smearing paste on the furniture, or drawing on the walls is not acceptable.

Preschool teachers also must be careful how they talk to children about their artwork. See the "Focus on Communicating with Children" feature in this chapter. It is important for teachers to refrain from either pretending to know what the child has drawn or from asking, "What is it?" As discussed earlier in the chapter, a child in an early representational stage of drawing may create pictures that do not represent anything in particular or represent something not discernible to the adult eye. If asked to identify or label his picture, a child may feel pressured to come up with an answer or feel incompetent because the adult cannot readily identify it. In the scenario at the beginning of the chapter, Mrs. Nakamura commented on the color of the children's paintings and the way they chose to use materials, to show her interest and provide positive feedback, but she did not ask the children directly to identify their paintings. Kaya and Anthony talked about their paintings on their own, in response to Mrs. Nakamura's interest. It is helpful as well for teachers to talk to parents about how they should react to and discuss their own children's art. Parents can be unintentionally discouraging if they do not know how to comment appropriately on their children's work.

Sometimes, teachers need to encourage children who are shy or do not like to get dirty to become involved in a creative art activity. If necessary, children need to know that they can be creative in "clean" ways. The teacher should communicate in a way that does not embarrass the child or cause anxiety. For example, when a child is afraid of getting dirty or sticky, the teacher can reassure him by showing him how his clothes will be protected by smocks or aprons, where he can clean up, and how easily paint washes off. The teacher may even dip his or her own hand into paste or paint and then wash it as the child watches. Very young children often want just to watch for a while before joining an activity. Watching is a perfectly acceptable way for children to learn and should be respected by the teacher, although children eventually should be encouraged to participate. Some children get frustrated quickly and will ask the teacher to do an activity for them. Teachers should resist doing a creative activity for a child, but they can make suggestions and offer encouragement.

Process Orientation

Because young children are not skillful with art materials and tools, much of their creative effort is focused on the process of trying out materials and tools and becoming acquainted with them. Teachers who adopt a *process orientation* to children's art emphasize that it is the process of creating that is important to children and not any product that may result from that effort. They acknowledge that children's satisfaction and joy come from the process of using and exploring materials. Teachers, however, often need to demonstrate how new materials and equipment are used. For example, children may be unfamiliar with how to use a hole punch or how to apply glitter. Through guidance and simple suggestions, teachers can help children learn how to use new materials and tools.

The artwork of young children is simply an expression of their own experiences in and exploration of the world, which relates to the constructivist approach to curriculum (see Chapter 2 and Chapter 12). Olive Francks wrote that children's art "need not be understood by the adult in order to be valid

FOCUS ON **Activities**

Making Props for Dramatic Play

One way to spur children's creativity is to have children make their own props for dramatic play. You might start during group time by asking the children to talk about places in the community they like or about favorite story characters. Create a list of items used in those places or by those characters. Encourage the children to think about which items on the list they could make. These items might include airline tickets or travel posters for a travel agency, menus for a restaurant, paper hats for a play birthday party or a sea voyage, books for a bookstore, play money for a bank, or postcards for a post office.

With the children, choose one type of dramatic play scenario to focus on first, such as a doctor's office or the public library. Save the other ideas for subsequent weeks. Put together materials to create the props. Materials might include old magazines, different kinds of papers, glue, scissors, crayons and pens, cardboard, and different types of fabric.

When the props are completed, you might create a "prop box," based on a selected theme. For example, a prop box for a grocery store might include child-constructed items—paper bags decorated with a logo or design, play money, cardboard boxes with pictures of food

items, coupons, advertisement circulars that feature a special theme or category—such as party/holiday food or canned goods—and props to set beside new product displays—such as a smiling snowman to be placed next to a display of ice cream treats. An assortment of magazines, newspaper advertisements, sample coupons, food labels from cans and jars, and similar materials would need to be available to the children to make these items. The contents of the prop box should include products that appeal to children's imaginations and inventiveness.

The prop box also can contain other items, such as a butcher's apron, a dustpan and a broom (for cleaning up spills in the aisles), plastic food, hand-held grocery baskets, and a play cash register.

Encourage children to think of their own ideas for props. For example, as you read stories during group time, point out unusual items that the children might make. A fairy's wand could be made with a short stick, aluminum foil, glue, streamers, and glitter. "Magic carpets" could be made from sample carpet squares. Soon, children will begin to point out similar items and offer their own ideas.

---

for the child. The child's art validates itself by its very existence" (Francks, 1982, p. 184).

The Value of Variety

Variety relates both to creative materials and to the activities that are offered by the teacher in the curriculum. Creativity is stifled when a child faces the same easel with the same kind of paintbrush and the same colors of paints day after day. With foresight and planning, teachers can easily add variety to stimulate interest and creativity. For example, teachers can provide papers of different colors or textures to paint on and such objects as stiff feathers, cut potatoes, or sponges instead of or along with brushes. Children can "paint" in sand with their fingers or with the handle of a paintbrush. Children are stimulated and motivated by having a wide variety of materials from which to choose each day.

It is also important for teachers to provide a variety of activities. Art is very individual. Some children are drawn to finger painting, some to clay, and others to music or dance. Teachers should make sure that children are able to pursue their own interests and should encourage them to pursue a variety of others.

Teachers must tap their own creativity to come up with new materials and creative activities for children. To gather new materials, teachers might ask parents to save such items as old coffee cans, used greeting cards or postcards, paper towel or toilet paper tubes, sponges, egg cartons, and plastic containers. See the "Focus on Communicating with Parents" feature in Chapter 5 for tips on talking to parents about free materials. Teachers also can ask members of the community for materials—such as fabric swatches from upholstery shops, wallpaper sample books from wallpaper stores, and surplus newsprint from the local newspaper office. Found objects such as leaves, keys, pinecones, and Styrofoam packing materials can be put to a variety of uses. Hunting for art materials, such as taking a nature walk or a walk in the park, can become a curriculum activity in itself. The "Applications" section at the end of this chapter includes further suggestions for adding variety to creative materials and activities.

Creativity and Children with Special Needs

Teachers who have children with special needs in their classrooms may find it necessary to adapt creative activities in certain ways. Children who have physical or mental disabilities need the same opportunities for self-expression and emotional release through creative activities as other children. In many cases, the teacher will have to make a few adjustments in an activity to accommodate special-needs children.

Some children with hearing impairments can hear bass notes or feel vibrations from music. The teacher can enhance music experiences by providing visual cues, such as making hand signals, or by situating the children where they can get visual cues from other children as they clap, stomp, dance, and move to music. Using realistic props also is helpful, as children with hearing impairments can express themselves through dramatic play.

Some children with visual impairments can be given three-dimensional materials, such as clay, which utilize their sense of touch. Music activities with these children can help them sharpen their listening skills. Moving to music, with the help of a teacher or a partner, is a good way for these children to gain a better awareness of their bodies and to improve their orientation and mobility skills (Deiner, 1993).

Teachers should help children with physical handicaps adapt creative activities to their own abilities. For example, a child who is in a wheelchair cannot dance to music, but he can clap his hands or beat a drum along with

Children who are visually impaired benefit from creative activities—such as manipulating play dough—that stimulate and sharpen their other senses.

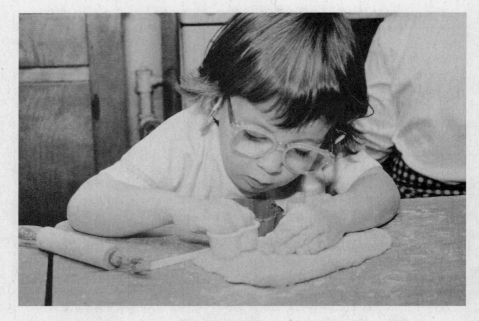

the music. It is important to help these children feel included in the group. A teacher might hold a child on his or her lap and guide the child through the motions of a song (Deiner, 1993). Children who have mental disabilities can practice fine motor skills with art activities. Repetition is especially important with these children. They should be encouraged to perform activities—such as dipping a sponge into paint and applying it to paper—repeatedly until the children feel that they have mastered the activity. Similarly, because these children's small-motor skills are not well controlled, creative movement activities should begin with large movements of the whole body.

It also is important to make sure that children with special needs understand the teacher's directions. Teachers should keep directions simple and short. They may need to use body language, broad gestures, props, and visual cues as well as words to interest children in activities.

Applications

Although teachers need to encourage creative expression, exploration, and problem solving in all areas of the curriculum, art activities have traditionally made up the main part of the creative curriculum. The following are some general guidelines for preparing and presenting art activities, as well as suggestions for variations.

- Look for equipment and materials that are developmentally appropriate. Items may include a variety of paintbrushes (large brushes with 12-inch handles work well), crayons, chalk sticks, blunt scissors, nontoxic paints, low tables and chairs, and easels.

- Paint containers can be made from cut-down quart milk cartons, empty frozen-juice containers, baby-food jars, muffin tins, or plastic jars. To help children put brushes back into the right container, label each with, for example, a piece of blue paper with the word *"Blue"* written on it (Mayesky, 1985).

- Encourage children to place paint to their left (whether they are standing at a table or at an easel) to help them develop a left-to-right orientation important for reading and writing (Cherry, 1990). To avoid unnecessary drips of paint (and to avoid children's frustration), teach children how to press the brush against the lip of the container to remove excess paint.

- Store materials on low, open shelves so that children can access them easily and put them away. Place materials in appropriate locations. For example, place painting and clay activities close to a water supply for easy cleanup. Store musical instruments near a large, open space where children can march, dance, or move freely.

- Whenever possible, allow children to help make, set up, and clean up creative materials. Children enjoy assisting with making finger paint, paste, and play dough. When children help make these materials, they learn, for example, about how dry materials can be transformed when wet ingredients are added and how textures change.

- When you are planning manipulative materials, remember to include Plasticine in addition to homemade or commercially made play dough. Plasticine does not stick to the hands (unlike clay, it contains oil), and it may be especially helpful for children who do not like to get dirty.

- See Figure 13.2 for suggestions for collage materials. Note that some preschools avoid using food items such as dried pasta or beans, in light of food shortages in some parts of the world or because the preschool may have families with low incomes who need food.

Suggestions for Collage Materials

Dried pasta of different shapes and sizes	Wallpaper scraps
Dried beans	Aluminum foil
Feathers	Large beads
Pebbles	Buttons
Fabrics	Bottle caps
Pieces of foam	Cotton balls
Yarn, lace, ribbons	Magazine pictures
Old or found keys	Old or chipped tiles
Leaves, bark, acorns, pine cones	Tongue depressors
Used gift wrap, tissue paper	Paper clips
Paper towel or toilet paper tubes	Pipe cleaners
Styrofoam packing material	Straws
Used greeting cards, postcards	Dried flowers
	Shells, seaweed
	Confetti

FIGURE 13.2 Suggestions for Collage Materials.

- Set up collage items in individual trays, shoe-box lids, aluminum baking pans, or clear plastic tubs, so that children can see the different items easily. Provide children with a strong, large surface such as cardboard on which to create the collage.
- Use table coverings, newspapers under easels, smocks, plastic aprons, and other protective materials to make cleanup easier and to protect children's clothing. Alternatives to smocks include adult-size T-shirts or old shirts with the sleeves cut down.
- In teaching songs, remember that short songs, especially those with repetitive melodies, work best with preschoolers. It is actually more effective to teach songs using just your voice and not a piano.

The following are specific suggestions for adding variety to each of four creative-activity areas—drawing and painting, play dough and clay, collage, and music and movement.

Drawing and Painting

- Mix sawdust, sand, glitter, or rock salt with paint to vary its texture.
- To make your own finger paint, see Figure 13.3.
- Look for interesting surfaces or objects other than paper to paint on—such as smooth rocks, large boxes, corrugated cardboard, seashells, and wood scraps.
- Take painting and drawing materials outside in good weather. Let children draw with fat chalk on an asphalt surface. The following two ideas from Clare Cherry's *Creative Art for the Developing Child: A Teacher's Handbook for Early Childhood Education* (1990) add variety to painting activities and work well outside.

Foot Painting.   Spread out large sheets of paper. Add small quantities of tempera paint to buttermilk. Have the children sit on low chairs (the paper

Art activities to foster creativity can take place outdoors as well as indoors. This painting activity also promotes cooperation, as children share wide brown paper for their "canvas."

Art Recipes

Finger Paint
1 c. flour
1½ tsp. salt
1 c. water
food coloring

Mix flour, salt, and water. Add food coloring. A more satisfying texture of finger paint can be obtained by combining dry tempera paint with one-half cup of liquid starch or one-half cup of liquid dishwashing detergent.

Play Dough
3 parts flour
1 part salt
1 part water

Combine flour, salt, and water in a large bowl. Knead the ingredients. If you wish, add food coloring or tempera paint to the water before adding it to the mixture. Store the play dough in a plastic bag.
Note: Adding one teaspoon of alum for every two cups of flour helps keep the play dough for several months. To make the dough more elastic, add one tablespoon of vegetable oil per cup of flour. For alternative recipes for play dough, see Chapter 10, Figure 10.3.

Flour Paste
½ c. flour
⅔ c. water
½ tsp. powdered resin (available at pharmacies)
Few drops of oil of peppermint or oil of wintergreen (as a preservative)

Add the water to the flour a little at a time, stirring to avoid lumps. Continue stirring the paste until it has a creamy consistency. Add the resin and oil of peppermint or oil of wintergreen. Makes one-half pint of paste.

Cornstarch Paste
1½ c. water
2 tbsp. light corn syrup
1 tsp. white vinegar
½ c. cornstarch
Few drops of oil of peppermint or oil of wintergreen

Mix the syrup, vinegar, and half the water (¾ cup) in a saucepan. Bring the mixture to a full boil. In a separate container, mix the cornstarch with the remaining water, stirring well until smooth. Add this mixture slowly to the boiled mixture. Stir constantly to avoid lumps. Add the oil of peppermint or oil of wintergreen. Let the mixture stand overnight before use. The paste will be good for about two months. Makes one pint of paste.

FIGURE 13.3 Four recipes from *Creative Art for the Developing Child: A Teacher's Handbook for Early Childhood Education, 2nd edition* by Clare Cherry. Copyright © 1990 by Fearon Teacher Aids. Reprinted by permission of Fearon Teacher Aids, 250 James St., Morristown, NJ 07960. All rights reserved.

surface will be too slippery for standing) and paint with their feet. Children can make their own footprints or walk across the paper while holding your hand. Have soapy water and towels ready for easy cleanup.

Drop Painting.   Place large pieces of butcher paper on plastic sheets. Let each child stand at the edge of the paper. Give each child a container of paint that is thinned out but not watery, and a large, full brush. Let children drop and splash paint onto the paper. As always, do not forget the smocks.

Manipulatives

- Add glitter or scented oil to play dough. Use nature scents such as pine, as opposed to vanilla, to discourage children from eating the dough.
- Provide trays or small plastic tubs of twigs, buttons, string, or pebbles for children to use to embellish their clay figures. In some cases, the clay will not be able to be reused.

Collage

- Take children on a nature walk, and let them gather leaves, twigs, bark, acorns, pinecones, seeds, pebbles, and other materials for a nature collage. Use glue on cardboard to create the collage, or try sticking items into clay.
- Ask the children each to bring different kinds of materials from home to make a group collage or a collage about their homes and families.
- Try gathering materials so that children can make a one-color collage with different textures, such as a green collage with buttons, ribbons, cloth scraps, leaves, moss, and gift wrap. Materials for a shiny collage might include aluminum foil, gold and silver gift wrap, and small scraps of metal.

Music and Movement

- Hold your hands up high or place them down low to provide visual cues to help children learn about high and low tones. Or spread your arms wide for a loud part of a song, and hold them in tight (as if cupping your hands) for a soft part.
- Fast and slow music can be combined with movement to help children discriminate among different tempos.
- Help children appreciate different kinds of music by using children's songs, folk songs, polkas, marches, classical music, and popular music. Children can explore different emotional states, such as scary, silly, or sad, through listening and moving to music.
- Find a recording of different sounds of nature (waves, a waterfall, rain, bird calls, and whales, for example), and play it for children as they lie on the floor with their eyes closed. This activity will help them learn that nature can make music, too.

- Music is a wonderful way to learn about other cultures. See the "Focus on Cultural Diversity" feature in this chapter.
- Children love to imitate animal sounds and animal movements, such as hopping like a bunny, crawling like a snake, flying like a bird, or galloping like a horse.
- Outdoors, give each child a long crepe paper streamer. Let children run around as they hold the streamer in one hand, to experience how the wind created by their movements moves the streamer.
- Ask children to move in response to open-ended questions, such as "How would it feel to float on a cloud or on a flying carpet?", "How would you move if your legs had bowling balls attached to them?", or "How would you move like a rag doll?"

CHAPTER 13 / REVIEW

SUMMARY

- Creativity refers to the ability to be original, to have new ideas, and to create something that did not exist before. Creativity in the preschool curriculum is not limited to the arts but occurs in any activity that requires original thought or problem solving.
- Creative activities in preschool help children grow and develop in a number of ways: physically, by developing large- and fine-motor control; emotionally, by expressing feelings and developing self-esteem; socially, by communicating and cooperating with others; and cognitively, by developing concepts, memory, language skills, and problem-solving abilities.
- Developmental theorist W. Lambert Brittain emphasized that children's drawing and painting abilities reflect three developmental stages: the exploratory stage, the early representational stage, and the preschematic stage.
- Cognitive theorists believe that children's art reveals what they know about the world. As children mature, their artwork becomes more sophisticated and complex.
- Manipulatives provide children with a variety of sensory experiences and with the opportunity to explore shapes and textures in three dimensions.
- Music, song, and movement are natural and essential aspects of children's lives and should be an important part of the daily preschool curriculum.
- Children learn about music by making music—by singing, dancing, playing simple instruments, and playing musical games.
- Creative activities can be included in every part of the curriculum and in every activity area. They are not confined to art and music but also apply

to block play, dramatic play, science, health, safety, and other curriculum areas.

- Teachers can encourage creativity by providing long periods of self-selected time and space to pursue activities and by offering children a variety of materials. They also can foster creativity by communicating acceptance and enthusiasm about children's involvement in creative activities and by asking open-ended questions.
- Teachers should assume an accepting, supportive, and noncritical attitude toward children's creative endeavors.
- Teachers who adopt a process orientation emphasize the process of exploring materials and creating rather than any end product.
- Creative activities can be adapted for children with special needs to allow them to express their individuality and emotions and to build certain skills, such as fine motor skills.
- Appropriate setup of materials, with a focus on variety, will help teachers incorporate creative elements into all aspects of the curriculum.

ACQUIRING KNOWLEDGE

1. How do most early childhood educators define creativity?
2. Describe the four characteristics of creativity identified by Torrance.
3. How is kinesthetic activity related to creativity in preschool children?
4. What type of motor control is developed by such activities as working with art supplies or musical instruments?
5. How can creative activities help a child develop communication skills?
6. How can a preschool teacher help foster self-esteem and independence in creative activities?
7. What social skills can be developed through creative activities?
8. Explain how creative activities can help children master symbolic thinking.
9. According to Brittain, through what developmental stages do children progress as they use new artistic materials?
10. In what developmental stage is a child who creates a picture that no one else can identify?
11. Describe the developmental stages identified by Kellogg.
12. Into what two groups did Goodnow categorize children in her comparison of children's art?
13. How does the cognitive view of children's creative development differ from the developmental view?
14. Explain how Gardner applies his theory of multiple intelligences to creative ability.
15. Why are manipulatives important to creative and emotional development?
16. What are the stages of musical development in young children?
17. What guidelines should a teacher follow in selecting musical activities that are developmentally appropriate for preschoolers?

18. How can open-ended questions encourage creative development?
19. Describe how science, premathematics, and dramatic play activities can encourage creativity.
20. When are art and music activities not creative activities?
21. How should a teacher talk to a child about her artwork?
22. How might a teacher encourage a child who is hesitant to get dirty to use art materials?
23. Why is a process orientation to children's art beneficial to creative development?
24. Why is variety an important element of a creative curriculum?
25. Explain how a teacher might adapt activities that foster creativity to suit a child who is visually impaired.

THINKING CRITICALLY

1. Preschool teachers can foster creativity in almost all areas of the curriculum. How can outdoor play encourage creative development? What might a teacher do to encourage creativity outdoors, without prescribing specific play activities?
2. Making collages out of pictures, seeds, buttons, and other materials is a common preschool art activity. If all the materials for the collage are already on hand, the child simply assembles them. Do you think that this activity encourages creative development? Explain your answer.
3. Adults should refrain from asking "What is it?" when looking at children's drawings. However, many children will tell a teacher what they have drawn, even though the elements will be recognizable only to the child. How might a teacher respond to the child's statement if the teacher cannot recognize any representational elements in the artwork?
4. Musical activities are a fundamental part of a preschool curriculum. There are many ways that recorded music can be incorporated into a classroom. Do you think that sitting and listening quietly to songs will effectively promote creative development? Why or why not?
5. Adopting a process orientation can help avoid frustration and disappointment as children explore creative activities. Teachers who adopt this orientation provide different activities from those with a goal- or results-oriented approach. What signs might indicate that a teacher has adopted a process orientation?

OBSERVATIONS AND APPLICATIONS

1. Observe a group of four- to five-year-olds during an art activity in a preschool setting. Describe the activity, and note the materials being used. How does the activity provide exposure to properties of objects, such as color, shape, or texture? Does it expose children to contrasting concepts, such as light/dark, wet/dry, or shiny/dull? Are the children creating their own work or copying from the teacher's example?

2. Visit a preschool group during music time. Describe the music activity. For example, are the children clapping, moving, or dancing to the music? Are they learning songs or finger plays? Are they playing instruments? In what ways does the activity foster the development of language skills, motor skills, or social skills? Are the children required to follow specific instructions, or can they use their own creativity to respond to the music? Does the activity reflect a particular culture and, if so, how?

3. Four-year-old Kristen is visually impaired. Although she knows the lay-out of the classroom well enough to get around, she sometimes needs help from the other children to find specific items. You are thinking about Kristen as you plan some activities related to Native Americans. How might you adjust the creative movement, music, and art projects you have planned to make sure that Kristen can participate and use her own creativity?

4. Three-year-old Samantha takes special care not to dirty the beautiful dresses that she wears to preschool. She is so concerned about getting dirty or sticky, however, that she refuses to participate in any of the art projects or other potentially messy activities. She will draw, but she will not paint, use glue, or play with clay. Instead, she prefers to watch the other children do their projects. You are afraid that Samantha will not get the chance to really explore her own creativity unless she participates. How might you help her to become more comfortable with these activities?

FOR FURTHER INFORMATION

Books and Journal Articles

Andress, B. (1991). From research to practice: Preschool children and their movement responses to music. *Young Children, 47*(1), 22–26.

Clemens, S. G. (1991). Art in the classroom: Making every day special. *Young Children, 46*(2), 4–11.

Deiner, P. L. (1993). *Resources for teaching children with diverse abilities: Birth through eight* (2nd ed.). Fort Worth, TX: Harcourt Brace Jovanovich.

Dodge, D. T. (1988). *The creative curriculum for early childhood.* Washington, DC: Teaching Strategies.

Edwards, L. C., & Nabors, M. L. (1993). The creative arts process: What it is and what it is not. *Young Children, 48*(3), 77–81.

Gardner, H. (1980). *Artful scribbles: The significance of children's drawings.* New York: Basic Books.

Golumb, C. (1974). *Young children's sculpture and drawing: A study in representational development.* Cambridge, MA: Harvard.

Goodnow, J. (1977). *Children drawing.* Cambridge, MA: Harvard University Press.

Hitz, R. (1987). Creative problem solving through music activities. *Young Children, 42*(2), 12–20.

Jalongo, M. R., & Collins, M. (1985). Singing with young children: Folk singing for nonmusicians. *Young Children, 40*(2), 17–21.

Kellogg, R. (1970). *Analyzing children's art.* Palo Alto, CA: Mayfield.

Myhre, S. (1991). With prop boxes we're always ready for creative movement. *Young Children, 46*(2), 29.

Curriculum and Resource Guides

Cherry, C. (1971). *Creative movement for the developing child: A nursery school handbook for non-musicians* (rev. ed.). Belmont, CA: Fearon Teacher Aids.

Cherry, C. (1990). *Creative art for the developing child: A teacher's handbook for early childhood education* (2nd ed.). Morristown, NJ: Fearon Teacher Aids.

Croft, D. J. (1990). *An activities handbook for teachers of young children* (5th ed.). Boston: Houghton Mifflin.

Church, E. B. (1993). *Learning through play: Music and movement.* New York: Scholastic.

Mayesky, M. (1990). *Creative activities for young children* (4th ed.). Albany, NY: Delmar.

Williams, R. A., Rockwell, R. E., & Sherwood, E. A. (1987). *Mudpies to magnets: A preschool science curriculum.* Mt. Rainier, MD: Gryphon House.

Zeitlin, P. (1982). *A song is a rainbow: Music, movement, and rhythm instruments in the nursery school and kindergarten.* Glenview, IL: Scott, Foresman.

Videotape

Frank Porter Graham Child Development Center, University of North Carolina at Chapel Hill (1988). *Thinking and creativity.* Chapel Hill, NC: DC/TATS MEDIA.

PART 3

Curriculum and the Child's Expanding World

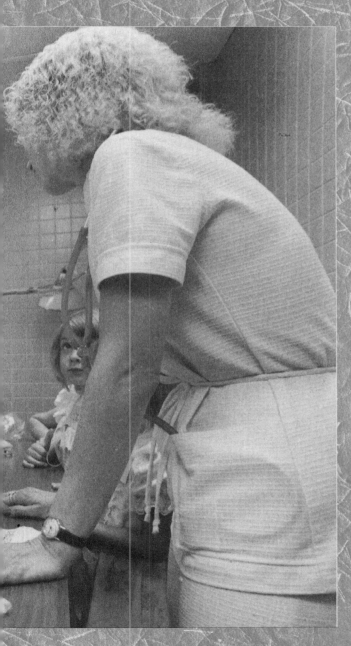

OBJECTIVES

Studying this chapter
will enable you to

- Discuss how children's identities
  affect how they relate to others
- Discuss how the preschool
  curriculum helps enhance
  children's awareness of a growing
  social environment that includes
  family, preschool, and community
- Explain the importance of a
  positive self-concept and strong
  communication skills in helping
  children succeed socially
- Describe the importance of
  friendships in learning to handle
  change and other aspects of social
  development
- List several strategies teachers can
  use to foster anti-bias attitudes and
  social skills through the curriculum

CHAPTER TERMS

gender constancy
gender identity
role identity

MS. MARSH sighed as she looked at the calendar. June 5. Summer was here, and she would soon have to say good-bye to her five-year-olds at the Canterbury Preschool. They would be entering kindergarten in September.

"I have a special treat for you this week and next week," Ms. Marsh told the children during group time. "We will be breaking up into groups to go visit the schools you will be attending and meet your kindergarten teachers." She pointed to Thursday on the felt-board calendar. "The first group will be Bobby, Sidney, Alexis, and Miranda. On Thursday, we're going to go to Green Gate Elementary School, while the rest of you will stay here with Mary."

"But why do we have to go somewhere else?" Bobby asked. "Why can't we stay with you?"

"You are all ready to start kindergarten, and we don't have a kindergarten here," Ms. Marsh answered. "Many of us have been together for two years, and I will miss you. But an important thing to remember is that most of you will have friends from Canterbury in your kindergarten classes. And you will also meet new people and make new friends."

"I can't wait," said Alexis.

"I'm scared," said Sidney.

"I know some of you are excited, but it's OK to be scared of something new, too," Ms. Marsh reassured them. "I think that going to see the new school will help you feel more comfortable there."

On the day that Ms. Marsh and the group of five-year-olds visited Green Gate Elementary School, they were greeted outside by Mrs. Lyons, the kindergarten teacher.

"Welcome, everybody. I'm happy to meet all of you. Let's go inside, and I'll take you to my classroom," Mrs. Lyons said. She then led the way through a maze of corridors.

"Please sit anywhere," Mrs. Lyons said, motioning to the tables. As the children took their seats, Miranda walked up to Mrs. Lyons.

"I have to go to the bathroom," she said.

"One of the things that is different about our room from your preschool room is that the bathrooms are outside in the hall," Mrs. Lyons replied. "In fact, in just a quick moment, I'll take all of you to show you. I'll also show you our playground."

She then turned to the rest of the group and said, "Today, I'm going to tell you all about our classroom and some of the wonderful activities you can look forward to when we start in September. I think lots of things—like our easels and the big sandbox outdoors—will be familiar. But you'll find some new things."

For preschool children, moving on to kindergarten can be an exciting, yet somewhat frightening, prospect. They are leaving behind familiar places, people, and routines. They are moving from a secure environment to unknown territory and are beginning to understand that their world of home and preschool is part of a much larger universe. But by the time they leave preschool, children have a sense of who they are and how to communicate with others. These and other aspects of social development will help them adjust to and enjoy new social environments, just as they adjusted to leaving home for preschool.

This chapter serves two purposes. It summarizes the material in the book about how the preschool curriculum helps young children develop the social skills that enable them to succeed in their expanding social world. Important elements of this process include forming an identity, establishing peer relationships, developing communication skills, and learning how to handle transitions such as entering kindergarten. The chapter also provides a preview of some of the social issues children will encounter in elementary school—such as prejudice and gender bias. In light of these issues, the chapter reiterates how an anti-bias preschool curriculum can help children develop positive attitudes—regardless of gender, race, or disabilities—so that they can successfully interact with a wide variety of people.

How the Child Builds an Identity

Young children learn about different roles in society and construct their own identities through observation, play, and preschool curriculum activities. In addition, the self-concepts children form early in life—for example, their view of how competent or attractive they are—affects their social interaction with others for the rest of their lives. Learning about and forming gender and cultural identity is part of the process children go through in developing their own roles in society.

Gender Identity

Very early in life, children hear adults talk about boys versus girls and see how adults interact with boys versus girls. Learning about one's gender and basic sexuality contributes positively or negatively to the formation of each child's self-concept.

By encouraging girls and boys to play in all areas of the classroom, teachers foster nonsexist attitudes and help children understand that girls and boys have the same choices and opportunities.

There are two basic aspects to gender. The first is *gender identity*, a person's biologically based identity—male or female. The second is *role identity,* a culturally based identity that is determined largely by the values and beliefs of the family and society. Awareness of gender identity begins at a very young age. Research has shown, for example, that children begin to recognize the difference between "boy" and "girl" at about age two or three (MacKain, 1987). They learn about such characteristics as height that are associated with age, and other characteristics, such as genitals and breasts, that define gender. Four- or five-year-olds can understand that characteristics associated with age change as people grow older. The primary characteristics associated with gender, however, remain unchanged regardless of age, behaviors, feelings, or activities (Harter, 1983; MacKain, 1987). The understanding that gender identity remains the same forever is a concept known as *gender constancy.* At the preschool level, it is important for adults to communicate and reinforce the idea that a child's gender will remain the same, and that neither physical growth nor behavior (for example, a boy's liking art or a girl's liking to play baseball) will change a person's gender.

Children's understanding of gender differences affects their interactions with other children. At 18 months of age, children do not differentiate the gender of their playmates. As they get older, however, children increasingly prefer to play with children of the same sex (Maccoby & Jacklin, 1990). Moreover, once children reach this stage, they tend to maintain that preference despite attempts by teachers or parents to change their behavior. In investigating reasons for the preference of same-sex playmates, researchers have found that girls often select same-sex playmates to avoid dominant behavior by boys (Maccoby & Jacklin, 1990).

During the preschool years, children also begin to form questions about their role identity, for example, "How should I act because I'm a girl?" By age three, children begin to develop attitudes about role identity based on what they perceive as normal. They may display prejudice on the basis of gender, such as making fun of a boy who is crying (Derman-Sparks, 1989).

FOCUS ON   **Cultural Diversity**

Fostering an Anti-Bias Curriculum with Classroom Visitors

The preschool curriculum can foster anti-bias attitudes in many ways. Activities that center on people in the community, for example, help children learn that people can become involved in a variety of careers and community services based on their talents and interests and not on their gender, disabilities, or cultural background.

For example, if a teacher wants to focus on challenging gender stereotypes, he or she might seek out classroom visitors who hold jobs or who have hobbies that break traditional gender stereotypes. Visitors might include a male nurse or ballet dancer (only if from a reputable school of dance, dance company, or local college) or a female engineer or scientist. As these people talk about how they became involved in their careers and the kinds of things they do every day, children will learn that they can choose activities based on their interests and not on traditional expectations for boys or girls.

To find nontraditional classroom visitors, teachers can survey the people they know, including colleagues, friends, neighbors, and the children's parents. They can call local busi-

nesses, police stations, hospitals, and community organizations.

It is important that the teacher talk with the visitor prior to the visit. The visit will have a much greater impact if the guest has prepared a simple but engaging activity related to his or her job—one in which the children can participate. For example, a dancer could teach the children some simple dance movements. A nurse might show the children how to find their pulse points and talk about how the pulse indicates that blood is flowing to the heart and throughout the body. An engineer might show the children the design for an industrial robot or an artificial limb. A scientist could conduct a simple experiment or bring in items to show the children under a magnifying glass.

Prior to the visit, the teacher should prepare the children so that they will use their best listening skills and not become overexcited. The teacher can discuss who the visitor is, what he or she will be doing, and how the children will be able to participate. A relaxing or quiet activity just before the visit will help prepare the children.

By age four or five, most children clearly exhibit socially defined behaviors appropriate for their gender, and they reinforce their role identity themselves during free play and structured activities (Honig, 1983; Roopnarine, 1984).

As children learn about gender and role identity, they also absorb the biases, stereotypes, and feelings about gender that are expressed by the society in which they live, and they tend to cling to these ideas. Teachers can help children foster positive, anti-bias attitudes and behaviors by providing nonsexist examples of boys and girls behaving in a variety of ways. They can, for example, use stories and posters to reinforce anti-bias attitudes. They also can communicate that boys and girls can do all the same things by emphasizing that both boys and girls can run fast and climb. See the "Focus on Cultural Diversity" feature in this chapter for a discussion of how to foster nonsexist attitudes with classroom visitors.

Cultural Identity

Just as gender can affect how children think about themselves, so can their cultural background. As discussed in Chapters 3 and 9, the cultural identities of children are formed both by their knowledge of and their pride in their own cultural heritage, traditions, and customs and by how others react to their cultural background—positively, negatively, or indifferently.

As soon as children, sometimes as young as age two, learn to categorize objects and point out the object in a group that is "different," they begin to categorize people and point out those who are "different." Young children need guidance to help them focus on similarities among people who look or act differently from them, and to understand that making fun of differences hurts people's feelings. The preschool curriculum can do much to foster in children positive attitudes about their own and other cultural backgrounds.

The "Applications" section later in this chapter summarizes how the antibias curriculum helps children feel good about who they are and where they come from, so that they establish and carry a strong identity—both from a gender and a cultural perspective—into their expanding social world.

Expanding Relationships

The first relationships of very young children are with their parents and siblings. Their "social universe" consists mainly of their homes and neighborhoods (Medrich, Roizen, Rubin, & Buckley, 1982). It also includes any extended family, such as grandparents, aunts, uncles, and cousins who may live in the same house or nearby, or whom they may visit on a regular basis. To a large extent, the social life of two- and three-year-olds is determined by the characteristics of their homes and neighborhoods. Playing with parents, siblings, or friends in their apartments or backyards, trips to the park, play dates, going to the store, and visits to relatives, are among the typical events of their social world.

However, during the preschool years, when children enter a group care situation, they come into contact with a growing number of adults and other children and gradually expand their social circles. They experience different kinds of relationships with different people. They may become very close to their preschool teacher, but they may only say a shy hello to the lady at the dry cleaners. They may have a best friend, and that best friend may change. Children develop relationships with a wide range of people who help shape their emotional, social, and cognitive development. For example, they may imitate the behaviors of people they admire or avoid interaction with children or adults they do not like. Although their families remain the focal point of preschoolers' lives, children at this age begin to spend a large part of their day seeking social acceptance from peers and approval from others.

FOCUS ON Activities

Our Town: A Social-Awareness Activity

The community is a vital part of a child's expanding social world. An effective way to teach children about their community is to have them build a model of selected buildings from their community using large cardboard boxes for buildings. Through dramatic play, the children also can experiment with various roles of people in the community.

Begin with a discussion about the different buildings that make up the community. Ask the children whether there are houses, apartment buildings, churches and synogogues, schools, and a post office in the community. Ask them to name different types of structures, building uses, and jobs that people might have in the different buildings.

Encourage the children to talk about why these buildings are important to them and their families. Identify the various physical features of the buildings. For example, churches and synogogues have steeples or stained glass windows. Banks and stores have signs, but houses do not. A post office or a school might have a sign and a flag. Suggest ways to beautify the community, such as by planting flowers, using brightly colored paint for awnings, and adding other decorations.

After this discussion, the children will be ready to build their own "town." Provide large, sturdy boxes to serve as the buildings and houses. Moving boxes and large appliance boxes work well. Group the children so that a maximum of four work on a box, one on each side. If possible, let all children have their own box. Then, provide the paints or markers and let the children create the buildings and houses.

Encourage the children to tell stories to the rest of the group about their buildings and who works or lives inside.

Extend the Experience

- Bring the buildings outside into the playground. Create lines with chalk or colored or white tape on the asphalt to represent streets. Involve the children in dramatic play scenarios, such as going to the post office, visiting a neighbor, or making a special delivery.
- Take a field trip to learn more about one of the buildings in your town, such as the public library, the police station, or the post office.

Family, Preschool, Community

The family plays a key role in the social development of children. Research suggests that children who have strong attachments to their families tend to have better peer relationships and are more socially accepted than those who have weak relationships with their families (Sroufe, 1983). Although many children enter family day care, group care, or preschool because of parents' work responsibilities, many parents put their children in this type of setting so that their children can develop socially through interacting with a variety of peers. In fact, most parents feel that social development is a major consideration in selecting a preschool. They regard increased peer interaction to be one of the most important aspects of the preschool experience (Bhavnagri, 1987).

The preschool creates an important link for children between their families and their community. Classroom visitors, such as this mother who works part-time as a clown, can help children learn about different roles and jobs that adults have in the community.

Parents must decide at what age the child should begin preschool and how many years the child should remain in preschool. These decisions may affect the child's social experiences. It has been found, for example, that children who stay in the same care arrangements for a substantial amount of time, such as two years, tend to benefit from having a stable peer group. This stability can have a positive effect on the quality of the relationships that children develop (Ladd & Coleman, 1993).

The preschool experience can create an important link for the child between the home and the community. Curriculum activities, field trips, and classroom visitors can help children learn about people, places, things, and events beyond their immediate families and the preschool itself. Children's concept of "community" is broadened by such activities as making gifts or cards for children in a local hospital or collecting canned goods for a local soup kitchen. Such activities also encourage the development of prosocial behavior and of social skills such as empathy.

Field trips provide another opportunity for children to experience the world beyond their homes and neighborhoods. Trips to the zoo, a farm, a fire station, a recycling center, a store, a bakery, or an office broaden children's social experiences. They also contribute to children's cognitive development, as children learn how the various parts of the community work separately and as a whole. The "Focus on Activities" feature in this chapter describes a social awareness activity that helps children explore their understanding of community.

Classroom visitors also can help broaden the perspectives of young children. Guests such as police officers, mail carriers, firefighters, and contractors or engineers can tell children stories about their jobs. They also may be able to add a new dimension to ongoing curriculum topics, such as safety and communicating. For example, a police officer may talk about safety rules for playing in the park, and a mail carrier may talk about how a letter gets from a child's mailbox to a grandparent in another town. This type of activity also makes community members become more familiar to the children and helps children feel more comfortable around them.

Peer Relationships

Friendships are an important part of any young child's social world. Friendships can have a positive impact on children's emotional, social, and cognitive development. Children develop friendships through many preschool activities, indoors and outdoors. Research indicates that outdoor playgrounds can stimulate as much, or even more, social play as indoor environments (Frost, 1986). Research also has shown that a less structured playground environment—for example, one that contains a variety of moveable equipment such as crates and boards—stimulates more social play among young children than a traditional playground equipped with swings, a slide, and seesaws (Campbell & Frost, 1985). See the "Applications" section at the end of this chapter for types of outdoor activities that foster cooperative play.

Peer relationships built through learning activities have many positive benefits. One study has shown that, when confronted with a novel situation or an unfamiliar environment, children are more likely to be adventuresome and to adjust to the new situation or environment when a friend is present than when they are alone or with a child they do not know (Schwartz, 1972). Interacting with peers and working in peer groups also positively affect children's cognitive development. L. S. Vygotsky suggests that work involving interaction among adults and children and among children and their peers has a more positive effect on cognitive growth than independent work (Vygotsky, 1978). Other research supports this view, suggesting that as children work in peer groups they learn from one another by sharing viewpoints and knowledge (Meisel, 1986). Similar findings have shown that children involved in a peer group freely contribute ideas that help the group identify a problem and formulate solutions to it (Forman & Cazden, 1985). The project approach to curriculum, described in Chapter 2, reflects these ideas.

The importance of peer relationships to cognitive and social development also can be seen by examining the effects of low or poor peer interaction. Research has shown that children with no or few peer relationships tend to fall behind and are less competent in cognitive skill development (Ladd & Coleman, 1993). Friendships help children develop feelings of self-worth, enjoy social situations, and perform well academically. Children who are unable to form friendships may suffer from negative self-esteem and feelings of inferiority (Bredekamp, 1987). Over the long term, the emotional support children experience through their peer relationships and relationships with family members and other adults gives them confidence to explore the world beyond their homes, neighborhoods, and schools.

Dramatic play fosters positive peer relationships, as children create pretend scenarios together and focus on a common goal—such as these four-year-olds who are driving a "fire truck."

Helping Children Succeed in Their Social World

What aspects of development and skills help children function well in their expanding social world? Among the most important are a positive self-concept, communication skills, and the ability to handle change, which will be discussed in this section. Other important skills include the ability to work cooperatively (see Chapter 9) and problem-solving skills (see Chapter 12). These elements play a key role in the social success of children and should be fostered both in the home and throughout the preschool curriculum.

Building a Positive Self-Concept

Self-concept—how a child perceives himself or herself—plays an important role as the child's social world expands. Studies show that parents who provide guidance and unconditional love, create a secure environment, and encourage independence tend to raise confident children (Sears, 1982). A positive self-concept motivates children to interact with others and to learn from them.

In the preschool setting, teachers help children build a positive self-concept through a curriculum that offers developmentally appropriate activities and a variety of choices. Making choices helps children become more independent and self-directed, and these traits contribute to a positive self-concept ("Ideas that work," 1987). Also, a curriculum that allows children to work at their own pace enables them to be more motivated and learn more than children who are always directed toward particular tasks. If the curriculum, or a teacher, however, denies children choices or pressures them to perform beyond their abilities, the result may be frustration, isolation, or feelings of failure in the children.

In addition to gaining a sense of competence by having and making choices, children build a positive self-concept by mastering skills. Thus, preschool teachers can help children by structuring the preschool curriculum to lay the groundwork for acquiring the knowledge and skills that are considered important to the society in which they live—such as reading and writing (Bredekamp, 1987). The child's self-concept also is discussed in Chapters 3 and 8.

Fostering Communication Skills

Communication skills contribute to young children's ability to establish and maintain positive relationships in their expanding social world. For example, as their language skills expand, children begin to enjoy increasingly richer and more complex conversations with both adults and other children. Research shows that conversation strengthens the ability of children not only to communicate with others but also to express themselves and to think logically (Nelson, 1985). As preschoolers' communication skills improve, children also become better able to understand another's point of view. This ability makes it easier for them to interact with others and helps them respond positively to one another.

Communication skills may be both a cause and an effect of whether or not children are liked or disliked by their peers. Research suggests, for example, that children who are well liked are better able to initiate and maintain conversations with other children and to involve other children in

Small-group activities help children practice communicating with one another. A play telephone booth creates an opportunity to develop language skills in a real-life context.

conversation (Hazen & Black, 1989). Children who are well liked also are better able to respond to comments made by others in a group situation. In contrast, children who are not well liked tend to be less skilled than other children during conversations with peers.

Certain types of curriculum activities can help children become more well liked. For example, activities such as creating a class list of ways to vent anger constructively (for example, vigorous physical activity, painting an "angry" painting, or going outdoors to use an "outdoor voice" can help children learn to control their anger, and thus be more well liked. Activities that require pairs of children or that group three or four children together based on a similar interest help children learn to recognize similarities in one another, learn to communicate, and learn to cooperate. Outdoor activities, such as sand, mud, and water play, encourage children to interact in a positive, peaceful way. Activities that focus on people helping one another show children qualities that are well liked by others. See the "Applications" sections at the end of Chapters 4 and 9 for more ideas on fostering social play.

Learning to Handle Change

Another factor that contributes to succeeding in a growing social world is the ability to handle change. Children of preschool age are likely to experience change in a number of ways, such as the transition from the home environment to the preschool environment and leaving preschool to attend kindergarten or elementary school. Although most children view such changes with excited anticipation, moving from a familiar to an unfamiliar environment can be stressful for some children (Bredekamp, 1987; U.S. Department of Health and Human Services, 1987). In the scenario at the beginning of the chapter, some of the children expressed fear of leaving preschool for elementary school. Toward the end of the preschool years, however, as children mature, make friends, and meet new people, their ability to handle these transitions and cope with new environments improves.

Friendships help make transitions easier. As stated earlier in the chapter, friendships contribute to a positive self-concept. This confidence in turn helps children through the transitions they will experience during their school years. One study has shown, for example, that children who move from preschool to kindergarten with one or more friends tend to develop more positive attitudes toward school and learning than children who come to school alone (Ladd & Price, 1987). These preschool friendships are likely to last throughout the kindergarten year, contributing further to children's ability to adapt.

Although friendships are an important factor in handling transitions, there are a number of things that preschool teachers can do to facilitate transitions. For example, trips to visit their new school, with parents or preschool teachers—such as Ms. Marsh's trip to the elementary school with her preschoolers—can help relieve children's anxiety and help them become acquainted with a new environment. Setting up a "Big Kids School" in the dramatic play area is a common end-of-year preschool activity that allows children to practice going to "school." Children enjoy playing with writing implements, using different kinds of paper such as computer paper and lined paper, setting up desks and chairs, and playing the roles of teacher and student.

While kindergartens vary from community to community, preschool teachers can discuss, in general ways, how kindergarten will be different from preschool and how it will be similar. These discussions help reduce the stress and fear surrounding the transition. Teachers also can read or make up stories about children going to a new school to prepare children for the experience. Another important aspect of easing the transition involves helping children realize that their preschool experiences have prepared them for the demands of elementary school. A good preschool experience is the best preparation for kindergarten. A child who sees herself as a competent learner will adjust better to any type of kindergarten program.

Children who have developed satisfying peer relationships, a positive self-concept, and the necessary skills to succeed on a personal and social level believe that they can succeed in all areas. In contrast, children who have weak social skills and an inability to form friendships easily tend to experience feelings of incompetence, which can lead to low self-confidence and low self-esteem. Children who struggle in social interaction often find it difficult to succeed in other areas as well.

Applications

The preschool setting can play a significant role in developing the positive attitudes and social skills that children need to function successfully in their expanding social world. Both the curriculum and the physical environment are important tools in this effort. For example, an environment that shows boys and girls and men and women performing a variety of activities in a variety of everyday settings will foster positive attitudes in young children about their own gender and the opposite gender. For this reason, you must try to create a curriculum and classroom environment that is as bias-free as possible. This section focuses on ways to structure your curriculum, present activities, and assess your teaching materials to achieve this important goal.

The Anti-Bias Curriculum

The anti-bias curriculum helps children foster positive attitudes about themselves and others, regardless of gender, physical characteristics, cultural background, or disabilities. A number of strategies can be used to promote anti-bias behaviors and attitudes. Multicultural activities were the focus of Chapter 9. The following suggestions offer guidelines for developing nonsexist attitudes.

To foster cross-gender play, you might place housekeeping props—such as stuffed animals, dolls, and telephones—in the block area to encourage their use by children of both sexes. Putting props related to a variety of occupations in the dramatic play area will encourage both boys and girls to role-

The anti-bias curriculum encourages boys and girls to work together on a variety of activities.

play different occupations. For example, you might add a teacher's tote bag with books and instructional supplies or a sportscaster's blazer or jacket with pretend microphone and clipboard. Make sure that props represent careers from different socioeconomic levels.

You might create an activity in which children look through magazines to find pictures of boys and girls doing a range of activities or showing a variety of emotions. Children might then create a collage showing boys and girls performing the same tasks in a variety of everyday environments—at home, in school, on the playground, or in different areas of the community, such as in stores, on the city bus or subway, or in the park.

In some cases, rearranging materials or providing new props may be enough to encourage children to play, for example, in both the block and housekeeping areas. In other cases, children may require more direct involvement by the teacher in planning or carrying out specific activities.

You might, for example, pair up boys and girls in the block area to construct different parts of the same object, such as a train. Suggest train cars that lend themselves to props. For example, one pair might make the engine and another pair the dining car. The engine might contain a mock control panel, a whistle, and a flashlight. The dining car might be stocked with play food, dishes, utensils, tablecloths, and menus. The sleeping car might contain blankets and pillows, and the baggage car might be filled with suitcases, bags, and boxes. Provide other realistic props, including cardboard replicas of train crossing signals and writing materials to make signs such as "Café Car."

The following are some other ideas for encouraging both boys and girls to engage in various activities.

- Make sure that you encourage girls as well as boys to be leaders when one is required in different activities.
- Girls need opportunities to explore spatial relationships. Create a treasure hunt indoors or outdoors.
- Boys need extra opportunities to promote listening and speaking skills. Create group-time activities that encourage boys to talk.
- Encourage boys to participate in small-muscle activities—such as making miniature blocks out of Styrofoam—and nurturing activities—such as caring for classroom pets. Fixing "broken" toys or dolls helps boys with small-muscle development as well as the development of responsibility and nurturing skills.
- Boys may shy away from activities that are too much like "dance." In creative movement, include activities with big movements, such as walking like an elephant and swinging your arms with clasped hands as the elephant's trunk. This activity is good for girls, too, because they need encouragement to use their large-muscle groups.

Regardless of the responsibility or the activity, the goal should be to encourage all children to try activities or materials they might not otherwise try. At the same time, however, you should avoid requiring every child to engage in the same activities for the same amount of time. Each child's own interests and abilities also must be respected.

Evaluating Materials to Reduce Bias

It is important for you to evaluate classroom materials for signs of bias, on a consistent basis. For example, such materials as posters and books in the classroom should show boys and girls performing similar activities. They also should depict boys and girls from diverse cultures and with differing abilities. Be aware of books, games, posters, pictures, or play props that portray people in a biased manner or in stereotypical roles. Decorate the classroom so as to include illustrations of cultural diversity, nontraditional sex roles, people of differing abilities, and the elderly. In the language arts area, for example, include books that show boys and girls involved in nonsexist roles and activities. See Table 14.1 for a list of books that foster nonsexist attitudes. Also select poetry and children's literature written by authors representing a variety of ethnic and cultural groups (see Table 11.2 in Chapter 11). Although it is impossible to eliminate biased materials completely, they should be avoided whenever possible and should not be displayed on a daily basis. You may even wish to use them as examples to help children identify situations in which bias exists.

Carefully review classroom materials to determine how gender, race, culture, and disabilities are portrayed. Since it is often difficult to find unbiased materials, you might alter existing materials to create new materials with an anti-bias focus. For example, alphabet blocks can be altered by pasting new

TABLE 14.1
Children's Books to Foster Nonsexist Attitudes

Ernst, Lisa Campbell. (1983). *Sam Johnson and the blue ribbon quilt*. New York: Lothrop. An awning rips while Sam's wife is away, so Sam sews his own patches. When the Women's Quilting Club refuses to let him join, he draws the farmers into a competition that results in friendly cooperation with the women.

Hilton, Nette. (1989). *A proper little lady*. Illustrated by Cathy Wilcox. New York: Orchard. Annabella decides that she will dress up as "a proper little lady." But she discovers that her spiffy clothes do not work well with her energetic activities, such as climbing trees and playing soccer.

Hoffman, Mary. (1991). *Amazing Grace*. Illustrated by Caroline Binch. New York: Dial. Imaginative Grace has the grit to be whatever she wants to be, despite advice to the contrary.

Hughes, Shirley. (1988). *The Big Alfie and Rose storybook*. New York: Lothrop. This book is a series of stories about family and school, featuring two preschoolers in a well-integrated neighborhood. Males and females participate in a number of different activities.

Lasky, Kathryn. (1988). *Sea Swan*. Illustrated by Catherine Stock. New York: Macmillan. On her 75th birthday, Elzibah Swan decides to learn something new. First she learns to swim, then to cook; and finally she builds and moves into a new house.

Mahy, Margaret. (1992). *The horrendous hullabaloo*. Illustrated by Patricia MacCarthy. New York: Viking. Peregrine the pirate takes advantage of his aunt, who cooks and cleans for him. But when he refuses to take her along to a party, she throws one of her own.

McKee, David. (1987). *Snow woman*. New York: Lothrop. Rupert builds a snowman ("You mean snowperson," says his father), while his sister Kate builds a snow woman.

Rabe, Berniece. (1981). *The balancing girl*. Illustrated by Lillian Hoban. New York: Dutton. Margaret (wheelchair-bound), uses intellect, ingenuity, and dexterity to triumph over a bully and earn money for her school class.

Ringgold, Faith. (1991). *Tar beach*. New York: Crown. This book tells the fanciful adventures of an imaginative African American girl who wants to own the George Washington Bridge in New York City.

Wells, Rosemary. (1992). *The island light* (A Voyage to the Bunny Planet series). New York: Dial. Feliz, sick at school, feels better after a visit to "the Bunny Planet," where his dad makes pancakes and offers comfort.

Wild, Margaret. (1988). *Mr. Nick's knitting*. Illustrated by Dee Huxley. San Diego: Harcourt Brace Jovanovich. Mr. Nick and his friend, Mrs. Jolley, love to knit together on their commuter train. One day, Mrs. Jolley gets sick, prompting Mr. Nick to knit her a special get-well gift.

Source: Compiled by Youth Services Department, Princeton Public Library, Princeton, NJ.

pictures over the existing ones. If the letter *F* is portrayed by a male firefighter, replace this picture with a picture of a fire truck or a fire. If the letter *I* is portrayed by a stereotypical "Indian," use another *I* picture, such as ice cream. Materials that show only white children in stereotypical gender roles—such as a girl washing her doll—could be altered by replacing some of the pictures with pictures of children from diverse backgrounds—such as an African American boy setting the dinner table. You might retell a story from a book that you consider biased, changing the text and characters to create an unbiased story.

An important factor in the success of an anti-bias curriculum is helping children feel unique and respected as individuals. Teachers need to treat all children as equals and to communicate that they are well liked.

You also can create your own anti-bias materials. A useful starting point is to search through magazines and keep a collection of nonstereotypical pictures of men and women of various cultures and races and people with disabilities performing a variety of everyday tasks. Use these pictures to create nonsexist puzzles, posters, books, or other materials.

Helping Children Respect Themselves and Others

You can help children respect themselves and others through your own attitudes and actions. When you make the effort to create a supportive environment, children are made to feel that they are each unique and special. Let children know that you really enjoy being in the classroom with them and that you accept them as they are. Make sure that all the children in the classroom feel that you like them unconditionally. You can convey these feelings in a number of ways.

- Encourage children to make choices free of sex-role conditioning.
- When children speak, listen attentively to what they have to say, and do not rush them or finish sentences for them.
- Speak privately with children about problems, away from the group, to avoid embarrassing them.
- Be generous with hugs, handshakes, and other signs of affection and caring.
- Enforce classroom rules fairly and consistently.
- Encourage each child to contribute to group efforts.
- Show confidence in children's decision-making abilities.
- Accept the use of more than one language in the classroom when bilingual children are in your group.

You also should examine and resolve your own biases, so that you can convey acceptance and respect for all the children in your classroom. By acknowledging that you have your own prejudices and that you adhere to a certain degree to some stereotypes, you heighten your own awareness. This acknowledgment is an important step toward feeling more comfortable about the differences among children. See the "Focus on Cultural Diversity" feature in Chapter 3 for tips on confronting your own biases.

Promoting Social Skills through the Curriculum

While a supportive environment provides the context in which positive social skills can develop, the preschool curriculum can provide specific opportunities to promote the development of social skills in young children. Curriculum activities can foster working cooperatively, communicating, group problem solving, and making and keeping friends.

Small-group activities can be especially useful because they offer children the opportunity to interact and talk with a few children rather than having to compete for attention in a large group. Cooperative group activities might include block or art projects—such as making a play sports car out of a large

FOCUS ON Communicating with Children

Talking about Violent or Upsetting Current Events

Although some young children in the United States witness violent events first hand in their own community, the vast majority of children experience violence through television. Can violence on television "hurt" a child who is merely watching it? Research shows that violent events—especially real news stories—can deeply trouble preschoolers.

Janie is upset by a violent event that she watched with her mother on a morning news program. Janie arrives at school teary-eyed, which prompts her teacher, Ms. Martin, to bring her into a quiet corner. After several minutes of discussion, Ms. Martin figures out that Janie has seen a news report on the Waco tragedy, in which a religious community of adults and children was destroyed in a fire following a mass suicide. Janie says that she saw children in the TV report.

Ms. Martin: I know that you feel upset because you saw people who were hurt.

Janie: They were my age.

Ms. Martin: Yes, they were. It is very sad.

Janie: Am I going to be burned up, too?

Ms. Martin: No, Janie. You're safe with us at school and at home.

Janie: But I was bad. Sometimes I hit my brother. I don't want the man from the TV to get me.

Ms. Martin: Janie, that man can't get you.

Janie: He took those children. My mother said so.

Ms. Martin: Yes, he did. But many of their mothers and fathers were with those children. Your mother and father would never let you go with someone like that man. And Janie, those children weren't bad. What happened to them had nothing to do with their being good or bad. The adults in their lives made a mistake.

Janie: But they still got killed.

Ms. Martin: Yes, but that man and the other adults are gone.

Janie: Really?

Ms. Martin: Really. You know, it might help you to draw a picture about how you feel. If the fire makes you sad, you can show it in your picture.

Do you think that Ms. Martin dealt effectively with Janie's fear? Why or why not? What other types of discussion or activities might Ms. Martin consider if her suggestions do not help Janie to alleviate her fear?

cardboard box—in which children must share supplies and work together. Dramatic play with small groups creates a natural opportunity for communication and interaction.

Small-group activities also provide opportunities for informal conversation and cooperative problem solving. For example, a group of children playing with blocks might discuss and experiment with ways to keep their structure from falling or determine what size to make a garage to accommodate a certain number of toy cars. Cooperative decision making helps all children feel that they have contributed to developing successful solutions. This feeling in turn helps build a positive self-concept. As you plan your curriculum, look for ways to turn some solitary or large-group activities into small-group activities.

Outdoor play also provides opportunities for children to practice social skills. When children use playground equipment, such as the rocking boat, requiring more than one child, they must communicate and cooperate in order to play. Most outdoor games, such as "Hide-and-Seek" and throwing and catching games, involve two or more children and offer a good opportunity for children to practice their social skills. Planting an outdoor garden can present interesting opportunities for social interaction and decision making over a period of time.

An important part of developing social skills is learning to see another's point of view. Group-time activities can help children learn to see situations from different points of view. Sit in a circle with the children. Ask them to help you create a list for the topic "A friend is someone who . . ." or "If I found a baby bird, I would . . ." or "Things That Make Us Angry . . . ," for instance. Taking another's point of view is essential to understanding and respecting cultural differences (Ramsey, 1982). Multicultural activities can be planned for group time. They will help children learn that there are different ways that people can perform the same task. For example, you might create an activity around different ways of carrying things—such as a basket, a suitcase, a knapsack, or carrying on the head. Be sure to include books, posters, or pictures to illustrate the different methods. Chapter 9 includes several suggestions for anti-bias and multicultural activities.

CHAPTER 14   REVIEW

SUMMARY

- Children learn about gender and culture at an early age. Their attitudes about these aspects of identity are largely derived from family experiences and observations of adults and older siblings.
- There are two basic aspects to gender: gender identity and role identity.
- Learning about gender and culture can contribute either positively or negatively to a child's self-concept, self-esteem, and ability to interact with others.
- Very young children's "social universe" consists of their homes and neighborhoods.
- As children grow older, their circles of social contact expand beyond their neighborhoods to include adults and other children in the community.

Their relationships with these people help shape their emotional, social, and cognitive development.

- Preschool creates an important link between the home and the community. Classroom activities, field trips, and classroom guests help expand children's awareness of the community outside their classroom.

- Friendships with other children play an important role in a child's social development and adaptation to new environments and transitions, such as entering kindergarten.

- Children develop friendships through a variety of school activities and in different community settings.

- Friendships help children develop feelings of self-worth and competence.

- Children who are unable to form positive peer relationships may suffer from negative self-esteem and feelings of inferiority.

- Vygotsky suggested that social interaction between adults and children, and between children and their peers, encourages cognitive as well as social growth.

- Research has shown that children in groups improve their problem-solving skills as they share viewpoints and knowledge.

- A positive self-concept, strong communication and problem-solving skills, and the ability to work cooperatively and make friends with others, all contribute to the development of social competence.

- Children improve their communication skills by interacting with adults and peers.

- How easily children handle transitions is largely determined by how well they are prepared for the transition by adults, how confident they are, and whether they make the transition with a friend.

- Teachers can use a variety of strategies to foster social skills and to help children develop positive attitudes about gender and cultural identity. These strategies include creating a supportive environment and utilizing an anti-bias curriculum.

- Teachers can develop an anti-bias curriculum by encouraging all children to engage in all activities regardless of gender, by providing opportunities for children to interact with people of different cultures and backgrounds, and by adapting or creating nonbiased materials.

ACQUIRING KNOWLEDGE

1. What does the "social universe" of a very young child include?
2. How does a child's social group change during the preschool years?
3. How is the strength of a child's attachment to family related to peer relationships and social acceptance?
4. How does the preschool curriculum form a link between a child and the community?
5. What aspects of social development are encouraged through field trips?
6. How do less structured playgrounds effectively stimulate social play?
7. Describe some benefits of positive peer relationships.

8. What problems may be experienced by children who do not form friendships?
9. How do a child's social skills affect self-confidence and self-concept?
10. How can the preschool curriculum contribute to a child's development of a positive self-concept?
11. Why are communication skills an important aspect of social development?
12. How is the ability to form friendships related to the ability to handle change?
13. What types of preschool activities can help children make transitions?
14. What is the difference between gender identity and role identity?
15. When does a child's awareness of gender identity begin?
16. Why is it important for children to develop a sense of gender constancy?
17. What has research suggested about why girls often select same-sex playmates?
18. How do small-group activities foster social skills differently than large-group activities?
19. What types of activities help children learn to see another's point of view?
20. What types of props might a teacher select for the dramatic play area to promote anti-bias attitudes?
21. To build children's feelings of competence and foster nonsexist behavior, describe the particular types of skills girls need to practice. Also list the types of skills boys need to practice.
22. What should a teacher keep in mind when evaluating materials for use in an anti-bias curriculum?
23. Name several ways teachers create a supportive environment in which children understand that they are accepted and respected as individuals.

THINKING CRITICALLY

1. Classroom visitors to preschools might include parents, local residents, or various members of the community. Choose one possible classroom visitor, and explain how his or her visit could help children to develop socially.
2. Preschool teachers can track progress in children's social-skill development in many different ways. How might a teacher keep notes about a child's social development?
3. In every class, there will be some children who are especially popular or well-liked. Do you think that being popular encourages or discourages the development of communication skills? Why?
4. Boys often rely on large-muscle skills while ignoring or avoiding activities that promote small-muscle development. What types of activities might a teacher use to encourage boys to develop small-muscle skills?
5. Children's artwork is often displayed in the classroom. What guidelines do you think that teachers should follow when selecting and displaying art so as to positively affect children's self-esteem?

OBSERVATIONS AND APPLICATIONS

1. Observe two different groups of children (with two or more children in each group) playing together. Record and compare the kinds of verbal interaction you hear. Are conversations brief or long? Is there any child (or children) who seem(s) to initiate and maintain the dialogue more often than the others? In what ways does the conversation relate or provide direction to the children's play?

2. Visit a preschool classroom during free play. How many girls are playing only with girls? How many boys are playing only with boys? How many children are playing with children of the opposite sex? Do you notice any stereotypical gender play—such as girls playing with dolls or boys playing with trucks? What materials, games, or activities do you notice that challenge gender stereotypes?

3. Five-year-old Heather is a bright, outgoing child in your preschool group. One day, Heather's mother approaches you in a panic. She explains that Heather is extremely upset about the family's impending move to another state. The family cannot mention the move without having Heather cry or plead to stay in their old house. What advice or suggestions for activities might you talk about with Heather's mother?

4. Four-year-old Danny has trouble making friends at preschool. He shies away from other children and tells you that they do not want to play with him. When he does occasionally play with the others, you see that he has difficulty communicating without hitting, or jumping on, them. In addition, he often has trouble maintaining a conversation. You also notice that Danny is reluctant to try new things at preschool because he thinks that he will fail. What strategies might you use to help develop Danny's feelings of self-worth, so that he will enjoy interacting with other children and in new situations?

FOR FURTHER INFORMATION

Books and Journal Articles

Beaty, J. J. (1992). Building a positive self-concept. In J. J. Beaty, *Skills for preschool teachers*. New York: Merrill.

Brown, M. H., Althouse, R., & Anfin, C. (1993). Guided dramatization: Fostering social development in children with disabilities. *Young children*, 48(2), 68–73.

Doescher, S. M., & Sugawara, A. I. (1989). Encouraging prosocial behavior in young children. *Childhood Education*, 65(4), 213–216.

Kostelnik, M. J., Stein, L. C., & Whiren, A. P. (1988). Children's self-esteem: The verbal environment. *Childhood Education*, 65(1), 29–32.

Videotape

National Association for the Education of Young Children. (1992). *Teaching the whole child in the kindergarten*. Washington, DC: Author.

Looking Ahead to the School Years

I want to put this paper in my folder," Bethany said to Mrs. Chen, her kindergarten teacher. The paper contained a drawing and a caption in Bethany's own writing.

"I think that's a great idea," Mrs. Chen answered. "You worked very hard on this paper and did a fine job."

Mrs. Chen was very pleased with the progress Bethany had made in the three months since school had started. She made some notes on the literacy skills page of the report written by Bethany's preschool teacher.

"We can look at some of the other papers in your folder, too, if you like," Mrs. Chen said. Although Bethany seemed reluctant to do so, she nodded and sat down next to Mrs. Chen.

"Look at this paper you did the first week of school," Mrs. Chen urged. "Well now, let's put this new paper next to the first one," she suggested, and she arranged the sheets so that Bethany could see her progress. "Tell me what you see."

"I have lots of letters in my name now," Bethany said, pointing to the full first and last names she had just printed on the latest paper. Her earlier paper had only her first name printed on it—spelled BETH.

"You also have a caption for your drawing. That's new, too. You seem pleased to be using a lot more letters. I'm pleased, too. You have learned many new things about writing."

"I guess so!" Bethany answered, grinning.

Mrs. Chen took the time to sit down with Bethany and talk to her about her progress and her interests—such as using words to tell more about her drawing. This individual attention made Bethany feel comfortable. It was like preschool. And Bethany's learning experiences in kindergarten were a continuation of activities she had had in preschool. Mrs. Chen had received the preschool teacher's report on Bethany's physical, emotional, social, and cognitive development. Such communication helped ease the transition from preschool to primary school for Bethany.

This chapter shows how preschools that teach in developmentally appropriate ways can help children be successful in primary school. It provides an overview of developmental tasks in the primary years. It also relates the whole child approach to curriculum that is used by many preschools to the integrated curriculum that is now utilized by many primary schools. The chapter concludes with a discussion of the assessment issues that are connected with preschoolers' entering kindergarten and first grade.

A Preview of the Primary-School Years

Earlier chapters of this book discussed how the preschool curriculum fosters various aspects of young children's physical, emotional, social, cognitive, and creative development. Growth in all these domains continues in the primary years. It is important for preschool teachers to have an understanding of what lies ahead for children ages six to eight because the preschool curriculum lays the groundwork for later learning. This preview of the early elementary school years describes several perspectives on cognitive development. It also discusses key areas of growth in emotional and social development.

Views of Cognitive Development

Children reach several significant milestones in terms of cognitive development during the primary years. Looking at cognitive development from three leading perspectives—the Piagetian, the sociohistorical, and the information processing views—is helpful for understanding the abilities of six- to eight-year-olds, who are in the upper range of early childhood.

The Piagetian Perspective.   According to Piaget, most children are beginning to shift in a gradual way from the preoperational stage of cognitive development to the concrete operations stage between the ages of six and eight. Children who have reached Piaget's concrete operations stage have an increased ability to solve problems "in their heads," with less hands-on exploration or experimentation than was necessary in the preoperational period. They also are better able than children in the preoperational stage to think logically and to use reasoning to draw conclusions and create solutions. Children of these ages are better able to understand another person's point of view and to consider more than one variable in a task simultaneously. In other words, the thinking of children becomes more like that of adults.

Although children in the preoperational stage begin to think symbolically—that is, to represent objects or concepts abstractly—this ability improves significantly in children who have reached the next stage. For example, children in the concrete operations stage are able to mentally reverse a physical action. This advanced aspect of symbolic thinking is called reversibility, and it was first discussed in Chapter 12. Thus, children are more apt to understand that "Don't fidget" means the same as "Sit still," and "Don't run" means "Walk." They also can understand, without actually needing to touch it, that a flattened piece of clay can be rolled back, or "reversed," into a ball or other shape.

According to Piagetian theory, the concrete operations stage, which occurs during the primary-school years, is marked by children's ability to perform increasingly complex tasks. Language skills are richer, and vocabulary is more extensive. Children are beginning to understand more abstract concepts beyond basic facts. Although they are still generally obedient with respect to classroom or parental rules, children begin to have opinions about rules.

The Sociohistorical Perspective.   According to sociohistorical theorists, cognitive development cannot be understood without considering its social

The sociohistorical theory of cognitive development asserts that children grow intellectually through interaction with older children and adults. This teacher knows that providing positive verbal feedback and asking open-ended questions play a key role in interaction.

context. Sociohistorical theory is thus based on observations of the interactions of children within social situations, and it attempts to explain how children's thinking and learning are shaped by their interaction with peers and adults.

The sociohistorical view was inspired largely by Lev Vygotsky, a well-known Russian psychologist who studied the relationship between children's social and cognitive development (see Chapter 12). Vygotsky believed that thinking originates as a shared experience and that children refine and gain new cognitive skills through interaction with peers and adults (Vygotsky, 1978). Language plays an important role in this process. For example, as older children and adults converse with young children—engaging them in longer conversations, adding new thoughts, and posing open-ended questions—children's thinking skills are challenged and enhanced. Vygotsky believed that the inherently social nature of language is of major importance in helping children learn about and construct meaning from their environment (Williams, 1991). Although this process takes place throughout development, when children enter elementary school, they are exposed to much more peer interaction in a different social setting than in preschool.

The Information Processing Perspective.   A third view of cognitive development, known as the *information processing theory*, likens thinking to the functioning of a computer. This view emerged during the last few decades with the rapid growth of computer technology and is based on research conducted in the 1970s and 1980s. The information processing theory focuses on the thinking process as being highly detailed, extremely precise, and sequential—as opposed to Piagetian theory, which looks at the thinking process in terms of broad stages (Gelman & Baillargeon, 1983).

According to the information processing theory, the mind, like a computer, has distinct parts that have specific functions that drive the thinking process (Seifert, 1993). Computers take in data from various sources—such as the keyboard, a disk, and a modem—and process this data in a sequential and logical manner. Similarly, people collect information through their various senses and use that information to develop concepts, solve problems, or draw conclusions.

Another aspect of the information processing theory applies to short- and long-term memory. According to this view, people receive stimuli through their senses, and this input is transferred by their mental processes to short-term memory. This short-term memory will fade and disappear, however, unless further mental processing occurs. By using different mental strategies, the contents of short-term memory are "transferred" to long-term memory. For example, when a child smells a scent, the scent is stored first in short-term memory. If the scent is especially pleasing or unpleasant, it may be transferred to long-term memory for future reference. Otherwise, it is "erased" from short-term memory and forgotten. This series of steps—from attention to short-term memory to long-term memory—forms the sequentially organized model of thinking on which the information processing theory is based.

FOCUS ON **Communicating with Parents**

Talking about Portfolios

Angela Margolis, the teacher of the four-year-old group at Buckingham Preschool, is holding the first parent conferences this year. Angela has talked with Vishal Daneesh about the school's developmental curriculum approach and about the way the theme of "families" will be used next month. Vishal asks about his daughter's portfolio.

VISHAL: I understand that Anitra's portfolio is made up of samples of her work in different areas. But something has been bothering me— I'd like to know why that material can't be sent home.

ANGELA: One of the most important aspects of portfolio assessment—in fact, one of the main ways it differs from formal testing—is that it tracks children's progress over time. We need to keep samples of Anitra's work in order to track her development. At the end of the year, portfolios go with the child from preschool into elementary school. At that time, I will go over Anitra's portfolio, pare it down, and send the rest of her material home.

VISHAL: I understand that. But I feel as if Anitra's best work is being kept from me. Anitra went on about this great picture she made of the fireworks she saw on the pier. We'd like to keep something like that.

ANGELA: I'll tell you what. If you hear Anitra talking about something we've put in her portfolio, and you feel it's very important for you to have it, let us know, and we can take a photograph of it, and keep that in the portfolio. We've done that before.

VISHAL: I would appreciate that. I'll try to keep it to a minimum!

Do you think that Angela should let original pieces go home just because Vishal wants them? Or do you think that Angela should have been more forceful about keeping the work? Explain your answer. If Angela's preschool did not have a camera for the teachers to use, how else might Angela have addressed Vishal's concerns?

Memory is, of course, an important aspect of cognitive development. As children enter the primary-school years, they become more adept at processing information and utilizing both short-term and long-term memory. Their increased memory capabilities allow children to develop more complex language skills and vocabulary as well as strategies for remembering information more efficiently. Children learn to read, for example, by first recognizing letters as a combination of shapes, then stringing letters together to form a word, and finally recognizing that word when they see it again alone or in context with other words. This process involves paying attention to letters and words, registering them in short-term memory, and storing that information in long-term memory for future use.

It is helpful for preschool teachers to consider these various views of cognitive development as they plan activities in the curriculum. See Figure 15.1 on the next page for teaching strategies, such as asking open-ended

Preparing Preschoolers for the Cognitive Tasks of Elementary School

1. Ask open-ended questions to stimulate children's thinking.

2. Give children real problems to solve—for example, figuring out how many cups are needed at snacktime, determining the best way to move a box of blocks from one location to another, or deciding what to name the gerbil.

3. Provide many opportunities for children to sort objects into self-determined categories—such as asking children to "Put the objects that are alike together." Also, have children put objects in descending or ascending order—for example, tallest to shortest, roughest to smoothest, softest to loudest, and smallest to biggest.

4. Encourage children to engage in measuring tasks using non-standard units of measure—for example, hands, cubes, or teddy bears. You might ask, "How many cubes tall is this table?" or "How many teddy bears wide is this carpet?"

5. Prompt children to engage in counting activities directly related to their real-life experiences—such as counting the number of children present for the day, counting the number of cubbies in the classroom, or counting how many napkins are needed for lunch.

6. Give children real-life experiences with nature.

7. Give children opportunities to experiment with simple machines, such as levers, wedges, and inclined planes. Encourage exploration with magnets.

8. Offer numerous cooking activities in which children count, measure, and see the effects of heating, cooling, mixing, or dissolving.

9. Help children develop their observation skills. For example, you might say to children, "Look closely at this shell. Tell me what you see." Or you might say, "Look carefully at this frog. Make a mark on your paper to help you remember what you see."

10. Give children opportunities to make predictions. Ask questions such as "What do you think will happen when . . .?" Or say, "Let's see what happens when . . .", followed by, "Tell me what you see." Encourage children to test out and evaluate their predictions.

FIGURE 15.1 **Preparing Preschoolers for the Cognitive Tasks of Elementary School.**

questions and helping children develop their observation skills, that will help children prepare for the cognitive tasks of elementary school.

Emotional-Social Development

During the primary-school years, children are increasingly interested in developing friendships with children their own age. Positive and productive relationships with their peers are important for children. These relationships help children develop feelings of competence and self-esteem, which in turn increase their interest in school and learning (Bredekamp, 1987).

As children compare themselves with others and become aware of differences, they also become more aware of what they perceive as limitations of their own abilities. Children experiencing difficulties in learning to read, for example, may be painfully aware of classmates who read easily. Continued lack of success in any classroom task can lead to feelings of inferiority that can hamper future performance.

Another area of growth for primary-school children is in moral behavior. By about age six, children begin to internalize moral rules about what is right and wrong, and, in the process, they develop a conscience. They learn how to behave appropriately in various situations, and they attempt to modify their own behavior according to moral standards. Although they are more independent than preschoolers, primary-school children still require a high level of adult supervision and assistance.

During the primary-school years, children also become increasingly aware of cultural and racial differences. Just as in preschool, primary-school teachers can turn these differences into positive classroom experiences. They can help children discover how people are similar—for example, the universal need for food, clothing, and shelter. They can foster respect for the differences—for example, by having children share and enjoy different foods and customs. See the "Focus on Cultural Diversity" feature in this chapter for a discussion of how primary schools are eliminating bias from the curriculum.

An understanding of the emotional-social and cognitive development of children ages six to eight is important for preschool teachers as they develop and implement curriculum. It is helpful for the future as well as for the present for preschool activities to focus on fostering social skills—such as learning to work in small groups, and empathy—both of which play a role in making friends and being liked by others. In terms of supporting children's moral development, preschool teachers who establish and enforce rules in a positive and consistent manner—and include children in this process—help children to understand the meaning of rules and to begin to formulate concepts of right and wrong. Teachers also should use positive techniques, such as modeling, rather than negative techniques, such as punishment or criticism, to foster social skills.

The Development of the Whole Child

In addition to understanding what lies ahead developmentally for six- to-eight-year-olds, it is also helpful for preschool teachers to see how the preschool curriculum compares and contrasts with the curriculum of the primary grades. The kindergarten curriculum always has been similar to the preschool curriculum in its focus on the development of social skills. It also has been traditionally considered, until recent years, a "stepping stone" to the academic content of the primary grades. Kindergarten activities often are related to specific subject areas, such as reading or language arts, mathematics, science, and social studies.

In preschool, on the other hand, the curriculum focuses mainly on the children themselves—how they develop and learn. This approach to early

FOCUS ON Activities

Create a Recycling Center

Recycling teaches children respect for the environment and responsibility for their own actions. It also sets a positive example and helps children form the habit of recycling on their own.

Start by talking with the children about recycling. Most of them are likely to be familiar with recycling if their families do it at home. Show examples of materials such as plastic and paper before and after they are recycled. You might invite a guest, such as an employee from a recycling plant, to talk about what happens to the material from school that is collected for recycling.

Once children understand the concept of recycling, you are ready to set up a recycling center. Start with four large bins. One bin will hold paper. Another will hold recyclable plastic. The third will hold aluminum or tin. And the last will hold materials that can be reused for curriculum projects. Provide examples of these materials to the children, and create an art activity out of decorating the bins with pictures of the items to go in them.

Bring in various items for the bins. Create a sorting activity as the children place the items in the corresponding bins. As recyclable materials are used in the classroom (for example, newspaper under paintings) or gathered from walks to the park or around the neighborhood, remind children to place the items in the appropriate bins. You may wish to spend some time each day as a group, filling the containers. Soon, the children will begin to recycle independently.

Don't forget to use the materials in the last bin for projects. "Found" materials—such as buttons, fabric scraps, and bottle corks—are terrific for art projects. To involve parents in the recycling center, you might send a note home to encourage them to contribute used items for Bin #4. Spark their imaginations with a descriptive list that could include driftwood from a beach trip, used gift wrap from a birthday party, and pictures from desk or wall calendars and holiday cards at the end of the year.

---

childhood education emphasizes the "whole child" and centers on the child's physical, emotional, social, cognitive, and language needs, as well as on the child's developing awareness of cultural diversity. However, this approach now is being seen more frequently in kindergarten and grades 1 and 2—grades considered to be a part of early childhood education (Bredekamp, 1987).

The Whole Child Approach

The whole child approach, sometimes called the developmental/whole child approach (see Chapter 2), reflects the belief that young children learn in different ways from older children. Proponents of the whole child approach assert that young children learn through the interaction of all their capabilities—including their physical, cognitive, and creative capabilities (Bredekamp, 1987). As Leslie Williams has written, "Learning in any of these domains must necessarily involve all the others. Effective teaching, as a consequence, must draw upon those inner connections, with recognition of the distinctive ways in which young children take in and utilize knowledge of the world around them" (Williams, 1992, p. 1). Activities created by teachers who subscribe to the whole child approach focus on integrating cognitive, social, emotional, and physical elements simultaneously, rather than focusing on any one in isolation.

There is evidence to support the validity of the whole child approach. According to some studies, problems arise when certain aspects of development are neglected. For example, children in classrooms where academic achievement is emphasized often lack adequate social and emotional skills (Spodek, 1986). Research also indicates that when intellectual development is favored over physical development, children begin to show signs of poor health and fitness (Reuschlein & Haubenstricker, 1985).

The whole child approach stresses the process of learning rather than the products of learning. For example, it favors developing vocabulary through interaction of dramatic play, storytelling, and story reading, rather than through completion of a vocabulary worksheet or a workbook page. The whole child approach also recognizes the importance of play as an ongoing form of learning and discovery. The interaction of children in small-group activities is another key aspect of this approach. These activities provide opportunities for children to communicate and to work together, exchanging information and expressing feelings, as they are developing physical, cognitive, and social skills.

How does the whole child approach work when it is put into practice in a classroom? Imagine a small group of preschool or primary children playing in the block area. As they build a hospital together, they use their fine motor skills to balance the blocks. They use language skills to communicate directions and ideas and social skills to work as a team. They use cognitive skills to solve problems, such as how wide to make the driveway to accommodate two "ambulance" cars. They use creative skills to decide what the hospital will look like.

The Holistic View of How Children Learn

The whole child approach to curriculum reflects a number of basic assumptions about how young children learn. They learn in a variety of different ways, which reflect various aspects of the three views of cognitive development discussed earlier. They learn through their senses, through exploration, through play; through interaction with others; and by making significant connections as they absorb and process information. Children also learn through reflection and through the process of maturation. The key idea is that young children learn through the interaction of a number of different, yet related processes. This theory behind the whole child approach is known as *holistic learning*.

As active learners, children instinctively move around, touch, run, and jump. These explorations provide children with stimulation and also increase

Holistic learning reflects the belief that children learn through the interaction of many "selves." This activity involves the physical self (eye-hand coordination) as children catch the bubbles and the cognitive self (experiencing cause and effect) as children see how air creates bubbles.

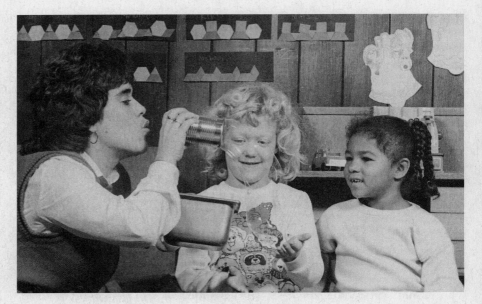

their opportunities for learning. As they explore their environment, children utilize their senses. They absorb and organize a great deal of information through touching, tasting, smelling, seeing, and hearing.

As children play and work together, they interact, communicating feelings and exchanging information and ideas. Disagreements and seeing others perform action in new ways challenge a child. The child reacts to the challenge either by taking in the new information or action or ignoring it. Social interaction helps children expand and refine their knowledge and understanding of the world around them. Thus, children not only acquire information from physical exploration of the environment but also through interacting with others. (Kostelnik, Soderman, & Whiren, 1993).

As children learn about their environment, they reflect on what they know and what they have done. The mental process of reflection helps increase children's self-awareness and enhances children's potential for learning and remembering what they have learned. It is important for teachers to provide time in the curriculum for children to have the opportunity to reflect on their experiences or to discuss them in small groups.

In the whole child approach, environment also plays an important role in the learning process. A child's environment includes biological aspects, such as nutrition, medical care, and exercise; physical or external aspects, such as climate, shelter, and clothing; and social aspects, including family, friends, community, and culture (Santrock, 1990). The nature of a child's environment can either interfere with or enhance the learning process. For example, research has found that children who are well fed and healthy and who feel safe, secure, and loved learn better than children whose basic needs are not being met. (Maslow, 1954; Bredekamp, 1991). The different aspects of a child's environment are interrelated, and the influence of one part of the environment is felt in the others. For example, a child's home environment will affect the preschool experience, and vice versa.

The whole child approach recognizes individual differences in the rate at which children develop and the way they learn. As children mature, they become capable of learning things and performing activities that were previously beyond their stage of development. For example, toddlers lack the cognitive ability to recognize connections between behaviors and events, but preschoolers are beginning to draw such connections. While maturation follows a general timetable in which children reach specific developmental milestones at approximately the same age, this timetable varies with individual children. Teachers need to be aware of developmental stages and of each child's progress on a developmental continuum, so that they will not ask children to perform tasks beyond their level of maturity.

The way young children process information and experiences also varies. Such differences are referred to as an individual's *learning style*. Some people learn primarily through vision and respond best to things they can see. Others may learn best through hearing and talking. Still others learn primarily through kinesthetics (physical movement) or their sense of touch. Children with a kinesthetic or touch-oriented learning style might learn to write by tracing the shapes of letters or numbers with their fingers or learn to count by manipulating rods or other objects. Although people learn through all these means in differing degrees, individuals learn most effectively when their own preferred learning style is highlighted. Two leading researchers in the area of learning styles, particularly as they relate to learning to read, are Marie Carbo and Rita Dunn (see the section "For Further Information" at the end of this chapter for suggested reading).

The whole child approach seeks to create early learning experiences that both integrate the various aspects of young children's development and accommodate children's differing learning styles. The next section examines how the primary-school curriculum can take some of the concepts of the whole child approach and to apply them to six- to eight-year-olds.

The Integrated Curriculum

Primary schools today are seeking ways to prepare children for the 21st century, when the ability to utilize information from myriad sources, to think creatively, and to remain flexible in various situations may be more important than knowledge of specific or predefined subject areas. For this reason, many early childhood educators continue to advocate a more integrated approach to learning. This approach focuses attention on the child and the learning process rather than on traditional subject areas (New, 1992). Often referred to as an *integrated curriculum,* this curriculum approach places more emphasis on the development of creative thinking skills ("learning how to learn"), rather than on knowledge of subjects alone.

The integrated curriculum combines experiences in several subject areas so that students can explore one theme or issue in depth from many different aspects. For example, if the children are learning about communication,

Eliminating Bias from the Elementary School Curriculum

It is projected that by the year 2000 the number of African American, Hispanic, Asian, and Native American children attending elementary school will increase dramatically. The changing face of the school population has another element. More school districts are adopting a policy of mainstreaming (also called inclusion) to integrate children with physical and learning disabilities into the regular classrooms.

This growing diversity in the elementary schools makes it extremely important to have a curriculum that reflects and addresses the needs of a diverse student body. To reduce bias, elementary schools across the country are following these recommendations or strategies.

- Obtain staff support. Schools are implementing faculty training programs so that teachers understand the importance of a bias-free curriculum. Schools also are providing curriculum planning strategies and materials so that teachers can present topics in new ways.
- Enlist the support of parents. Without parental support, schools may have difficulty implementing an anti-bias curriculum.

Schools are initiating communication with parents specifically to explain the rationale for and changes needed to implement an anti-bias curriculum.

- Establish a task force. A task force will systematize the approach of the school (or school district) toward an anti-bias curriculum. Made up of faculty, principals, and parents, a task force will review the topics covered within the curriculum, evaluate whether they are biased, and determine if the curriculum reflects a variety of cultures. The task force will make recommendations for changes. In addition, a task force will meet regularly to review existing and new classroom materials—such as books or educational games—for signs of bias. The task force will research speakers that the school might sponsor, and recommend assembly topics about diverse cultures and other activities.
- Treat multiculturalism in materials and activities as an integral part of the curriculum, rather than as a special unit or a weeklong celebration.

they might explore written, verbal, and nonverbal communication (such as body language, art, dance, or facial expressions). They might learn through books, creative movement, dramatic play, and materials in the writing or art center. They might devise ways of having two groups communicate with each other from opposite ends of the playground. They also might draw up lists, such as "How Communication Helps People in Their Everyday Lives." The aim of the integrated approach to curriculum is to help children master skills, acquire knowledge, formulate concepts, and solve problems that can be applied over a broad range of subjects.

The concept of an integrated curriculum has its roots in the works of Jean-Jacques Rousseau, Johann Pestalozzi, Friedrich Froebel, Maria Montessori, John Dewey, and others (New, 1992; Williams, 1992). Over the years, many integrated curriculum models have appeared. In the 1980s, a new curriculum movement developed in response to the changing requirements in public school kindergarten programs.

Within this movement, two viewpoints emerged. One group of experts held that kindergarten programs should provide children with formal academic skills to prepare them for elementary school. The other group considered this focus to be developmentally inappropriate for young children. Experts in this second group believed that the curriculum could have academic elements. Yet they believed that it was more important for these elements to be integrated into a focus on developing young children's thinking processes and fostering literacy and mathematics skills in a context relevant to the interests and everyday lives of the children. Creative-thinking skills would serve as a foundation for problem solving and skills acquisition. Advocates of this view believed that the elements of all subject areas could be integrated into activities that would engage children socially, emotionally, cognitively, and sensorily. The idea of an integrated curriculum has gained increasing support among early childhood educators in elementary schools.

The Role of the Teacher

The teacher plays a vital role in setting the stage for an integrated curriculum. Teachers act as guides to the learning process rather than as imparters of knowledge. Teachers should be able to talk with the children, sharing information and ideas and responding to children's questions in a thoughtful, serious manner. They also should pose questions that challenge children's ability to analyze information and respond appropriately and that encourage them to consider implications, conclusions, or alternatives rather than just facts (New, 1992). Teachers must provide activities that children will consider significant and worthwhile. Scheduling is another important aspect of an integrated curriculum. The time allotted for activities must be flexible enough to accommodate both long, involved projects and short ones.

In an integrated curriculum, the teacher helps make connections between and among developmental domains and acknowledges that learning in different areas overlaps. When children discuss their artwork or participate in storytelling, they are practicing language skills. In the same way, when they research a social studies or science project, they are using reading and writing skills (Van Deusen-Henkel & Argondizza, 1987). This overlapping recognizes the fact that children can learn the same skills in different ways, and it allows teachers to relate each skill to a number of subject areas.

Different Paths to an Integrated Curriculum

An integrated curriculum can be implemented in two main ways—through theme-based projects and through self-directed learning centers. A theme-based project is best when it grows out of the children's interests. If, for example, the elementary school is located near a river, several projects and activities in the first-grade class might relate to rivers. These activities will

Theme-based projects and self-directed learning centers play important roles in an integrated curriculum. This "travel agency" helps children learn about planning trips with maps, posters, books about different places, and telephones to make hotel and flight reservations.

integrate subject areas, such as reading (finding and reading books about the formation of rivers or freshwater fish); social studies (researching how the river has shaped the economic and cultural life of the town); science (identifying plants and animals that live near or in the river); art (re-creating the river with art materials or creating a terrarium with moss and plant life from the riverbank); writing (writing stories about the river or writing to the town council about preventing pollution in the river); and physical education (canoeing in the river or having a recreation day along the river).

A theme-based project requires cooperative effort and involvement of both teachers and children. Projects generally take several days or weeks to complete. See Chapter 2 for a discussion of the project approach, a type of preschool curriculum closely related to the integrated curriculum.

Another way to implement an integrated curriculum is through learning centers or activity areas, in which children choose and plan their own learning opportunities. Although most preschool activity areas are largely planned and set up by teachers, some elementary school learning centers develop with the children's involvement. For example, children might create a "bookshop" where they use reading skills (reading the books in the bookshop); language skills (discussing stories with other children or asking the "manager" for book recommendations); and writing skills (making signs to label sections of the "bookshop"). They also might use mathematics skills in the "bookshop" (collecting play money and making change when children "buy" books). Learning centers such as the "bookshop" also require children to use problem-solving, social, and organizational skills.

These two avenues of implementing an integrated curriculum—theme-based activities and self-directed learning centers—provide learning opportunities in a context that is meaningful to the children. They also encourage children to develop their skills in several domains as they interact with one another and with adults.

The Assessment Debate

Most teachers, regardless of the curriculum approach they use, conduct frequent assessments of the children in their classrooms. At the preschool level, these assessments tend to be informal, individualized, and based on anecdotal notes from observations over time. The results are used to make decisions about each child's developmental progress and as a basis for creating curriculum activities geared to children's interests and needs.

In contrast, elementary schools often rely on more formal testing to provide information for a variety of purposes. These purposes include *placement decisions*—assigning children to particular learning groups; special-needs assessment; and curriculum planning. In addition, tests are used for *formative decisions* early on and throughout the school year, to provide ongoing feedback about curriculum instruction to both the teacher and the child. Tests also are used for *summative decisions* at the end of a unit or a year of instruction, to evaluate what the child has learned and the overall success of the instruction. The most commonly used assessment measures for primary-school children are developmental screening tests, intelligence tests, and readiness tests. This section will include a discussion of each of these types of tests, as well as alternative assessment methods.

Decisions about test selection generally are made on a local rather than on a state or national level. Tests may be selected because school administrators have chosen them before; because the tests have been marketed energetically; or on the basis of the lowest costs involved in purchasing, administering, and scoring the test. Unfortunately, test purchasers often ignore the question of whether test results provide useful information or adequately reflect the child's abilities.

Before purchasing any test, educators should investigate two specific aspects—the test's reliability and its validity. *Reliability* is a measure of a test's consistency in producing the same score if it is taken more than once. *Validity* measures whether the test actually provides information about the areas it claims to assess. The test is said to be valid if its stated objectives match what is actually being assessed.

The more reliable and valid a test, the more useful its results in helping teachers modify the curriculum to address children's needs. Curriculum and placement decisions that are based on the results of tests with limited reliability and validity may overlook some children who require additional services or provide special services for children who do not need them. Unfortunately, using results of tests with limited reliability and validity is one of the more frequent abuses of testing (Meisels, 1987).

Important decisions about children and the curriculum never should be made on the basis of just one set of test results. To make informed decisions, teachers need a substantial amount of information about children's skills, abilities, and accomplishments. Several types of standardized tests can help provide some of this information. By incorporating the information from those sources, along with information from alternative methods—such as performance and portfolio assessments (discussed later in this chapter)—

teachers will be able to make meaningful and appropriate decisions about each child's educational program.

Developmental Screening

Developmental screening tests assess those developmental abilities that are related to a child's current functioning and future success. These tests may include screening for hearing, vision, or physical development. They also may include performance assessments of tasks requiring cognitive, language, perception, and motor skills. Developmental screening tests, by comparing the child to a norm, generally are used to identify children who may need extra assistance or special services because of some type of handicap—such as a hearing impairment or a learning disability. It should be noted that developmental screenings provide only preliminary findings and alert the teacher to the need for additional testing. They sometimes are used inappropriately as predictors of success to deny kindergarten entry or to keep children home for an extra year (Gnezda & Bolig, 1988).

One example of a developmental screening test is the Denver Developmental Screening Inventory (DDSI), for infants through children age six. This test is designed to assess four developmental areas—personal-social, fine motor, gross motor, and language. Other tests in this category include the Brigance Diagnostic Inventory of Early Development and the Developmental Indicators for Assessment of Learning (Revised) (DIAL-R).

Intelligence Tests

Intelligence tests, also called IQ tests or individual intelligence tests, are broad measures of a child's reasoning, memory, language skills, perceptual-motor abilities, and social awareness. While IQ tests measure some of the same skills as developmental screenings, they are much more complex and provide more in-depth information. Only specially trained individuals should administer IQ tests.

IQ tests are most useful for identifying children who are functioning either in the very high or very low range of academic abilities. However, when interpreting IQ-test results, teachers should understand that the results can be strongly influenced by a child's prior learning experiences (Shepard & Graue, 1993). For example, primary-school children who are familiar with the type of content included on the test or who have had a number of enriching experiences—such as attending preschool or visiting zoos, museums, and theaters—tend to score higher on IQ tests than do their peers.

The leading intelligence tests are the Stanford-Binet and the Wechsler Preschool and Primary Scale of Intelligence-Revised (WPPSI-R). Studies have shown these two tests to have high reliability and validity. These tests are able to predict with some accuracy how well children will perform in an academic setting (Shepard & Graue, 1993). They do not predict how well a child will do in other areas of life. See Table 15.1 for an example of categories and questions from the WPPSI-R. Twelve subtests compose the WPPSI-R.

TABLE 15.1
Sample questions from the *Wechsler Preschool and Primary Scale of Intelligence-Revised* **test**

Category	Sample Question
Information	How many legs does a cat have?
Comprehension	What makes a sailboat move?
Similarities	In what way are a quarter and a dime alike?
Arithmetic	Judy had four books. She lost one. How many books does she have left?
Vocabulary	Name pictures like boot and book.
Sentences	Repeat a sentence like, "Ted likes to eat apples."
Picture Completion	Identify missing parts in a picture like a doll without a leg.
Block Design	Use three or four blocks to reproduce the design presented in a picture.
Object Assembly	Put together puzzle pieces to form a complete object.
Animal Pegs	Children must learn an association between certain colors and animals and perform a matching task.
Mazes and Geometric Design	Children must first pick matching shapes and then draw a circle, triangle, square, and diamond.

Source: Items adapted from *Wechsler Preschool and Primary Scale of Intelligence - Revised.* Reprinted by permission of the Psychological Corporation.

These subtests are designed to assess children's capacity to understand and their knowledge of events and objects in the world around them.

Readiness Testing

Readiness tests assess the curriculum-related skills children currently have rather than developmental potential. They are administered before children begin particular programs to determine whether these children have the necessary skills to succeed. As with other tests, readiness tests often are used inappropriately to make decisions about school entry or grade placement. Instead, these tests should be used to plan a child's individual program within the regular classroom, such as deciding on the next phase of reading instruction (Meisels, 1987).

Some of the readiness tests in use today reflect theories of learning that were popular 60 years ago. These tests are based on the assumption that complex tasks, such as reading comprehension, can be broken down into specific skills, which can be improved through practice. Critics have said that these tests do not recognize a child's capability to reconstruct such skills

Alternative assessment techniques are designed to track children's development within the context of a normal learning environment. In the Concepts About Print Test, a teacher sits with a child and asks the child to identify parts of a book, such as words and pictures.

into higher-order thinking skills. Many early childhood educators within the whole language movement argue against the use of these tests.

Before making instructional decisions based on readiness tests, teachers should consider whether the tests are compatible with their own approach to teaching. Teachers who organize instruction around the belief that children learn holistically would find little use for testing skills in isolation.

Alternative Approaches to Testing

Traditional, group-administered, paper-and-pencil tests frequently have been criticized for being too abstract and for penalizing children who are not raised in a white, middle-class environment (Stallman & Pearson, 1990). Critics say that children are tested on skills in a context to which they cannot relate, rather than in a natural setting close to their own real-life experiences.

With such criticisms in mind, educators have begun to develop some alternative approaches to testing children. Many of these alternative approaches are more flexible than the tests just described and take into account a child's development over time (Shepard & Graue, 1993). They may present questions in a context that is more meaningful to children than questions in traditional tests. Also, rather than testing skills in isolation, they reflect the relationships among several different skills, as well as the interactive relationship between teacher and child (Meisels, 1993). For example, Marie Clay (1985) developed the *Concepts About Print Test,* which is administered by a teacher sitting with a child and a book. The teacher says to the child, for example, "Show me a word," and the child responds by pointing. The test assesses the child's language and listening skills simultaneously within the context of a normal learning environment (Shepard & Graue, 1993).

Among the new methods that are being widely adopted by school systems today are performance assessment and portfolio assessment. These methods are characterized by their flexibility and their ability to monitor and reflect a child's developmental and academic progress. Both forms of assessment are useful in programs based on age- and developmentally appropriate activities. Whereas standardized tests reflect a child's performance at one point in time, performance and portfolio assessments document continuous progress in an ongoing manner over the course of a school year.

Performance assessment is a method based on observation—teachers observe and document how a child in the classroom interacts with peers and with materials—and on a child's performance on specific tasks. It reflects an individualized approach to achievement and includes narrative records of observations, journals, and samples of children's work. Gathered from all areas of children's development, this information helps teachers monitor and plan the curriculum for individual children and groups.

Portfolio assessment, one type of performance assessment, is a systematic collection of children's work gathered by both children and teachers over time. The portfolio is used to assess development, progress, and achievement and thus can be used to shape the curriculum (Tierney, 1991). Portfolios demonstrate performance through a diverse cross section of a child's work in many areas. They may include drawings, dictated stories, and even photographs of block structures. Portfolios actively involve children in the process of self-reflection on their own work, as the children choose what they would like to put in their portfolios.

Even though most preschools are not part of the public school system, they are starting to develop portfolios for all children. These portfolios will stay with the children as they enter the public school system (or private school), and straight through high school. With this approach, at the end of each school year, the child's best work (chosen by the student and the teacher) is kept in the portfolio, and the rest is sent home.

An important part of the use of portfolios is in influencing classroom practice. Researchers have found, for example, that elementary school teachers use portfolios to shape the curriculum (Koretz, Stecher, & Deibert, 1992). These teachers tend to rely less on textbooks and place less emphasis on drill and practice, plan more hands-on activities, use more interdisciplinary projects, and focus more on the development of skills (Dietel, 1992). See Figure 15.2, Paradigm Portfolio Assessment, for an illustration of how portfolio assessment is used to shape the curriculum.

FIGURE 15.2 Paradigm of Portfolio Assessment. This figure shows how portfolios help teachers in two distinct but related ways: assessing children's progress and developing curriculum activities based on children's interests and needs. *Source:* Adapted by Sherry Copeland and Dr. Muriel Drew, District 27Q, Ozone Park, NY, from *Alerta: A Multicultural, bilingual approach to teaching young children* by Leslie R. Williams and Yvonne De Gaetano. Copyright © 1985 by Addison-Wesley Publishing Company, Innovative Division. Reprinted by permission of the publisher.

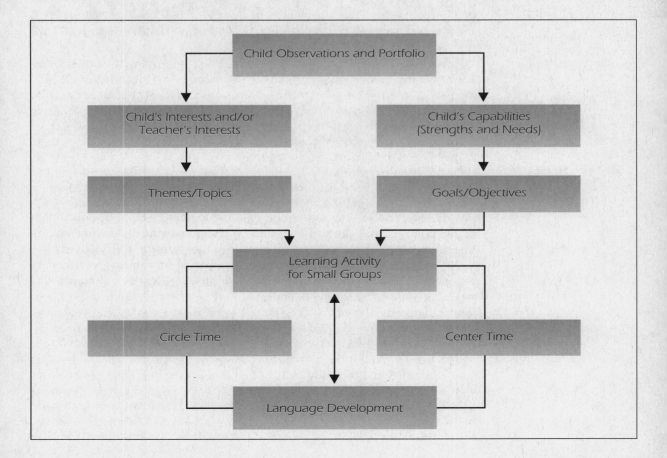

Preschooler's portfolios can include many different elements, such as paintings, drawings, and dictated stories. This teacher is taking a photograph of a small group's construction project, so that she can make multiple prints and include one in each child's portfolio.

Portfolios help children take responsibility for improving their own learning. By being able to review their own work as it is developed over time, many children are able to identify what they do well and what they need to improve—as Bethany did with Mrs. Chen in the scenario at the beginning of the chapter. By serving as mentors or guides rather than evaluators, teachers can capitalize on children's awareness of their strengths and weaknesses to help children modify and assess their own work.

In addition to evaluating the needs of individual children, information from alternative assessments also can be useful for group evaluation. By compiling the information about each individual child's progress into a class profile, the teacher may detect areas in which all children need additional assistance, or notice skills or competencies that all children have mastered. By matching these areas against the classroom curriculum, the teacher can modify class activities accordingly.

Unlike some traditional assessment tools, alternative assessment methods require a major commitment over time on the part of teachers, administrators, and schools. However, they do not require nearly as much time as devoting whole weeks to administering standardized tests. Also, the financial costs of administering and scoring traditional tests is very high.

Teachers utilizing the alternative assessment process need to be adequately trained and fully supported in their efforts to implement these types of assessments. Because there are no "right" and "wrong" answers in alternative assessments, as there are on standardized tests, teachers need to be trained to recognize patterns in a child's work that will help them assess the child's progress and development. Also, teachers need to learn to look at the portfolio with a critical eye so that they can recognize warning signs that the child may need additional attention in a particular area.

In addition, teachers should involve parents in the alternative assessment process and should keep them informed of their children's involvement in the process. Despite the greater demands of these assessment tools, studies indicate that teachers, students, and parents are quite enthusiastic about the process and its results (Dietel, 1992; Nardi, 1992).

Alternative assessment methods, such as portfolio assessment, are not without critics, however. For example, those educators and administrators who argue against the use of portfolios assert that teachers are not selective enough and put too many pieces of work and written observations into the portfolio. Opponents say that some teachers draw conclusions or overgeneralize from individual pieces of work instead of looking for important patterns—one of the key purposes of portfolios. Lastly—and this point applies to all types of assessment—if a teacher tries to pass the portfolio on to the teacher of the next grade (or if the preschool teacher passes it along to the kindergarten teacher), it may not be well received and may even be ignored.

Applications

The increasing popularity of the whole child approach to curriculum, the integrated curriculum, and alternative assessment methods has a number of implications and applications for preschool teachers. Most important are the ways in which these ideas can be applied to support early educational experiences in preschool that develop strong, self-confident learners who will be better able to cope with primary school. This section will discuss two types of applications—activities to use in the integrated curriculum and how to get started using portfolios at the preschool level.

Activities in the Integrated Curriculum

Activities in the integrated curriculum provide a comprehensive way to help children acquire developmental skills while simultaneously learning a subject area or topic. Consider, for example, a high-interest topic such as "Animals." This topic provides a rich project base from which children can learn language, problem-solving, physical, social, and cognitive skills in different areas of the classroom as well as outside.

To give a focus to this broad topic, you and the children might first decide together which kinds of animals will be included in the activity. Some children might bring play animals from home and talk about them during group time. These same animals might be used in the art center, as children draw or paint pictures of them.

Dramatic play areas can be stocked with masks, fake furs, and other props to provide opportunities for the children to pretend that they are animals. As part of a creative movement activity outdoors, you might suggest to the children that they walk like different animals or move like animals in an open field or a crowded forest.

FIGURE 15.3 A Sample Anecdotal Record. Anecdotal records can be formatted in several different ways. In one format, all the teachers contribute information about each child from informal observations. To make record keeping easy, the teachers make notes on small pieces of adhesive paper cut to fit the columns of the anecdotal record form. *Source: Cathy Albro, Executive Director, the creative learning center, Grand Rapids, MI.*

Field trips to a local farm or zoo can give children an opportunity to see animals in their natural habitats (or simulated ones in a zoo) and to see what they eat, how they sleep, their types of shelter, and what they do.

In each of these various activities, it is important that you encourage children to pool their information and create projects in small groups. They also should participate in planning activities and talk about their ideas.

Creating Portfolios: Getting Started

Interest in portfolios is growing at the preschool level, in part because portfolios build on ideas central to early childhood education. For example, preschool teachers always have recorded informal observations of individual children. These are now called anecdotal records (See Figure 15.3 and Figure 15.4), an important element of portfolios that will be discussed later

Child's Name: _Rachel_   Remember to date all entries

Language	Representation	Classification	Seriation	Number	Sphere	Time	Movement	Social/Emotional
11/16 Rachel helps Tara (sub) clean up after lunch. She explains what to do and says, "See the sponges in the sink?" T—"Yes." R—"Those are what you wash your dishes with." 1/3 Rachel said, "If you get hit by a car, you die."	*9/28 Hanna and Rachel set one big block over a smaller block and made a teeter totter. Both got on. Rachel said, "Hanna, you're too small. This doesn't work." They try out something else.* 10/9 Rachel piled cornmeal on her arm. When I asked what she was doing, she said,"I'm making a snowman." *11/10 Rachel made a "horse farm" out of her blocks for her ponies.*	1/7 Sees the dinosaur Scotty prints and says, "He looks like a shadow! He's all black!" 8/5 Rachel plays Uno successfully with Grant and Stacy— matches colors/#'s. *11/20 Rachel sorted the "jewels" by colors. Then she matched up each color pile with its dark or light partner, too.*	11/30 Rachel— "This is a 'wall' 'cuz it looks like a wall." (She did seriation right away.) *12/3 Rachel said, "Look! I have smallest to biggest. Also, they're different colors. It looks like stairs."*	10/12 Rachel said, "I made three pumpkins." *11/10 Rachel counted her six horses.*	8/14 Rachel sets the table in housekeeping. Then puts a full tablesetting in its proper place. 1/3 Rachel put a 30-piece puzzle together by herself. 1/13 Rachel does a 30-piece puzzle by herself.	1/12 Rachel— "I had to get three shots and a booster shot—just a little time ago." 1/21 Rachel said, "Hey, in the summer, leaves are on the trees and flowers come out." 1/30 Rachel said, "I saw a movie the other day."	10/20 Rachel can listen and follow movement directions. Can also recall the sounds from movement tape songs— listen and move. *12/1 Rachel listened to movement tape and did the movements suggested by the tape (clap, jump, wiggle, shake.)*	7/7 Rachel willingly shares her squirter with Stephen and shows him how to fill it. 7/10 Rachel shares her baby with Katie. "You can hold her, too." Katie says, "Rachel shared with me!" 7/10 Alex attempts to hold Rachel's baby by taking it. Rachel says, "Don't take my baby!" She leaves.

A Sample Anecdotal Record

Child's Name: Maria Villarruel   **Observer**: W. Sanchez
Date: 10/14/94   **Setting**: Game Table, kindergarten room
Time: Free Choice Period

Observation:

Four children, including M., were playing dinosaur bingo. L., the caller, held up a dinosaur picture for the group to look at. M. shouted in a loud voice, "I have that one." She immediately placed a chip on the corresponding dinosaur on her bingo card. M. pointed to the appropriate dinosaur on G.'s card. L. Held up a second picture, M. said in a quiet voice, "I don't have that one, but you do." She pointed to the appropriate picture on G.'s bingo card. L. held up a third picture, M. showed R. the corresponding place on his bingo card to cover with a chip.

G. 'won' the game. M. laughed and said, "Let's play again, okay?"

Interpretation:

M. exhibits good visual perception skills. She could accurately match the pictures in the caller's hand with the pictures on the bingo cards. M. seemed to enjoy the matching process regardless of whether the match was on her own card or not. Winning the game was not very important to M.

FIGURE 15.4   A Sample Anecdotal Record. In contrast to Figure 15.3, this anecdotal record is written by one teacher and focuses on a single activity of one child. It also includes a brief interpretation relating the child's actions to developmental areas such as visual perception skills and social skills. *Source: Marjorie Kostelnik, Professor and Acting Chairperson, Department of Family and Child Ecology, Michigan State University.*

in this section. Children's portfolios may stay with them through high school.

To introduce the idea of portfolios to preschoolers, show different kinds of portfolios, so that children understand the concept of a portfolio as a collection of someone's work. For example, you might invite a parent who is an artist, a photographer, or a designer to come in and show his or her portfolio to the class. Make sure that the parent talks about how and why the pieces of work in the portfolio were chosen. Another idea is to ask children to share any collection they might have, such as dolls or miniature cars. It is helpful for the collection to have at least five items. The point is to focus children's attention on why the items in a collection are important and have value to the owner.

The teacher also contributes to the preschooler's portfolio. *Anecdotal records* are narrative notes about children's behaviors, usually taken during informal observation. A simple means of recording this information is on

TABLE 15.2
Examples of portfolio elements

Area of Focus	Elements
Creativity and Spatial Relations	Assess drawings, easel paintings, and/or block structures. See the discussion of developmental stages in drawing in Chapter 13 and stages of block play in Chapter 10.
Literacy	Write down the title of one of a child's favorite books. Ask the child who is her favorite character, and ask her to draw the character. Create an open-ended question related to the story to stimulate creative thinking. Include unedited samples of the child's experimentation with writing, stories created by the child and dictated to you, and a record of the child's ability to retell a story at two or three different points in the year.
Expressiveness	Show the child a detailed illustration, such as a picture of several children playing in the park. Ask the child to describe the picture. Some children may name objects, others may be more descriptive.
Physical Development	You may measure progress in the development of fundamental gross motor skills—such as hopping on one foot, walking along a low board, and catching a ball with two hands—at two separate points in the year, such as November and May.
Self-awareness	Ask the child to draw a self-portrait at the beginning of the year and at the end of the year.
Various Curricular Areas	Look for "notable moments" in the child's activities—such as completion of a block structure the child has worked on for a long time or a creative solution to a problem. Write down a description of the notable moment. Attach a photograph, if possible.
Involving Children	When a child decides that something he has created should be included in his portfolio, you might ask him to finish the sentence, "I like this because . . ." or "I chose this because . . ." Write down the answer, and clip it to the item.
Involving Parents	You might send a letter home that says "Let me tell you about my child!" at the top, and that asks parents to describe some aspect of their child's behavior or personality at home—such as showing a sense of humor or showing care for another person.
Summary Card	At the end of the year, create a short document that summarizes progress achieved, and strengths and weaknesses in the various developmental domains.

index cards or notepaper, placed in a folder or a binder, one for each child in your class. Besides notes on behaviors and actions, anecdotal records also may contain hypotheses about the meaning of those behaviors. This information will help you develop appropriate objectives for each child and track progress and milestones reached.

A Sample Checklist

Date: 11/29/92

Teacher: Mrs. Gonzalez

	Robert	Joanna	Jerry	Larue	Donna	Gavin	Laura	Paul	Rosalie	William
Knows telephone number	✓			✓	✓	✓		✓	✓	
Can give full address	✓			✓	✓					
Buttons with no help	✓	✓		✓	✓	✓	✓	✓	✓	✓
Zips	✓			✓	✓		✓			✓
Can tie shoes	✓			✓		✓				
Puts materials away without being reminded	✓		✓	✓					✓	
Follows directions	✓		✓	✓	✓	✓			✓	
Cleans up after self	✓			✓					✓	
Asks for help when needed	✓			✓						

FIGURE 15.5   A Sample Checklist. Checklists like this one are often used in portfolio assessment. Checklists can track progress in a variety of developmental areas for an individual child or for a group of children. *Source: Kostelnik, M. J., Soderman, A. K., & Whiren, A. P. (1993). Developmentally appropriate programs in early childhood education.* New York: Macmillan.

Another way of tracking children's progress is with checklists. Checklists can be developed to track a particular aspect of development or behavior. Designed to match specific objectives, they provide an excellent way of determining whether educational objectives have been met. A checklist can be a list of anything the teacher believes is important—curricular activities, individual behaviors, or various skills, for example. Checklists enable the teacher to note each child's participation behavior, skill achievement, and other progress. See Figure 15.5 for an example of a checklist. See Table 15.2

for examples of other informal assessments that might be included in a preschooler's portfolio.

The information gained from alternative assessment methods can help you monitor each child's progress over time in various curriculum areas. It also is helpful in identifying children with delayed development or children who excel in a particular area. This information can be used to make program changes for each child as needed and for the class as a whole.

CHAPTER 15 REVIEW

SUMMARY

- Piaget believed that six- to eight-year-old children shift from the preoperational stage of cognitive development to the concrete operations stage. They are better able to think symbolically, to mentally reverse physical actions, to see others' points of view, and to act on more than one variable in a task simultaneously.

- Sociohistorical theory attempts to show how thinking is shaped by social interactions of children with peers and adults.

- The information processing view of cognitive development likens the process of thinking to the functioning of a computer.

- The primary-school years are an important time for social and emotional development. Children's positive relationships and friendships with peers promote the development of feelings of self-esteem and competence.

- The whole child approach reflects the belief that young children ages six to nine learn in different ways from older children ages nine to twelve and upward. Young children learn through the interaction of all developmental domains—physical, emotional, social, cognitive, and creative. They learn through their senses, through explorations, through play, and through interaction with others.

- The whole child approach stresses the process of learning rather than the products of learning.

- A learning style refers to the way the child processes information and learns from it. Learning styles vary among children as well as among adults.

- An integrated curriculum focuses on creative thinking, or "learning how to learn," rather than on acquiring compartmentalized knowledge about specific or predetermined subjects.

- The teacher plays a vital role in setting the stage for an integrated curriculum. The teacher acts as a guide to the learning process rather than as an imparter of knowledge.

- Theme-based activities and self-directed learning centers are two ways of implementing an integrated curriculum.
- Most teachers conduct frequent assessments of their students. In the primary grades, evaluation often involves formal testing for purposes of placement, curriculum planning, and special-needs assessment.
- To be useful, tests should be both reliable and valid and related to what is being taught.
- Several categories of standardized tests are used in primary grades, including developmental screening tests, intelligence tests, and readiness tests.
- Alternate assessment methods are being developed to more closely reflect a child's developmental progress.
- Alternative assessment methods include performance assessment and portfolio assessment.
- Performance assessment is an observation-based assessment in which teachers observe and document how children in the classroom interact with their peers and with materials.
- Portfolio assessment involves a collection of children's work that is gathered over time for the purpose of measuring development and progress and for shaping the curriculum to meet individual and group needs and interests.

ACQUIRING KNOWLEDGE

1. How did Piaget believe that a child's cognitive abilities develop between the ages of six and eight?
2. How is the concept of reversibility related to cognitive development?
3. How does the sociohistorical perspective differ from Piagetian theory?
4. To what is cognitive development commonly compared from the information processing perspective?
5. How does the information processing perspective apply to short- and long-term memory?
6. What social skills do children typically develop during the early years of primary school?
7. How can a preschool teacher support a child's moral development?
8. How does a whole child approach differ from an academic curriculum?
9. Why is the process of learning so important in a whole child approach?
10. Does the theory of holistic learning support activities that include physical components? Why or why not?
11. Why are small-group activities common in the whole child approach?
12. Describe three different learning styles.
13. What is a primary goal of an integrated curriculum?
14. What is the role of the teacher in an integrated curriculum?
15. What are two ways an integrated curriculum can be implemented?
16. How is placement different from assessment?

17. What two aspects of a test should be evaluated before it is used with children?
18. What are some appropriate uses for developmental screening tests?
19. What does an intelligence test assess? Name one purpose for which this type of test often is used.
20. How should readiness tests be used?
21. What type of assessment is based primarily on teacher observation?
22. What is a portfolio? In what way do portfolios offer an alternative to traditional testing?
23. How can portfolios help children take responsibility for their own learning?
24. What activities might a preschool use to introduce the idea of portfolios to young children?
25. What purpose do anecdotal records serve in a portfolio?

THINKING CRITICALLY

1. Piaget's theories suggest that children develop cognitive abilities through their interaction with their surroundings. Do you think that Piaget would advocate the use of an integrated curriculum? Why or why not?
2. Development screening tests and readiness tests should not be used for placement purposes. What assessment tools do you think might be useful when determining placement?
3. Intelligence tests are a requirement of many school systems. Do you think that these tests should be required? Do you think that children should be told the results of their own tests?
4. Theme-based projects are most successful when they grow out of children's interests. Suggest one theme on which a preschool group might develop a series of activities. Explain why you think that this theme might work in a preschool setting.
5. Portfolios require a commitment from teachers, administrators, and parents. They are not as easy to maintain or analyze as standardized tests. What do you think are some benefits of portfolios that have persuaded many schools to use this alternative form of assessment?

OBSERVATIONS AND APPLICATIONS

1. Look for examples of activities that reflect the whole child approach to learning in a preschool group. Observe and describe specific aspects (materials, actions, dialogue) of an activity that combines two or more of the following elements: language skills, gross or fine motor skills, emotional or social skills, cognitive skills, and creative skills.
2. Look for examples of an integrated curriculum in a kindergarten class in a public or private elementary school. Describe in what ways related activities throughout the classroom help the children explore one theme from many different aspects—for example, through books, art, science, mathematics, creative movement, or dramatic play. Is there a learning

center dedicated to the theme? Observe the interaction between the teacher and the students. Does the teacher pose questions that encourage the children to consider implications or alternatives rather than just facts?

3. Sandy is a seven-year-old girl in first grade. She can do simple addition problems in her head and can solve other number-oriented problems, such as how to divide two apples among three people. She sometimes questions classroom rules—even though she is generally well behaved. In terms of the Piagetian perspective of cognitive development, how might you classify Sandy? Would you say that Sandy reached this stage at an appropriate age, or was she early or late?

4. During a parent conference toward the end of the year, Brian's mother questions you about the preschool's portfolio assessment process. She tells you that she is worried that the more formal assessment methods being used in her older son's elementary school might make it more difficult for Brian to show his achievements. You know that the local elementary school uses alternative assessment methods in addition to some standardized tests. What might you tell Brian's mother to alleviate her concerns?

FOR FURTHER INFORMATION

Beaty, J. J. (1990). *Observing development of the young child* (2nd ed.). Columbus, OH: Merrill.

Brewer, J. A. (1992). *Early childhood education through the primary years.* Boston: Allyn & Bacon.

Carbo, M. (1986). *Teaching students to read through their individual learning styles* (rev. ed.). Englewood Cliffs, NJ: Prentice Hall.

Dunn, R. & Dunn, K. (1992). *Teaching elementary students through their individual learning styles: A practical approach.* Boston: Allyn & Bacon.

Dunn, R., Dunn, K., & Price, G. E. (1981). *Learning style manual.* Lawrence, KS: Price Systems.

Goodwin, W. L., & Driscoll, L. A. (1980). *Handbook for measurement and evaluation in early childhood education.* San Francisco: Jossey-Bass.

Kamii, C. (1990). *Achievement testing in the early grades: The games grown-ups play.* Washington, DC: National Association for the Education of Young Children.

McCracken, J. B. (1993). *Valuing diversity: The primary years.* Washington, DC: National Association for the Education of Young Children.

Meisels, S. J. (1987). Uses and abuses of developmental screening and school readiness testing. *Young Children, 42*(2), 4–6, 68–73.

Tierney, R. J. (1991). *Portfolio assessment in reading-writing classrooms.* Norwood, MA: Christopher-Gordon.

Appendix A
Child Development Stages in the Preschool Years

Table 1

Chart of normal development: 24–36 months (two-year-olds)

Areas of Development	Tasks	
Gross Motor Skills	• Runs forward well • Jumps in place, with two feet together • Stands on one foot, with aid	• Walks on tiptoe • Kicks ball forward
Fine Motor Skills	• Strings four large beads; snips with scissors • Turns pages singly • Holds crayons with thumb and fingers, not flat • Uses one hand consistently in most activities	• Imitates circular, vertical, horizontal strokes • Paints with some wrist action; makes dots, lines, circular strokes • Rolls, pounds, squeezes, and pulls clay
Understanding Language	• Points to pictures of common objects when they are named • Can identify objects when told their use • Understands question forms *what* and *where*	• Understands negatives *no, not, can't,* and *don't* • Enjoys listening to simple storybooks
Spoken Language	• Joins vocabulary words together in two-word phrases • Gives first and last name	• Asks *what* and *where* questions • Makes negative statements (such as *Can't open it*) • Shows frustration at not being understood
Cognitive Skills	• Responds to simple directions (such as *Give me the ball and the block, Get your shoes and socks*) • Selects and looks at picture books, names pictures and objects, identifies several objects within one picture • Matches and uses associated objects (for example, given cup, saucer, and bead, puts cup and saucer together) • Stacks rings on peg in order of size • Recognizes self in mirror, saying, *baby,* or own name	• Can talk briefly about what he or she is doing • Imitates adult action (as in housekeeping play) • Has limited attention span; learning is through exploration and adult direction (as in reading of picture stories) • Is beginning to understand functional concepts of familiar objects (for example, that a spoon is used for eating) and part/whole concepts (such as parts of the body)
Self-Help Skills	• Uses spoon, with little spilling • Gets drink from fountain or faucet unassisted	• Opens door by turning handle • Takes off coat; puts on coat with assistance • Washes and dries hands with assistance
Social Skills	• Plays near other children, joins briefly in their play • Defends own possessions	• Symbolically uses objects, self in play • Participates in simple group activity • Knows gender identity

Table 2

Chart of normal development: 36–48 months (three-year-olds)

Areas of Development	Tasks	
Gross Motor Skills	• Runs around obstacles • Walks on a line • Balances on one foot for five to ten seconds • Hops on one foot • Pushes, pulls, steers wheeled toys • Rides (that is, steers and pedals) tricycle	• Uses slide without assistance • Jumps over 6"-high object, landing on both feet • Throws ball overhead • Catches ball bounced to him or her
Fine Motor Skills	• Builds tower of nine small blocks • Drives nails and pegs	• Copies circle; imitates cross • Manipulates clay materials
Understanding Language	• Begins to understand sentences involving time concepts (such as *We are going to the zoo tomorrow*) • Understands size comparatives, such as *big* and *bigger*	• Understands relationships expressed by *if. . . then* or *because* sentences • Carries out a series of two to four related directions • Understands when told *Let's pretend*
Spoken Language	• Talks in sentences of three or more words, which take the form agent-action-object (such as *I see the ball*) or agent-action-location (*Daddy sit on chair*) • Tells about past experiences • Uses *s* on nouns to indicate plurals	• Uses *ed* on verbs to indicate past tense • Refers to self using pronouns *I* or *me* • Repeats at least one nursery rhyme and can sing a song • Speech is understandable to strangers, but there are still some sound errors
Cognitive Skills	• Recognizes and matches six colors • Intentionally stacks blocks or rings in order of size • Draws somewhat recognizable picture that is meaningful to child, if not to adult; briefly explains picture • Asks questions for information (*why* and *how*) • Knows own age; knows own last name	• Has short attention span; learns through observing and imitating adults, and by adult instruction and explanation; is very easily distracted • Has increased understanding of concepts of the functions and groupings of objects and part/whole • Begins to be aware of past and present
Self-Help Skills	• Pours well from small pitcher • Spreads soft butter with knife • Buttons and unbuttons large buttons	• Washes hands unassisted; blows nose when reminded • Uses toilet independently
Social Skills	• Joins in play with other children; begins to interact • Shares toys; takes turns with assistance	• Begins dramatic play, acting out whole scenes (such as traveling, playing house, pretending to be animals)

Appendix A: continued

Table 3

Chart of normal development: 48–60 months (four-year-olds)

Areas of Development	Tasks	
Gross Motor Skills	• Walks backward toe-heel • Jumps forward 10 times, without falling	• Walks up and down stairs alone, alternating feet • Turns somersault
Fine Motor Skills	• Cuts on line continuously • Copies cross	• Copies square • Prints a few capital letters
Understanding Language	• Follows three unrelated commands in proper order • Understands comparatives and superlatives like *pretty, prettier,* and *prettiest* • Listens to long stories but often misinterprets facts	• Incorporates verbal directions into play activities • Understands sequencing of events when told them (such as *First we have to go to the store, then we can make the cake*)
Spoken Language	• Asks *when, how,* and *why* questions • Uses modals like *can, will, shall, should, might* • Joins thoughts together (such as *I like chocolate chip cookies and milk*)	• Talks about causality by using *because* and *so* • Tells the content of a story but may confuse facts
Cognitive Skills	• Plays with words (creates own rhyming words, says or makes up words having similar sounds) • Points to and names four to six colors • Matches pictures of familiar objects (such as apple, orange) • Draws a person with two to six recognizable parts, such as head, arms, legs; can name or match drawn parts to own body • Draws, names, and describes recognizable picture • Rote counts to five, imitating adults	• Knows own street and town • Has more extended attention span; learns through observing and listening to adults as well as through exploration; is easily distracted • Has increased understanding of concepts of function, time, part/whole relationships; function or use of objects may be stated in addition to names of objects • Time concepts are expanding; the child can talk about yesterday or last week (a long time ago), about today, and about what will happen tomorrow
Self-Help Skills	• Cuts "easy" foods with knife	• Laces shoes
Social Skills	• Plays and interacts with other children	• Dramatic play is closer to reality, with attention paid to detail, time, and space; plays dress-up

Source: Adapted from Healy, A., McAreavey, P., Saaz von Hippel, C., & Jones, S. H. (1978). *Mainstreaming preschoolers: Children with health impairments*. Washington, D.C.: U.S. Department of Health, Education, and Welfare, Office of Human Development Services, Administration for Children, Youth, and Families, Head Start Bureau.

Appendix B
Curriculum Themes

Theme teaching involves offering children an array of activities created around a central idea. Early childhood educators select such ideas, keeping in mind children's interests, their developmental capacities, and the family/community context in which children live and learn. Related activities are integrated into all aspects of the curriculum and take place within a concentrated time frame. This integration creates a common thread among activities that facilitates children's generalization of knowledge and skills from one experience to another. Preschool teachers who implement themes also will incorporate into their teaching the principles of developmentally appropriate practice as described throughout this volume. Such principles are the foundation on which effective theme teaching builds.

What follows is a list of thematic ideas for teachers of young children. Each theme is composed of several subthemes teachers might consider adopting. When choosing a theme for one's classroom, it is important to bear in mind these principles:

1. Select a theme that is relevant to the children in your group. Themes are relevant when the concepts they represent are tied directly to children's real-life experiences and build on their interests. Such units highlight concepts with which children are already somewhat familiar and expand their understanding of life around them.

2. Choose themes that easily lend themselves to the development of hands-on activities. Only units whose content children can experience through the direct manipulation of objects are suitable for children in the early childhood period. Also make sure that the themes you select can be addressed in a variety of ways—through art and music activities, language lessons, physical development experiences, cognitive activities, pretend play, and construction experiences. Themes that lend themselves to only one activity type, such as arts and crafts, are too narrow to promote children's conceptual understanding and should be rejected in favor of other topics for which a broader activity base can be developed.

3. During the course of the year, it is desirable for children to experience a broad array of themes. Choose a cross section of topics that represent diversity across the curriculum. That is, select some mathematics-based topics, some language arts-focused ideas, some science units, and some social studies-based themes.

Animals
Mammals
Reptiles and Amphibians
Fish
Insects
Birds

Art and Artists
Visual Arts
Performing Arts
Usable Arts

Bears
Storybook Bears
Teddy Bears

Bears in Nature

The Body
Body Parts
The Senses
Caring for the Body
Bodies in Motion

Backyard Animals
Spiders
Worms
Frogs and Toads

Books
General Information
  about Books

How Books Are Created
  and Produced
Caring for and about
  Books
Libraries and Bookstores

Cats
General Information
  about Cats
Domestic Cats
Wild Cats

Classroom Animals
Rabbits
Fish

Guinea Pigs, Gerbils, and
  Hamsters

**Changes in People's
Lives**
Growing Older
Moving
Family Changes

Clothing
Dressing and Self-Help
  Skills
Functions and Uses of
  Clothing
Origins of Clothing
  Materials

Communication
Communication between Individuals
Community Communication (Newspapers, Magazines, and TV)
Communication, Machines and Tools

Dinosaurs
Dinosaur Characteristics
Dinosaur Behavior
The Time of the Dinosaurs
Discovering Dinosaurs
Extinction

Dogs
Dogs as Pets
Working Dogs
Wild Dogs

Exploring Space
Stars, Planets, and Moons
Exploration (Astronomers and the Tools They Use)
Direct Space Exploration

Families
Family Members
Family Life
Family Traditions

Food
Food and Food Preparation
Where Food Comes From
How the Body Uses Food

Friends
Friends and Friendship
Making Friends
Getting Along with Friends

Foundations of Mathematical Understanding
Shapes
Parts and Wholes
Grouping, Ordering, and Patterning

Homes
People's Homes
Building Homes
Moving from One Home to Another

Insects
Flying Insects
Ground Insects
How Insects Eat
How Insects Communicate
Butterflies and Moths
Bees
Ants
Grasshoppers and Crickets

Lights
Natural Light
Artificial Light
How People Use Light

Machines
Simple Machines (Wheel, Lever, and Inclined Plane)
Complex Machines
Machines in Daily Life
Machines and Safety

Measuring
Measuring Weight
Measuring Linear Dimensions
Measuring Volume
Measuring Time

Music Makers
Music; General Information
Creating Musical Sounds
Making, Writing, and Responding to Music

Numbers and Numerals
General Exploration
Numbers and Numerals in Day-to-Day Living

Pets
Pet Selection
What Pets Need
Caring for Pets
Pets that Live on Land
Pets that Fly
Pets that Live on or in Water

Plants
Parts of Plants
Types of Plants
Plants as a Food Source
Plants as a Source of Clothing and Shelter
Plants in the Ecological Balance of Life

Rocks
Characteristics of Rocks
People and Rocks
Other Living Things and Rocks

Safety
Safety at Work and Play
Fire Safety
Personal Safety

Seasons
The Four Seasons
Temperature
Weather

Self-awareness
Myself
My Neighborhood
My School

The Sky
The Daytime Sky (Sun, Clouds, and Rainbows)
The Nighttime Sky (Stars, Moon, and Weather)

Stores
People in a Store
Products and Merchandise
Using Money in the Store

Storytelling
Story Types
Story Characters
Telling Stories
Story Preferences

Trees
Characteristics of Trees
Kinds of Trees
Uses of Trees

Water
Water and Its Properties
How People Use Water Each Day
How Animals and Plants Use Water

Vehicles
Types of Vehicles
Vehicles that Move on Roads
Vehicles that Move on Rails
Vehicles that Move through the Air

Wild Birds
Local Birds
Characteristics of Birds
Bird Behavior

Source: Courtesy of Marjorie Kostelnik, Professor and Acting Chairperson, Department of Family and Child Ecology, Michigan State University.

Daily Plans of Five Curriculum Approaches

Developmental Daily Plan for Four-Year-Olds with "Pets" Theme

8:30– 9:40   **Choice Activities.**   Children self-select from among the following activities:
Dramatic Play: Animal hospital
Sensory: Play dough, animal cookie cutters. Water table, sheared sheep's wool
Blocks: Blocks with plastic animal figures
Prereading/Prewriting: "Writing" (dictating) stories about pets
Art: Gluing shapes to make an animal
Fine Motor: "Lacing" yarn through holes along edges of precut rabbit shapes.

9:40– 9:45   **Cleanup.**

9:45–10:05   **Large Group.**   Calendar time; music and movement; introduction of pet rabbit, which has been brought in by one of the children; discussion of rabbit's needs.

10:05–10:25   **Snack and Transition.**   Children eat snack at tables, clean up themselves, and put on coats.

10:25–11:05   **Outside Play.**   Put pet rabbit in "fenced area" made from big wooden blocks. Teacher lets a few children at a time pet, brush, feed rabbit. (Different child each day will bring in a pet.) Outside equipment includes climbing equipment, tricycles, sidewalk chalk, and sandbox. If windy, activities may include dancing with crepe paper streamers.

11:05–11:25   **Story Time and Group Time.**   Teacher divides children into two groups. Teacher reads *The Velveteen Rabbit* to one group; assistant teacher reads *Rabbit's Loose Tooth* to the other group. Finish with group discussion of the stories and what the children did that day.

Academic Daily Plan for Four-Year-Olds with "Pets" Theme

8:30– 9:00   **Large Group Time.**   Calendar time, music, and movement; pictures of rabbits; discussion of rabbits and their needs; introduction of Triad Activities.

9:00–10:00   **Triad Activities.**   Teacher divides children into three groups, and each group moves from one activity to the next every 20 minutes.

9:00– 9:20   *1. Art:* Gluing shapes to make a rabbit.

9:20– 9:40   *2. Reading/Writing:* Writing the letters *R* and *r*. Finding toys that start with the *r* sound.

9:40– 10:00   *3. Math:* Using precut paper rabbits, matching the correct number of baby rabbits to the mother rabbits (each mother rabbit has a numeral from 1–10 written on her).

10:00–10:10   **Cleanup.**   Children clean up in the last activity where they played and put on coats.

10:10–10:30   **Outside Play.**   Equipment includes climbing equipment, sandbox, tricycles, sidewalk chalk.

10:30–10:45   **Snack.**   Children take off coats, wash hands, eat snack at assigned seat. Children clean up.

10:45–11:00   **Story Time.**   Teacher reads stories about rabbits, such as *The Velveteen Rabbit.*

11:00–11:20   **Free Play.**   Blocks; housekeeping corner; play dough with animal cookie cutters.

11:20–11:30   **Cleanup and Going Home.**   Children gather artwork, writing papers, and coats to go home. They line up for parents at the door.

Source: Courtesy of Jane Billman, Department of Human Development and Family Studies, University of Illinois at Urbana-Champaign.

Project Approach Daily Plan for Four-Year-Olds with "Making a Movie" Theme

The children will participate in a variety of activities over several days or weeks, leading to the eventual filming of a video. Rationale for movie theme: The children have been seeing a lot of movies with their families. They have been talking about the movies and acting out movie scenes in the dramatic play area.

8:30	**Arrival.**
8:30– 9:50	**Free-Choice Activities.** Children are free to choose from among the following activities; *Art:* Painting a movie poster *Dramatic Play:* Costume shop (a variety of dress-up clothes to suggest different roles) *Sensory:* Popcorn in pans with bowls and scoops *Small Motor:* Creating masks using paper plates, glitter, sequins, and feathers *Large Motor:* Trampoline, mats, and balance beams *Blocks:* Unit blocks with wooden people figures to suggest actors *Library:* Books about making movies, in addition to favorite stories *Woodworking:* Construction of the stage, backdrop, and props for the movie set *Language:* "Writing" a script for the movie *Science:* Creating colored lights for the stage (attaching colored cellophane to flashlights; experimenting with mixing colors on the stage) *"Always" art:* Free-choice art materials
9:50–10:00	**Cleanup.**
10:00–10:15	**Group Time.** Singing time, group discussion of plans for the movie, reading a book about how movies are made
10:15–10:20	**Handwashing prior to snack.**
10:20–10:30	**Snack.**
10:30–11:30	**Outside Free-Choice Activities.**

Source: Anne Lytle and Donna Morris, University of Illinois, Child Development Lab.

Montessori Daily Plan for Multi-Age Group with Afternoon Child Care

7:00	**School Opening.** Traditional preschool activities as the children arrive.
8:30– 9:00	**Children Proceeding to Classrooms.** Preparatory activities, such as browsing, care of the environment, and socializing, as the children gather for the day.
9:00–11:15	**"Work" Time.** Children choose self-directed activities from the various Montessori classroom areas as the teacher moves from child to child working with each on a one-on-one basis.

Practical Life Activities introduce the child to normal daily living experiences. These exercises assist the child in developing concentration, coordination, independence, and order. Exercises include activities that promote care of one's self, such as handwashing, and care of the environment, such as dusting and sweeping. They also include activities in the social graces, such as learning to offer assistance to a friend and safe travel through the classroom.

Sensorial Activities educate all the senses. By using these jobs, children learn to sort, order, and compare. Jobs include such activities as building a tower, matching smells, sorting colors, and working with puzzles. See Appendix D for an example lesson plan of a Sensorial Activity.

Cultural Studies Activities include art, music, social studies, and science activities with a hands-on process orientation.

Time for outside activity also is an option.

Snack is prepared by the children during this period and offered to one another (part of Practical Life Activities).

11:15–11:30	**Preparation for Lunch.** Table setting and handwashing.
11:30–12:00	**Lunch.**
12:00–12:30	**Lunch cleanup and preparation for resting and naps in napping area.**
12:30– 2:15	**Nap time for younger children; afternoon "work" time for older children who no longer nap.** Activities for older children may include learning number and letter concepts through hands-on manipulative materials.
2:15– 2:45	**Nappers returning to class as they wake up.**
2:45– 3:00	**Afternoon Work Closure and Group Time.**
3:00– 3:15	**Afternoon Snack.**
3:15– 6:00	**Afternoon child care activities as children wait for their parents to pick them up.** Activities may include traditional games, creative movement, stories, art, and so on.
6:00	**School Closing.**

Source: Cheryll R. Ruszat, Executive Director, Montessori Schools of Irvine, Irvine, California.

Appendix C: continued

High/Scope Daily Plan for Four-Year-Olds

7:00– 8:30	**Breakfast/Quiet Activity.**	Books, play dough, puzzles.
8:30– 8:45	**Cleanup.**	
8:45– 9:30	**Gym/Outside Play.**	Half organized, half free play.
9:30– 9:45	**Snack.**	
9:45–10:00	**Small-Group Activity.**	Uses key experiences.

10:00–11:45 **Small-Group Planning/Work Time/Cleanup/Recall Time.**   Children choose their own activities during this time, using the High/Scope Plan-Do-Review process.

11:45–12:00 **Lunch.**

12:00–12:15 **Circle Time/Movement Activity/Story.**

12:15– 1:00 **Outside Play.**

1:00– 1:15 **Inside/Bathroom Time.**

1:15– 2:30 **Rest.**   For long sleepers.

1:15– 1:45 **Quiet Shelf.**   For short resters or those children who no longer need a nap.

1:45– 2:00 **Quiet Shelf Cleanup.**

2:00– 2:30 **Short Resters Time.**   Children go to their cots. (By law, in Michigan, even children who no longer need a nap are required to rest quietly for ½ hour.)

2:30– 2:45 **Rise and Shine.**   Transition time—finger plays, small-group activities, and so on, as children wake up on their own.

2:45– 3:15 **Gym or Quiet Activity.**   Children may choose.

3:15– 3:30 **Small-Group Language Activity.**   Uses key experiences.

3:30– 3:45 **Snack.**

3:45– 6:00 **Free-Choice or Outside Play.**   Activities might include a walk in the neighborhood with a teacher or teacher's assistant, a cooking activity such as making snack for the following day, visiting siblings in another room (this school offers after-school care up to 6th grade), cleanup duty (such as kitchen or outdoor storage shed), sledding or running through the sprinkler (depending on season), story reading or storytelling, and so on. The teachers find out what the children want to do during this time. Children are picked up between 4:00 and 6:00. They must clean up whatever activity they are doing before leaving the preschool.

Source: Cathy Albro, Executive Director, the creative learning center, Grand Rapids, Michigan.

Activity Plan: Developmental Model and Play Dough Pizza

Name: *Marguerite Lanza*   **Date to be implemented:** *October 10*

Activity Title: *Making Play Dough "Pizza"*

Developmental Area(s): *Social, fine motor, cognitive*   **Curriculum Area(s):** *Cooking, sensory*

Objectives: *Social:* Children will work together cooperatively to make large "pizzas." They will share materials, space, and the common goal of making the "pizza."

Fine Motor: Children will use fine motor skills to roll, pinch, and stretch play dough for the "pizza."

Cognitive: Children will plan how to make a "pizza" using sequencing, decision-making, and memory skills.

Materials: 2 large pizza pans; Play dough in the following colors: white (for dough and cheese), red (for pizza sauce), brown (for meat), green (for peppers); 5 rolling pins; 5 smocks

Procedure:
1. Setup. Before the children arrive at the activity, place one smock and one rolling pin at each chair. Place the pizza pans and play dough in the middle of the table.
2. Motivation. Two of the children in your group have been playing superheroes often, and it has been hard for you to get them to play at table games. You know that they love to eat pizza. Say to them, "You could make some of the superheroes' favorite food!"
3. Process. Explain that the children will work together to make a "pizza." Ask what ingredients are needed to make a pizza. Help the children decide what colors of play dough could be used for each pizza ingredient. Then have the children decide in what order (sequence) the ingredients should be used. They will work together to place the sauce on the "pizza." The children will decide how to make the cheese and place it on the "pizza." The children will decide if and how much meat and green peppers should be added. If you know that one child in the group is allergic to cheese, for example, you might ask the children if anyone is allergic to cheese and what they should do about this.
4. Variation. The children could vary the ingredients used or make a "giant cookie," instead of a "pizza."
5. Closure. After making the "pizza," the children could cut it up and pretend to eat it, or pretend to bake it in the oven in the housekeeping corner. Then they will clean up the table and pans, just as if they actually had been cooking.

No. of Children: *5*   **Location in Room:** *Table near the sink*

Limits: Keep all materials at the table.

Safety Factors: Keep "food" out of the children's mouths.

Appendix D: continued

Activity Plan: Montessori Model

There is a "lesson plan" for each activity within the Montessori curriculum, with variations and extensions to vary the work according to the specific and individualized needs of the child.

Name of Activity:	Each "work" or activity should have its own name. This facilitates communication when an activity is being referred to.
Materials:	List anything that is necessary for the successful assembly and completion of an exercise.
Direct Aim:	This is the immediate goal for the child.
Indirect Aim:	This includes the benefits derived from the exercise, which will aid the future learning processes for the child.
Indirect Preparation:	This includes those activities which must precede the exercise described in the lesson plan. Success sometimes requires specific developmental abilities or prior experience with easier activities.
Presentation:	This is a numbered, step-by-step description of the teacher's first demonstration to the child. Conservation of language—that is, using only the specific language needed for concept understanding—is used to help the child concentrate his or her attention on the activity being presented. Appropriate language is important.
Points of Interest:	These are the elements of the activity that make it attractive to the child. Also include elements of the activity that will help hold the child's attention so that the child wants to work with the material in progressive phases toward new conceptual understanding.
Control of Error:	This includes built-in safeguards or hints that assist the child in completing the activity successfully or in self-correction. The purpose is to free the child from needing constant teacher correction and assistance.
Language:	This includes the new words introduced that are pertinent to the activity.
Variations:	After the child has successfully done the exercise, variations help the child adapt the activity creatively. Vary the original lesson plan here.
Extensions:	These are more advanced variations that can be presented to the child and that will lead the child logically to new activities.
Age:	This is the suggested developmentally appropriate age range for this activity.

Tower of Cubes Activity Using Montessori Model

Name of Activity: Pink Tower/Tower of Cubes (Sensorial Activity/Visual)

Materials:
1. Ten wooden cubes, painted pink. Their sizes progress sequentially from 1 cubic centimeter (often referred to as "Tiny Tim" or the "baby" pink tower), 2 cubic centimeters, 3 cubic centimeters, and so on up to 10 cubic centimeters.

Direct Aims:
1. To improve visual discrimination of differences in dimension.
2. To advance muscular control of hand and arm.
3. To introduce seriation.

Indirect Aims:
1. To educate the voluntary movement.
2. To prepare the hands for the movements of grasping, gripping, and stretching.
3. To develop a sense of relative sizes.
4. Preparation for the mathematical mind.
5. Preparation for the concepts of volume, cubing, and so on.

Presentation:
1. Invite the child.
2. Carry and unroll a rug on the floor.
3. Take the child to the location of the pink tower.
4. Take the cubes one by one from the tower to the rug. Note: To carry the two smallest cubes, remove them with the right hand, place them in the palm of the left hand, and cup the right hand over the left in a protective way. The next cubes are lifted by stretching the right hand over the cube to lift it and carry it, with the left hand holding the cube from underneath, for additional support.
5. Walk to the rug; place the smallest cube on the rug, starting on the lower left side. Place the next pieces above the previous pieces and up the left edge of the rug in sequence.
6. Sit down on the rug, and look over the cubes to select the largest cube.
7. Place the largest cube in the center of the rug. This is the base cube for the tower.
8. Select the second largest cube in the sequence, and place it on top of the largest cube, aligning one side of the cube with the previous cube. In other words, one side is flush, and the other three sides have a small, even edge showing (step effect).
9. Continue selecting, placing, and aligning the remaining cubes until the tower is built.
10. Using the smallest cube from the top of the tower, show the child how the cube fits exactly on the exposed "step" edges.
11. Return the cube to the top of the tower.
12. Disassemble the tower by taking the top smallest cube and placing it at the top left of the rug. Continue taking the next cube and placing it on the rug under the smallest until all cubes are placed on the rug.
13. Select the largest cube with two hands, carry back to location where cubes are kept.

14. Repeat the same procedure, replacing all cubes until the tower is "built" back in the previous location. Note: To keep the smallest cube from being lost, place it in a special container. The child may ask for the container when needed, or you might keep the special container with the tower so that the child is aware of the special place for the smallest cube.

Points of Interest:	**1.** Carrying and placing the blocks properly. **2.** Volume of the cube.
Control of Error:	**1.** Visual disharmony **2.** Blocks falling
Language:	**1.** Pink **2.** Cube **3.** Tower **4.** Small/smaller/smallest **5.** Large/larger/largest **6.** Middle
Variations:	**1.** Change the shelf storage arrangement of the material. For example, place the tower horizontally, or place the cubes in a basket. **2.** Build the tower horizontally.

Extensions: (for children ages four to five)

(Preparation for extensions: The child must have worked successfully with the pink tower.)

Extension I:	**1.** Have the child build the pink tower vertically. **2.** Ask the child to think of another way to build it, and allow the child to try several ways.
Extension II: Distance Game	**1.** Place the pink cubes in a random array on one rug. **2.** Take the largest cube to another rug. **3.** Ask the child to bring you the cube that is the next largest. **4.** Repeat the request, building the tower as the child brings you the cubes.
Extension III: Visual Memory Game	**1.** Have the child build the tower vertically. **2.** Ask the child to close the eyes. **3.** Remove one of the cubes, leaving the tower intact, and place the cube behind you. **4.** Ask the child to look and tell you which cube is missing. **5.** Replace the cube, and repeat the game as many times as the child wishes to.
Age:	2 ½–5, depending on extensions.

Source: Cheryll R. Ruszat, Executive Director, Montessori Schools of Irvine, Irvine, California.

Activity Plan: Theme Planning Model with "Friends" Theme

Curriculum Domain	Monday	Tuesday	Wednesday	Thursday	Friday
Aesthetics	Rainbow Song	Junk Art	Song: "If You're Friendly . . ."	Friendly Hands Mural	Beautiful Letters
Affective	Small Groups: A Tour of My School				These are MY Initials
	Independent Computer Use				
Cognition	Small Groups: Pattern Block Walls				
	What's in the Square?	Shadow Box		Broken Hearts	Sink/Float
Construction	Bolt and Play Constructions				Woodworking
	Build Structures to Save				
Language	Class Surveys	Big Book: *Why Can't I Fly?*	My Friend Is. . .	Notes to the Custodian	Story: *Peter's Pocket*
Physical	Small Groups: Cutting Activity				
	Stair Safety	FIRE DRILL		The Freeze	Musical Hoops
Pretend Play	THE RAINBOW POST OFFICE				
Social	Work Together to Create Rainbow	My Friend Likes . . .	Cooperative Color Mixing	Trace a Friend's Hand	Play a Game with Friends
Large-Group Focus	Doll Talk: "I Want to Play"	Helping	Safe at School	Friendly Touches	Group Cooperation
Red Group	Sharing Day	Pattern Block Wall	Cutting Activity	School Tour	LIBRARY DAY
Yellow Group	School Tour	Sharing Day	Pattern Block Wall	Cutting Activity	Please
Green Group	Cutting Activity	School Tour	Sharing Day	Pattern Block Wall	return
Blue Group	Pattern Block Wall	Cutting Activity	School Tour	Sharing Day	books
	Sharing Day Item: Something that Starts with a *K*				

Source: Donna Howe, Child Development Laboratories, Department of Family and Child Ecology, Michigan State University, East Lansing, MI.

Activity Plan: High/Scope Model

Small-Group Time-Planning Sheet: Comparing

Key Experience:	Comparing. Which one is longer/shorter?
Activity:	Stringing straws on yarn.
Materials:	Straws precut into different lengths.
	Different lengths of yarn—one end should be knotted, and the other end wrapped with masking tape.
Procedure:	*Beginning*. Give each child a container with precut straws. Ask the children to tell you what they notice about the materials. Refer children to one another. For example, "David, Mary said she has a long straw in her container. Do you have a long straw, too?" After a few minutes, pass out the yarn for stringing.
	Middle. While children are stringing (some may choose to simply make designs on the table with the straws), talk with them about what they are doing. "I'm going to put a short straw on first, and then I'm going to put a long straw on next. How are you going to do yours?" Make comparisons about the length of the strings also. "If you wanted to wear it as a bracelet, which size string would you use—a short one or a long one?"
	End. Encourage children to talk about what they did and to make comparisons with the other children. "Frankie, do you think your necklace is as long as Cecelia's, or do you think it's shorter? Ask them to put any extra straw pieces away in containers by length.
Observations and Assessments:	Note children who identify the materials as *straws*.
	Notice children who use the language *long* and *short*.
	Observe children who sort in appropriate containers.
Extensions and Follow-Ups:	Add materials to art or quiet area.
	Play a game at outdoor time using long and short steps.

Source: Cathy Albro, Executive Director, the creative learning center, Grand Rapids, Michigan.

Activity Plan: Curriculum Web Model

Curriculum Web: Water

Activity Title: Sounds of the Rain

Learning Center: Art/Writing

"The lightning."

Learner Outcomes: Developing representational thought.
Participating in sensory learning.

Objective: Children will imitate actions and sounds.
Children will describe objects and events.

Materials: Tape of rain or thunderstorms
Gray, white, and black paint
Paper
Easels
Markers
Pencils

"The rain is hitting the puddles."

Motivation and Procedures: Begin by doing the following activity to make the sound of rain. Children should sit quietly in a large circle. Demonstrate "making rain" using the following technique: rub hands gently, snap fingers, slap hands on thighs, continue slapping hands on thighs and stamp feet, return to slapping hands on thighs, snap fingers, rub hands, stop all movement. Let children participate by following the same sequence. A more complicated activity involves the children's following the teacher's cue as he or she walks around inside the circle of children creating sounds. After the children have created their rainstorm, play the tape or listen to the rain outdoors. Compare the sounds. Allow children to choose a method for symbolizing the sounds of the rain. Record their language.

Key Questions: What does rain sound like?
What does thunder sound like?
How does it sound falling on an umbrella? On a car roof?
How could you draw that sound?

Language to Use: Rain, sprinkle, drizzle, storm, thunder

Adaptations/ Extensions: Follow up by playing parts of Beethoven's *Pastoral Symphony* and talking about what might be happening.

Source: "Curriculum Web: Water" from *Myself and My Surroundings: An Early Childhood Curriculum Resource* by S. Workman, S. Bradley, S. Nipper, and D. Workman (1991). San Juan College, Farmington, MN.

Glossary

A

academic approach   An approach to curriculum content in which the majority of activities are specifically designed to help children develop the skills they will need in grade school, such as reading and writing. [Ch. 2]

academic objective   An objective that focuses on mastering a skill, which will help children learn academic subjects in grade school. [Ch. 6]

activity area   In developmentally oriented preschools, the term used to describe a section of the classroom where specific types of activities are carried out. [Ch. 5]

adventure playground   A play area that is equipped with several large boxes, large wooden spools, tires, barrels, boards, and crates that children can manipulate in many different ways. [Ch. 5]

aesthetics   Elements that contribute to the appearance and atmosphere of a physical environment. [Ch. 5]

amblyopia   A visual problem in which a person has weak eye muscles that make an eye difficult to control. [Ch. 10]

analysis question   A question that focuses on solving a problem by examining its parts. [Ch. 12]

anecdotal record   Narrative notes about children's behaviors, usually taken by the teacher during informal observation. [Ch. 15]

anti-bias curriculum   A curriculum approach designed to promote positive attitudes in young children toward themselves and toward other people based on gender, race, differing abilities, and culture. [Ch. 3]

associative play   According to Parten, a type of play in which children play together in a similar but loosely organized manner. [Ch. 4]

attitude   A person's feeling, belief, and/or opinion about himself, herself, or others. [Ch. 3]

auditory discrimination   The ability to hear and identify sounds. [Ch. 10]

autonomy   The ability to make choices and act on one's own. [Ch. 3]

autonomy versus shame and doubt   The second stage of Erikson's theory of psychosocial development, when children begin to assert their "separateness" from their primary caregivers. [Ch. 8]

B

behavioral objective   An objective that focuses on behavior that can be observed. [Ch. 6]

behaviorist theory   A leading theory of child development, which holds that a child develops and learns as a result of forces outside the child, such as external stimuli and praise by adults. [Ch. 2]

bibliotherapy   A teaching technique that involves reading books out loud about children who have learned how to deal with their emotions or difficult situations. [Ch. 8]

bilingual   Having the ability to speak and function in two different languages. [Ch. 11]

bimodal perception   See *sensory integration*. [Ch. 10]

body management skill   A physical skill, such as balancing, in which a person must handle or control the body but does not travel anywhere; also known as a *nonlocomotor skill.* [Ch. 7]

C

cephalocaudal principle   A pattern of physical development in which control over the head, shoulders, and trunk is acquired before control over the arms, legs, hands, and feet. [Ch. 7]

child care center   A type of child care facility that provides early educational experiences for young children, with a schedule that is geared toward working parents; also called a *day-care center.* [Ch. 1]

child-initiated curriculum   A curriculum approach in which children make choices about the activities they will do; based on the theory that children learn by exploring their environment and experimenting with objects rather than by being taught directly about them. [Ch. 2]

cognitive-developmental theory   A theory of child development, which states that children learn by interacting with their world. [Ch. 2]

competence   The ability to accomplish tasks and succeed at endeavors. [Ch. 8]

complex play unit   Play equipment that has two types of materials or parts that can be manipulated or used in different ways. [Ch. 5]

conservation   According to Piaget, the understanding that a given quantity does not change when its appearance changes. [Ch. 10]

constructive play   See *symbolic play*. [Ch. 4]

constructivist or process approach   A curriculum approach to early literacy in which teachers do not teach specific skills in a set sequence but rather provide curriculum activities that surround preschoolers with the spoken and written word. [Ch. 11]

contemporary playground   A play area consisting of one or more multiuse play structures. [Ch. 5]

controlled scribbling   W. Lambert Brittain's second developmental art stage, in which children gain mastery of the drawing tool and create more intricate patterns. [Ch. 13]

convergent question   A question that has a preconceived "right" answer. [Ch. 12]

cooperative play According to Parten, a type of play involving structured play within a group with a common purpose. [Ch. 4]

cooperative preschool   A private preschool in which parents cooperatively govern all facets of the school and also work as volunteers in order to control costs. [Ch. 1]

corporate child care center   A privately funded child care facility provided for the children of employees of a corporation, hospital, or large professional organization. [Ch. 1]

creativity   The ability to be original, to have new ideas, to create something that did not exist before, or to put things together in new ways. [Ch. 13]

culturally responsive curriculum   A curriculum approach in which the teacher devises activities that reflect various aspects of diverse cultures, notably the cultural backgrounds of the children in the class. [Ch. 11]

curriculum   In the preschool setting, the goals and plans to provide early educational experiences for young children. [Ch. 1]

curriculum web   An aspect of the project approach in which children's interests serve as a starting point from which different activities grow, with each activity relating to a central concept. [Ch. 2]

daily plan   A schedule of one day's activities, sometimes including the steps or materials needed for each activity, prepared by the teacher for children in a preschool setting. [Ch. 6]

design stage   Rhoda Kellogg's third developmental art stage, in which the child draws more elaborate shapes and begins to combine shapes. [Ch. 13]

developmental-interactionist theory   A theory of child development, which asserts that learning takes place not only through the interaction of children with their environment but also through interaction of the children's various "selves." [Ch. 2]

developmental motor pattern   An interim pattern of motor skill development combining several fundamental motor skills. [Ch. 7]

developmental objective   An objective that relates to one of the areas of development—physical, emotional, social, cognitive, or creative. [Ch. 6]

developmental screening test   A test that assesses those developmental abilities that are related to a child's current functioning and future success. [Ch. 15]

developmental task   An ability or a skill that children acquire or learn at various ages in different developmental domains, such as walking, feeling empathy, or matching similar objects. [Ch. 2]

developmental/whole child approach   An approach to curriculum content in which activities are designed to en courage development of the "whole child." [Ch. 2]

developmentally appropriate   Referring to a curriculum approach in which the activities are geared to the developmental level of the child. [Ch. 2]

developmentally at risk   Referring to a child whose language or motor skills are significantly below the norm. [Ch. 1]

disposition   A person's personality traits and tendencies to respond to situations or experiences in a certain way. [Ch. 3]

divergent thinking   Thinking that promotes imaginative reflection and the consideration of different options and solutions. [Ch. 12]

dramatic play   Play in which children use their imaginations to act out different roles, transforming themselves and objects to enact various real or imagined scenarios. [Ch. 4]

dramatist   A child who, during play, responds more to the symbolic potential of objects than to the realistic qualities or properties of objects. [Ch. 4]

E

early literacy   The language arts components of curricula that promote early forms of reading and writing by young children. [Ch. 11]

early representational stage   W. Lambert Brittain's fourth art stage, in which children have gained some skill in manipulating the material and are beginning to use it in a purposeful and creative way. [Ch. 13]

egocentrism   A personality characteristic in which a person is concerned primarily with his or her own needs and wants and has difficulty understanding a situation from another's point of view. [Ch. 8]

emergent literacy   A theory of learning, which asserts that learning to read and write involves a combination of social, linguistic, and psychological aspects and is not just a cognitive skill. [Ch. 11]

empathy   The ability to understand and relate to the feelings and viewpoints of others. [Ch. 8]

encouragement   Specific, sincere, direct, and informative praise that focuses on a person's persistence, effort, and increasing competence in performing a task; also known as *effective praise*. [Ch. 8]

exploratory stage   W. Lambert Brittain's first developmental art stage, in which children intently examine and manipulate the material, employing all their senses in doing so. [Ch. 13]

eye-hand coordination   A fine motor skill that requires coordinating what the hands do with what the eyes see. [Ch. 10]

F

family day care   A type of child care in which providers take care of small groups of children in their own homes. [Ch. 1]

finger play   A verbal and fine-motor activity that does not require music but uses the fingers to represent characters or movements to accompany songs and nursery rhymes. [Ch. 13]

formative decision   A decision about curriculum instruction, early on and during the school year, based on formal testing. [Ch. 15]

functional play   See *sensorimotor play*. [Ch. 4]

fundamental motor skill   A basic physical movement, such as running or jumping. [Ch. 7]

G

gender constancy   The understanding that gender identity remains the same forever. [Ch. 14]

gender identity   A person's biologically based identity—male or female. [Ch. 14]

global quality-assessment instrument   A set of standards formulated to help preschool directors evaluate their curricula, and facilities. [Ch. 5]

goal   In a preschool setting, one of the physical, intellectual, social, or emotional skills and behaviors that preschool teachers believe children should develop within a certain broad time period; also called a *broad objective*. [Ch. 6]

group home care   A type of family day care in which two or more providers care for 7 to 12 children in a home setting. [Ch. 1]

guided play   Play in which adults are directly involved. [Ch. 4]

H

hardness-softness factor   The balance of hard and soft surfaces in a classroom. [Ch. 5]

heterogeneous classroom   A classroom in which the children come from diverse backgrounds. [Ch. 9]

hierarchical learning   A theory of learning, which states that learning proceeds in stages. [Ch. 2]

High/Scope   A specialized curriculum approach that uses a predetermined set of "key experiences" to encourage children to learn through interaction with their environment. [Ch. 2]

holistic learning   The theory that young children learn through the interaction of a number of different, yet related processes; the theory behind the whole child approach to curriculum. [Ch. 15]

homogeneous classroom   A classroom in which the children come from a similar background; also known as a *monocultural classroom*. [Ch. 9]

hostile aggression   Purposeful physical or verbal behavior that is intended to hurt another person or to destroy property. [Ch. 9]

hygiene   The science of preventing the spread of diseases. [Ch. 7]

I

individual objective   An objective that is set for one child in the class; designed by the teacher for growth in physical, emotional, and social areas as well as in academic areas. [Ch. 6]

information processing theory   The view of cognitive development that likens thinking to the functioning of a computer. [Ch. 15]

initiative versus guilt   The third stage of Erikson's theory of psychosocial development, when children begin to develop a sense of responsibility and accomplishment. [Ch. 8]

instrumental aggression   Belligerent behavior that is intended to fulfill a specific goal. [Ch. 9]

integrated curriculum   The curriculum approach that focuses attention on the child and the learning process rather than on traditional subject areas. [Ch. 15]

intelligence test   A broad measure of a child's reasoning, memory, language skills, and perceptual-motor abilities as well as social awareness; also called an *IQ test* or an *individual intelligence test.* [Ch. 15]

interactionist/constructivist theory   A theory of language acquisition, which holds that language is learned in social settings and that children construct their own ideas about language as they interact with others in a meaningful context. [Ch. 11]

K

key experience   One of a preset group of experiences used in the High/Scope curriculum that is designed to stimulate teacher-child discussion and problem-solving tasks. [Ch. 2]

kinesthetic   Referring to a movement-oriented experience. [Ch. 13]

L

learning center   In academically oriented preschools, the term used to describe a section of the classroom where specific types of activities are carried out. [Ch. 5]

learning style   The way individual young children process information and experiences. [Ch. 15]

limited English proficiency (LEP)   Referring to a person who does not have a working understanding of English. [Ch. 11]

locomotor skill   A physical skill, such as walking, in which the body moves from one place to another. [Ch. 7]

long-term plan   A schedule comprising a week's or a month's worth of activities prepared by the teacher for children in a preschool setting; may focus on a theme or particular skills. [Ch. 6]

M

mandala   A sunburst pattern, one of the most recognizable of universal shapes that children draw. [Ch. 13]

manipulative   A malleable material, such as clay, play dough, Plasticine, or wet sand; also a material that promotes small-motor skill development, such as a peg board or a set of snap cubes. [Ch. 13]

manipulative skill   A physical skill that involves throwing or catching an item such as a ball; also known as *object control skill*. [Ch. 7]

maturationist theory   Arnold Gesell's theory of child development, which contends that children generally master the same skills and perform the same behaviors in the same sequence, but on their own timetable. [Ch. 2]

mature motor pattern   The highest level of motor skill development, which can be adapted to specific activities such as batting a baseball. [Ch. 7]

meta communications   The communications that children have about dramatic play to give it direction, such as negotiating or determining who will play what role. [Ch. 4]

monocultural classroom   See *homogeneous classroom*. [Ch. 9]

Montessori   A specialized curriculum approach in which the activities are academic in focus and are designed to develop independence, a sense of empowerment, and self-help in children. [Ch. 2]

multicultural curriculum   A curriculum approach designed to foster positive attitudes and respect for diverse cultures. [Ch. 3]

multisensory environment   In the preschool setting, surroundings that offer a variety of activities and materials that stimulate children's senses. [Ch. 10]

N

named scribbling   W. Lambert Brittain's third developmental art stage, in which children identify their own scribbling as standing for an object in real life. [Ch. 13]

narrative competence   The ability to create characters and their behaviors and language in the context of a particular situation. [Ch. 11]

nativist theory   A theory of language acquisition, which asserts that people are born with the ability to learn language. [Ch. 11]

negotiation   The process of moving from a problem toward a solution, requiring communication, compromise, the ability to see other points of view, and the ability to see how aspects of a conflict are related to one another. [Ch. 9]

nonlocomotor skill   See *body management skill*. [Ch. 7]

nonstandard English   A dialect of English that has its own structure and vocabulary. [Ch. 11]

O

object control skill   See *manipulative skill*. [Ch. 7]

objective   In a preschool setting, the written statement identifying a skill, behavior, or ability that a teacher wants a group of children or individual children to master or learn. [Ch. 6]

object permanence   The understanding that objects exist even if they are out of sight. [Ch. 2]

object substitution   The ability to transform, or substitute, one object for another in imaginative ways. [Ch. 4]

open-ended question   A question that does not have just one "right" answer; designed to stimulate the exploration of ideas and solutions. [Ch. 11]

ossification   The hardening of cartilage into bone. [Ch. 7]

P

parallel play   According to Parten, a type of play in which children play independently but are engaged in the same activity as other children near or beside them. [Ch. 4]

patterner   A child who, during play, responds more to the realistic qualities and properties of objects than to the symbolic potential of objects. [Ch. 4]

perceived competence   A person's own beliefs about his or her ability to succeed at particular tasks. [Ch. 3]

perception   The organization of sensory information. [Ch. 10]

perceptual development   The process of learning to coordinate information from the senses with physical motions and activities; also called *perceptual-motor development*. [Ch. 10]

performance assessment A method of educational evaluation based on observation and on a child's performance on specific tasks. [Ch. 15]

phoneme A small unit of sound that distinguishes one word from another. [Ch. 10]

physical environment In a preschool setting, the surroundings, including the walls and shape of the room, the furniture, the materials, the toys, and the equipment. [Ch. 5]

pictorial stage Rhoda Kellogg's fourth and final developmental art stage, in which children begin to draw recognizable pictures. [Ch. 13]

placement decision A decision about assigning a child to a particular learning group; made based on results of formal testing. [Ch. 15]

placement stage Rhoda Kellogg's first developmental art stage, in which very young children begin scribbling spontaneously in certain places on a sheet of paper. [Ch. 13]

play structure A large wooden and/or metal apparatus that combines separate areas for slides, ramps, poles, steps, ladders, tires, jungle gyms, and swings into one large piece of equipment. [Ch. 5]

portfolio assessment A method of assessment based on a systematic collection of children's work gathered by both children and teachers over time; a type of performance assessment. [Ch. 15]

praise A positive statement intended to reward and reinforce what is judged by the person giving the praise as appropriate behavior. [Ch. 8]

preoperational stage Jean Piaget's second stage of intellectual development, which lasts from about age two to about age six or seven. [Ch. 2]

preschematic stage W. Lambert Brittain's fifth and final developmental art stage, in which children begin to use materials to produce recognizable objects; also called *representational stage*. [Ch. 13]

preschool A type of child care facility designed to provide early educational experiences for three- to five-year-old children; also called a *prekindergarten school* or a *nursery school*. [Ch. 1]

pretend communications The dialogue that children use within a dramatic play situation. [Ch. 4]

print-rich environment Classroom surroundings with plenty of reading and writing materials throughout all areas. [Ch. 11]

private speech According to Vygotsky, the speech of children talking to themselves out loud to practice language and behavior. [Ch. 11]

process approach See *constructivist or process approach*. [Ch. 11]

process of construction The process of developing an understanding of conflict and how to resolve it. [Ch. 9]

process orientation An approach to children's art that emphasizes the importance of the process of creating and deemphasizes any product that may result from that effort. [Ch. 13]

proficiency barrier An indicator of the fundamental motor skills that children should master by age five so as to avoid difficulty with the physical skills needed in elementary school and beyond. [Ch. 7]

project approach A variation of the child-initiated approach to curriculum structure in which groups of children explore one topic, from several different aspects, over the course of several days or weeks. [Ch. 2]

Project Head Start A government-supported early childhood education program designed to give children from low-income families and children with physical disabilities a "head start" so that they will be more likely to succeed in school. [Ch. 1]

prosocial behavior Actions that are positive and constructive and that show caring and concern for others. [Ch. 9]

proximodistal principle A pattern of physical development in which physical mastery is acquired from the center of the trunk outward to the hands and feet and gross-motor movements are learned before fine-motor movements. [Ch. 7]

psychosocial Referring to Erikson's theory of child development, which addresses the psychological and emotional aspects of people through their lives, as well as how people interact with one another. [Ch. 2]

R

random scribbling   W. Lambert Brittain's first developmental art stage, in which toddlers randomly create lines on paper. [Ch. 13]

rapport   A warm, positive, and open relationship with another person. [Ch. 6]

readiness test   A test that assesses the curriculum-related skills children currently have rather than developmental potential. [Ch. 15]

reading readiness   A theory of learning, which contends that preschool is the time for formal, direct instruction in specific language skills, such as learning letter names. [Ch. 11]

receptivity   The ability of a person to be open to new experiences, reflective, attentive to others, perceptive, and curious. [Ch. 3]

redirection   A discipline technique in which the teacher steers a child's attention away from one activity and to another. [Ch. 8]

relationship question   A question that requires children to focus on the relationship among objects, actions, and events. [Ch. 12]

reliability   A measure of a test's consistency in producing the same score if it is taken more than once. [Ch. 15]

representational stage   See *preschematic stage*. [Ch. 13]

responsive planning   Curriculum planning based on following the children's interests. [Ch. 12]

reversibility   The ability to mentally split a whole into two or more parts and put the parts back together again, or to mentally retrace one's steps back to the beginning of a sequence. [Ch. 12]

role identity   A culturally based identity that is determined largely by the values and beliefs of the family and society. [Ch. 14]

rough-and-tumble play   A type of play that involves chasing, wrestling, and pretend fighting. [Ch. 7]

S

scaffolding   A teaching strategy in which the teacher verbally "builds on" what children say in order to expand their spoken language skills. [Ch. 11]

scheme   A general, established mental concept or structure. [Ch. 2]

selectivity   An aspect of children's art in which children omit certain details, such as a nose on a person's face, and choose only those details that are relevant to them at the moment. [Ch. 13]

self-concept   The perception that a person has of himself or herself. [Ch. 3]

self-esteem   An aspect of self-concept involving how a person evaluates or judges his or her own worth as a person. [Ch. 3]

self-report   A discipline technique in which children, following a fight or a conflict, are encouraged to describe how they are feeling and then the teacher describes the feelings back to them. [Ch. 8]

sensorimotor play   According to Piaget, a type of play that is characterized by simple, repeated movements; also known as *functional play*. [Ch. 4]

sensory integration   The ability to use information from two or more senses simultaneously; also called *bimodal perception*. [Ch. 10]

sequencing   The order in which activities and lessons will be presented over time. [Ch. 6]

shape stage   Rhoda Kellogg's second developmental art stage, in which children begin to draw common, recognizable shapes. [Ch. 13]

simple play unit   Play material that has one obvious use. [Ch. 5]

skills approach   See *transmission or skills approach*. [Ch. 11]

sociohistorical theory   A theory of cognitive development that asserts that people pass knowledge down to younger generations within each culture and society. [Ch. 12]

solitary play   According to Parten, a type of play in which a child plays with toys or materials alone and independently and is not involved in any way with other children. [Ch. 4]

spatial relations   The physical dimensions of objects and their position in relation to the environment. [Ch. 10]

strabismus   The medical term for crossed eyes. [Ch. 10]

stress   The body's physiological reaction to the demands and strains of daily life that exceed a person's ability to cope. [Ch. 8]

summative decision   A decision made at the end of a unit or a year of instruction; based on formal testing results that evaluate what the child has learned and the overall success of the instruction. [Ch. 15]

super-complex play unit   Play material that combines three or more types of materials or parts. [Ch. 5]

symbolic distancing   A developmental sequence in childhood in which the need for realism in objects or props during play diminishes. [Ch. 4]

symbolic play   According to Piaget, a type of play that is characterized by the manipulation of objects to either represent or construct something; also known as *constructive play*. [Ch. 4]

T

teachable moment   A spontaneous opportunity for learning. [Ch. 6]

teacher-directed curriculum   An approach to curriculum structure in which the teacher decides what activities the children will do, when they will participate in the activities, for how long, and how the materials will be used. [Ch. 2]

theme   In a preschool setting, a subject on which the teacher plans interrelated activities; also known as a *topic* or a *unit*. [Ch. 6]

time-out   Time out from play or from an activity; a common form of discipline in the preschool setting. [Ch. 9]

traditional playground   A play area consisting of separate large, fixed pieces of equipment, such as slides and swings. [Ch. 5]

transition   The time needed between activities to shift from one activity to another. [Ch. 6]

transmission or skills approach   A curriculum approach to early literacy in which teachers "transmit" meaning about language by breaking down the complex skills of reading and writing into individual steps or components. [Ch. 11]

trust versus mistrust   The first stage of Erikson's theory of psychosocial development, which occurs when infants learn to trust or mistrust their caregivers and the immediate world around them. [Ch. 8]

U

unit blocks   Solid hardwood blocks that come in various shapes. [Ch. 5]

V

validity   A measure of whether a test actually provides information about the areas it claims to assess. [Ch. 15]

visual discrimination   The ability to identify differences and similarities among shapes, objects, or people. [Ch. 10]

visual perception   The ability to use the sense of sight to recognize, differentiate, and recall objects. [Ch. 10]

visual perceptual disorder   The inability to identify and interpret what the eye perceives. [Ch. 10]

W

whole language approach   A learning environment in which speaking, listening, reading, and writing are combined into one interrelated process rather than treated as separate skills to be mastered. [Ch. 11]

will   The desire to control or direct the events in one's own life. [Ch. 8]

Z

zone of proximal development   The zone of knowledge just slightly more advanced than children comprehend on their own. [Ch. 12]

References

AHRMES, E. H., JR., & CONNOR, W. E. (1979). Symposium report of the task force on the evidence relating dietary factors to the nation's health. *American Journal of Clinical Nutrition, 32*, 2621–2748.

ARNHEIM, D. D., & SINCLAIR, W. A. (1979). *The clumsy child* (2nd ed.). St. Louis: Mosby.

AU, K. H. (1993). *Literacy instruction in multicultural settings.* Fort Worth, TX: Holt, Rinehart & Winston, Inc. a division of Harcourt Brace & Company.

BAGLEY, C., VERMA, G. K., MALLICK, K., & YOUNG, L. (1979). *Personality, self-esteem and prejudice.* Westmead, Farnborough, Hants, England: Saxon House.

BAKER, B. R. (1986, Summer). Transition time: Make it a time of learning for children. *Day Care and Early Education,* 36–38.

BANDURA, A. (1977). *Social learning theory.* Englewood Cliffs, NJ: Prentice Hall.

BANDURA, A. (1986). *Social foundations of thought and action: A social cognitive theory.* Englewood Cliffs, NJ: Prentice Hall.

BARBOUR, N. H. (1992). Language. In C. Seefeldt (ED.), *The early childhood curriculum: A review of current research.* New York: Teachers College Press.

BAYLESS, K. M. (1990). *Music: A way of life for the young child* (4th ed.). New York: Macmillan.

BECKER, W. C., & GERSTEN, R. (1982, Spring). A follow-up of Follow Through: The later effects of the direct instruction model on children in fifth and sixth grades. *American Educational Research Journal, 19*(1), 75–92.

BEST, C. T. (ED.). (1985). *Hemispheric function and collaboration in the child.* Orlando, FL: Academic Press.

BHAVNAGRI, N. (1987). *Parents as facilitators of preschool children's peer relationships.* Unpublished doctoral dissertation, University of Illinois at Urbana-Champaign.

BIBER, B. (1984). *Early education and psychological development.* New Haven, CT: Yale University Press.

BLOOM, B. S. (1956). *Taxonomy of educational objectives: Handbook I: Cognitive domain.* New York: McKay.

BOUTTE, G. S., KEEPLER, D. L., TYLER, V. S., & TERRY, B. Z. (1992). Effective techniques for involving "difficult" parents. *Young Children, 47*(3), 19–22.

BREDEKAMP, S. (ED.). (1987). *Developmentally appropriate practice in early childhood programs serving children from birth through age 8* (expanded ed.). Washington, DC: National Association for the Education of Young Children.

BREDEKAMP, S. (1991). Guidelines for appropriate curriculum content and assessment in programs serving children ages three through eight. *Young Children, 46*(3), 21–38.

BRENNER, B. (1989). *The preschool handbook.* New York: Pantheon Books.

BRITTAIN, W. L. (1979). *Creativity, art, and the young child.* New York: Macmillan.

BROOKS, C. K. (ED.). (1985). *Tapping potential: English and language arts for the Black learner.* Urbana, IL: National Council of Teachers of English.

BRUNER, J. S. (1972). The nature and uses of immaturity. *American Psychologist, 27*, 687–708.

BUZZELLI, C. (1992). Young children's moral understanding: Learning about right and wrong. *Young Children, 47*(6), 47–53.

BYRNES, J. P. (1988). Formal operations: A systematic reformulation. *Developmental Review, 8*, 66–87.

CAMPBELL, P. F., & CASEY, D. A. (1992). New directions for the early childhood mathematics curriculum. In C. Seefeldt (Ed.), *The early childhood curriculum: A review of current research* (2nd ed.). New York: Teachers College Press.

CAMPBELL, S. D., & FROST, J. L. (1985). The effects of playground type on the cognitive and social play behaviors of grade two children. In J. L. Frost & S. Sunderlin (Eds.), *When children play.* Wheaton,

MD: Association for Childhood Education International.

CARLSSON-PAIGE, N., & LEVIN, D. E. (1992). Making peace in violent times: A constructivist approach to conflict resolution. *Young Children, 48*(1), 4–13.

CAZDEN, C. B. (1988). *Classroom discourse: The language of teaching and learning.* Portsmouth, NH: Heinemann.

CELIS, W. (1993, April 20). Study suggests Head Start helps beyond school. *The New York Times*, p. A23.

CENTERS FOR DISEASE CONTROL. (1988, October 21). Playground-related injuries in preschool children—United States, 1983–87. *Morbidity and Mortality Weekly Report*, Issue 37(41). Washington, DC: U.S. Department of Health and Human Services.

CHERRY, C. (1990). *Creative art for the developing child: A teacher's handbook for early childhood education* (2nd ed.). Eden Prairie, MN: Fearon Teacher Aids.

CHIRA, S. (1993, September 14). Working-class parents face shortage of day care centers, a study finds. *The New York Times*, p. A20.

CHOMSKY, N. (1965). *Aspects of the theory of syntax.* Cambridge, MA: MIT Press.

CHOMSKY, N. (1972). Stages in language development and reading exposure. *Harvard Educational Review, 42*(1), 1–33.

CHRISTIE, J. F., JOHNSON, E. P., & PECKOVER, R. B. (1988). The effects of play period duration on children's play patterns. *Journal of Research in Childhood Education, 3*(2), 123–131.

CLARK, A. H., WYON, S. M., & RICHARDS, M. P. M. (1969). Free play in nursery school children. *Journal of Child Psychology and Psychiatry, 10,* 205–216.

CLARK, M. (1976a). Language and reading: A study of early reading. In W. Latham (Ed.), *The road to effective reading.* London: United Kingdom Reading Association.

CLARK, M. (1976b). *Young fluent readers.* London: Heinemann.

CLAY, M. (1985). *Emergent reading behavior.* Unpublished doctoral dissertation, University of Auckland, New Zealand.

CROSSER, S. (1992). Managing the early childhood classroom. *Young Children, 47*(2), 23–29.

COATES, S., LORD, M., & JAKABOVICS, E. (1975). Field dependence-independence, social-non-social play and sex differences in preschool children. *Perceptual and Motor Skills, 40,* 195–202.

DAMON, W. (1983). *Social and personality development: Infancy through adolescence.* New York: Norton.

DAVIDSON, J. (1982). Wasted time: The ignored dilemma. In J. F. Brown (Ed.), *Curriculum planning for young children.* Washington, DC: National Association for the Education of Young Children.

DEINER, P. L. (1993). *Resources for teaching young children with diverse abilities: Birth through eight* (2nd ed.). Fort Worth, TX: Harcourt Brace Jovanovich.

DERMAN-SPARKS, L., & THE A.B.C. TASK FORCE. (1989). *Anti-bias curriculum: Tools for empowering young children.* Washington, DC: National Association for the Education of Young Children.

DEVRIES, R., & KOHLBERG, L. (1990). *Constructivist early education: Overview and comparison with other programs.* Washington, DC: National Association for the Education of Young Children.

DIAZ, R. M., PADILLA, K. A., & WEATHERSBY, E. K. (1991). The effects of bilingualism on preschoolers' private speech. *Early Childhood Research Quarterly, 6,* 377–393.

DIETEL, R. (1992, Fall). Portfolios as worthwhile burdens? *The CRESST Line, Newsletter of the National Center for Research on Evaluation, Standards, & Student Testing.* Los Angeles: University of California at Los Angeles, pp. 3–5.

DODGE, K. A. (1983). Behavioral antecedents of peer social status. *Child Development, 54.*

DREIKURS, R., & CASSEL, P. (1972). *Discipline without tears.* New York: Hawthorne Books.

DURKIN, D. (1966). *Children who read early: Two longitudinal studies.* New York: Teachers College Press.

DURKIN, D. (1972). *Teaching young children to read.* Boston: Allyn & Bacon.

EDWARDS, L. C., & NABORS, M. L. (1993). The creative arts process: What it is and what it is not. *Young Children, 48*(3), 77–81.

EISENBERG, N. (1982). Introduction. In N. Eisenberg (Ed.), *The development of prosocial behavior.* New York: Academic Press.

EISNER, E. W. (1985). *The art of educational evaluation: A personal view.* London: Falmer Press.

ELKIND, D. (1983). The nature and function of play. In H. N. Schefler (Ed.), *Resources for early childhood: An annotated bibliography and guide for educators, librarians, health care professionals, and parents.* New York: Garland.

ELKIND, D. (1986, May). Formal education and early childhood education: An essential difference. *Phi Delta Kappan*, pp. 631–636.

ELKIND, D. (1988). *The hurried child: Growing up too fast too soon.* Reading, MA: Addison-Wesley.

EPSTEIN, A. S. (1993). New forces promote early childhood programs. *High/Scope Resources, 12*(1), 4–6.

ERIKSON, E. (1963). *Childhood and Society* (2nd ed.). New York: Norton.

FAGAN, J. F., & SINGER, L. T. (1979). The role of simple feature differences in infants' recognition of faces. *Infant Behavior and Development, 2,* 39–45.

FEENEY, L. (1993). Pre-K today tips: Resolving playground conflicts. *Scholastic Pre-K Today, 7*(7), 40.

FEIN, G. (1979). Play and the acquisition of symbols. In L. Katz (Ed.), *Current topics in early childhood education* (Vol. 2). Norwood, NJ: Ablex.

FEIN, G. (1986). Pretend play: New perspectives. In J. Brown (Ed.), *Curriculum planning for young children.* Washington, DC: National Association for the Education of Young Children.

FEIN, G. G., & STORK, L. (1981). Sociodramatic play: Social class effects in integrated preschool classrooms. *Journal of Applied Developmental Psychology, 2,* 267–279.

FIELD, T. M. (1980). Preschool play: Effects of teacher/child ratio and organization of classroom space. *Child Study Journal, 10,* 191–205.

FIELDS, M. V., SPANGLER, K. S., & LEE, D. M. (1991). *Let's begin reading right: Developmentally appropriate beginning literacy.* Columbus, OH: Merrill.

FLAVELL, J. H. (1963). *The developmental psychology of Jean Piaget.* Princeton, NJ: Van Nostrand.

FORMAN, E. A., & CAZDEN, C. B. (1985). Exploring Vygotskian perspectives in education: The cognitive value of peer interaction. In J. Wertsch (Ed.), *Culture, communication and cognition: Vygotskian perspectives.* New York: Cambridge University Press.

FORMAN, G., & KUSCHNER, D. (1983). *The child's construction of knowledge: Piaget for teaching children.* Washington, DC: National Association for the Education of Young Children.

FOX, R., & ROUTH, D. K. (1976). Phonemic analysis and synthesis as word attack skills. *Journal of Educational Psychology, 68,* 70–74.

FRANCKS, O. R. (1982). Scribbles? Yes, they are art! In J. F. Brown (Ed.), *Curriculum planning for young children.* Washington, DC: National Association for the Education of Young Children.

FRANKLIN, M. B., & BIBER, B. (1977). Psychological perspectives and early childhood education: Some relationships between theory and practice. In L. G. Katz (Ed.), *Current topics in early childhood education* (Vol. 1). Norwood, NJ: Ablex.

FREYBERG, J. T. (1973). Increasing the imaginative play of urban disadvantaged kindergartners through systematic training. In J. L. Singer (Ed.), *The child's world of make-believe: Experimental studies of imaginative play.* New York: Academic Press.

FRIEDMAN, D. E., & GALINSKY, E. (1991). *Work and family trends.* New York: Families and Work Institute.

FROSCHL, M., & SPRUNG, B. (1983). Providing an anti-handicappist early childhood environment. *Interracial Books for Children Bulletin, 14.*

FROST, J. L. (1986). Children's playgrounds: Research and practice. In G. Fein & M. Rivkin (Eds.), *The young child at play: Reviews of research,* Vol. 4. Washington, DC: National Association for the Education of Young Children.

FROST, J. L., & KLEIN, B. L. (1983). *Children's play and playgrounds.* Austin, TX: Playgrounds International.

GALLAHUE, D. (1993). Motor development and movement skill acquisition in early childhood education. In B. Spodek (Ed.), *Handbook of research on the education of young children.* New York: Macmillan.

GARCIA, E. E. (1982). Bilingualism in early childhood education. In J. F. Brown (Ed.), *Curriculum planning for young children*. Washington, DC: National Association for the Education of Young Children.

GARDNER, H. (1984). *Art, mind, and brain: A cognitive approach to creativity*. New York: Basic Books.

GARDNER, H. (1993). *Frames of mind: The theory of multiple intelligences* (10th anniv. ed.). New York: Basic Books.

GARVEY, C. (1977). *Play*. Cambridge, MA: Harvard University Press.

GARVEY, K., & BERNDT, R. (1977). Organization of pretend play. *Catalogue of Selected Documents in Psychology, 7*. Washington, DC: American Psychological Association.

GELMAN, R., & BAILLARGEON, R. (1983). A review of some Piagetian concepts. In P. Mussen (Ed.), *Handbook of child psychology* (Vol. 3). New York: John Wiley.

GENISHI, C. (1992). Developing the foundation: Oral language and communicative competence. In C. Seefeldt (Ed.), *The early childhood curriculum: A review of current research*. New York: Teachers College Press.

GIBSON, J. J. (1979). *The ecological approach to visual perception*. Boston: Houghton Mifflin.

GIBSON, J. J. (1986, October). *The concept of affordance in development*. Paper presented at the Symposium on Human Development and Communication Sciences, University of Texas at Dallas, Richardson, TX.

GILLIGAN, C. (1982). *In a different voice: Psychological theory and women's development*. Cambridge, MA: Harvard University Press.

GINOTT, H. (1972). *Teacher and child*. New York: Macmillan.

GNEZDA, M. T., & BOLIG, R. (1988). *A national survey of public school testing of pre-kindergarten and kindergarten children*. Washington, DC: National Research Council, National Forum on the Future of Children and Families.

GOODMAN, K. S., SMITH, E. B., MEREDITH, R., & GOODMAN, Y. M. (1987). *Language and thinking in school: A whole-language curriculum* (3rd ed.). Katonah, NY: Richard C. Owen.

GOODNOW, J. (1977). *Children drawing*. Cambridge, MA: Harvard University Press.

GORDON, A. M., & BROWNE, K. W. (1989). Planning for the heart and soul: Emotional, social, and creative growth. In A. M. Gordon & K. W. Browne, *Beginnings and beyond* (2nd ed.). Albany, NY: Delmar.

GREENBERG, P. (1990). Why not academic preschool? Part 1. *Young Children, 45*(2), 70–80.

GREENBERG, P. (1992). How to institute some simple democratic practices pertaining to respect, rights, roots, and responsibilities in any classroom (without losing your leadership position). *Young Children, 47*(5), 10–17.

GREENBERG, P. (1992). Why not academic preschool? Part 2. *Young Children, 47*(3), 54–63.

GREENBERG, P. (1993). How and why to teach all aspects of preschool and kindergarten math naturally, democratically, and effectively—Part 1. *Young Children, 48*(4), 75–84.

GRIFFING, P. (1980). The relationship between socioeconomic status and sociodramatic play among black kindergarten children. *Genetic Psychology Monographs, 101*, 3–34.

HANLINE, M. F. (1985). Integrating disabled children. *Young Children, 40*(2), 45–48.

HARMS, T., & CLIFFORD, R. M. (1980). *Early childhood environment rating scale*. New York: Teachers College Press.

HARRILL, I., SMITH, C., & GANGEVER, J. A. (1972, Summer). Food acceptance and nutrition intake of preschool children. *Journal of Nutrition Education, 4*, 103–106.

HARRIS, D. B., & GOODENOUGH, F. (1963). *Children's drawings as measures of intellectual maturity*. New York: Harcourt Brace Jovanovich.

HARTER, S. (1983). Developmental perspectives on the self-system. In P. H. Mussen (Ed.), *Handbook of child psychology* (4th ed.), Vol. 4. New York: John Wiley.

HASWELL, K. L., HOCK, E., & WENAR, C. (1993). Techniques for dealing with oppositional behavior in preschool children. In J. F. Brown (Ed.), *Curriculum planning for young children*. Washington, DC: National Association for the Education of Young Children.

HAUBENSTRICKER, J., & SEEFELDT, V. (1986). Acquisition of motor skills during childhood. In V. Seefeldt, *Physical activity and well-being*. Reston, VA: American Alliance for Health, Physical Education, Recreation and Dance.

HAVIGHURST, R. (1952). *Developmental tasks and education*. New York: David McKay.

HAZEN, N. L., & BLACK, B. (1989). Preschool peer communication skills: The role of social status and interaction context. *Child Development, 60*, 867–876.

HENNINGER, M. (1987). Learning mathematics and science through play. *Childhood Education, 63*(3), 167–171.

HERNANDEZ, H. (1989). *Multicultural education: A teacher's guide to content and process*. Columbus, OH: Merrill.

HERR, J., & MORSE, W. (1982). Food for thought: Nutrition education for young children. In J. F. Brown (Ed.), *Curriculum planning for young children*. Washington, DC: National Association for the Education of Young Children.

HERRERA, J. F., & WOODEN, S. L. (1988). Some thoughts about effective parent–school communication. *Young Children, 14*(6), 78–80.

HILDEBRAND, V. (1991). *Introduction to early childhood education*. New York: Macmillan.

HINE, C. (1993). *Building a developmentally appropriate preschool program: Resource handbook*. Bellevue, WA: Bureau of Education and Research.

HITZ, R., & DRISCOLL, A. (1988). Praise or encouragement? New insights into praise: Implications for early childhood teachers. *Young Children, 43*(5), 6–13.

HOFFMAN, L. (1983). Sexism: Related problems, research and strategies. *Interracial Books for Children Bulletin, 14*.

HOHMANN, M., BANET, B., & WEIKART, D. P. (1979). *Young children in action: A manual for preschool educators*. Ypsilanti, MI: High/Scope Press.

HONIG, A. S. (1983). Sex role socialization in early childhood. *Young Children, 38*(6), 57–70.

HONIG, A. S. (1986). Stress and coping in children—Part 1. *Young Children, 41*(4), 50–63.

HONIG, A. S. (1987). The shy child. *Young Children, 42*(4), 54–64.

Ideas that work with young children: Child choice—Another way to individualize—Another form of preventive discipline. (1987). *Young Children, 43*(1), 48–54.

JAVERNICK, E. (1988). Johnny's not jumping: Can we help obese children? *Young Children, 43*(2), 18–23.

JOHNSON, J. E., & ERSCHLER, J. (1982). Curricular effects on the play of preschoolers. In D. J. Pepler & K. H. Rubin (Eds.), *The play of children: Current theory and research*. Basel, Switzerland: S. Karger.

JONES, E. (1977). *Dimensions of teaching-learning environments: Handbook for teachers*. Pasadena, CA: Pacific Oaks.

JONES, E., & DERMAN-SPARKS, L. (1992). Meeting the challenge of diversity. *Young Children, 47*(2), 12–18.

JUEL, C. (1988). Learning to read and write: A longitudinal study of fifty-four children from first through fourth grades. *Journal of Educational Psychology, 80*, 437–447.

KAGAN, J. (1984). *The nature of the child*. New York: Basic Books.

KALLIOPUSKA, M., & RUOKONEN, I. (1986). Effects of music education on development of holistic empathy. *Perceptual and Motor Skills, 62*, 187–191.

KAMII, C. (1985). Leading primary education toward excellence: Beyond worksheets and drill. *Young Children, 40*(6), 3–9.

KAMII, C., WITH DECLARK, G. (1985). *Young children reinvent arithmetic: Implications of Piaget's theory*. New York: Teachers College Press.

KAMII, C., & DEVRIES, R. (1993). *Physical knowledge in preschool education: Implications of Piaget's theory.* New York: Teachers College Press.

KATZ, L. (1988, Summer). What should young children be doing? *American Educator,* pp. 28–33, 44–45.

KATZ, L., & CHARD, S. (1989). *Engaging children's minds: The project approach.* Norwood, NJ: Ablex.

KATZ, P. (1982). Development of children's racial awareness and intergroup attitudes. In L. Katz (Ed.), *Current topics in early childhood education.* Vol. 4. Norwood, NJ: Ablex.

KELLER, A., FORD, L., & MEACHAM, J. (1978). Dimensions of self-concept in preschool children. *Developmental Psychology, 14*(5), 48–49.

KELLOGG, R. (1970). *Analyzing children's art.* Palo Alto, CA: Mayfield.

KELMAN, A. (1990). Choices for children. *Young Children, 45*(3), 42–45.

KOHLBERG, L. (1971). From is to ought: How to commit the naturalistic fallacy and get away with it in the study of moral development. In T. Mischel (Ed.), *Cognitive development and epistemology.* New York: Academic Press.

KOHLBERG, L., & LICKONA, T. (1990). Moral discussion and the class meeting. In R. DeVries & L. Kohlberg (Eds.), *Constructivist early education: Overview and comparison with other programs.* Washington, DC: National Association for the Education of Young Children.

KOOIJ, R. VAN DER. (1989). Research on children's play. *Play and Culture, 2.*

KORETZ, D., STECHER, B., AND DEIBERT, E. (1992). *The Vermont Portfolio Assessment Program: Interim Report on Implementation and Impact, 1991–92 School Year.* Los Angeles: University of California at Los Angeles, Center for Research on Evaluation, Standards, and Student Testing (CRESST).

KOSTELNIK, M. J., SODERMAN, A. K., & WHIREN, A. P. (1993). *Developmentally appropriate programs in early childhood education.* New York: Macmillan.

KOSTELNIK, M. J., STEIN, L. C., WHIREN, A. P., & SODERMAN, A. K. (1993). *Guiding children's social development.* Albany, NY: Delmar.

KOSTELNIK, M. J., STEIN, L. C., & WHIREN, A. P. (1988). Children's self-esteem: The verbal environment. *Childhood Education, 65*(1), 29–32.

KRITCHEVSKY, S., PRESCOTT, E., & WALLING, L. (1969). *Planning environments for young children: Physical space.* Washington, DC: National Association for the Education of Young Children.

KUTNER, L. (1993, September 16). Parent & Child: Helping clumsy children even out the playing field. *The New York Times,* p. C10.

LADD, G. W., & COLEMAN, C. C. (1993). Young children's peer relationships: Forms, features, and functions. In B. Spodek (Ed.), *Handbook of research on the education of young children.* New York: Macmillan.

LADD, G. W., & PRICE, J. M. (1987). Predicting children's social and school adjustment following the transition from preschool to kindergarten. *Child Development, 58,* 1168–1189.

LAMB, M. W. (1969). Food acceptance, a challenge to nutrition education—A review. *Journal of Nutrition Education, 1*(2), 20–22.

LAMME, L. L. (1982). Handwriting in an early childhood curriculum. In J. F. Brown (Ed.), *Curriculum planning for young children.* Washington, DC: National Association for the Education of Young Children.

LAY-DOPYERA, M., & DOPYERA, J. E. (1992). Strategies for teaching. In C. Seefeldt (Ed.), *The early childhood curriculum: A review of current research,* (2nd ed.). New York: Teachers College Press.

LAZAR, I., DARLINGTON, R., MURRAY, H., ROYCE, J., & SNIPPER, A. (1982). Lasting effects of early education: A report from the Consortium for Longitudinal Studies. *Monographs of the Society for Research in Child Development, 47*(2–3, No. 195).

LENNEBERG, E. (1967). *Biological foundations of language.* New York: John Wiley.

MACCOBY, E. E., & JACKLIN, C. N. (1990). Gender segregation in nursery school: Predictors and outcomes. In M. A. Jensen & Z. W. Chevalier (Eds.),

Issues and advocacy in early education. Boston: Allyn & Bacon.

MACKAIN, S. J. (1987, April). *Gender constancy: A realistic approach.* Paper presented at the Biennial Meeting of the Society for Research in Child Development, Baltimore, MD.

MARKUS, H. R., & KITAYAMA, S. (1991). Culture and the self: Implications for cognition, emotion, and motivation. *Psychological Review, 98*(2), 224–253.

MAROTZ, L. R., RUSH, J. M., & CROSS, M. Z. (1989). *Health, safety, and nutrition for the young child.* Albany, NY: Delmar.

MARSHALL, H. (1989). The development of self-concept. *Young Children, 44*(5), 44–51.

MASLOW, A. H. (1954). *Motivation and personality.* New York: Harper & Row.

MASON, J., KERR, B., SINHA, S., & MCCORMICK, C. (1990). Shared book reading in an Early Start program for at-risk children. In J. Zutell & S. McCormick (Eds.), *Literacy theory and research: Analysis from multiple paradigms.* Chicago: National Reading Conference.

MASON, J. M. (1992). Reading stories to preliterate children: A proposed connection to reading. In P. B. Gough, L. C. Ehri, & R. Treiman (Eds.), *Reading acquisition.* Hillsdale, NJ: Erlbaum.

MASON, J. M., & SINHA, S. (1993). Emerging literacy in the early childhood years: Applying a Vygotskian model of learning and development. In B. Spodek (Ed.), *Handbook of research on the education of young children.* New York: Macmillan.

MAYESKY, M., NEUMAN, D., & WLODKOWSKI, R. J. (1985). *Creative activities for young children* (3rd ed.). Albany, NY: Delmar.

MCDONALD, D. T., & RAMSEY, J. H. (1982). Awakening the artist: Music for young children. In J. Brown (Ed.), *Curriculum planning for young children.* Washington, DC: National Association for the Education of Young Children.

MCLANE, J. B., & MCNAMEE, G. D. (1990). *Early literacy.* Cambridge, MA: Harvard University Press.

MCMILLAN, M. (1921). *The nursery school.* New York: Dutton.

MECCA, A. M., SMELSER, N. J., & VASCONCELLOS, J. (1989). *The social importance of self-esteem.* Berkeley: University of California Press.

MEDRICH, E. A., ROIZEN, J., RUBIN, V., & BUCKLEY, S. (1982). *The serious business of growing up: A study of children's lives outside of school.* Berkeley: University of California Press.

MEISEL, C. J. (ED.). (1986). *Mainstreaming handicapped children: Outcomes, controversies, and new directions.* Hillsdale, NJ: Erlbaum.

MEISELS, S. J. (1987). Uses and abuses of developmental screening and school readiness testing. *Young Children, 42*(2), 4–6, 68–73.

MEISELS, S. J. (1993). Remaking classroom assessment with the work sampling system. *Young Children. 48*(5), pp. 34–40.

MEYER, W. (1979). Informational value of evaluative behavior: Influences of praise and blame on perceptions of ability. *Journal of Educational Psychology, 71*(2), 259–268.

MILLER, C. S. (1984). Building self-control: Discipline for young children. *Young Children, 40*(1), 15–19.

MONTESSORI, M. (1912). *The Montessori method: Scientific pedagogy as applied to child education in "The Children's House" with additions and revisions by the author* (A. E. George, Trans.). New York: Frederick A. Stokes.

MONTESSORI, M. (1975). *Childhood education* (A. M. Joosten, Trans.). New York: New American Library.

MOORE, G. T. (1983). *The role of the socio-physical environment in cognitive development* (WP83–5). Milwaukee: University of Wisconsin, Center for Architecture and Urban Planning Research.

MORGAN, E. L. (1989). Talking with parents when concerns come up. *Young Children, 44*(2), 52–56.

MORROW, L. M. (1985). Retelling stories: A strategy for improving young children's comprehension, concept of story structure, and oral language complexity. *Elementary School Journal, 85*(5), 647–661.

MORROW, L. M. (1990). Preparing the classroom environment to promote literacy during play. *Early Childhood Research Quarterly, 5,* 537–554.

MORROW, L. M., & SMITH, J. K. (1990). The effects of group size on interactive storybook reading. *Reading Research Quarterly, 25*(3), 213–231.

MUSSEN, P., & EISENBERG-BERG, N. (1977). *Roots of caring, sharing, and helping.* San Francisco: Freeman.

NARDI, W. M., (ED.). (1992). Exploring the feasibility and educational potential of performance-based testing. *ETS Developments.* Princeton, NJ: Educational Testing Service, *37*(4), 4–5.

NAYLOR, H. (1985). Outdoor play and play equipment. *Early Child Development and Care, 19*, 109–130.

NELSON, K. (1985). *Making sense: The acquisition of shared meaning.* New York: Academic Press.

NEW, R. S. (1992). The integrated early childhood curriculum: New interpretations based on research and practice. In C. Seefeldt (Ed.), *The early childhood curriculum: A review of current research* (2nd ed.). New York: Teachers College Press.

NOUROT, P. M., & VAN HOORN, J. L. (1991). Symbolic play in preschool and primary settings. *Young Children, 46*(6), 40–49.

OLSON, G. M. (1976). An information-processing analysis of visual memory and habituation in infants. In T. J. Tighe & R. N. Leaton (Eds.), *Habituation.* Hillsdale, NJ: Erlbaum.

OXFORD-CARPENTER, R., POL, L., LOPEZ, D., STUPP, D., GENDELL, M., & PENG, S. (1984). *Demographic projections of non-English-language background and limited-English-proficient persons in the United States to the year 2000 by state, age, and language group.* Rosslyn, VA: InterAmerica Research Associates.

PARTEN, M. (1932). Social participation among preschool children. *Journal of Abnormal Psychology, 27,* 243–269.

PAYNE, V. G., & ISAACS, L. D. (1991). *Human motor development: A life-span approach.* Mountain View, CA: Mayfield.

PEASE-ALVAREZ, L., GARCIA, E. E., & ESPINOSA, P. (1991). Effective instruction for language-minority students: An early childhood case study. *Early Childhood Research Quarterly, 6,* 347–361.

PEERY, J. C. (1993). Music in early childhood education. In B. Spodek (Ed.), *Handbook of research on the education of young children.* New York: Macmillan.

PELLEGRINI, A. D. (1983). Sociolinguistic contexts of the preschool. *Journal of Applied Developmental Psychology, 4,* 389–397.

PELLEGRINI, A. D. (1986). Communicating in and about play: The effect of play centers on preschoolers' explicit language. In G. Fein & M. Rivkin (Eds.), *The young child at play.* Washington, DC: National Association for the Education of Young Children.

PELLEGRINI, A. D., & PERMUTTER, J. C. (1988). Rough and tumble play on the elementary school playground. *Young Children, 43*(2), 14–17.

PHILLIPS, C. (1988). Nurturing diversity for today's children and tomorrow's leaders. *Young Children, 43*(2), 42–47.

PIAGET, J. (1948). *The moral judgment of the child.* Glencoe, IL: Free Press.

PIAGET, J. (1962). *Play, dreams, and imitation in childhood.* New York: Norton.

PIAGET, J. (1963). *The origins of intelligence in children.* New York: Norton.

PICK, JR., H. L. (1983). Some issues on the relation between perceptual and cognitive development. In T. Tighe & B. Shepp, *Perception, cognition, and development.* Hillsdale, NJ: Erlbaum.

PITCHER, E. G., FEINBURG, S. G., & ALEXANDER, D. (1989). *Helping young children learn* (5th ed.). Columbus, OH: Merrill.

PRESCOTT, E. (1984). The physical setting in day care. In J. T. Greenman & R. W. Fuqua (Eds.), *Making day care better.* New York: Teachers College Press.

PULASKI, M. A. (1973). Toys and imaginative play. In J. L. Singer (Ed.), *Child's world of make-believe.* New York: Academic Press.

RADKE-YARROW, M., ZAHN-WAXLER, C., & CHAPMAN, M. (1983). Children's prosocial dispositions and behavior. In P. H. Mussen (Ed.), *Handbook of child psychology.* New York: John Wiley.

RAMSEY, L. F., & PRESTON, J. D. (1990). *Impact attenuation performance of playground surfacing materials.* Washington, DC: Consumer Product Safety Commission.

RAMSEY, P., & DERMAN-SPARKS, L. (1992). Multicultural education reaffirmed. *Young Children, 47*(2), 10–11.

RAMSEY, P. G. (1982). Multicultural education in early childhood. In J. F. Brown (Ed.), *Curriculum planning for young children.* Washington, DC: National Association for the Education of Young Children.

READ, K., GARDNER, P., & MAHLER, B. (1993). *Early childhood programs: Human relations and learning* (9th ed.). Fort Worth, TX: Harcourt Brace Jovanovich.

REIFEL, S. (1984). Block construction: Children's developmental landmarks in representation of space. *Young Children, 40*(1), 61–67.

REIMER, B. (1989). *A philosophy of music education* (2nd ed.). Englewood Cliffs, NJ: Prentice Hall.

RESNICK, L. B. (1983). A developmental theory of number understanding. In H. P. Ginsburg (Ed.), *The development of mathematical thinking.* New York: Academic Press.

REUSCHLEIN, R., & HAUBENSTRICKER, J. (EDS.). (1985). *1984–1985 physical education interpretive report: Grades 4, 7, and 10.* Lansing, MI: Michigan Department of Education, Michigan Educational Assessment Program.

RHEINGOLD, H. L., & EMERY, G. N. (1986). The nurturant acts of very young children. In D. Olweus, J. Block, & M. Radke-Yarrow (Eds.), *Development of antisocial and prosocial behavior: Research, theories, and issues.* Orlando, FL: Academic Press.

RHO, L., & DRURY, F. (1978). *Space and time in early learning.* Cheshire, CT: Cheshire Board of Education.

RIGG, P., & ENRIGHT, D. S. (EDS.). (1986). *Children and ESL: Integrating perspectives.* Alexandria, VA: Teachers of English to Speakers of Other Languages.

ROBISON, H., & SCHWARTZ, S. (1982). *Designing curriculum for early childhood.* Boston: Allyn & Bacon.

ROGERS, D., & ROSS, D. D. (1986). Encouraging positive social interaction among young children. *Young Children, 41*(3), 12–17.

ROGERS, D. L. (1985). Relationships between block play and the social development of young children. *Early Child Development and Care, 20,* 245–261.

ROOPNARINE, J. (1984). Sex-typed socialization in mixed age preschool children. *Child Development, 55,* 1078–1084.

RUBIN, K. H. (1977). The play behaviors of young children. *Young Children, 32*(6), 16–24.

RYAN, R., CONNELL, J., & DECI, E. (1985). A motivational analysis of self-determination and self-regulation in education. In C. Ames & R. Ames (Eds.), *Research on motivation in education, Vol. 2: The classroom milieu.* New York: Academic Press.

SANDERS, K. M., & HARPER, L. V. (1976). Free-play fantasy behavior in preschool children: Relations among gender, age, season, and location. *Child Development, 47,* 1182–1185.

SANTROCK, J. W. (1990). *Children* (2nd ed.). Dubuque, IA: William C. Brown.

SARACHO, O. N. (1991). The role of play in the early childhood curriculum. In B. Spodek & O. N. Saracho (Eds.), *Issues in early childhood curriculum.* New York: Teachers College Press.

SARAFINO, E. (1986). *The fears of childhood: A guide to recognizing and reducing fearful states in children.* New York: Human Sciences.

SATTLER, J. M. (1988). *Assessment of children* (3rd ed.). San Diego, CA: Author.

SAVA, S. G. (1987). Development, not academics. *Young Children, 42*(3), 15.

SCHRADER, C. T. (1990). Symbolic play as a curricular tool for early literacy development. *Early Childhood Research Quarterly, 5,* 79–103.

SCHWARTZ, J. C. (1972). Effects of peer familiarity on the behavior of preschoolers in a novel situation. *Journal of Personality and Social Psychology, 24,* 276–284.

SCHWEINHART, L. J., WEIKART, D. P., & LARNER, M. B. (1986). Consequences of three preschool curriculum models through age 15. *Early Childhood Research Quarterly, 1,* 15–45.

SEAGOE, M. V., & MURAKAMI, K. (1961). A comparative study of children's play in America and Japan. *California Journal of Educational Research*, II.

SEARS, W. (1982). *Creative parenting.* New York: Dodd, Mead.

SEEFELDT, C. (1990). *Continuing issues in early childhood.* New York: Macmillan.

SEEFELDT, V. (1980). Developmental motor patterns: Implication for elementary school physical education. In C. Nadeau, W. Halliwell, K. Newell, & G. Roberts (Eds.), *Psychology of motor behavior and sport—1979.* Champaign, IL: Human Kinetics.

SEEFELDT, V., & VOGEL, P. G. (1986). *The value of physical activity.* Reston, VA: American Alliance for Health, Physical Education, Recreation and Dance.

SEIFERT, K. L. (1993). Cognitive development and early childhood education. In B. Spodek (Ed.), *Handbook of research on the education of young children.* New York: Macmillan.

SELYE, H. (1982). History and present status of the stress concept. In L. Goldberger & S. Breznitz (Eds.), *Handbook of stress: Theoretical and clinical aspects.* New York: Free Press.

SHEPARD, L. A., & GRAUE, M. E. (1993). The morass of school readiness screening: Research on test use and test validity. In B. Spodek (Ed.), *Handbook of research on the education of young children.* New York: Macmillan.

SHOTWELL, J., WOLF, D., & GARDNER, H. (1979). Exploring early symbolization: Styles of achievement. In B. Sutton-Smith (Ed.), *Play and learning.* New York: Gardner Press.

SINGER, J. L. (ED.). (1973). *The child's world of make-believe: Experimental studies of imaginative play.* New York: Academic Press.

SINGER, J. L., & SINGER, D. G. (1985). *Make-believe: Games and activities to foster imaginative play in young children.* Glenview, IL: Scott, Foresman.

SLOBIN, D. I. (ED.). (1985). *The crosslinguistic study of language acquisition.* Hillsdale, NJ: Erlbaum.

SMILANSKY, S. (1968). *The effects of sociodramatic play on disadvantaged children.* New York: John Wiley.

SMITH, C. A. (1982). *Promoting the social development of young children: Strategies and activities.* Palo Alto, CA: Mayfield.

SMITH, C. A. (1988). *I'm positive: Growing up with self-esteem.* Manhattan, KS: Cooperative Extension Service, Kansas State University.

SMITH, F. (1979). The language arts and the learner's mind. *Language Arts, 56*(2), 118–145.

SMITH, P. K., & CONNOLLY, K. J. (1980). *The ecology of preschool behavior.* Cambridge, UK: Cambridge University Press.

SODERMAN, A. K. (1985). Dealing with difficult young children: Strategies for teachers and parents. *Young Children, 40*(5), 15–20.

SPACHE, E. (1976). *Reading activities for child involvement.* Boston: Allyn & Bacon.

SPODEK, B. (1986). *Today's kindergarten: Exploring the knowledge base, expanding the curriculum.* New York: Teachers College Press.

SPODEK, B., & BROWN, P. C. (1993). Curriculum alternatives in early childhood education: A historical perspective. In B. Spodek (Ed.), *Handbook of research on the education of young children.* New York: Macmillan.

SPODEK, B., SARACHO, O. N., & DAVIS, M. D. (1991). *Foundations of early childhood education* (2nd ed.). Englewood Cliffs, NJ: Prentice Hall.

SROUFE, L. A. (1983). Individual patterns of adaptation from infancy to preschool. In M. Perlmutter (Ed.), *Proceedings of the Minnesota Symposium on Child Psychology.* Hillsdale, NJ: Erlbaum.

STACKER, J. (1978). *The effects of altering the physical setting for dramatic play upon cognitive and social play levels of preschool children.* Master's thesis. Ohio State University, Columbus, OH.

STALLMAN, A. C., & PEARSON, P. D. (1990). Formal measures of early literacy. In L. M. Morrow & J. K. Smith (Eds.), *Assessment for instruction in early literacy.* Englewood Cliffs, NJ: Prentice Hall.

STEDT, J. D., & MOORES, D. F. (1987). Developmental differences in hearing. In J. T. Neisworth & S. J. Bagnato (Eds.), *The young exceptional child.* New York: Macmillan.

STEEL, C., & NAUMANN, M. (1985). Infants' play on outdoor play equipment. In J. L. Frost & S. Sunderlin (Eds.), *When children play.* Wheaton, MD: Association for Childhood Education International.

STEVENS, J. H., HOUGH, R. A., & NURSS, J. R. (1993). The influence of parents on children's development and education. In B. Spodek (Ed.), *Handbook of research on the education of young children*. New York: Macmillan.

STONE, J. G. (1992). *A guide to discipline* (rev. ed.). Washington, DC: National Association for the Education of Young Children.

STONE, L. J., & CHURCH, J. (1984). *Childhood and adolescence*. New York: Random House.

STRAYER, J. (1986). Children's attributions regarding the situational determinants of emotion in self and others. *Developmental Psychology, 22*(5), 649–654.

STRICKLAND, D. (1990). Emergent literacy: How young children learn to read and write. *Educational Leadership, 47*, 18–23.

SUTTON-SMITH, B. (1967). The role of play in cognitive development. *Young Children, 22*(6), 361–370.

SYLVA, K. (1977). Play and learning. In B. Tizard & D. Harvey (Eds.), *Biology of play*. London: Heinemann.

TEALE, W., & SULZBY, E. (1989). Emergent literacy. In D. S. Strickland & L. M. Morrow (Eds.), *Emerging literacy: Young children learn to read and write*. Newark, DE: International Reading Association.

TEMPLE, C. A., NATHAN, R. G., & BURRIS, N. A. (1982). *The beginnings of writing*. Boston: Allyn & Bacon.

TIERNEY, R. J. (1991). *Portfolio assessment in reading-writing classrooms*. Norwood, MA: Christopher-Gordon.

TINSWORTH, D. K., & KRAMER, J. T. (1990). *Playground equipment-related injuries and deaths*. Washington, DC: U.S. Consumer Product Safety Commission, Directorate for Epidemiology, Division of Hazard Analysis.

TIZARD, B., PHILPS, J., & PLEWIS, I. (1976). Play in preschool centers—I: Play measures and their relation to age, sex and IQ. *Journal of Child Psychology and Psychiatry, 17*, 241–264.

TORRANCE, E. P. (1970). *Encouraging creativity in the classroom*. Dubuque, IA: William C. Brown.

TOWNSEND-BUTTERWORTH, D. (1992). *Your child's first school: A handbook for parents*. New York: Walker.

VAKIL, E., SOROKER, N., & BIRAN, N. (1992). Differential effect of right and left hemispheric lesions on two memory tasks: Free recall of items and recall of spatial location. *Neuropsychologia, 30*(12), 1041–1051.

VANDER ZANDEN, J. W. (1993). *Human development* (5th ed.). New York: McGraw-Hill.

VAN DEUSEN-HENKEL, J., & ARGONDIZZA, M. (1987). Early elementary education: Curriculum planning for the primary grades. In *A framework for curriculum design: People, process, and product*. Augusta, ME: Maine Department of Educational and Cultural Services, Division of Curriculum.

VUKELICH, C. (1991). Material and modeling: Promoting literacy during play. In J. F. Christie (Ed.), *Play and early literacy development*. Albany: State University of New York Press.

VURPILLOT, E. (1968). The development of scanning strategies and their relation to visual differentiation. *Journal of Experimental Child Psychology, 6*, 632–650.

VYGOTSKY, L. S., (1967). Play and its role in the mental development of the child. *Soviet Psychology, 12*, 62–76.

VYGOTSKY, L. S. (1978). *Mind in society*. Cambridge, MA: Harvard University Press.

WALLACH, L. B. (1993). Helping children cope with violence. *Young Children, 48*(4), 4–11.

WARREN, D. L. (1984). *Blindness and early childhood development* (2nd ed.). New York: American Foundation for the Blind.

WEIKART, D. P., & SHOUSE, C. (1993). What years of inservice training have taught us. *High/Scope Resources, 12*(1), 7–9.

WERNER, J. S., & SIQUELAND, E. R. (1978). Visual recognition memory in the preterm infant. *Infant Behavior and Development, 1*, 79–94.

WHITE, B. L., KABAN, B. T., ATTANUCCI, J., & SHAPIRO, B. B. (1973). *Experience and environment: Major in-*

fluences on the development of the young child. Englewood Cliffs, NJ: Prentice Hall.

WHITE, B. L., & WATTS, J. C. (1973). *Experience and environment.* Englewood Cliffs, NJ: Prentice Hall.

WICKSTROM, R. L. (1983). *Fundamental motor patterns* (3rd ed.). Philadelphia: Lea and Febiger.

WIEDER, S., & GREENSPAN, S. I. (1993). The emotional basis of learning. In B. Spodek (Ed.), *Handbook of research on the education of young children.* New York: Macmillan.

WILLIAMS, H. (1983). *Perceptual and motor development.* Philadelphia: Lea and Febiger.

WILLIAMS, L., & DE GAETANO, Y. (1985). *ALERTA: A multicultural, bilingual approach to teaching young children.* Reading, MA: Addison-Wesley.

WILLIAMS, L. R. (1991). Curriculum making in two voices: Dilemmas of inclusion in early childhood education. *Early Childhood Research Quarterly, 6,* 303–311.

WILLIAMS, L. R. (1992). Determining the curriculum. In C. Seefeldt (Ed.), *The early childhood curriculum: A review of current research.* New York: Teachers College Press.

WOLFORD, G., & FOWLER, C. A. (1983). The perception and use of information by good and poor readers. In T. Tighe & B. Shepp, *Perception, cognition, and development.* Hillsdale, NJ: Erlbaum.

WONG FILLMORE, L. (1991). Language and cultural issues in early education. In S. L. Kagan (Ed.), *The care and education of America's young children: Obstacles and opportunities: Part I.* 90th Yearbook of the National Society for the Study of Education. Chicago: National Society for the Study of Education.

WORKMAN, S., & ANZIANO, M. (1993). Curriculum webs: Weaving connections from children to teachers. *Young Children,* 48(2), 4–9.

WORKMAN, S., & STAFF. (1992). *Integrating culture into an early childhood classroom: A photo-essay.* Farmington, NM: San Juan College.

ZINSMEISTER, K. (1988, Spring). Brave new world: How day-care harms children. *Policy Review,* pp. 40–48.

Index